How To Brew

How To Brew

Ingredients, Methods, Recipes, and Equipment for Brewing Beer at Home

2nd Edition

by John J. Palmer

Defenestrative Publishing Co.

How To Brew

2nd Edition
by John J. Palmer

First time in hardcopy print–2001. Second Printing 2002

Defenestrative Publishing Co.
PO Box 1781
Monrovia, CA 91017
Email: john@howtobrew.com

About this book
Cover design: John Palmer
Interior design: John Palmer
Graphics: John Palmer
Photography: Naomi K. Palmer and John Palmer
This book was designed and laid out using QuarkXpress 4.1
on an Apple PowerMac computer.
All graphics were constructed using Deneba's Canvas 3.5 and 7.
All photographs were prepared using Adobe PhotoDeluxe 2.0
and Photoshop 5.5
Years of work were rescued by Alsoft's Diskwarrior.
I typically stayed up late and drank green tea.

Library of Congress Card Number: 00-109877

ISBN–0-9710579-0-7

Printed in the United States of America

Let There Be Peace On Earth.

Acknowledgments

My success and enjoyment of homebrewing would not be possible without the advice and encouragement from the brewers on the Home Brew Digest. Never has there been a more helpful worldwide group of friends to exchange and debate information on one hobby.

Nor would any of this have been possible without the good-natured indulgence of my wife, Naomi. I will never forget the time I spilled a gallon and a half of wort into the dining room carpeting. When she got home later and I explained what had happened, her first question was, "Was (the beer) ruined?" Thank you, Sweetie.

I would like to thank my friends Norm Pyle and Martin Lodahl for a lot of help and advice in preparing this book–they provided the impetus and early reviews that I needed to get this project off the ground. Many thanks also to Jim Liddil, Glenn Tinseth, Maribeth Raines, Steve Alexander, Dave Logsdon, Chris White, Rob Moline, Patrick Weix, Don Put, Dave Draper, AJ Delange, Laurel Maney, Jim Busch, George and Laurie Fix, Jeff Donovan, Guy Gregory, Brian Kern, Ken Schwartz, Dan Listermann, and Jeff Renner for contributing their knowledge to the Sanitization, Hops, Yeast, Water, Malts, Mashing, Lautering, and Recipe chapters.

My sincere thanks to Stephen Mallery, Deb Jolda, and all the wonderful people of New Wine Press for their guidance and commitment to the project and the opportunities they gave me as a beer writer. The legacy of Brewing Techniques is priceless.

Thanks also to all the people at the Real Beer Page for hosting the online version of this book. From the very beginning of this project I have wanted to be able to share this information with the world, and they have enabled me to do that.

Finally, I am indebted to Glenn Tinseth for his many, many hours of editing the drafts of this work, both for checking my technical accuracy and for improving my writing by an order of magnitude. His contributions have turned this compilation of facts and procedures into a book worth reading. Thank you.

Table of Contents

List of Tips, Tables, & Significant Figures

Section I—Brewing With Malt Extract

Chapter 1
A Crash Course in Brewing

Chapter Two
Brewing Preparations

Chapter 3
Malt Extract and Beer Kits

Chapter 4
Water For Extract Brewing

Chapter 5
Hops

Section II—Brewing With Extract and Specialty Grain

Chapter 12
What is Malted Grain?

Chapter 13
Steeping Specialty Grains

Section III—All-Grain Brewing

Chapter 14
How the Mash Works

Chapter 15
Understanding the Mash pH

Chapter 16
The Methods of Mashing

Chapter 17
Getting the Wort Out (Lautering)

Chapter 18
Your First All-Grain Batch

Section IV—Recipes, Experimentation, and Troubleshooting

Chapter 19
Some of My Favorite Beer Styles and Recipes

Chapter 20
Developing Your Own Recipes

Chapter 21
Is My Beer Ruined?

Section V—Appendices

Appendix A
Using Hydrometers

Appendix B
Brewing Metallurgy

Appendix C
Building Wort Chillers

Appendix D
Building a Mash/Lauter Tun

Introduction

There are many good books on homebrewing currently available, so why did I write one you ask? The answer is: a matter of perspective. When I began homebrewing several years ago, I read every book I could find; books often published 15 years apart. It was evident to me that the state of the art had matured a bit. Where one book would recommend using baking yeast and covering the fermenting beer with a towel, a later book would insist on brewing yeast and perhaps an airlock. So I felt that another point of view, laying out the hows and whys of the brewing processes, might help more new brewers get a better start.

As an engineer, I am intrigued with the process of brewing. I want to know what each step is supposed to be doing so I can understand how to better accomplish them. For instance, when adding the yeast to the beer wort, some books emphasize getting the yeast fermenting as soon as possible to prevent wild yeast or microbes from gaining a foothold. There are actually several factors that influence yeast lagtime, and I didn't find them all in any single book. This kind of editing was an effort by the authors to present the information that they felt was most important to overall success and enjoyment of the hobby. Each of us has a different perspective, and I hope my nuts and bolts approach will serve you well.

Here is a synopsis of the brewing process:

1. Malted barley is soaked in hot water to release the malt sugars.
2. The malt sugar solution is boiled with hops for seasoning.
3. The solution is cooled and yeast is added to begin fermentation.
4. The yeast ferments the sugars, releasing CO_2 and ethyl alcohol.
5. When the main fermentation is complete, the beer is bottled with a little bit of added sugar to provide the carbonation.

Sounds fairly simple doesn't it? It is, but as you read this book you will realize the incredible amount of information that I glossed over with those five steps. But brewing is easy. And it's fun. Some people may be put off by the technical side of things, but learning about the processes of beer making will help ensure a successful batch. As my history teacher used to chide me, "It's only boring until you learn something about it. Knowledge makes things interesting." Besides, brewing unsuccessful batches in not much fun.

Fortunately for me, I discovered the Internet and the homebrewing discussion groups it contained. With the help of veteran brewers on the Home Brew Digest (an Internet mailing list) and Rec.Crafts.Brewing (an Internet newsgroup) I soon discovered why my first beer had turned out so brilliantly clear, yet fit only for mosquitoes to lay their eggs in.

As I became more experienced, and was able to brew beer that could stand proudly with any commercial offering, I realized that I was seeing new brewers on the 'net with the same basic questions that I had. They were reading the same books I had, and some of those were excellent books.

Well, I decided to write an electronic document that contained everything that a beginning brewer would need to know to get started. It contained equipment descriptions, process descriptions and some of the why's of homebrewing. I posted it to electronic bulletin boards and homebrewing ftp sites such as sierra.stanford.edu. (Would you believe that the World Wide Web didn't exist back then?) It was reviewed by other brewers and accepted as one of the best brewing guides available. It has been through five revisions as comments were received and I learned more about the why's of brewing. That document, "How To Brew Your First Beer", is still available and free to download and/or reproduce for personal use. It was written to help the first-time brewer produce a fool-proof beer–one they could be proud of. That document has apparently served quite well, it has been requested and distributed to every continent (including Antarctica) and been translated into Spanish, Italian, Czech, Korean, and Japanese. Probably tens of thousands of copies have been distributed by now. Glad I could help.

As time went by, and I moved on to "partial mashes" (half extract, half malted grain) and "all-grain" brewing, I actually saw requests on the 'net from brewers requesting "Palmer-type" documents explaining these more complex brewing methods. There is a lot to talk about with these methods though, and I realized that it would be best done with a book. After years and years of writing and re-writing, I published *How To Brew* online with the help of the Real Beer Page. It is at www.howtobrew.com for free. But I immediately started receiving requests for hard copy. Of course, in the process of laying it out, I couldn't resist the chance to improve it. This book in your hands is the second edition of *How To Brew*.

Oh, one more thing–I should mention that malt extract brewing should not be viewed as inferior to brewing with grain, it is merely easier. It takes up less space and uses less equipment. You can brew national competition winning beers using extracts. The reason I moved on to partial mashes and then to all-grain was because brewing is FUN. These methods really let you roll up your sleeves, fire up the kettles and be the inventor. You can let the mad-scientist in you come forth, you can combine different malts and hops at will, defying conventions and conservatives, raising your creation up to the storm and calling down the lightening...Hah hah HAH....

But I digress, thermo-nuclear brewing methods will be covered in another book. Okay, on with the show...

Glossary

One of the first things a new brewer asks is, "What do I need to buy to get started?" and "What does that word mean?" For guidance to simple starter equipment setups for home brewing, see the List of Equipment. The glossary is divided into two groups–Basic and Advanced–to help you get started right away without burying you in details.

Basic Terms

The following fundamental terms will be used throughout this book.

Aerate–To mix air into solution to provide oxygen for the yeast.

Ale–A beer brewed from a top-fermenting yeast with a relatively short, warm fermentation.

Alpha Acid Units (AAU)–A homebrewing measurement of hops. Equal to the weight in ounces multiplied by the percent of alpha acids.

Attenuation–The degree of conversion of sugar to alcohol and CO_2.

Beer–Any beverage made by fermenting a wort made from malted barley and seasoned with hops.

Blow-off–A type of airlock arrangement consisting of a tube exiting from the fermenter, submerging into a bucket of water, that allows the release of carbon dioxide and removal of excess fermentation material.

Cold Break–Proteins that coagulate and fall out of solution when the wort is rapidly cooled prior to pitching the yeast.

Conditioning–An aspect of secondary fermentation in which the yeast refine the flavors of the final beer. Conditioning continues in the bottle as long as there are active yeast present.

Fermentation–The total conversion of malt sugars to beer, defined here as three phases: adaptation, primary, and secondary.

Hops–Hop vines are grown in cool climates and brewers make use of the cone-like flowers. The dried cones are available in pellets, plugs, or whole.

Hot Break–Proteins that coagulate and fall out of solution during the wort boil.

Gravity–Like density, gravity describes the concentration of malt sugar in the wort. The specific gravity of water is 1.000 at 59°F. Typical beer worts range from 1.035-1.055 before fermentation (the "Original Gravity").

International Bittering Units (IBU)–A more precise method of measuring hops. Equal to the AAU multiplied by factors for percent utilization, wort volume and wort gravity. An IBU estimates the amount of bitterness in the resultant beer.

Krausen (kroy-zen)–Refers to the foamy head that builds on top of the beer during fermentation. Also an advanced method of priming.

Lager–A beer brewed from a bottom-fermenting yeast and given a long cool fermentation. Lager beer is characterized by a lack of esters, maltier flavor, and high clarity.

Lagtime–The period of adaptation and rapid aerobic growth of yeast upon pitching to the wort. The lag time typically lasts from 2-12 hours.

Pitching–Term for adding the yeast to the fermenter.

Primary Fermentation–The vigorous fermentation phase marked by the evolution of carbon dioxide and krausen. Most of the total attenuation occurs during this phase.

Priming–The method of adding a small amount of fermentable sugar prior to bottling to give the beer carbonation.

Racking–The careful siphoning of the beer away from the trub to another fermentor or bottles.

Sanitize–To reduce microbial contaminants to insignificant levels.

Secondary Fermentation–A period of settling and conditioning of the beer after primary fermentation and before bottling.

Sterilize–To eliminate all forms of life, especially microorganisms, either by chemical or physical means.

Trub (trub or troob)–The sediment at the bottom of the fermenter consisting of hot and cold break material, hop bits, and dead yeast.

Wort (wart or wert)–The malt-sugar solution that is boiled prior to fermentation. The wort before boiling is called "sweet wort," after boiling (with hops) it is called "bitter wort."

Zymurgy–The science of brewing and fermentation.

Advanced Terms

The following terms are more advanced and are more likely to come up as you progress in your home brewing skills and experience.

Amylase–An enzyme group that converts starches to sugars, consisting primarily of alpha and beta amylase. Also referred to as the diastatic enzymes.

Adjunct–Any non-enzymatic fermentable. Adjuncts include: unmalted cereals such as flaked barley or corn grits, syrups, and refined sugars.

Acrospire–The beginnings of the plant shoot in germinating barley.

Aerobic–A process that utilizes oxygen.

Anaerobic–A process that does not utilize oxygen or may require the absence of it.

Aldehyde–A chemical precursor to alcohol. In some situations, alcohol can be oxidized to aldehydes, creating off-flavors.

Alkalinity–The condition of pH between 7-14. The chief contributer to alkalinity in brewing water is the bicarbonate ion (HCO_3^{-1}).

Aleurone Layer–The living sheath surrounding the endosperm of a barley corn, containing enzymes.

Amino Acids–An essential building block of protein, being comprised of an organic acid containing an amine group (NH_2).

Amylopectin–A branched starch chain found in the endosperm of barley. It can be considered to be composed of amylose.

Amylose–A straight-chain starch molecule found in the endosperm of barley.

Autolysis–When yeast run out of nutrients and die, they release their innards into the beer, producing off-flavors.

°Balling, °Brix, or °Plato–These three nearly identical units are the standard for the professional brewing industry for describing the amount of available extract as a weight percentage of cane sugar in solution, as opposed to specific gravity. e.g., 10 °Plato is equivalent to a specific gravity of 1.040.

Beerstone–A hard organo-metallic scale that deposits on fermentation equipment; chiefly composed of calcium oxalate.

Biotin–A colorless crystalline vitamin of the B complex, found especially in yeast, liver, and egg yolk.

Buffer–A chemical species, such as a salt, that by disassociation or re-association stabilizes the pH of a solution.

Cellulose–Similar to a starch, but organized in a mirror aspect; cellulose cannot be broken down by starch enzymes, and vice versa.

Decoction–A method of mashing whereby temperature rests are achieved by boiling a part of the mash and returning it to the mash tun.

Dextrin–A complex sugar molecule, left over from diastatic enzyme action on starch.

Diastatic Power–The amount of diastatic enzyme potential that a malt contains.

Dimethyl Sulfide (DMS)–A background flavor compound that is desirable in low amounts in lagers, but at high concentrations tastes of cooked vegetables like corn or cabbage. Actually this is only one of a group of sulfur compounds that contribute to these aromas and flavors. Others are dimethyl disulfide, dimethyl trisulfide, diethyl sulfide, et cetera.

Dry Basis, Fine Grind (DBFG)–A measure (percentage by weight) of the total soluble extract or maximum extraction achievable for a particular malt in a laboratory mash and lauter. This number, when applied to the reference standard sucrose, is the basis for both PPG and HWE.

Enzymes–Protein-based catalysts that effect specific biochemical reactions.

Endosperm–The nutritive tissue of a seed, consisting of carbohydrates, proteins, and lipids.

Esters–Aromatic compounds formed from alcohols by yeast action. Typically smell fruity.

Ethanol–The type of alcohol in beer; formed by yeast from malt sugars.

Extraction–The soluble material derived from barley malt and adjuncts. Not necessarily fermentable.

Fatty Acid–Any of numerous saturated or unsaturated aliphatic monocarboxylic acids, including many that occur in the form of esters or glycerides, in fats, waxes, and essential oils.

Finings–Ingredients such as isinglass, bentonite, Polyclar, and gelatin, that improve clarity by helping the yeast, suspended proteins, and polyphenols to flocculate and settle out of the beer after fermentation.

Flocculation–The state of being clumped together. In the case of yeast, it is the clumping and settling of the yeast out of solution.

Fructose–Commonly known as fruit sugar, fructose differs from glucose by have a ketone group rather than an aldehydic carbonyl group attachment.

Fusel Alcohol–A group of higher molecular weight alcohols that esterify under normal conditions. When present after fermentation, fusels have sharp solvent-like flavors and are thought to be partly responsible for hangovers.

Gelatinization–The process of rendering starches soluble in water by heat, or by a combination of heat and enzyme action, is called gelatinization.

Germination–Part of the malting process where the acrospire grows and begins to erupt from the hull.

Glucose–The most basic unit of sugar. A single sugar molecule.

Glucanase–An enzyme that acts on beta glucans, a type of gum found in the endosperm of unmalted barley, oatmeal, and wheat.

Grist–The term for crushed malt before mashing.

Hardness–The hardness of water is equal to the concentration of dissolved calcium and magnesium ions. Usually expressed as ppm of ($CaCO_3$).

Hydrolysis–The process of dissolution or decomposition of a chemical structure in water by chemical or biochemical means.

Hopback–A vessel that is filled with hops to act as a filter for removing the break material from the finished wort.

Hot Water Extract (HWE)–The international unit for the total soluble extract of a malt, based on specific gravity. HWE is measured as liter degrees per kilogram, and is equivalent to points/pound/gallon (ppg) when you apply metric conversion factors for volume and weight. The combined conversion factor is 8.3454 x ppg = HWE.

Infusion–A mashing process where heating is accomplished via additions of boiling water.

Invert Sugar–A mixture of dextrose and fructose found in fruits or produced artificially by the inversion of sucrose (e.g., hydrolyzed cane sugar). Also known as Candy Sugar.

Isinglass–The clear swim bladders of a small fish, consisting mainly of the structural protein collagen, acts to absorb and precipitate yeast cells, via electrostatic binding. Isinglass is used as a fining agent after primary fermentation in the fermenter or keg.

Irish Moss–An emulsifying agent, Irish moss promotes break material formation and precipitation during the boil and upon cooling. Irish moss promotes clarity but is not a fining agent because it is used before fermentation. Irish moss is sold as dehydrated flakes and should be rehydrated before use. Use by adding it to the boil during the last 15 minutes. Recommended dose (as flakes) is 2-3 tsp/5 gallons, or 1/16-1/8 grams per liter.

Lactose–A nonfermentable sugar, lactose comes from milk and has historically been added to Stout, hence Milk Stout.

Lactic Acid–A tart, sour, but not vinegary acid that is produced by bacterial fermentation. While usually a contaminant and off-flavor, it is a hallmark of some styles, including Lambics and Berliner Weisse.

Lauter–To strain or separate. Lautering acts to separate the wort from grain via filtering and sparging.

Lipid–Any of various substances that are soluble in nonpolar organic solvents, and include fats, waxes, phosphatides, cerebrosides, and related and derived compounds. Lipids, proteins, and carbohydrates compose the principal structural components of living cells.

Liquefaction–As alpha amylase breaks up the branched amylopectin molecules in the mash, the mash becomes less viscous and more fluid; hence the term liquefaction of the mash and alpha amylase being referred to as the liquefying enzyme.

Lupulin Glands–Small, bright yellow nodes at the base of each of the hop petals, which contain the resins utilized by brewers.

Maillard Reaction–A browning reaction caused by external heat wherein a sugar (glucose) and an amino acid form a complex, and this product has a role in various subsequent reactions that yield pigments and melanoidins.

Maltose–The preferred food of brewing yeast. Maltose consists of two glucose molecules joined by a 1-4 carbon bond.

Maltotriose–A sugar molecule made of three glucoses joined by 1-4 carbon bonds.

Melanoidins–Strong flavor compounds produced by browning (Maillard) reactions.

Methanol–Also known as wood alcohol, methanol is poisonous but cannot be produced in any significant quantity by the beer-making process.

Mash–The hot water steeping process that promotes enzymatic breakdown of the grist into soluble, fermentable sugars.

Modification–An inclusive term for the degree of degradation and simplification of the endosperm and the carbohydrates, proteins, and lipids that comprise it.

pH–A negative logarithmic scale (1-14) that measures the degree of acidity or alkalinity of a solution for which a value of 7 represents neutrality. A value of 1 is most acidic, a value of 14 is most alkaline.

ppm–The abbreviation for parts per million and equivalent to milligrams per liter (mg/l). Most commonly used to express dissolved mineral concentrations in water.

Peptidase–A proteolytic enzyme which breaks up small proteins in the endosperm to form amino acids.

Points per Pound per Gallon (PPG)–The US homebrewers unit for total soluble extract of a malt, based on specific gravity. The unit describes the change in specific gravity (points) per pound of malt, when dissolved in a known volume of water (gallons).

Protease–A proteolytic enzyme which breaks up large proteins in the endosperm that would cause haze in the beer.

Phenol, Polyphenol–A hydroxyl derivative of an aromatic hydrocarbon that causes medicinal flavors and is involved in staling reactions.

Proteolysis–The degradation of proteins by proteolytic enzymes, e.g., protease and peptidase.

Saccharification–The conversion of soluble starches to sugars via enzymatic action.

Sparge–To sprinkle. To rinse the grainbed during lautering.

Sterols–Any of various solid steroid alcohols widely distributed in plant and animal lipids.

Sucrose–This disaccharide consists of a fructose molecule joined with a glucose molecule. It is most readily available as cane sugar.

Tannins–Astringent polyphenol compounds that can cause haze and/or join with large proteins to precipitate them from solution. Tannins are most commonly found in the grain husks and hop cone material.

List of Necessary Equipment for Beginning Brewers

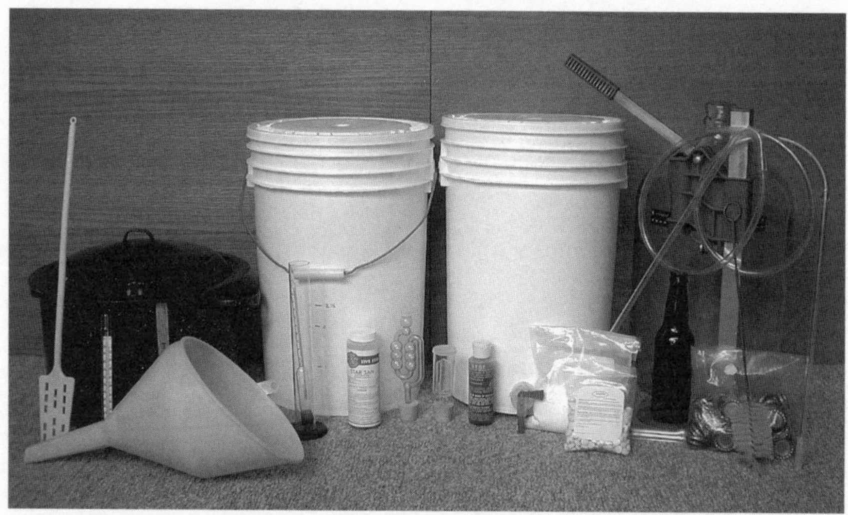

Here you see all the possible equipment a beginning brewer might use. Fermentors, pot, funnel, hydrometer, bottle brush, bottle capper, bottle caps, sanitizer, racking cane and siphon, and a bottle. But you don't have to have all of this stuff to get started.

Required Equipment

Airlock–Two basic kinds are available: the single piece or "bubbler", and the three piece. They are filled with water or sanitizer to prevent contamination from the outside atmosphere. The three piece has the advantage of disassembly for cleaning, but can inadvertantly allow the water to be sucked back inside the fermenter if the internal pressure drops due to lagering,

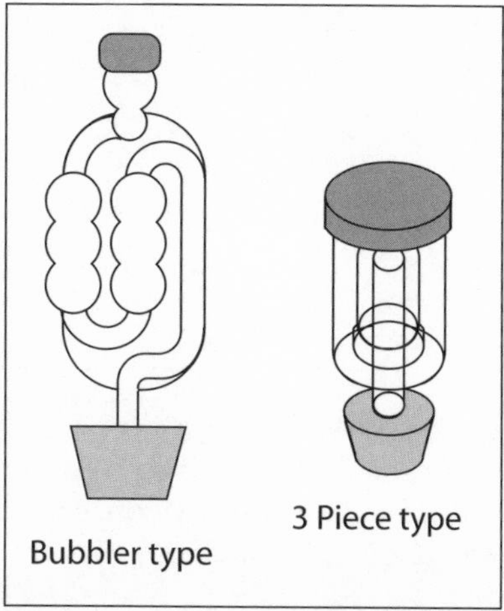

or from lifting the plastic bucket. The bubbler type will not suck liquid back inside but are more easily clogged by fermentation gunk and cannot be dissasembled for cleaning.

Boiling Pot–Must be able to comfortably hold a minimum of 3 gallons; bigger is better. Use quality pots made of stainless steel, aluminum, or porcelain enamel steel. A 5 gallon home canning pot (those black, speckled ones) is the least expensive and a good choice for getting started.

Bottles–You will need (48) recappable 12 oz bottles for a typical 5 gallon batch. Alternatively, (30) of the larger 22 oz bottles may be used to reduce capping time. Twist-offs do not re-cap well and are more prone to breaking. Used champagne bottles are ideal if you can find them.

Bottle Capper–Two styles are available: hand cappers and bench cappers. Bench cappers are more versatile and are needed for the champagne bottles, but are more expensive.

Bottle Caps–Either standard or oxygen absorbing crown caps are available.

Bottle Brush–A long handled nylon bristle brush is necessary for the first, hard-core cleaning of used bottles.

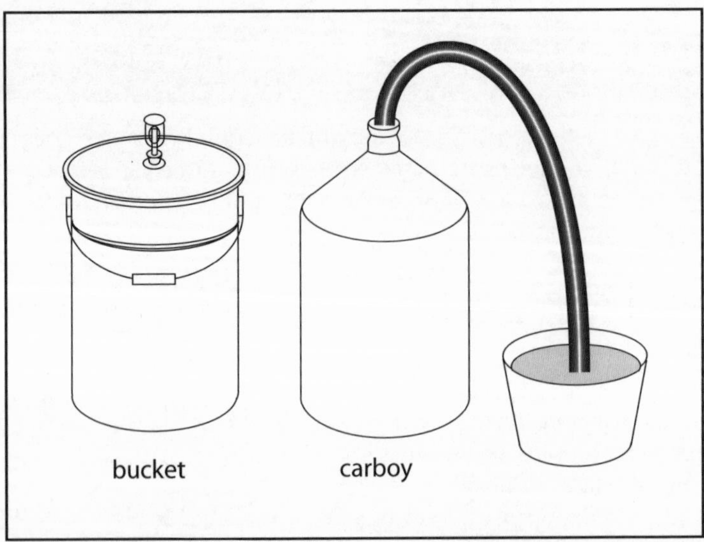

Fermentor–The 6 gallon food-grade plastic pail is recommended for beginners. These are very easy to work with. Glass carboys are also available, in 3, 5, and 6.5 gallon sizes. The carboy is shown with a blowoff hose which ends in a bucket of water.

Pyrex™ Measuring Cup–The quart-size or larger measuring cup will quickly become one of your most invaluable tools for brewing. The heat resistant glass ones are best because they can be used to measure boiling water and are easily sanitized.

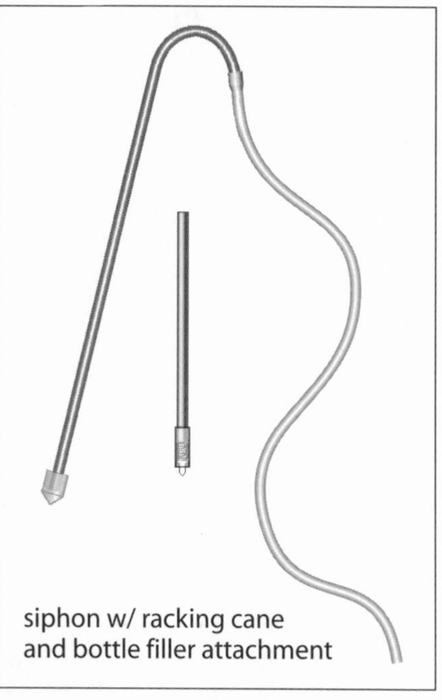

siphon w/ racking cane and bottle filler attachment

Siphon–Available in several configurations, usually consisting of clear plastic tubing with a racking cane and optional bottle filler.

Racking Cane–Rigid plastic tube with sediment stand-off used to leave the trub behind when siphoning.

Bottle Filler–Rigid plastic (or metal) tube often with a spring loaded valve at the tip for filling bottles.

Stirring Paddle–Food grade plastic paddle (or spoon) for stirring the wort during the boil.

Thermometer–Obtain a thermometer that can be safely immersed in the wort and has a range of at least 40°F to 180°F. The floating dairy thermometers work very well. Dial thermometers read quickly and are inexpensive.

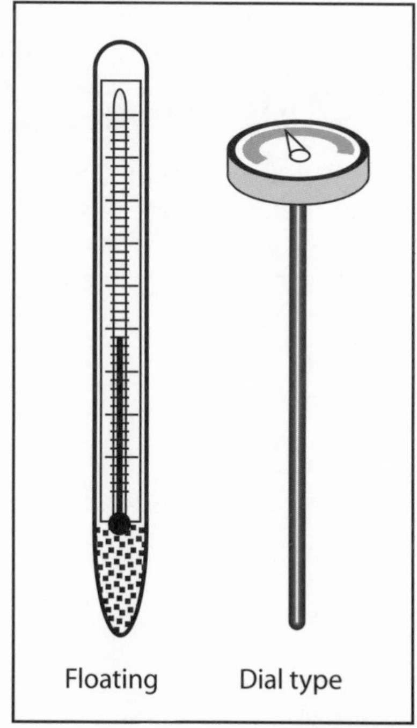

Optional but Highly Recommended

Bottling Bucket– A 6 gallon food-grade plastic pail with attached spigot and fill-tube. The finished beer is racked into this for priming prior to bottling. Racking into the bottling bucket allows clearer beer with less sediment in the bottle. The spigot is used instead of the bottle filler, allowing greater control of the fill level and no hassles with a siphon during bottling.

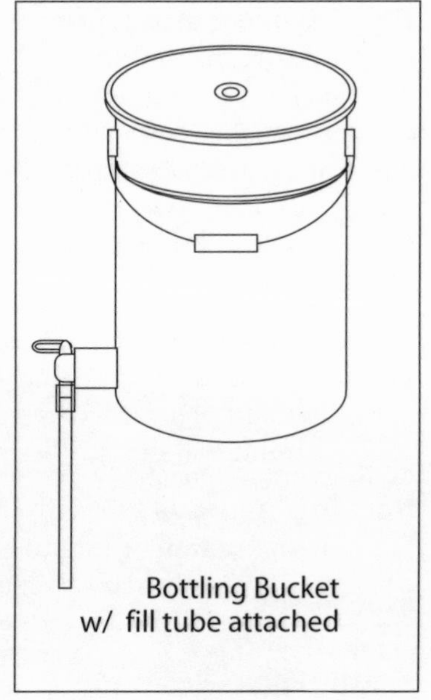

Bottling Bucket w/ fill tube attached

Hydrometer–A hydrometer measures the relative specific gravity between pure water and water with sugar dissolved in it by how high it floats when immersed. The hydrometer is used to gauge the fermentation progress by measuring one aspect of it, attenuation. Hydrometers are necessary when making beer from scratch (all-grain brewing) or when designing recipes. The first-time brewer using known quantities of extracts usually does not need one, but it can be a useful tool. See Appendix A–Using Hydrometers.

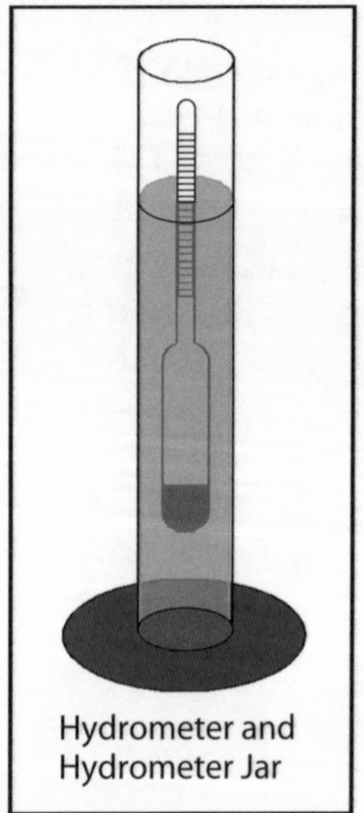

Hydrometer and Hydrometer Jar

Wine Thief or Turkey Baster– These things are very handy for withdrawing samples of wort or beer from the fermentor without risking contamination of the whole batch. *(not shown)*

Equipment Kit Comparison

(2001 prices)

Basic Beginner Package		**Complete Beginner Package**	
Porcelain Enamel Pot (5 gal.)	$20	Porcelain Enamel Pot (5 gal)	$20
1 Fermentor with Airlock	$10	2 Fermentors with Airlocks	$20
		(Use one as Bottling Bucket)	
Siphon	$4	Siphon w/ Bottle Filler	$8
Bottle Capper (hand)	$15	Bottle Capper (Bench)	$25
Bottle Caps (gross)	$3	Bottle Caps (gross)	$3
Large Stirring Spoon	$2	Large Stirring Spoon	$2
Bottle Brush	$3	Bottle Brush	$3
		Thermometer	$6
		Hydrometer	$5
Ingredients Kit	$20	Ingredients Kit	$20
Total	$77		$112

You will usually find beginner's kit packages at homebrew supply shops containing the majority of these items for $60–80. The prices shown above are for estimating your costs if you purchased items separately.

Section I

Brewing With Malt Extract

Welcome to How To Brew! In this first section of the book, we are going to lay the groundwork for the rest of your brewing education. As with every new skill, it helps to learn to do things the right way the first time, rather than learning via short cuts that you will have to unlearn later on. On the other hand, you don't need to know *how* an internal combustion engine works when you are learning how to drive. You just need to know that it does work when you keep it supplied with air and gasoline for fuel, oil for lubrication, and water for cooling.

To learn to brew beer, you don't need to learn how the yeast metabolize the malt sugars. But, you need to understand that metabolizing is what they do, and you need to understand what they need from you to get the job done. Once you understand that, you can do your part, they can do theirs, and the job should turn out right. Once you gain some familiarity with the brewing processes, you can delve deeper into the inner workings and make your beer better.

So, in *Brewing With Malt Extract,* you will learn to drive. *Chapter 1–A Crash Course in Brewing*, will provide an overview of the entire process for producing a beer. *Chapter 2–Brewing Preparations*, explains why good preparation, including sanitation, is important, and how to go about it. *Chapter 3–Malt Extract and Beer Kits,* examines the key ingredient of do-it-yourself beer and how to use it properly. *Chapter 4–Water For Extract Brewing,* cuts to the chase with a few do's and don'ts about a very complex subject. *Chapter 5–Hops,* covers the different kinds of hops, why to use them, how to use them, and how to measure them for consistency in your brewing. The last ingredient chapter in *Section I, Chapter 6–Yeast,* explains what yeast are, how to prepare them, and what they need to grow.

From there, *Section I* moves into the physical processes of brewing. *Chapter 7–Boiling and Cooling,* walks you thru a typical brew day: mixing the wort, boiling it, and cooling it to prepare it for fermentation. *Chapter 8–Fermentation,* examines how the yeast ferments wort into beer so you will understand what you are trying to do, without going into excruciating detail. *Chapter 9–Fermenting Your First Beer,* does just what it says: it takes what you have just learned and walks you through the practical application.

Everybody wants to brew their favorite beer that they buy at the store, and it's usually a lager. So, *Chapter 10–What is Different for Brewing Lager Beer?* examines the key differences of lager brewing, building on what you have already learned about ale brewing. *Section I* finishes with *Chapter 11–Priming and Bottling,* explaining each step of how to package your five gallons of new beer into something you can really use.

It is a long section, but you will learn to brew, and brew right the first time. Later sections of the book will delve deeper into malt and malted barley so you can take more control over the ingredients, and thus, your beer. A later section, *Section IV–Recipes, Experimentation, and Troubleshooting,* will give you the roadmaps, the tools, and the repair manual you need to drive this hobby to new horizons. Have Fun!

Chapter 1

A Crash Course in Brewing

What Do I Do?

If you are like me, you are probably standing in the kitchen, wanting to get started. Your beer kit and equipment are on the counter, and you are wondering how long this will take and what to do first. Frankly, the first thing you should do is read all of *Section I–Brewing With Malt Extract.* This section is going to teach you the fundamentals of how to brew beer; you won't be confused by conflicting instructions on a beer kit, and you will have an outstanding first batch.

But if you are like me, you probably want to do this right now while you have some time. (It's going to take about 3 hours, depending.) So, in this first chapter, I will walk you through the steps necessary to get your first batch bubbling in the fermentor, and give you an overview of what you will do to ferment and bottle your beer.

The instructions in this chapter may not explain *why* you are doing each step or even *what* you are doing. To understand the Whats and Whys of brewing, you will need to read the rest of this section. Each of the chapters in *Section I* discuss the brewing steps in detail, giving you the purpose behind each step. You will *know* what you are doing, rather than doing it that way because "that's what it said..." You will know how long to boil the wort, how to really use hops, why to bother cooling the wort, why to bother re-hydrating the yeast, why to wait two weeks before bottling... Get the picture?

But, if you can't wait, this chapter should see you through. Beer production can be broken down into 3 main events: Brew Day, Fermentation Week(s), and Bottling Day. If you have questions about terminology or equipment, be sure to review the *Glossary* and *Required Equipment* sections at the beginning of the book.

Brew Day

Equipment Needed

Let's review the minimum equipment you will need for this first batch:

- a 20 qt. brew pot (large canning pot)
- large stirring spoon (non-wood)
- ordinary table spoon
- measuring cup (preferably Pyrex glass)
- glass jar (at least 12 oz)
- fermentor (food-grade plastic bucket or glass carboy)
- airlock (get from homebrew shop)
- sanitizer (chlorine bleach or other)
- thermometer

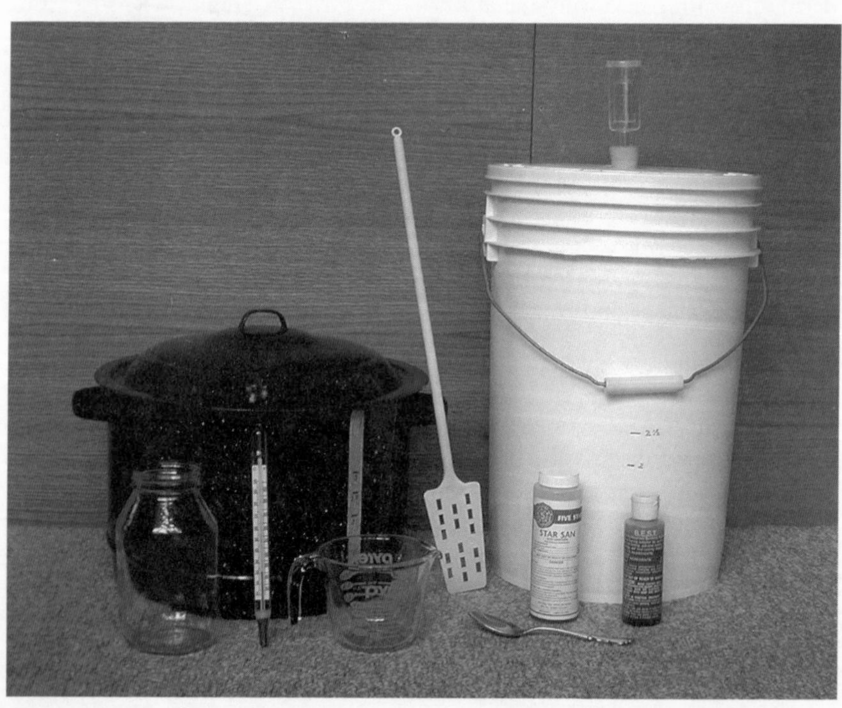

Preparation
(45 minutes)

1. Assemble ingredients. Gather together the ingredients for the brew. You may have purchased a brewing kit at a homebrewing shop, and it will contain the ingredients needed to brew a particular style of beer. A kit usually consists of malt extract, yeast, and hops. The extract may already be "hopped" and the kit may not include any hops.

If you don't have a kit, then head to a homebrew supply store and buy the ingredients outlined in the recipe here. You will notice that the recipe calls for various quantities of hops measured in AAUs. AAU stands for alpha acid units. Briefly, an AAU is a measuremet unit for hops, which add balancing bitterness to the beer. The actual unit for measuring bitterness in beer is the IBU, for which the AAU is a constituent. The AAU is obtained by multiplying the alpha acid rating of the hop (a percentage value) by the weight (ounces) that you intend to use. For example, 2 oz of a 6% alpha acid hop equals 12 AAUs. Every package of hops you buy will list the hop's alpha acid rating. To figure out how much of a hop you will need for this recipe, just divide the AAU target by the alpha acid percentage on your hops. For example, 12 AAUs divided by 12 (Nugget hop's alpha acid rating) equals 1 oz; 12 AAUs divided by 8 (Northern Brewer hop's alpha rating) equals 1½ oz. (See *Chapter 5–Hops,* for more info.)

2. Boil water. You will need at least a gallon of sterile water for a variety of small tasks. Start by boiling about 1 gallon of water for 10 minutes and let it cool, covered, to room temperature.

3. Clean and sanitize. It may seem strange to the first-time brewer, but probably the most important factor for success in brewing is good cleaning and sanitization. Clean all equipment that will be used during the brew with a mild, unscented dishwashing detergent, and be sure to rinse well. Some equipment will need to be sanitized for use after the boiling stage.

RECIPE

Cincinnati Pale Ale

Ingredients for a 5 gallon batch

- 3-4 lb. Pale malt extract syrup, unhopped
- 2 lb. Amber dry malt extract
- 12 AAU of bittering hops (any variety)
  For example, 1 oz. of 12% AA Nugget, or 1.5 oz. of 8% AA Northern Brewer
- 5 AAU of finishing hops (Cascade or other)
  For example, 1 oz. of 5% Cascade or 1.25 oz. of 4% Liberty
- 3 packets of dry ale yeast

You can easily make a simple sanitizing solution by filling the fermentor bucket with 5 gallons of water and adding 5 tablespoons of chlorine bleach (a concentration equivalent to 1 tbs./gallon, or 4 ml/L). Soak all items that need to be sanitized in this bucket for 20 minutes.

After soaking, dump the sanitizing solution and pour in some of the preboiled water for a quick rinse to remove any excess sanitizer. Place the small spoon and the thermometer in the glass jar and cover it with plastic wrap to keep them sanitary. Cover the fermentor with the lid to keep it sanitary also. (See *Chapter 2–Preparations,* for more info.)

BREWING CHECKLIST

Table 1—Cleaning and Sanitization Check List

Item	Clean	Sanitize
Brewpot	☐ Clean	
Stirring spoon	☐ Clean	
Table spoon	☐ Clean	☐ Sanitize
Measuring Cup	☐ Clean	☐ Sanitize
Yeast Starter Jar	☐ Clean	☐ Sanitize
Fermentor and lid	☐ Clean	☐ Sanitize
Airlock	☐ Clean	☐ Sanitize
Thermometer	☐ Clean	☐ Sanitize

Making Wort
(1 1/2 hours)

Now we begin the fun part of the work, creating the wort. Wort is what brewers call the sweet, amber liquid extracted from malted barley that the yeast will later ferment into beer.

Figure 3—Start boiling the water and get your ingredients ready. Do you have yeast?

4. Boil the brew water. In the brewpot, bring about 3 gallons of water to a boil. Pour this water into the fermentor and leave it to cool. Now bring another 3 gallons of water to boil in the brewpot. You will be boiling the extract in this water and diluting this concentrated wort with the water in the fermentor to make the total 5 gallons. Some water will evaporate during the boil, and some will be lost to the trub. Starting out with something closer to six gallons will ensure that you hit your five gallon recipe volume. (See *Chapter 4–Water for Extract Brewing,* and *Chapter 7–Boiling and Cooling*, for more info.)

Note: If your beer kit includes some crushed specialty grain, you will need to steep that first, before adding the extract. (See *Chapter 13–Steeping Specialty Grain,* for more info.)

5. Rehydrate the dried yeast. Although many people skip this step with fair results, rehydrating it assures the best results. While you are waiting for the brew water to boil, rehydrate two packets of dried ale yeast. Put 1 cup of warm (95-105°F, 35-40°C), preboiled water into your sanitized jar and stir in the yeast. Cover with plastic wrap and wait 15 minutes.

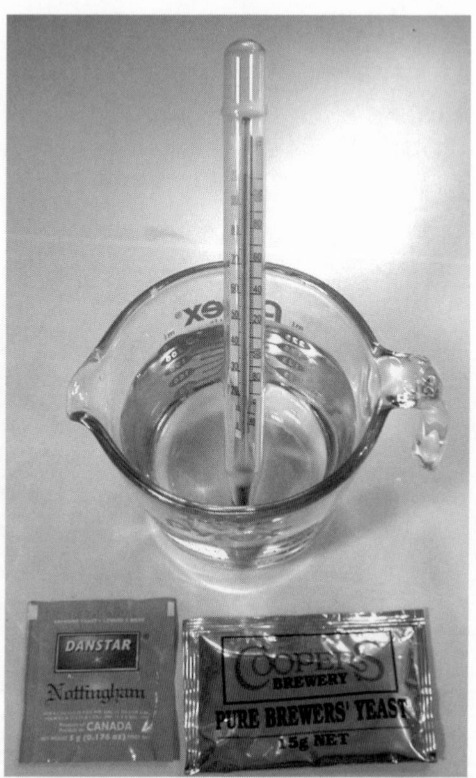

Next, "proof" the yeast. Start by adding one teaspoon of malt extract or table sugar to a small amount of water (1/4 cup, for example) and boil it to sanitize. (A microwave oven is good for this step.) Allow the sugar solution to cool and then add it to the yeast. Cover the yeast with plastic wrap and place in a warm area out of direct sunlight. Check it after 30 minutes, it should be showing some signs of activity –foaming and/or churning. If it just seems to sit on the bottom of the jar, then it is probably dead. Repeat the rehydration procedure with more yeast. (See *Chapter 6–Yeast,* for more info.)

Figures 4 and 5—Rehydrating and proofing the yeast.

6. Add malt extract. When the water in the brewpot is boiling, turn off the stove and stir in the malt extract. Be sure the extract is completely dissolved (if your malt extract is the dry variety, make sure there are no clumps; if the extract is syrup, make sure that none is stuck to the bottom of the pot). Next, turn the heat back on and resume the boil. Stir the wort regularly during the boil to be sure that it doesn't scorch.

The boil time for extract beers depends on two things: waiting for the "hot break" (See Step 8) and boiling for hop additions. In a nutshell, if you are using hopped extract without any added hops then you only need to boil through the hot break stage, about 15 minutes. With some extracts, the hot break will be very weak, and you may have little foam to begin with. If you are using hopped extract but adding flavoring or aroma hops, then you will probably want to boil for 30 minutes. If you are using unhopped extract, then you will need to add hops for bittering and should boil for an hour. (See *Chapter 3–Malt Extract and Beer Kits, Chapter 5–Hops,* and *Chapter 7–Boiling and Cooling,* for more info.)

7. Add hops. If you are using unhopped extract, add the first (bittering) hop addition and begin timing the hour-long boil. *(See Chapter 5–Hops* for more info.)

8. Watch for boilovers. As the wort boils, foam will form on the surface. This foam will persist until the wort goes through the "hot break" stage. The wort will easily boil over during this foaming stage, so stay close by and stir frequently. Blow on it and turn the heat down if it begins to boil over. Put a few copper pennies into the pot to help prevent boilovers. (See *Chapter 7–Boiling and Cooling* for more info.)

9. Add finishing hops (optional). If you are using unhopped malt extract or want to add more character to hopped extract, add finishing hops during the last 15 minutes of the hour-long boil. (See *Chapter 5–Hops* for more info.)

10. Cool the wort. After the boil, the wort must be cooled to yeast pitching temperature (65-90°F, 18-32°C) as quickly as possible. To do this, immerse the pot in a cold water bath. A sink, bathtub, or a handy snowbank all work well. Be sure to keep the lid on the pot while cooling to prevent any cooling water or other potential contaminants from getting in. (See *Chapter 7–Boiling and Cooling,* for more info.)

Figure 8—Chilling the wort in an ice bath.

Fermentation Week(s)

The science of fermentation is discussed in *Chapter 8–Fermentation. Chapter 9–Fermenting Your First Batch,* walks you through the application of that science, so that you too will be able to amaze your family and friends with a bubbling airlock! (You laugh *now*...)

1. Pitch the yeast. Pour the rehydrated yeast solution into the fermentation bucket.

2. Add cooled wort. Pour the cooled wort into the fermentation bucket *aggressively*, so that it splashes and churns in the bucket. This action adds the oxygen yeast need for growth. For best results, pour some back into the boiling pot, and then pour it into the fermenter again. This is the only time during the brewing process that you want the beer to be aerated or exposed to oxygen. All other transfers should be done *quietly*, using a sanitized siphon, and with very little disturbance in the flow and minimal contact with the air.

If you had added hops during the boil, you can remove them during this step by pouring the wort into the fermentor through a strainer. It is not necessary to remove the hops, however.

Figure 9—Pouring the chilled wort.

3. Store the fermentor. Put the lid tightly on the fermentor and carry it to a secure location where it will be undisturbed for two weeks. Choose a location that has a stable temperature of 65-70°F (18-21°C). A warmer temperature of 75°F (24°C) is okay, but above 80°F (26°C) the flavor of the beer will be affected. As soon as you have finished moving it, insert the airlock.

4. Leave it alone! After about 24 hours, the airlock will be bubbling steadily, the exciting evidence of fermentation. At right you can see what it looks like inside. The fermentation will proceed like this for two to four days, depending on the conditions of your fermentation. The activity will decrease as most of the malt sugars are consumed by the yeast, though the yeast will continue to ferment the beer long after the bubbling diminishes. Leave the beer in the fermentor for a total of two weeks.

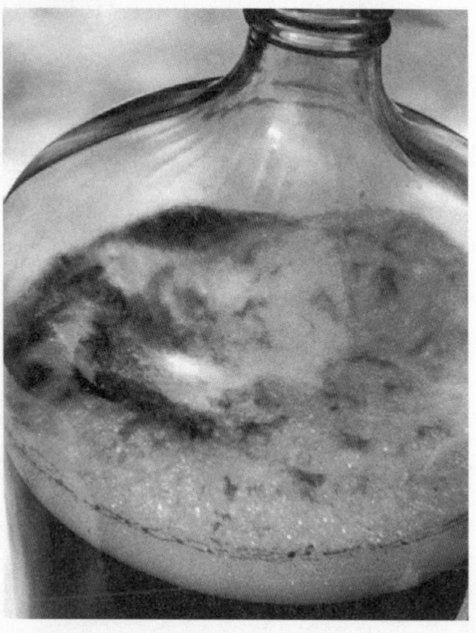

5. Clean Up. Now is the time to wash out your brewpot and other equipment. Only use mild unscented dishwashing detergents, or the cleaners recommended in *Chapter 2–Preparations,* and rinse well.

Bottling Day

The second big day in your career as a homebrewer comes two weeks later, after fermentation is complete. Everything outlined below is thoroughly discussed in *Chapter 11–Priming and Bottling.*

To bottle your beer, you will need:

- 48 (12 oz) bottles
- bottle brush (baby bottle variety is okay)
- bottle capper (from homebrew shop)
- bottle caps (from homebrew shop)
- bottling bucket (basically another fermentor bucket with a spigot and bottle filler attached)
- racking cane/siphon/bottle filler (from homebrew shop)
- Sugar (6 oz)

1. Prepare your bottles. A typical 5-gallon batch requires two cases (48) of 12-oz bottles for bottling. Thoroughly clean and sanitize the bottles before use. If you are using old bottles, check them inside for dirt or mold deposits. They may need to be scrubbed with a bottle brush to get them really clean. Always clean first, then sanitize.

2. Prepare your bottle caps. Bottle caps should be sanitized before use, and the best way is to soak them in sanitizing solution. Some brewers use flip-top (Grolsch-style) bottles. The ceramic part of the flip tops can be sanitized along with the bottles. The rubber seals can be sanitized like the bottle caps.

3. Prepare your priming sugar. We add a priming solution just before bottling to provide carbonation to the beer in the bottle. Boil ¾ cup (4 oz by weight) of corn sugar or ⅔ cup (3.8 oz by weight) of table sugar in two cups of water. Cover the pan and allow it to cool.

Figure 12—Racking to the bottling bucket.

4. Combine beer and priming sugar. The best method for preparing the beer and priming sugar solution is to use a separate container the same size as your fermentor as a "bottling bucket." Clean and sanitize it and gently pour the priming solution into it. Next, siphon the beer from the fermentor into the bottling bucket. Don't simply pour the beer into the bucket, and don't let the beer splash as you siphon it in. Instead, put the end of the siphon under the surface of the beer as it fills. The swirling motion of the beer as it enters the bucket will be sufficient to evenly mix the priming solution into the beer without aeration. *See Figure 13.*

If you don't have a bottling bucket, you can gently pour the priming solution into the fermentor and gently stir it. Allow the sediment in the fermentor to settle for 15-30 minutes before proceeding. You can fill the bottles using the bottle filler attachment on your siphon. *See Figure 14.*

5. Bottle. Carefully fill the bottles with the primed beer, place a sanitized bottle cap on each bottle, and crimp it using the bottle capper. At this stage it is helpful to have a friend operate the capper while you fill the bottles.

6. Store the bottles. Place the capped bottles out of the light in a warm environment (room temperature–65-75°F, 18-24°C). The bottles will take about two weeks to carbonate. The bottles will have a thin layer of yeast on the bottom.

Figure 13—Filling bottles from the bottling bucket (preferred method).

Figure 14—Filling bottles from a siphon with a bottle filler attachment.

Serving Day

At last, you get to sample the fruit of your labors. It's been about a month since Brew Day, and you are ready to open your first bottle and see what kind of wonderful beer you have created. During the past two weeks, the yeast still swimming around in the beer have consumed the priming sugar, creating just enough carbon dioxide to carbonate your beer perfectly.

Okay, so maybe you couldn't wait this long and you already opened a bottle. You may have noticed the beer wasn't fully carbonated or that it seemed carbonated but the bubbles had no staying power. You may have also noticed a "green" flavor. That flavor is the sign of a young beer. The two-week "conditioning" period not only adds carbonation but also gives the beer flavors time to meld and balance out.

1. Chill your beer. The bottled beer does not need to be stored cold. It will keep for approximately six months, depending on how well you managed to avoid exposure to oxygen during the last stage of fermentation and the bottling process. You will probably want to chill it before serving, however. The optimal temperature for serving beer depends on the style, varying from 40-55°F (4-12°C). In general, the darker the beer, the warmer you serve it.

2. Pouring your beer. To pour the beer without getting yeast in your glass, tip the bottle slowly to avoid disturbing the yeast layer on the bottom of the bottle. With practice, you will be able to pour everything but the last quarter inch of beer without getting any yeast in your glass.

3. Savor the flavor. Finally, take a deep draught and savor the flavor of the beer you created. Take time to evaluate the flavor, its bitterness qualities, its sweetness, the level of carbonation. These observations are your first steps to beer appreciation and designing your own recipes.

But Wait! There's More!

If you want to learn more about brewing beer–how it works, why it works, and how to have fun creating your own recipes and trying advanced techniques–then I encourage you to keep reading. The next chapters in this book will lead you through extract brewing again, but this time with more explanation. They include descriptions of the great variety of hops, yeast strains, and malts that can make each brewing session and every beer unique. In later chapters, I will teach you how to brew beer from scratch, without extracts, using the malted barley itself. This kind of brewing really puts you in control of the final product, and many brewers find this "all-grain" type of brewing to be the most satisfying.

It is my sincere hope that this book will help you to derive the same sense of fun and enthusiasm for this hobby that I have experienced, and that it will enable you to brew some really outstanding beer.

The next chapter describes brewing preparation in more detail. Good preparation is the most important step to assuring a successful batch.

Chapter Two

Brewing Preparations

The Road to Good Brewing

There are three important things to keep in mind every time you brew: Preparation, Sanitation, and Good Record Keeping. Good preparation prevents nasty surprises. You don't want to be halfway through your brewing and realize that you don't have any yeast. You don't want to pour good wort into a fermentor that you forgot to clean. Cleaning and Sanitizing are part of your preparation but are the most important factors for assuring a successful batch of beer. During an interview, Bob Brandt, the head brewer at a very successful brewpub, told me, "Good brewing is 75% cleaning." And I agree–spoiled batches are not good.

Likewise, there are two types of brewers–lucky and consistent. The lucky brewer will sometimes produce an outstanding batch of beer, but just as often one that is not. He brews from the seat-of-his-pants, innovating and experimenting with mixed results. The consistent brewer has more outstanding batches than poor ones. He may be an innovator and an experimenter, the difference is that he takes note of what he did and how much he did of it so that he can always learn from his results. Good record keeping will make the difference between luck and skill.

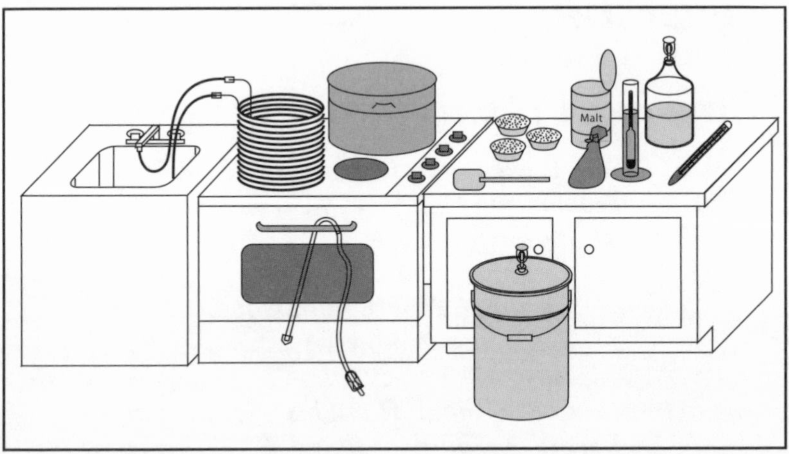

Figure 16—All the equipment and ingredients for the day's brew are set out on the counter and ready to go. The crushed specialty grain is tied in a muslin grainbag, and the hops have been weighed and put in three separate bowls.

Preparation

Preparing your brewing equipment is principally a matter of cleaning and sanitizing, but organization is a part of the process too. For each of the brewing processes, some preparation can be done to make the process work better. Consider what you are going to do:

Check the Recipe—Make a shopping list of your ingredients and amounts. Plan ahead on how you are going to measure them. Do you need extra bowls or measuring cups? Do you have good water out of the tap, or should you buy some?

Equipment—Make a checklist of the equipment you will be using and note whether it needs to be sanitized or only cleaned. Don't try to clean something at the last minute just as you need it, you are inviting trouble. Use a

BREWING CHECKLIST

Table 1—Cleaning and Sanitization Check List

Brewpot	☐ Clean	
Stirring spoon	☐ Clean	
Table spoon	☐ Clean	☐ Sanitize
Measuring Cup	☐ Clean	☐ Sanitize
Yeast Starter Jar	☐ Clean	☐ Sanitize
Fermentor and lid	☐ Clean	☐ Sanitize
Airlock	☐ Clean	☐ Sanitize
Thermometer	☐ Clean	☐ Sanitize

checklist to organize your thoughts and see if you have overlooked anything. You may want to purchase utensils expressly for brewing; don't stir with a spatula that you often use to cook onions. More instruction on cleaning is given later in this chapter.

Sanitizing—Anything that touches the cooled wort must be sanitized. This includes the fermentor, airlock, and any of the following, depending on your transfer methods: Funnel, strainer, stirring spoon and racking cane. Sanitizing techniques are discussed later in this chapter.

Preparing The Yeast—This step is paramount; without yeast, you can not make beer. The yeast should be prepared at the beginning of the brewing session (if not before) so you can tell if it's alive and ready to work beforehand. If you have spent time preparing the equipment and making the wort and then you have nothing to ferment it with, you will be very disappointed. See *Chapter 6–Yeast,* for detailed information on yeast preparation.

The Boil—Weigh out your hop additions and place them in separate bowls for the different addition times during the boil. If you are going to steep crushed specialty grain (see Chapter 12), then weigh, package and steep it before adding your extract to the boiling pot.

Cooling After The Boil—If you plan to chill the wort using a water bath, i.e., setting the pot in the sink or the bathtub, make sure you have enough ice on hand to cool the wort quickly. A quick chill from boiling is necessary to help prevent infection and to generate the Cold Break in the wort. A good cold break precipitates proteins, polyphenols and beta glucans which are believed to contribute to beer instability during storage. A good cold break also reduces the amount of chill haze in the final beer.

By taking the time to prepare for your brewday, the brewing will go smoothly and you will be less likely to forget any steps. Cleaning and sanitizing your equipment beforehand will allow you to pay more attention to your task at hand (and maybe prevent a messy boilover). Preparing your yeast by either re-hydrating and proofing, or making a Starter will ensure that the afternoon's work will not have been in vain. Having your ingredients laid out and measured will prevent any mistakes in the recipe. In short, preparing for each stage of the brewing process by having the equipment ready and the process planned out will make the whole operation simple and keep it fun. Your beer will probably benefit too. As in all things, a little preparation goes a long way to improving the end result.

Sanitation

Cleanliness is the foremost concern of the brewer. Providing good growing conditions for the yeast in the beer also provides good growing conditions for other micro-organisms, especially wild yeast and bacteria. Cleanliness must be maintained throughout every stage of the brewing process.

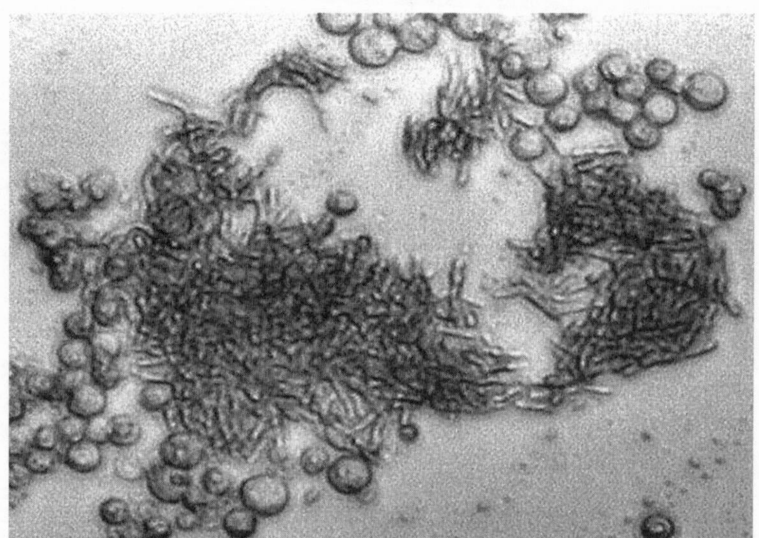

Figure 17—The yeast cells are the round things, the worms are bacteria. (Sample was taken from fermenting wort that was spit into.) 3000X

The definition and objective of sanitization is to reduce bacteria and contaminants to insignificant or manageable levels. The terms clean, sanitize and sterilize are often used interchangeably, but should not be. Items may be clean but not sanitized or vice versa. Here are the definitions:

Clean To be free from dirt, stain, or foreign matter.
Sanitize To kill/reduce spoiling microorganisms to negligible levels.
Sterilize To eliminate all forms of life, especially microorganisms, either by chemical or physical means.

Cleaning is the process of removing all the dirt and grime from a surface, thereby removing all the sites that can harbor bacteria. Cleaning is usually done with a detergent and elbow grease. None of the sanitizing agents used by homebrewers are capable of eliminating all bacterial spores and viruses. The majority of chemical agents homebrewers use will clean and sanitize but not sterilize. However, sterilization is not necessary. Instead of worrying about sterilization, homebrewers can be satisfied if they consistently reduce these contaminants to negligible levels.

All sanitizers are meant to be used on clean surfaces. A sanitizer's ability to kill microorganisms is reduced by the presence of dirt, grime or organic material. Organic deposits can harbor bacteria and shield the surface from being reached by the sanitizer. So it is up to you to make sure the surface of the item to be sanitized is as clean as possible.

Cleaning Products

Cleaning requires a certain amount of scrubbing, brushing and elbow grease. It is necessary because a dirty surface can never be a completely sanitized one. Grungy deposits can harbor bacteria that will ultimately contaminate your beer. The ability of a sanitizing agent to kill bacteria is reduced by the presence of any extra organic matter, so prior cleaning is necessary to assure complete sanitization. Several cleaning products available to the homebrewer are discussed below. Cleaning recommendations for the equipment you will be using follow.

Detergents Dishwashing detergents and cleansers should be used with caution when cleaning your brewing equipment. These products often contain perfumes that can be adsorbed onto plastic equipment and released back into the beer. In addition, some detergents and cleansers do not rinse completely and often leave behind a film that can be tasted in the beer. Several rinses with hot water may be necessary to remove all traces of the detergent. Detergents containing phosphates generally rinse more easily than those without, but because phosphates are pollutants, they are slowly being phased out. A mild unscented dish washing detergent like Ivory brand is a good choice for most of your routine equipment cleaning needs. Only stubborn stains or burnt-on deposits will require something stronger.

Bleach Bleach is one of the most versatile cleaners available to the homebrewer. When dissolved in cold water, it forms a caustic solution that is good at breaking up organic deposits like food stains and brewing gunk. Bleach is an aqueous solution of chlorine, chlorides and hypochlorites. These chemical agents all contribute to bleach's bactericidal and cleaning powers, but are also corrosive to a number of metals used in brewing equipment. Bleach should not be used for cleaning brass and copper because it causes blackening and excessive corrosion. Bleach can be used to clean stainless steel, but you need to be careful to prevent corrosion and pitting.

There are a few simple guidelines to keep in mind when using bleach to clean stainless steel.

- Do not leave the metal in contact with chlorinated water for extended periods of time (no more than an hour).
- Fill vessels completely so corrosion does not occur at the waterline.
- After the cleaning or sanitizing treatment, rinse the item with boiled water and dry the item completely if it is going to be stored.

Percarbonates Sodium percarbonate is sodium carbonate (i.e., Arm and Hammer Super Washing Soda) reacted with hydrogen peroxide and it is a very effective cleaner for all types of brewing equipment. It rinses easily. Several products containing percarbonates (e.g. Straight-A, Powder Brewery Wash, B-Brite, and One-Step) are approved by the FDA as cleaners in food-manufacturing facilities. One Step is labeled as a light cleaner and final rinse agent, and produces hydrogen peroxide in solution. Hydrogen peroxide will effectively sanitize surfaces and containers which are already clean. As with all sanitizers, the effectiveness of hydrogen peroxide as a sanitizing agent is comprimised by organic soil. Use these cleaners according to the manufacturer's instructions, but generally use one tablespoon per gallon (4 ml per liter) and rinse after cleaning.

In my opinion, percarbonate-based cleaners are the best choice for equipment cleaning, and Straight-A from Logic, Inc. and Powder Brewery Wash (PBW) from Five Star Chemicals, Inc. are the best of them. These products combine sodium metasilicate with the percarbonate in a stable form which increases its effectivity and prevents the corrosion of metals (like copper and aluminum) that strong alkaline solutions can cause.

Trisodium Phosphate Trisodium phosphate (TSP) and chlorinated TSP (CTSP) are effective cleaners for post-fermentation brewing deposits and the chlorinated form is also a sanitizer. TSP and CTSP are becoming harder to find, but are still available at hardware stores in the paint section. (Painters use it for washing walls because it can be rinsed away completely.) The recommended usage is one tablespoon per gallon of hot water. Solutions of TSP and CTSP should not be left to soak for more than an hour because a white mineral film can sometimes deposit on glass and metal which requires an acid (vinegar) solution to remove. This is not usually a problem however.

Automatic Dishwashers Using dishwashers to clean equipment and bottles is a popular idea among homebrewers but there are a few limitations:

- The narrow openings of hoses, racking canes and bottles usually prevent the water jets and detergent from effectively cleaning inside.
- If detergent does get inside these items, there is no guarantee that it will get rinsed out again.
- Dishwasher drying additives (Jet Dry™, for example) can ruin the head retention of beer. Drying additives work by putting a chemical film on the items that allows them to be fully wetted by the water so droplets don't form; preventing spots. The wetting action destabilizes the proteins that form the bubbles.

With the exceptions of spoons, measuring cups and wide mouth jars, it is probably best to only use automatic dishwashers for heat sanitizing, not cleaning. Heat sanitizing is discussed later in this chapter.

Oven Cleaner Commonly known as lye, sodium hydroxide (NaOH) is the caustic main ingredient of most heavy-duty cleaners like oven and drain cleaner. Potassium hydroxide (KOH) is also commonly used. Even in moderate concentrations, these chemicals are very hazardous to skin and should only be used when wearing rubber gloves and goggle-type eye protection. Vinegar is useful for neutralizing sodium hydroxide that gets on your skin, but if sodium hydroxide gets in your eyes it could cause severe burns or blindness. Spray-on oven cleaner is the safest and most convenient way to use sodium hydroxide. Brewers often scorch the bottoms of their brewpots resulting in a black, burned wort area that is difficult to remove for fear of scouring a hole in the pot. The easiest solution is to apply oven cleaner and allow it to dissolve the stain. After the burned-on area has been removed, it is important to thoroughly rinse the area of any oven cleaner residue to prevent subsequent corrosion of the metal.

Sodium hydroxide is very corrosive to aluminum and brass. Copper and stainless steel are generally resistant. Pure sodium hydroxide should not be used to clean aluminum brewpots because the high pH causes the dissolution of the protective oxides, and a subsequent batch of beer might have a metallic taste. Oven cleaner should not affect aluminum adversely if it is used properly.

Cleaning Your Equipment

Cleaning Plastic There are basically three kinds of plastic that you will be cleaning: opaque white polypropylene, hard clear polycarbonate and clear soft vinyl tubing. You will often hear the polypropylene referred to as "food grade plastic", though all three of these plastics are. Polypropylene is used for utensils, fermenting buckets and fittings. Polycarbonate is used for racking canes and measuring cups. The vinyl tubing is used for siphons and the like.

The main thing to keep in mind when cleaning plastics is that they may adsorb odors and stains from the cleaning products you use. Dish detergents are your best bet for general cleaning, but scented detergents should be avoided. Bleach is useful for heavy duty cleaning, but the odor can remain and bleach tends to cloud vinyl tubing. Percarbonate cleaners have the benefit of cleaning as well as bleach without the odor and clouding problems. Dishwashers are a convenient way to clean plastic utensils, but the heat might warp polycarbonate items.

Cleaning Glass Glass has the advantage of being inert to everything you might use to clean it with. The only considerations are the danger of breakage and the potential for stubborn lime deposits when using bleach and TSP in hard water areas. When it comes to cleaning your glass bottles and carboys, you will probably want to use bottle and carboy brushes so you can effectively clean the insides.

Cleaning Copper For routine cleaning of copper and other metals, percarbonate-based cleaners like PBW are the best choice. For heavily oxidized conditions, acetic acid is very effective, especially when hot. Acetic acid is available in grocery stores as white distilled vinegar at a standard concentration of 5% acetic acid by volume. It is important to use only white distilled vinegar as opposed to cider or wine vinegar because these other types just might contain live acetobacteria cultures, which are the last thing you want in your beer.

BREWING TIP

Cleaning and Sanitizing Bottles

Dishwashers are great for cleaning the outside of bottles and heat sanitizing, but will not clean the insides effectively.

If your bottles are dirty or moldy, soak them in a mild bleach solution or sodium percarbonate type cleaners (ex. PBW™) for a day or two to soften the residue. You'll still need to scrub them thoroughly with a bottle brush to remove any stuck residue.

To eliminate the need to scrub bottles in the future, rinse them thoroughly after each use.

Brewers who use immersion wort chillers are always surprised how bright and shiny the chiller is the first time it comes out of the wort. If the chiller wasn't bright and shiny when it went into the wort, guess where the grime and oxides ended up? Yep, in your beer. The oxides of copper are more readily dissolved by the mildly acidic wort than is the copper itself. By cleaning copper tubing with acetic acid once before the first use and rinsing with water immediately after each use, the copper will remain clean with no oxide or wort deposits that could harbor bacteria. Cleaning copper with vinegar should only occasionally be necessary.

Cleaning and sanitizing copper and brass with bleach solutions is not recommended. The chlorine and hypochlorites in bleach cause oxidation and blackening of copper and brass. If the oxides come in contact with the mildly acidic wort, the oxides will quickly dissolve, possibly exposing yeast to unhealthy levels of copper during fermentation.

Note: I discuss the cleaning of metals more thoroughly in *Appendix B–Brewing Metallurgy.*

Cleaning Brass Some brewers use brass fittings in conjunction with their wort chillers or other brewing equipment and are concerned about the lead that is present in brass alloys. The amount of lead on the surface of brass parts is miniscule and not a health concern. However, a solution of two parts white vinegar to one part hydrogen peroxide (common 3% solution) will remove tarnish and surface lead from brass parts when they are soaked for 5-15 minutes at room temperature. The brass will turn a buttery yellow color as it is cleaned. If the solution starts to turn green, then the parts have been soaking too long and the copper in the brass is beginning to dissolve. The solution has become contaminated and the part should be re-cleaned in a fresh solution.

Cleaning Stainless Steel and Aluminum For general cleaning, mild detergents or percarbonate-based cleaners are best for steel and aluminum. Bleach should be avoided because the high pH of a bleach solution can cause corrosion of aluminum and to a lessor degree of stainless steel. Do not clean aluminum shiny bright or use bleach to clean an aluminum brewpot because this removes the protective oxides and can result in a metallic taste. This detectable level of aluminum is not hazardous. There is more aluminum in a common antacid tablet than would be present in a batch of beer made in an aluminum pot.

There are oxalic acid based cleansers available at the grocery store that are very effective for cleaning stubborn stains, deposits, and rust from stainless. They also work well for copper. Examples are Bar Keeper's Friend Cleanser, Revere Ware Copper and Stainless Cleanser, and Kleen King Stainless Steel Cleanser. Use according to the manufacturer's directions and rinse thoroughly with water afterwards.

Sanitizing Products

Once your equipment is clean, it is time to sanitize it before use. Only items that will contact the wort after the boil need to be sanitized, namely: fermentor, lid, airlock, rubber stopper, yeast starter jar, thermometer, funnel, and siphon. Your bottles will need to be sanitized also, but that can wait until bottling day. There are two very convenient ways to sanitize your equipment: chemical and heat. When using chemical sanitizers, the solution can usually be prepared in the fermentor bucket and all the equipment can be soaked in there. Heat sanitizing methods depend on the type of material being sanitized.

Chemical

Bleach The cheapest and most readily available sanitizing solution is made by adding 1 tablespoon of bleach to 1 gallon of water (4 ml per liter). Let the items soak for 20 minutes, and then drain. Rinsing is supposedly not necessary at this concentration, but many brewers, myself included, rinse with some boiled water anyway to be sure of no off-flavors from the chlorine.

Star San Star San is an acidic sanitizer from the makers of PBW and was developed especially for sanitizing brewing equipment. It requires only 30 seconds of contact time and does not require rinsing. Unlike other no-rinse

Figure 19—The most commonly used chemical sanitizers: Iodophor, Star San, and Bleach.

sanitizers, Star San will not contribute off-flavors at higher than recommended concentrations. The recommended usage is one fluid ounce per 5 gallons of water. The solution can be put in a spray bottle and used as a spray-on sanitizer for glassware or other items that are needed in a hurry. The foam is just as effective as immersion in the solution. Also, the surfactant used in Star San will not affect the head retention of beer like those used in detergents.

Star San is my preferred sanitizer for all usages except those that I can conveniently do in the dishwasher. A solution of Star San has a long usage life and an open bucket of it will remain active for several days. Keeping a solution of Star San in a closed container will increase its shelf life. The viability of the solution can be judged by its clarity; it turns cloudy as the viability diminishes.

Star San is only effective when the pH of the solution is less than 3.5. At a pH above 3.5, the solution turns cloudy and loses its batericidal properties. This is also the reason it is a no rinse sanitizer–when the fermenter or bottle has been drained and filled with wort or beer, the higher pH of the wort and beer neutralizes the sanitizing capability so that the yeast are unaffected.

One last note on this product: Because it is listed as a sanitizer and bactricide by the FDA and EPA, the container must list disposal warnings that are suitable for pesticides. Do not be alarmed, it is less hazardous to your skin than bleach.

Iodophor Iodophor is a solution of iodine complexed with a polymer carrier that is very convenient to use. One tablespoon in 5 gallons of water (15ml in 19 l) is all that is needed to sanitize equipment with a two minute soak time. This produces a concentration of 12.5 ppm of titratable iodine. Soaking equipment longer, for 10 minutes, at the same concentration will disinfect surfaces to hospital standards. At 12.5 ppm the solution has a faint brown color that you can use to monitor the solution's viability. If the solution loses its color, it no longer contains enough free iodine to work. There is no advantage to using more than the specified amount of iodophor. In addition to wasting the product, you risk exposing yourself and your beer to excessive amounts of iodine.

Iodophor will stain plastic with long exposures, but that is only a cosmetic problem. The 12.5 ppm concentration does not need to be rinsed, but the item should be allowed to drain before use. Even though the recommended concentration is well below the taste threshold, I rinse everything with a little bit of cooled boiled water to avoid any chance of off-flavors, but that's me.

Heat

Heat is one of the few means by which the homebrewer can actually sterilize an item. Why would you need to sterilize an item? Homebrewers that grow and maintain their own yeast cultures want to sterilize their growth media to assure against contamination. When a microorganism is heated at a high enough temperature for a long enough time, it is killed. Both dry heat (oven) and steam (autoclave, pressure cooker or dishwasher) can be used for sanitizing.

Oven Dry heat is less effective than steam for sanitizing and sterilizing, but many brewers use it. The best place to do dry heat sterilization is in your oven. To sterilize an item, refer to *Table 2–Dry Heat Sterilization* for the temperatures and times required.

The times indicated in begin when the item has reached the indicated temperature. Although the durations seem long, remember this process kills all microorganisms, not just most as in sanitizing. To be sterilized, items need to be heat-proof at the given temperatures. Glass and metal items are prime candidates for heat sterilization.

Some homebrewers bake their bottles using this method and thus always have a supply of clean sterile bottles. The opening of the bottle can be covered with a piece of aluminum foil prior to heating to prevent contamination after cooling and during storage. They will remain sterile indefinitely if kept wrapped.

One note of caution: bottles made of soda lime glass are much more susceptible to thermal shock and breakage than those made of borosilicate glass and should be heated and cooled slowly (e.g. 5°F per minute). You can assume all beer bottles are made of soda lime glass and that any glassware that says Pyrex™ or Kimax™ is made of borosilicate.

STERILIZATION

Table 2—Dry Heat Sterilization

Temperature	Duration
338°F (170°C)	60 Minutes
320°F (160°C)	120 Minutes
302°F (150°C)	150 Minutes
284°F (140°C)	180 Minutes
250°F (121°C)	12 Hours

Autoclaves, Pressure Cookers and Dishwashers Typically when we talk about using steam we are referring to the use of an autoclave or pressure cooker. These devices use steam under pressure to sterilize items. Because steam conducts heat more efficiently, the cycle time for such devices is much shorter than when using dry heat. The typical amount of time it takes to sterilize a piece of equipment in an autoclave or pressure cooker is 20 minutes at 257°F (125°C) at 20 pounds per square inch (psi).

Dishwashers can be used to sanitize, as opposed to sterilize, most of your brewing equipment, you just need to be careful that you don't warp any plastic items. The steam from the drying cycle will effectively sanitize all surfaces. Bottles and other equipment with narrow openings should be precleaned. Run the equipment through the full wash cycle without using any detergent or rinse agent. Dishwasher Rinse Agents will destroy the head retention on your glassware. If you pour a beer with carbonation and no head, this might be the cause.

Cleaning and Sanitizing Final Thoughts

Clean all equipment as soon after use as possible. This means rinsing out the fermentor, tubing, etc. as soon as they are used. It is very easy to get distracted and come back to find that the syrup or yeast has dried hard as a rock and the equipment is stained. If you are pressed for time, keep a large container of water handy and just toss things in to soak until you can clean them later.

You can use different methods of cleaning and sanitizing for different types of equipment. You will need to decide which methods work best for you in your brewery. Good preparation will make each of the brewing processes easier and more successful.

Table 3—Cleaning Products Summary Table

Cleaners	Amount	Comments
Detergents	(squirt)	It is important to use unscented detergents that won't leave any perfumey odors behind. Be sure to rinse well.
Straight A, PBW	1/4 cup per 5 gal. (<1 tbs./gal)	Best all purpose cleaners for grunge on all brewing equipment. Most effective in warm water.
Sodium Percarbonates	1 tbs./gal	Effective cleaner for grungy brew ing deposits. Will not harm metals.
Bleach	1–4 tbs./gal	Good cleaner for grungy brewing deposits. Do not allow bleach to contact metals for more than an hour. Corrosion may occur.
TSP, CTSP	1 tbs./gal	Good cleaner for grungy brewing deposits. May often be found in paint and hardware stores. Mineral deposits may form after soaking for days.
Dishwasher	Normal amount of automatic dish-washer detergent.	Recommended for utensils and glassware. Do not use scented detergents or those with rinse agents.
Oven Cleaner (Spray-on)	Follow product instructions.	Often the only way to dissolve burned-on sugar from a brewpot.
White Distilled Vinegar	Full Strength as necessary.	Most effective when hot. Useful for cleaning copper wort chillers.
Vinegar and Hydrogen Peroxide	2:1 volume ratio of vinegar to peroxide.	Use for removing surface lead and cleaning tarnished brass.
Oxalic Acid based Cleansers	As Needed with scrubby.	Sold as stainless steel and copper cookware cleanser. Use for removing stains and oxides.

Table 4—Sanitizers Summary Table

Sanitizer	Amount	Comments
Star San	2 tablespoons per 5 gallons	Can be used via immersion or spraying. Will sanitize clean surfaces in 30 seconds. Allow to drain before use; does not need to be rinsed.
Iodophor	12.5—25 ppm 1 tablespoon per 5 gal = 12.5 ppm	Iodophor will sanitize in 10 minutes at 12.5 ppm and does not need to be rinsed. Allow to drain before use.
Bleach	1 tablespoon per gallon.	Bleach will sanitize equipment in 20 minutes. It does not have to be rinsed, but probably should be to prevent chlorophenol flavors.
Dishwasher	Full wash and Heat Dry cycle without detergent.	Bottles must be clean before being put in dishwasher for sanitizing. Place upside down on rack.
Oven	340°F for 1 hour	Renders bottles sterile, not just sanitized. Allow bottles to cool slowly to prevent thermal shock and cracking.

Record Keeping

Always keep good notes on what ingredients, amounts and times were used in the brewing process. There are several brewing spreadsheets and software programs available over the Internet that can be a big help. A brewer needs to be able to repeat good batches and learn from poor ones. If you have a bad batch and want to ask another brewer for their opinion, they are going to want to know all the brewing details. They will want to know your ingredients and amounts, how long you boiled, how you cooled, the type of yeast, how long it fermented, what the fermentation looked, what the temperature was, etc. There are so many possible causes for "it tastes funny", that you really need to keep track of everything that you did so you can figure where it might of gone wrong and fix it the next time. *Chapter 21—Is My Beer Ruined?*, will help you identify possible causes for most of the common problems.

Create a recipe form that will help you be consistent. See the example on the next page.

Example Recipe Form

Recipe Name: Cascade Ale

Recipe Volume: 5 gal

Yeast: Cooper's Ale Yeast (re-hydrated)

Malts:	**Amount**	**Type**
1. Northwestern Amber malt extract	2 lbs.	dry
2. Cooper's Pale malt extract	4 lbs.	liquid
3.		
Calculated Original Gravity	1.045	

Hops:	**Amount**	**Time**	**% Alpha Acid**
1. Perle	1.5 oz	60 min.	6.4%
2. Cascade	1/2 oz	30 min.	5%
3. Willamette	1/2 oz	30 min.	4%
4. Cascade	1/2 oz	15 min.	5%
Calculated IBUs			40

Procedure:

Boiled 3 gallons of water, turned off heat and stirred in extract. Returned to boiling. Added first hop addition. Boiled 30 minutes and added Cascade and Willamette hops. Boiled another 15 minutes and added final addition of Cascade. Turned off heat and chilled the pot in an ice water bath to 70°F. Added the 2.5 gallons of wort to 2.5 gallons of water in the fermentor. Aerated by pouring back and forth five times. Pitched yeast.

Fermentation:

Fermenter is sitting at 70°F and started bubbling within 12 hours. Bubbled furiously for 36 hours then slowed. After 4 days, bubbles had stopped completely. It remained in the fermentor for two weeks total. Racked to bottling bucket and primed with 3/4 cup of corn sugar (boiled). Bottles were allowed to condition for two weeks.

Results:

Beer is Good! Strong hop taste and aroma. Perhaps a little too bitter. Tone down the bittering hops next time or add more amber malt extract to better balance the beer.

Chapter 3

Malt Extract and Beer Kits

What is Malt Extract?

Beer is brewed from malted barley. More precisely, beer is made by fermenting the sugars extracted from malted barley (mostly maltose). Malt is a general term used as an abbreviation for several things associated with maltose and malted barley. Brewer's malt is not malted milk balls, malted milk shakes, nor is it malt extract. In those cases, malt refers to the use of maltose–the sugar. The malts that brewers talk about are the specific types of malted barley that are processed to yield a wide range of fermentable malt sugars. These include lager malts, pale malts, vienna malts, munich malts, toasted, roasted and chocolate malts. *But what is malt extract?*

Don't worry, I'm getting to that...

During malting, the barley is soaked and drained to initiate the germination of the plant from the seed. When the seed germinates, it activates enzymes which start converting its starch reserves and proteins into sugars and amino acids that the growing plant can use. The purpose of malting a grain is to release these enzymes and starch reserves for use by the brewer. Once the seeds start to sprout, the grain is dried in a kiln to stop the enzymes until the brewer is ready to use the grain.

The brewer crushes the malted barley and soaks it in hot water to reactivate and accelerate the enzyme activity, converting the barley's starch reserves into sugars in a short period of time. The resulting sugar solution (extract of malt!) is boiled with hops and fermented by the yeast to make beer.

When making malt extract, the sugar solution is drawn off, pasteurized, and run into vacuum chambers for dehydration. By boiling off the water under a partial vacuum, the wort sugars are not caramelized by the heat of full boiling and a lighter tasting extract is produced. To make a hopped extract, Iso-Alpha Acid extracts of hops are added along with hop oils to give a complete hop character to the final wort extract. These hop extracts are added at the end of the process to prevent loss during dehydration. Malt extract takes a lot of the work out of homebrewing.

Malt extract is sold in both liquid (syrup) and powdered forms. The syrups are approximately 20 percent water, so 4 pounds of Dry Malt Extract (DME) is roughly equal to 5 pounds of Liquid Malt Extract (LME). DME is produced by heating the liquid extract and spraying it from an atomizer in a heated chamber. Strong air currents keep the droplets suspended until they dry and settle to the floor. DME is identical to LME except for the additional dehydration and lack of hopping. DME is typically not hopped because hop compounds tend to be lost during the final dehydration.

Beer Kit Woes

Perhaps you've been to a homebrew supply store and seen some of the many commercial beer kits that are packaged for the beginning homebrewer. Usually these kits are composed of an attractively labeled can of hopped extract, a packet of yeast, and easy instructions–Just Add Sugar and Water. And if you follow those instructions you will be disappointed with the results. My first beer kit was a bitter disappointment due to the lame instructions on the can. The instructions said something like, "Add 2 pounds of corn sugar or table sugar; Boil if you want to; ferment for 1 week at room temperature; and bottle after that." The result? Sparkling pond water.

BREWING TIP

Canned Beer Kit Rules

1. Don't follow the instructions on the can to add table or corn sugar.

2. Don't use the yeast that came with the can. (Unless it's a name-brand and has a use-by date code.)

The reason is that the yeast that is supplied with the can may be more than a year old and has most likely experienced harsh shipping conditions. It may have been poor quality yeast to begin with. It is better to buy a name brand yeast that is more reliable and has been stored well. For more information on yeast, see Chapter 6.

You don't need a kit to make your first batch. (And for heaven's sake, don't buy one of those of beer-in-a-bag-type kits.) Brewing beer is not mysterious, it's very straightforward. And despite the many different names and packaging, many kits taste the same. The reason is the commonality of the dry yeast strain provided with the kits and the instructions. Most canned beer kits, even the top brands, instruct you to add a couple pounds of white table sugar to the malt extract to make up the beer fermentables. Adding plain sugar dilutes the malty flavor of a beer. In addition, a study was carried out several years ago which discovered that many malt extract manufacturers were adulterating their extracts with corn sugar or other simple sugars. Everything is good in moderation, but when the kit starts out as half sugar and then instructs the brewer to add a couple pounds more, the resulting beer will not measure up.

In the time since that study was published however, homebrewing has grown greatly in popularity and has become much more aware of the necessity for high quality ingredients. Malt extract producers have responded to the new awareness in the marketplace with renewed pride in their products. There are a lot of good extracts and beer style kits to choose from these days.

Figure 23—Building your own kit for Cincinnati Pale Ale.

Shopping for Extracts

The freshness of the extract is important, particularly for the syrup. Beer brewed with extract syrup more than a year old will often have a blunt, stale, even soapy flavor to it. This is caused by the oxidation of the fatty acid compounds in the malt. Dry malt extract has a better shelf life than the liquid because the extra de-hydration slows the pertinent chemical reactions.

Another quality of an extract that can have a particularly strong affect on the quality of the finished beer is Free Amino Nitrogen (FAN). FAN is a measure of the amount of amino acid nitrogen that is available to the yeast for nutrition during fermentation. Without sufficient FAN, the yeast are less efficient and produce more fermentation byproducts which result in off-flavors in the final beer. This is why it is important to not follow most canned kit instructions to add sugar to the wort. Corn, rice, and cane sugar contain little, if any, FAN. Adding large percentages of these sugars to the wort dilutes what little FAN there is and deprives the yeast of the nutrients they need to grow and function. FAN can be added to the wort in the form of yeast nutrient. See *Chapter 7–Yeast* for more information.

Malt Extract is available as either Hopped or Unhopped. Hopped extracts are boiled with hops prior to dehydration and usually contain a mild to moderate level of bitterness. Alexander's, Briess, Coopers, Edme, Ireks, John Bull, Mountmellick, Munton & Fison, and Northwestern are all high quality brands. Read the ingredient list to avoid refined sugar.

Malt extract is commonly available in Pale, Amber, and Dark varieties, and can be mixed depending on the style of beer desired. Wheat malt extract is also available and new extracts tailored to specific beer styles are arriving all the time. The quality of extracts and beer kits has improved greatly in the last 5 years. An all-extract brewer will be quite satisfied brewing entirely from beer kits as long as they ignore the instructions on the can and follow the guidelines in this book. With the variety of extract now available, there are few beer styles that cannot be brewed using extract alone. For more information on which kinds of extracts to use to make different styles of beer, see *Chapter 19–Some of My Favorite Beer Styles and Recipes.*

RECIPE

Cincinnati Pale Ale

Ingredients for a 5 gallon batch

- 3-4 lb. Pale malt extract syrup, unhopped
- 2 lb. Amber dry malt extract
- 12 AAU of bittering hops (any variety)
  For example, 1 oz. of 12% AA Nugget, or 1.5 oz. of 8% AA Northern Brewer
- 5 AAU of finishing hops (Cascade or other)
  For example, 1 oz. of 5% Cascade or 1.25 oz. of 4% Liberty
- 3 packets of dry ale yeast

Finding a Good Kit

In addition to the name brand beer kits available, many of the better homebrew shops package their own kits and provide more comprehensive instructions. Kits assembled by homebrewers for homebrewers are probably the best way to get started. If your supply shop does not offer this type of kit, you can assemble your own. The recipe given for Cincinnati Pale Ale is a basic American pale ale and quite tasty. You will be amazed at the full body and rich taste compared to most commercial beers. More recipes and style guidelines are given in *Chapter 19–Some of My Favorite Beer Styles and Recipes.* You can use any one of those recipes for your first batch by choosing the all-extract option, or you can read *Section II–Brewing with Extract and Specialty Grain,* and try that easy additional step for a bit more liveliness in your first batch.

How Much Extract to Use

A rule of thumb is one pound of liquid extract per gallon of water for a light bodied beer. One and a half pounds per gallon produces a richer, full bodied beer. A pound of LME typically yields a gravity of 1.034-38, as measured by a hydrometer, when dissolved in one gallon of water. DME yields about 1.040-43. These yield values are referred to as Points per Pound per Gallon. If someone tells you that a certain extract or malt's yield is 36 points, it means that when 1 pound is dissolved into 1 gallon of water, the gravity is 1.036. If that 1 pound is dissolved into 3 gallons, its gravity would be 36/3 = 12 or 1.012. The gravity is how the strength of a beer is described. Most commercial beers have an Original Gravity (OG) of 1.035-1.050.

CALCULATION

Gravity (OG) Calculations

Total gravity points
= an extract's yield x mass
= specific gravity x total volume.

If you want to brew 5 gallons of 1.040 gravity beer, this would call for:
5 lbs of DME having 40 pts/lb./gal, or
5.5 lbs of LME having 36 pts/lb./gal.

40 pts/gal x 5 gal = 200 pts total
200 pts = 36 pts/lb. x (?) lbs
=> (?) lbs = 200 / 36 = 5.55 lbs.

5.55 lb. of 36 pts/lb./gal LME are needed to make the same 5 gallons of beer.

Note: The same concept can be used with the SI units of Liter Degrees per Kilogram i.e., L°/kg or pts./kg/L.
The conversion factor between ppg and L°/kg is 8.3454 x ppg = L°/kg

Gravity vs. Fermentability

Different extracts have different degrees of fermentability. In general, the darker the extract, the more complex sugars it will contain and the less fermentable it will be. Amber extract will typically have a higher finishing gravity than pale extract and dark will be higher than amber. This is not always the case, though. By manipulating the mash conditions, the relative percentages of sugars that are extracted from the mash can be varied. A brewer can produce a wort that is almost entirely made up of highly fermentable sugars like maltose or he can produce one that has a higher percentage of unfermentable complex carbohydrates. Because these complex sugars are not very fermentable, the beer will have a higher finishing gravity. While most of the perception of a beer's body is due to medium length proteins, the unfermentable complex sugars will lend some of the same feel.

WORT SUGARS

Table 5—Typical Sugar Profile Extracted from Malted Barley

Maltose	50%
Maltotriose	18%
Glucose	10%
Sucrose	8%
Fructose	2%
Other complex carbohydrates, including Dextrins	12%

For example, Laaglander's DME from the Netherlands is a high quality extract that often has a finishing gravity (FG) as high as 1.020 from a common 1.040 OG. The heavier body is nice to have in a stout for example; all-grain brewers would add American Carapils malt (a.k.a. Dextrin Malt) to their mash to produce the same effect. Brewers using extract have the alternative of adding Malto-dextrin powder, which is a concentrated form. Malto-dextrin powder has no taste, i.e. it's not sweet, and is slow to dissolve. It contributes about 40 points per pound per gallon.

To summarize–malt extract is not some mysterious substance but simply a concentrated wort, ready for brewing. You don't need to agonize over which kit to buy, comparing labels and product claims; you can plan your own beer and buy the type of extract that you want to use to make it. Malt extract makes brewing easier by taking the work out of producing the wort. This lets a new brewer focus on the fermentation processes.

The biggest step for a homebrewer is to learn how to extract the sugars from the malted grain himself. This process, called mashing, allows the brewer more control in producing the wort. This type of homebrewing is referred to as all-grain brewing, because the wort is produced from the grain without using any malt extract, and it won't be discussed until *Section III–Brewing With All-Grain.* In *Section II–Brewing With Extract and Specialty Grain,* we will examine the middle ground of this transition and take advantage of the benefits of grain with less equipment. You can use steeped specialty grains to increase the complexity of extract-based beers, and you will probably want to try it for your second or third batch, but it is certainly not difficult and could be done for a first beer.

Chapter 4

Water For Extract Brewing

The Taste of Water

Water is very important to beer. After all, beer is mostly water. Some waters are famous for brewing: the soft water of Pilsen, the hard water of Burton, Midlands, and pure Rocky Mtn. spring water. Each of these waters contributed to the production of a unique tasting beer. But what about your water? Can it make a good beer? When using malt extract, the answer is almost always "Yes". If you are brewing with grain, the answer can vary from "Sometimes" to "Absolutely". The reason for this difference between the brewing methods is that the minerals in the water can affect the starch conversion of the mash, but once the sugars have been produced, the affect of water chemistry on the flavor of the beer is greatly reduced. When brewing with malt extract, if the water tastes good to begin with, the beer should taste good.

Home Water Treatment

If the water smells bad, many odors (including chlorine) can be removed by boiling. Some city water supplies use a chemical called chloramine instead of chlorine to kill bacteria. Chloramine cannot be easily removed by boiling and will give a medicinal taste to beer. However, chloramine can be removed by running the water through an activated-charcoal filter, or by adding 1 campden tablet (potassium metabisulfite). Campden tablets are used in winemaking and should be available at your brew shop. One tablet will treat 20 gallons, so use a quarter or half and crush it up to help it dissolve. Charcoal filters are a good way to remove most odors and bad tastes due to dissolved gases and organic substances. These filters are relatively inexpensive and can be attached inline to the faucet or spigot. Another alternative is to use bottled water from the grocery store.

If the water has a metallic taste or leaves hard deposits on the plumbing, then aeration, boiling, and letting it cool overnight will precipitate the excess minerals. Pour the water off into another pot to leave the minerals behind. Water softening systems can also be used to remove bad-tasting minerals like iron, copper, and manganese as well as the scale-causing minerals, calcium and magnesium. Salt-based water softeners use ion exchange to replace these heavier metals with sodium. Softened water works fine for extract brewing but should be used with caution for all-grain brewing. Depending on the type of beer, the mashing process requires a particular balance of minerals in the water that the softening process will remove.

A good bet for your first batch of beer is the bottled water sold in most supermarkets as drinking water. Use the 2.5 gallon containers. Use one container for boiling the extract and set the other aside for addition to the fermentor later.

Water Chemistry Adjustment for Extract Brewing

Some brewing books advocate the addition of brewing salts to the brewpot to imitate the water of a famous brewing region, like the Burton region of Britain. While some salts can be added to extract-based brews to improve the flavor profile, salts are more properly used to adjust the pH of the mash for all-grain brewing. Water chemistry is fairly complex and adding salts is usually not necessary for extract brewing. Most municipal water is fine for brewing with extract and does not need adjustment. So, if you are brewing from an extract recipe that calls for the addition of gypsum or Burton salts, do not add it. The proper amount of a salt to add to your water depends on the mineral amounts already present and the brewer who published the recipe probably had entirely different water than you do. You may end up ruining the taste of the beer by adding too much. Just leave it out; you probably won't miss it.

However, if in the course of time after you have brewed several batches of the same recipe and have decided that the beer is somehow lacking, there are three ions that can be used to tweak the flavor. These ions are sodium, chloride, and sulfate. Briefly, sodium and chloride act to round out and accentuate the sweetness of the beer, while sulfate (from gypsum, for example) makes the hop bitterness more crisp. You need to know and understand the initial mineral profile of your brewing water before you start adding anything to it though. Too much sodium and sulfate can combine to produce a very harsh bitterness.

Water chemistry becomes even more important for all-grain brewing. The mineral profile of the water has a large affect on the conversion of sugars from the mash. Water reports, brewing salts and their affects are discussed more in *Chapter 15–Understanding the Mash pH.* I suggest you read that chapter before you add any salts to your extract brewing.

Here are the main points to remember about water for extract brewing:

- If your water tastes good, your beer should taste good.
- Many odors will dissipate during the boil, but some bad tastes need to be removed via filtration or water treatment.
- The addition of brewing salts when brewing with extract is not strictly necessary, and is not recommended until you have gained experience with the intended recipe.

Chapter 5

Hops

What Are They?

Hops are the cone-like flowers of a climbing vine that is native to the temperate regions of North America, Europe and Asia. The species has separate male and female plants and only the female vines produce the cones. The vines will climb 20 ft or more up any available support and are commonly trained onto strings or wires when grown commercially. The leaves resemble grape leaves and the cones vaguely resemble pine cones in shape but are light green, thin and papery. At the base of the petals are the yellow lupulin glands which contain the essential oils and resins that are so prized by brewers for their bittering and aroma qualities.

Hops have been cultivated for use in brewing for over 1000 years. The earliest known cultivation was in Central Europe, and by the early 1500s, cultivation had spread to Western Europe and Great Britain. At the turn of the century, about one dozen varieties of hop were being used for brewing; today, there are over one hundred. The focus of breeding programs has been to maintain desirable characteristics, while improving yield and disease resistance.

How Are They Used?

Hops are a natural preservative and part of the early use of hops in beer was to preserve it. Hops were added directly to the cask after fermentation to keep it fresh while it was transported. This is how one particular style of beer, India Pale Ale, was developed. At the turn of the 18th century, British brewers began shipping strong ale with lots of hops added to the barrels to preserve it over the several month voyage to India. By journey's end, the beer had acquired a depth of hop aroma and flavor. Perfect for quenching the thirst of British personnel in the tropics.

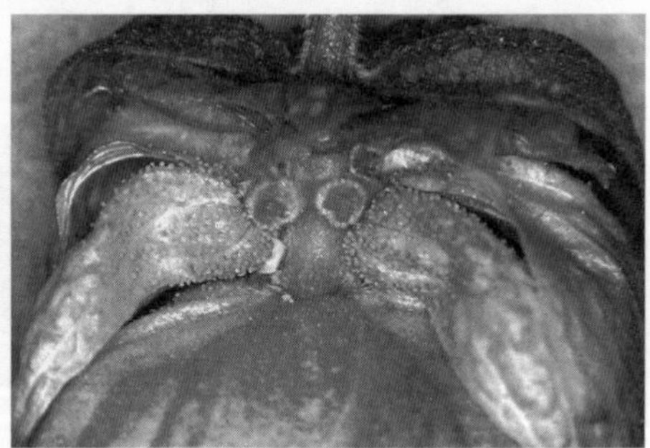

Figure 27—Lupulin glands at the base of the the petals.

Beer wouldn't be beer without hops–hops provide the balance, and are the signature in many styles. The bitterness contributed by hops balances the sweetness of the malt sugars and provides a refreshing finish. The main bittering agent is the alpha acid resin which is insoluble in water until isomerized by boiling. The longer the boil, the greater the percentage of isomerization and the more bitter the beer gets. However, the oils that contribute characteristic flavors and aromas are volatile and are lost to a large degree during the long boil. There are many varieties of hops, but they are usually divided into two general categories: Bittering and Aroma. Bittering hops are high in alpha acids, at about 10% by weight. Aroma hops are usually lower, around 5% and contribute a more desirable aroma and flavor to the beer. Several hop varieties are in-between and are used for both purposes. Bittering hops, also known as kettle hops, are added at the start of the boil and boiled for about an hour. Aroma hops are added towards the end of the boil and are typically boiled for 15 minutes or less. Aroma hops are also referred to as finishing hops. By adding different varieties of hops at different times during the boil, a more complex hop profile can be established that gives the beer a balance of hop bitterness, taste and aroma. Descriptions of the five main types of hop additions and their attributes follow.

First Wort Hopping

An old yet recently rediscovered process (at least among homebrewers), first wort hopping (FWH) consists of adding a large portion of the finishing hops to the boil kettle as the wort is received from the lauter tun. As the boil tun fills with wort (which may take a half hour or longer), the hops steep in the hot wort and release their volatile oils and resins. The aromatic oils are normally insoluble and tend to evaporate to a large degree during the boil. By letting the hops steep in the wort prior to the boil, the oils have more time to oxidize to more soluble compounds and a greater percentage are retained during the boil.

Only low alpha finishing hops should be used for FWH, and the amount should be no less than 30% of the total amount of hops used in the boil. This FWH addition therefore should be taken from the hops intended for finishing additions. Because more hops are in the wort longer during the boil, the total bitterness of the beer in increased but not by a substantial amount due to being low in alpha acid. In fact, one study among professional brewers determined that the use of FWH resulted in a more refined hop aroma, a more uniform bitterness (i.e. no harsh tones), and a more harmonious beer overall compared to an identical beer produced without FWH.

Bittering

The primary use of hops is for bittering. Bittering hop additions are boiled for 45-90 minutes to isomerize the alpha acids; the most common interval being one hour. There is some improvement in the isomerization between 45 and 90 minutes (about 5%), but only a small improvement at longer times (<1%). The aromatic oils of the hops used in the bittering addition(s) tend to boil away, leaving little hop flavor and no aroma. Because of this, high alpha varieties (which commonly have poor aroma characteristics) can be used to provide the bulk of the bitterness without hurting the taste of the beer. If you consider the cost of bittering a beer in terms of the amount of alpha acid per unit weight of hop used, it is more economical to use a half ounce of a high alpha hop rather than 1 or 2 ounces of a low alpha hop. You can save your more expensive (or scarce) aroma hops for flavoring and finishing.

Flavoring

By adding the hops midway through the boil, a compromise between isomerization of the alpha acids and evaporation of the aromatics is achieved yielding characteristic flavors. These flavoring hop additions are added 40-20 minutes before the end of the boil, with the most common time being 30 minutes. Any hop variety may be used. Usually the lower alpha varieties are chosen, although some high alpha varieties such as Columbus and Challenger have pleasant flavors and are commonly used. Often small amounts (¼–½ oz) of several varieties will be combined at this stage to create a more complex character.

Finishing

When hops are added during the final minutes of the boil, less of the aromatic oils are lost to evaporation and more hop aroma is retained. One or more varieties of hop may be used, in amounts varying from ¼–4 oz, depending on the character desired. A total of 1–2 oz. is typical. Finishing hop additions are typically 15 minutes or less before the end of the boil, or are added "at knockout" (when the heat is turned off) and allowed to steep ten minutes before the wort is cooled. In some setups, a "hopback" is used–the hot wort is run through a small chamber full of fresh hops before the wort enters a heat exchanger or chiller.

A word of caution when adding hops at knockout or using a hopback–depending on several factors, e.g., amount, variety, freshness, etc., the beer may take on a grassy taste due to tannins and other compounds which are usually neutralized by the boil. If short boil times are not yielding the desired hop aroma or a grassy flavor is evident, then I would suggest using FWH or Dry Hopping.

Dry Hopping

Hops can also be added to the fermentor for increased hop aroma in the final beer. This is called "dry hopping" and is best done late in the fermentation cycle. If the hops are added to the fermentor while it is still actively bubbling, then a lot of the hop aroma will be carried away by the carbon dioxide. It is better to add the hops (usually about a half ounce per 5 gallons) after bubbling has slowed or stopped and the beer is going through the conditioning phase prior to bottling. The best way to utilize dry hopping is to put the hops in a secondary fermentor, after the beer has been racked away from the trub and can sit a couple of weeks before bottling, allowing the volatile oils to diffuse into the beer. Many homebrewers put the hops in a nylon mesh bag–a "hop bag," to facilitate removing the hops before bottling. Dry hopping is appropriate for many pale ale and lager styles.

Don't worry about adding unboiled hops to the fermentor when you are dry hopping. Infection from the hops just doesn't happen.

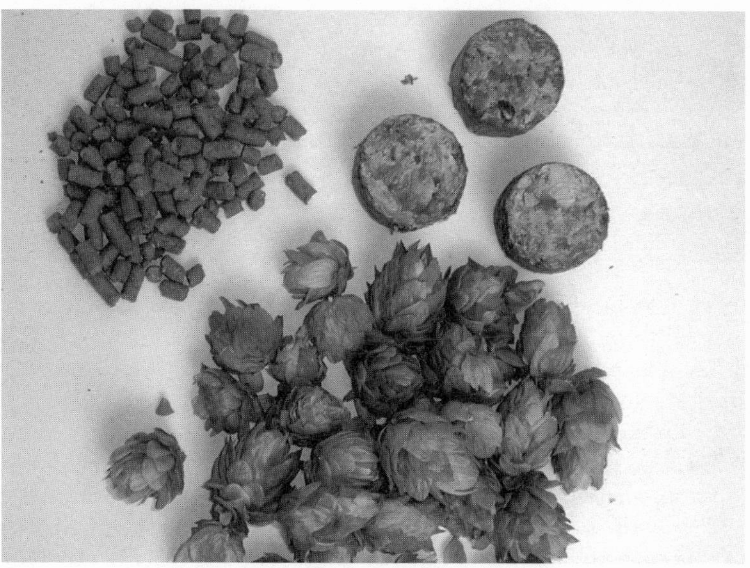

Hop Forms - Pellets, Plug and Whole

It's rare for any group of brewers to agree on the best form of hops. Each of the common forms has its own advantages and disadvantages. What form is best for you will depend on where in the brewing process the hops are being used, and will probably change as your brewing methods change.

HOP FORMS AND MERITS

Table 6—Hop Forms

Form	Advantages	Disadvantages
Whole	Easy to strain from wort. Best aroma, if fresh. Good for dry hopping.	They soak up wort, resulting in some wort loss after the boil. Bulk makes them more difficult to weigh.
Plug	Retain freshness longer than whole form. Convenient half ounce units. Plugs behave like whole hops in the wort.	Can only use in half ounce increments. Soak up wort just like whole hops.
Pellets	Easy to weigh Small increase in utilization due to shredding. Best storability.	Turn into hop sludge in bottom of kettle that is difficult to strain. Aroma content tends to be less than other forms due to amount of processing. Hard to contain when dry hopping–creates floaters.

Whichever form of hops you choose to use, freshness is important. Fresh hops smell fresh, herbal, and spicy, like evergreen needles and have a light green color like freshly mown hay. Old hops or hops that have been mishandled are often oxidized and smell like pungent cheese and may have turned brown. It is beneficial if hop suppliers pack hops in oxygen barrier bags and keep them cold to preserve the freshness and potency. Hops that have been stored warm and/or in non-barrier (thin) plastic bags can easily lose 50% of their bitterness potential in a few months. Most plastics are oxygen permeable; so when buying hops at a homebrew supply store, check to see if the hops are stored in a cooler or freezer and if they are stored in oxygen barrier containers. If you can smell the hops when you open the cooler door, then the hop aroma is leaking out through the packaging and they are not well protected from oxygen. If the stock turnover in the brewshop is high, non-optimum storage conditions may not be a problem. Ask the shop owner if you have any concerns.

Hop Types

Bittering Hop Varieties

Name: Brewer's Gold
Grown: UK, US
Profile: Poor aroma; Sharp bittering hop.
Usage: Bittering for ales
AA Range: 8-9%
Substitute: Bullion, Northern Brewer, Galena

Name: Bullion
Grown: UK (maybe discontinued), US
Profile: Poor aroma; Sharp bittering and black currant-like flavor when used in the boil.
Usage: Bittering hop for British style ales, perhaps some finishing
AA Range: 8-11%
Substitute: Brewer's Gold, Northern Brewer

Name: Centennial
Grown: US
Profile: Spicy, floral, citrus aroma, often referred to as Super Cascade because of the similarity; A clean bittering hop.
Usage: General purpose bittering, aroma, some dry hopping
Example: Sierra Nevada Celebration Ale, Sierra Nevada Bigfoot Ale
AA Range: 9-11.5%
Substitute: Cascade, Columbus

Name: Challenger
Grown: UK
Profile: Strong, fine spicy aroma widely used for English Bitters; A clean bittering hop.
Usage: Excellent bittering hop, also used for flavoring and aroma.
Example: Full Sail IPA, Butterknowle Bitter
AA Range: 6-8%
Substitute: Progress

Name: Chinook
Grown: US
Profile: Heavy spicy aroma; Strong versatile bittering hop, cloying in large quantities
Usage: Bittering
Example: Sierra Nevada Celebration Ale, Sierra Nevada Stout
AA Range: 12-14%
Substitute: Galena, Eroica, Brewer's Gold, Nugget, Bullion

Name: Cluster
Grown: US, Australia
Profile: Small, spicy aroma; Sharp, clean bittering hop
Usage: General purpose bittering (Aussie version has a better aroma and is used as finishing hop)
Example: Winterhook Christmas Ale
AA Range: 5.5-8.5%
Substitute: Galena, Eroica, Cascade

Name: Columbus
Grown: US
Profile: Strong fine herbal flavor and aroma;
Solid, clean bittering hop
Usage: Excellent general purpose bittering, flavoring and aroma hop.
Example: Anderson Valley IPA, Full Sail Old Boardhead Barleywine
AA Range: 13-16%
Substitute: Centennial, Chinook, Galena, Nugget

Name: Eroica
Grown: US
Profile: Good bittering hop;
Usage: Good general purpose bittering
Example: Blackhook Porter, Anderson Valley Boont Amber
AA Range: 12-14%
Substitute: Northern Brewer, Galena

Name: Galena
Grown: US
Profile: Strong, clean bittering hop
Usage: General purpose bittering
Example: The most widely used commercial bittering hop in the US.
AA Range: 12-14%
Substitute: Cluster, Northern Brewer, Nugget

Name: Northern Brewer
Grown: UK, US, Germany (called Hallertauer NB), and other areas (growing region affects profile greatly)
Profile: Hallertauer NB has a fine, fragrant aroma;
Dry, clean bittering hop
Usage: Bittering and finishing for a wide variety of beers
Example: Old Peculiar (bittering), Anchor Liberty (bittering),
Anchor Steam (bittering, flavoring, aroma)
AA Range: 7-10%
Substitute: Perle

Name: Northdown
Grown: UK
Profile: Similar to Northern Brewer, but with a better flavor and aroma than domestic NB; A clean bittering hop.
Usage: General purpose bittering, flavor and aroma for heavier ales.
Example: Fuller's ESB
AA Range: 7-8%
Substitute: Northern Brewer, Target

Name: Nugget
Grown: US
Profile: Heavy, spicy, herbal aroma; Strong bittering hop
Usage: Strong bittering, some aroma uses
Example: Sierra Nevada Porter & Bigfoot Ale, Anderson Valley ESB
AA Range: 12-14%
Substitute: Galena, Chinook, Cluster

Name: Perle
Grown: Germany, US
Profile: Pleasant aroma; Slightly spicy, almost minty, bittering hop
Usage: General purpose bittering for all lagers
Example: Sierra Nevada Summerfest
AA Range: 7-9.5%
Substitute: Northern Brewer, Cluster, Tettnanger

Name: Pride Of Ringwood
Grown: Australia
Profile: Poor, citric aroma;Clean bittering hop
Usage: general purpose bittering
Example: Most Australian beers.
AA Range: 9-11%
Substitute: Cluster

Name: Target
Grown: UK
Profile: Strong herbal aroma can be too strong for lagers; A clean bittering hop.
Usage: Widely used bittering and flavoring hop for strong ales.
Example: Fuller's Hock, Morrells Strong Country Bitter
AA Range: 8-10%
Substitute: Northdown

Figure 29— Cascade Hops on the vine.

The next group are common examples of Aroma hops. Aroma hops can be used for bittering also, and many homebrewers swear by this, claiming a finer, cleaner overall hop profile. I like to use Galena for bittering and save the good stuff for finishing. But making these decisions for yourself is what homebrewing is all about.

There is a category of aroma hops, called the "Noble Hops," that is considered to have the best aroma. These hops are principally four varieties grown in central Europe: Hallertauer Mittelfrüh, Tettnanger Tettnang, Spalter Spalt, and Czech Saaz. The location a hop is grown has a definite impact on the variety's character, so only a Tettnanger/Spalter hop grown in Tettnang/Spalt is truly noble. There are other varieties that are considered to be Noble-Type, such as Perle, Crystal, Mt. Hood, Liberty, and Ultra. These hops were bred from the noble types and have very similar aroma profiles. Noble hops are considered to be most appropriate for lager styles because the beer and the hops grew up together. This is purely tradition and as a homebrewer you can use whichever hop you like for whatever beer style you want. After all, we are doing this for the fun of it!

Aroma Hop Varieties

Name: British Columbia (BC) Goldings
Grown: Canada
Profile: Earthy, rounded, mild aroma; Spicy flavor
Usage: Bittering, finishing, dry hopping for British style ales. Used as a domestic substitute for East Kent Goldings. Not quite as good as EK.
AA Range: 4.5-7%
Substitute: EK Goldings

Name: Cascade
Grown: US
Profile: Strong spicy, floral, citrus (i.e. grapefruit) aroma.
Usage: The defining aroma for American style Pale ales. Used for bittering, finishing, and especially dry hopping.
Example: Anchor Liberty Ale & Old Foghorn Barleywine, Sierra Nevada Pale Ale
AA Range: 4.5-8%
Substitute: Centennial

Name: Crystal a.k.a. CJF-Hallertau
Grown: US
Profile: Mild, pleasant, slightly spicy. One of three hops bred as domestic replacements for Hallertauer Mittelfrüh.
Usage: Aroma/finishing/flavoring
AA Range: 2-5%
Substitute: Hallertauer Mittelfrüh, Hallertauer Hersbrucker, Mount Hood, Liberty, Ultra

Name: East Kent Goldings (EKG)
Grown: UK
Profile: Spicy/floral, earthy, rounded, mild aroma; spicy flavor
Usage: Bittering, finishing, dry hopping for British style ales
Example: Young's Special London Ale, Samuel Smith's Pale Ale, Fuller's ESB
AA Range: 4.5-7%
Substitute: BC Goldings, Whitbread Goldings Variety

Name: Fuggles
Grown: UK, US, and other areas
Profile: Mild, soft, grassy, floral aroma
Usage: Finishing / dry hopping for all ales, dark lagers
Example: Samuel Smith's Pale Ale, Old Peculiar, Thomas Hardy's Ale
AA Range: 3.5-5.5%
Substitute: East Kent Goldings, Willamette, Styrian Goldings

Name: Hallertauer Hersbrucker
Grown: Germany
Profile: Pleasant, spicy/mild, noble, earthy aroma
Usage: Finishing for German style lagers
Example: Wheathook Wheaten Ale
AA Range: 2.5-5%
Substitute: Hallertauer Mittelfrüh, Mt. Hood, Liberty, Crystal, Ultra

Name: Hallertauer Mittelfrüh
Grown: Germany
Profile: Pleasant, spicy, noble, mild herbal aroma
Usage: Finishing for German style lagers
Example: Sam Adam's Boston Lager, Sam Adam's Boston Lightship
AA Range: 3-5%
Substitute: Hallertauer Hersbruck, Mt. Hood, Liberty, Crystal, Ultra

Name: Liberty
Grown: US
Profile: Fine, very mild aroma. One of three hops bred as domestic replacements for Hallertauer Mittelfrüh.
Usage: Finishing for German style lagers
Example: Pete's Wicked Lager
AA Range: 2.5-5%
Substitute: Hallertauer Mittelfrüh, Hallertauer Hersbruck, Mt. Hood Crystal, Ultra

Name: Mt. Hood
Grown: US
Profile: Mild, clean aroma. One of three hops bred as domestic replacements for Hallertauer Mittelfrüh.
Usage: Finishing for German style lagers
Example: Anderson Valley High Rollers Wheat Beer
AA Range: 3.5-8%
Substitute: Hallertauer Mittelfrüh, Hallertauer Hersbrucker, Liberty, Tettnang, Ultra

Name: Progress
Grown: UK
Profile: Assertive fruity aroma
Usage: Widely used for real cask ales.
Example: Hobson's Best Bitter, Mansfield Bitter
AA Range: 5-6%
Substitute: Fuggles, Whitbread Goldings Variety

Name:	Saaz
Grown:	Czechoslovakia
Profile:	Delicate, mild, floral aroma
Usage:	Finishing for Bohemian style lagers
Example:	Pilsener Urquell
AA Range:	2-5%
Substitute:	Tettnang, Spalt, Ultra (some would claim there is no substitute)

Name:	Spalt
Grown:	Germany/US
Profile:	Mild, pleasant, slightly spicy
Usage:	Aroma/finishing/flavoring, some bittering
AA Range:	3-6%
Substitute:	Saaz, Tettnang, Ultra

Name:	Styrian Goldings
Grown:	Yugoslavia (seedless Fuggles grown in Yugoslavia), also grown in US
Profile:	Similar to Fuggles
Usage:	Bittering/finishing/dry hopping for a wide variety of beers. Popular in Europe, especially UK.
Example:	Ind Coope's Burton Ale, Timothy Taylor's Landlord
AA Range:	4.5-7%
Substitute:	Fuggles, Willamette

Name:	Tettnang
Grown:	Germany
Profile:	Fine, spicy aroma
Usage:	Finishing for German style beers
Example:	Gulpener Pilsener, Sam Adam's Oktoberfest, Anderson Valley ESB, Redhook ESB
AA Range:	3-6%
Substitute:	Saaz, Spalt, Ultra

Name:	Willamette
Grown:	US
Profile:	Mild, spicy, grassy, floral aroma
Usage:	Finishing / dry hopping for American / British style ales
Example:	Sierra Nevada Porter, Ballard Bitter, Anderson Valley Boont Amber, Redhook ESB
AA Range:	4-7%
Substitute:	Fuggles

Name: Whitbread Goldings Variety (WGV)
Grown: UK
Profile: Flowery, fruity, a cross between Goldings and a Fuggle.
Usage: Often combined with other varieties in Bitters
Example: Whitbread Best Bitter
AA Range: 4-5%
Substitute: Progress, Fuggles, EKG

Name: Ultra
Grown: US
Profile: Very fine, mild, spicy with floral notes
Usage: Excellent finishing hop for Pilsner and German style lagers.
Example: (too new)
AA Range: 2-5%
Substitute: Any Noble hop, Crystal, Liberty, Mt. Hood

How to Measure Hops

Alpha Acid Units (AAUs) As noted in the glossary, there are two ways to measure hops for use in brewing. The first way measures the bittering potential of the hops going into the boil. Alpha Acid Units (AAUs) or Homebrew Bittering Units (HBUs), are the weight of hops (in ounces) multiplied by the percentage of alpha acids. This unit is convenient for describing hop additions in a recipe because it indicates the total bittering potential from a particular hop variety while allowing for year to year variation in the percentage of alpha acids.

Whenever a brewer is using AAUs in a recipe to describe the quantity of hops, it is important to specify how long each addition is boiled. The boiling time has the largest influence on how bitter a hop addition makes the beer. If no times are specified, then the rule of thumb is that bittering hops are boiled for an hour and finishing hops are boiled for the last 10-15 minutes. Many brewers add hops at 15 or 20 minute intervals and usually in multiples of a half ounce (for ease of measurement).

International Bittering Units (IBUs) The second way estimates how much of the alpha acid is isomerized and actually dissolved into the beer. The equation for International Bittering Units (IBUs) takes the amount of hops in AAUs and applies factors for the boil gravity, volume, and boiling time. IBUs are independent of batch size, and to a large extent, independent of style, unlike the AAU.

Hop resins act like oil in water. It takes the boiling action of the wort to isomerize them, which means that the chemical structure of the alpha acid compounds is altered so that the water molecules can attach and these compounds can dissolve into the wort. The percentage of the total alpha acids that are isomerized and survive into the finished beer, i.e. utilized, is termed the "utilization". Under homebrewing conditions, utilization generally tops out at 30%.

Several factors in the wort boil influence the degree to which isomerization occurs. Unfortunately how all these factors affect the utilization is complicated and not well understood. Empirical equations have been developed which give us at least some ability to estimate IBUs for homebrewing.

The utilization is influenced by the vigor of the boil, the total gravity of the boil, the time of the boil and several other minor factors. The vigor of the boil can be considered a constant for each individual brewer, but between brewers there probably is some variation. The gravity of the boil is significant because the higher the malt sugar content of a wort, the less room there is for isomerized alpha acids. The strongest bittering factors are the total amount of alpha acids you added to the

AAU CALCULATION

Calculating Alpha Acid Units (AAU)

AAUs are a good way to state hop additions in your recipes. By specifying the amount of alpha acid for each addition, rather than just the weight, you don't have to worry about year to year variation in the hop.

An AAU is equal to the % AA multiplied by the weight in ounces.

For Example:

1.5 oz of Cascade at 5% alpha acid is 7.5 AAUs

If next year the alpha acid percentage in Cascade is 7.5%, you would only need 1 oz rather than 1.5 oz to arrive at the same bitterness contribution.

wort, and the amount of time in the boil for isomerization. Understandably then, most equations for IBUs work with these three variables (gravity, amount, and time) against a nominal utilization.

As mentioned earlier, the utilization for alpha acids in homebrewing is generally accepted as topping out at about 30%. The Utilization Table (Table 7 in the following section) lists the utilization versus time and gravity of the boil. This allows you to estimate how much each hop addition is contributing to the total bitterness of the beer. By incorporating a factor for gravity adjustment, the IBU equation allows for direct comparisons of total hop bitterness across beer styles. For instance, 10 AAUs in a Pale Ale would taste pretty bitter while 10 AAUs would hardly be noticed in a high gravity Stout. Gravity is not the total difference between styles however, the yeast also yields a particular flavor and sweetness profile which the hop bitterness balances against. As the maltiness of the beer increases, so does the relative balance between hop bitterness and malt sweetness. A very sweet American Brown Ale needs about 40 IBUs to yield the same balance of flavor as a Bavarian Oktoberfest of the same gravity does with 30 IBUs.

This brings up a good question, how bitter is bitter? Well, in terms of IBUs, 20 to 40 is considered to be the typical international range. North American light beers, like Coors™, have a bitterness of only 10-15 IBUs. More bitter imported light beers, like Heineken™, have a bitterness closer to 20-25. American microbrews like Samuel Adam Boston Lager™ have a bitterness of about 30 IBUs. Strong bitter ales like Anchor Liberty Ale™ and Sierra Nevada Celebration Ale™ have bitterness of 45 or more.

While more experimentation and analysis needs to be done to accurately predict hop bittering potential, the IBU equations described below have become the common standard by which most homebrewers calculate the final bitterness in the beer. Everyone who uses these equations is in the same ballpark and that is close enough for comparison.

Hop Bitterness (IBU) Calculations

For those of you who dislike math, I will make this as straightforward as possible. We will use the following "Joe Ale" recipe for our example:

The first step is to calculate the AAUs from the recipe.

$$AAU_{Perle} = 1.5 \text{ oz} \times 6.4\% = 9.6$$

$$AAU_{Liberty} = 1 \text{ oz} \times 4.6\% = 4.6$$

To calculate how much bitterness the final beer will have from these hop additions, we apply factors for the recipe volume (V), gravity of the boil, and the boil time. The time and gravity of the boil are expressed as the utilization (U). The equation for IBUs is:

IBU = AAU x U x 75 / Vrecipe

75 is a constant for the conversion of English units to metric. The proper units for IBUs are milligrams per liter, so to convert from ounces per gallon a conversion factor of 75 (74.89) is needed. For the metric world, using grams and liters, the factor is 10. (For those of you paying attention to the units, the missing factor of 100 was taken up by the % in the AAU calculation.)

EXAMPLE RECIPE

Joe Ale

Ingredients for a 5 gallon batch

- 6 lbs. of amber DME
- 1.5 oz. of 6.4% AA Perle hops (60 minutes)
- 1 oz. of 4.6% AA Liberty hops (15 minutes)

For a 5 gallon recipe, we will boil 1.5 oz of Perle hops for 60 minutes for Bittering, and 1 oz of Liberty for 15 minutes for Finishing. The recipe calls for 6 lbs. of dry malt extract and it will be boiled in 3 gallons of water because of the pot size. The remaining water will be added in the fermenter.

Gravity of the Boil

The recipe volume is 5 gallons. The gravity is figured by examining the amount and concentration of malt being used. As noted in the previous chapter, dry malt extract typically yields about 40 pts/lb./gal. Since this recipe calls for 6 lbs. of extract to be used in 5 gallons, the calculated OG is:

OG = 6 x 40 / 5 = 48 or 1.048

But, since we are only boiling 3 of the 5 gallons due to of the size of the pot, we need to take into account the higher gravity of the boil. The boil gravity becomes:

6 x 40 / 3 = 80 or 1.080

It is the gravity of the boil (1.080) that is used in figuring the utilization. As you will see in the next section, hop utilization decreases with increasing wort gravity. A higher concentration of sugars makes it more difficult for the isomerized alpha acids to dissolve. I use the initial boil gravity in my utilization calculation; others have suggested that the average boil gravity should be used. (The average being a function of how much volume will be boiled away during the boiling time.) This gets rather complicated with multiple additions, so I just use the initial boil gravity to be conservative. The difference is small–overestimating the total bitterness by 1-3 IBUs.

Utilization

The utilization is the most important factor. This number describes the efficiency of the isomerization of the alpha acids as a function of time. This is where a lot of experimentation is being conducted to get a better idea of how much of the hops are actually being isomerized during the boil. The utilization numbers that Tinseth published are shown in Table 7. To find the utilizations for boil gravities in-between the values given, simply interpolate the value based on the numbers for the bounding gravities at the given time.

For example, to calculate the utilization for a boil gravity of 1.057 at 30 minutes, look at the utilization values for 1.050 and 1.060. These are .177 and .162, respectively. There is a difference of 15 between the two, and 7/10ths of the difference is about 11, so the adjusted utilization for 1.057 would be .177 - .011 = 0.166

The Utilizations for 60 minutes and 15 minutes at a Boil Gravity of 1.080 are 0.176 and 0.087, respectively. Inserting these values into the IBU equations gives:

IBU_{60} = 9.6 x .176 x 75 / 5 = 25 (rounded to nearest whole number)
and
IBU_{15} = 4.6 x .087 x 75 / 5 = 6

Giving a grand total of 31 IBUs.

Utilization numbers are really an approximation. Each brew is unique; the variables for individual conditions, i.e. vigor of the boil, wort chemistry, or for losses during fermentation, are just too hard to get a handle on from the meager amount of published data available. Then why do we bother, you ask? Because if we are all working from the same model and using roughly the same numbers, then we will all be in the same ballpark and can compare our beers without too much error. Plus, when the actual IBUs are measured in the lab, these models are shown to be pretty close.

Hop Utilization Equation Details

For those of you who are comfortable with the math, the following equations were determined by Tinseth from curve fitting a lot of test data and were used to generate Table 7. The degree of utilization is composed of a Gravity Factor and a Time Factor. The gravity factor accounts for reduced utilization due to higher wort gravities. The boil time factor accounts for the change in utilization due to boil time:

Utilization = f(G) x f(T)
where: f(G) = 1.65 x 0.000125^(Gb - 1)
f(T) = [1 - e^(-0.04 x T)] / 4.15

Table 7—Utilization as a function of Time versus Boil Gravity

	1.030	1.040	1.050	1.060	1.070	1.080	1.090	1.100	1.110	1.120
0	0.000	0.000	0.000	0.000	0.000	0.000	0.000	0.000	0.000	0.000
5	0.055	0.050	0.046	0.042	0.038	0.035	0.032	0.029	0.027	0.025
10	0.100	0.091	0.084	0.076	0.070	0.064	0.058	0.053	0.049	0.045
15	0.137	0.125	0.114	0.105	0.096	0.087	0.080	0.073	0.067	0.061
20	0.167	0.153	0.140	0.128	0.117	0.107	0.098	0.089	0.081	0.074
25	0.192	0.175	0.160	0.147	0.134	0.122	0.112	0.102	0.094	0.085
30	0.212	0.194	0.177	0.162	0.148	0.135	0.124	0.113	0.103	0.094
35	0.229	0.209	0.191	0.175	0.160	0.146	0.133	0.122	0.111	0.102
40	0.242	0.221	0.202	0.185	0.169	0.155	0.141	0.129	0.118	0.108
45	0.253	0.232	0.212	0.194	0.177	0.162	0.148	0.135	0.123	0.113
50	0.263	0.240	0.219	0.200	0.183	0.168	0.153	0.140	0.128	0.117
55	0.270	0.247	0.226	0.206	0.188	0.172	0.157	0.144	0.132	0.120
60	0.276	0.252	0.231	0.211	0.193	0.176	0.161	0.147	0.135	0.123
70	0.285	0.261	0.238	0.218	0.199	0.182	0.166	0.152	0.139	0.127
80	0.291	0.266	0.243	0.222	0.203	0.186	0.170	0.155	0.142	0.130
90	0.295	0.270	0.247	0.226	0.206	0.188	0.172	0.157	0.144	0.132
100	0.298	0.272	0.249	0.228	0.208	0.190	0.174	0.159	0.145	0.133
110	0.300	0.274	0.251	0.229	0.209	0.191	0.175	0.160	0.146	0.134
120	0.301	0.275	0.252	0.230	0.210	0.192	0.176	0.161	0.147	0.134

The numbers *1.65* and *0.000125* in $f(G)$ were empirically derived to fit the boil gravity (Gb) analysis data. In the $f(T)$ equation, the number *-0.04* controls the shape of the utilization vs. time curve. The factor *4.15* controls the maximum utilization value. This number may be adjusted to customize the curves to your own system. If you feel that you are having a very vigorous boil or generally get more utilization out of a given boil time for whatever reason, you can reduce the number a small amount to 4 or 3.9. Likewise if you think that you are getting less, then you can increase it by 1 or 2 tenths. Doing so will increase or decrease the utilization value for each time and gravity in Table 7.

IBU Nomograph for Hop Additions *(next page)*

To use the nomograph, start on the right and draw a straight line from the *%Alpha Acids* of your hop, through the *Weight* of the addition, to arrive at the *AAUs* for that addition. Next, draw a line from the *AAUs* through the *Recipe Volume* to arrive at the *AAUs/gallon*. Now move to the left hand side of the chart and draw a line from your *Boil Gravity*, through your *Boil Time*, to determine the *Utilization*. Finally, draw a line through the points from the *Utilization* and *AAUs/gallon* lines to determine the *IBUs* of that hop addition.

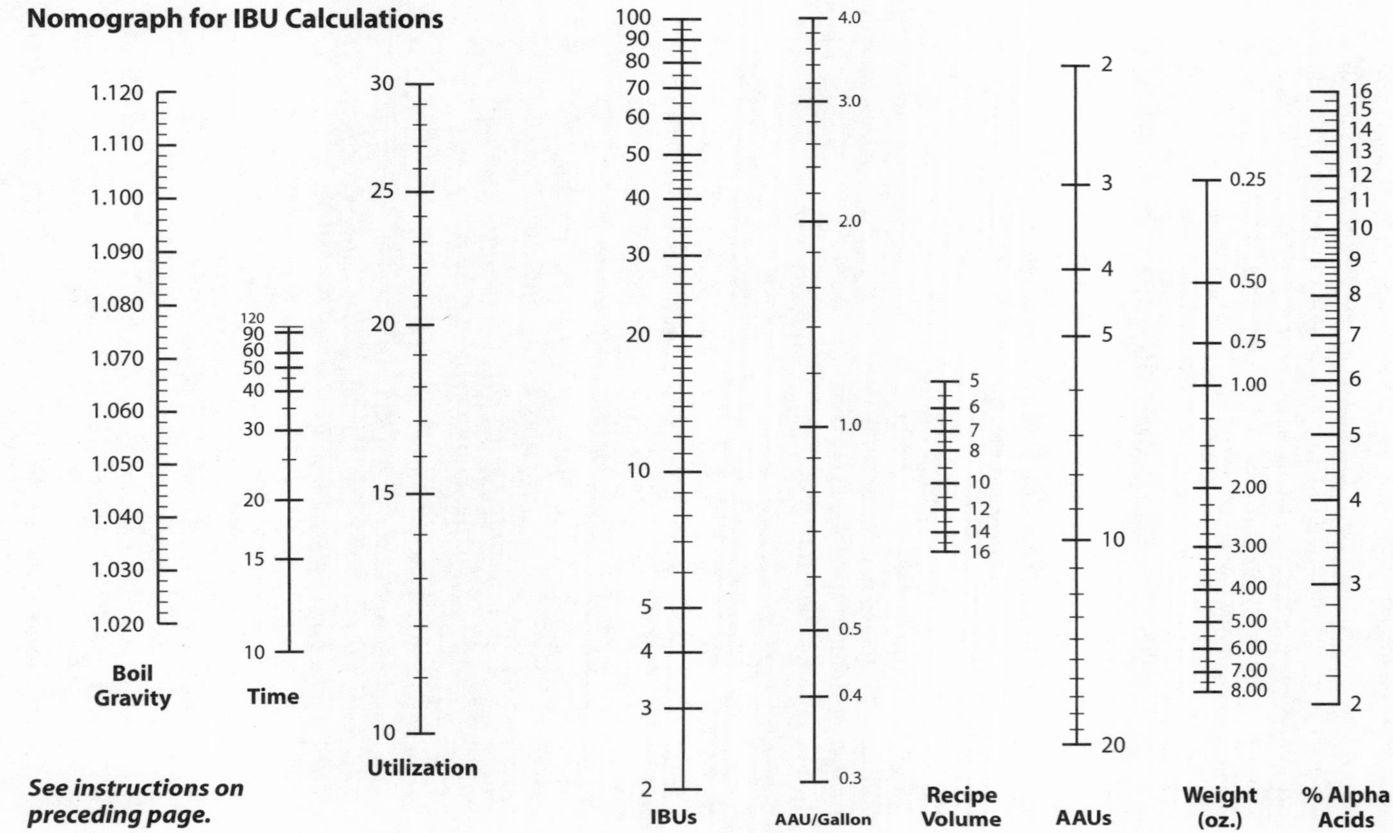

Nomograph for IBU Calculations
1.120 1.110 1.100 1.090 1.080 1.070 1.060 1.050 1.040 1.030 1.020
Boil Gravity
120 90 60 50 40 30 20 15 10
Time
30 25 20 15 10
Utilization
100 90 80 70 60 50 40 30 20 10 5 4 3 2
IBUs
4.0 3.0 2.0 1.0 0.5 0.4 0.3
AAU/Gallon
5 6 7 8 10 12 14 16
Recipe Volume
2 3 4 5 10 20
AAUs
0.25 0.50 0.75 1.00 2.00 3.00 4.00 5.00 6.00 7.00 8.00
Weight (oz.)
16 15 14 13 12 11 10 9 8 7 6 5 4 3 2
% Alpha Acids
See instructions on preceding page.

Chapter 6

Yeast

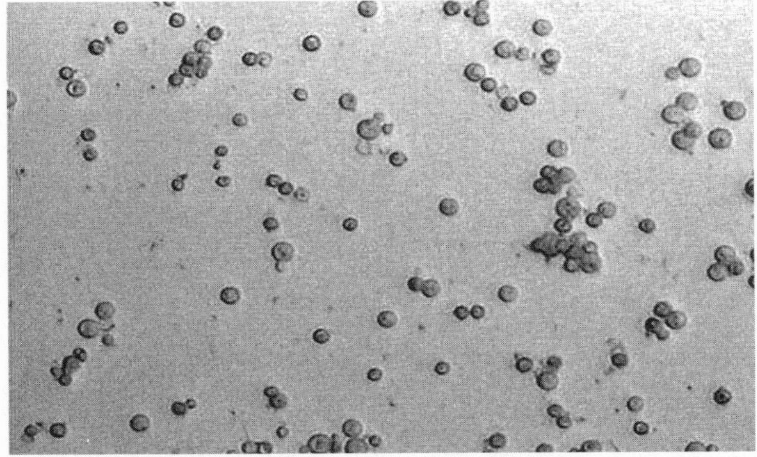

Figure 31—Aerial view of yeast ranch. 1500X

There was a time when the role of yeast in brewing was unknown. In the days of the Vikings, each family had their own brewing stick that they used for stirring the wort. These brewing sticks were family heirlooms because it was the use of that stick that guaranteed that the beer would turn out right. Obviously, those sticks retained the family yeast culture.

The German Beer Purity Law of 1516–The Reinheitsgebot, listed the only allowable materials for brewing as malt, hops, and water. With the discovery of yeast and its function in the late 1860's by Louis Pasteur, the law had to be amended.

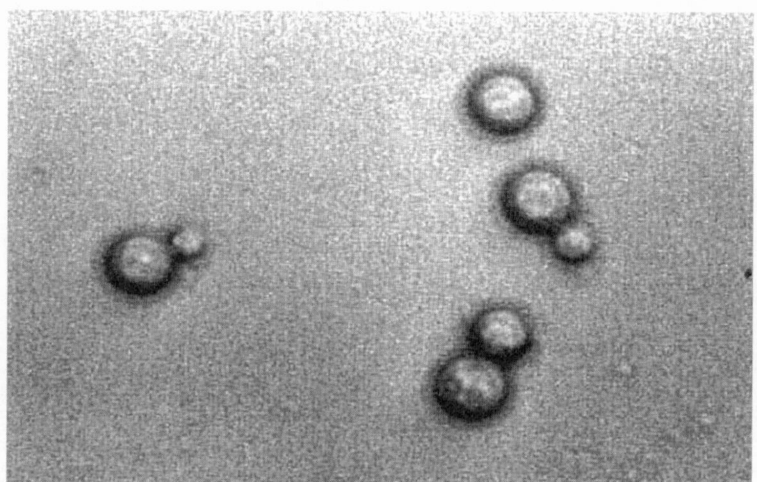

Figure 32—Budding yeast cells. 5000X

Brewer's Yeast (Saccharomyces cerevisiae) is considered to be a type of fungus. It reproduces asexually by budding–splitting off little daughter cells. Yeast are unusual in that they can live and grow both with or without oxygen. Most micro-organisms can only do one or the other. Yeast can live without oxygen by a process that we refer to as fermentation. The yeast cells take in simple sugars like glucose and maltose and produce carbon dioxide and alcohol as waste products.

In addition to ethyl alcohol and carbon dioxide, yeast produce many other compounds, including esters, fusel alcohols, ketones, various phenolics and fatty acids. Esters are the molecular compound responsible for the fruity notes in beer, phenols cause the spicy notes, and in combination with chlorine (chlorophenols)–medicinal notes. Diacetyl is a ketone compound that can be beneficial in limited amounts. It gives a butter or butterscotch note to the flavor profile of a beer and is desired to a degree in heavier Pale Ales, Scotch Ales and Stouts. Unfortunately, diacetyl tends to be unstable and can take on stale, raunchy tones due to oxidation as the beer ages. This is particularly true for light lagers, where the presence of diacetyl is considered to be a flaw. Fusel alcohols are heavier molecular weight alcohols and are thought to be a major contributor to hangovers. These alcohols also have low taste thresholds and are readily apparent as "sharp" notes. Fatty acids, although they take part in the chemical reactions that produce the desired compounds, also tend to oxidize in old beers and produce cardboard-like and soapy off-flavors.

Yeast Terminology

The following are some terms that are used to describe yeast behavior.

Attenuation This term is usually given as a percentage to describe the percent of malt sugar that is converted by the yeast strain to ethanol and CO2. Most yeast strains attenuate in the range of 67-77%. More specifically, this range is the "Apparent" attenuation. The apparent attenuation is determined by comparing the Original and Final gravities of the beer. A 1.040 OG that ferments to a 1.010 FG would have an apparent attenuation of 75%.

(From FG = OG - (OG x %) => % att. = (OG-FG)/OG)

The "Real" attenuation is less. Pure ethanol has a gravity of about 0.800. If you had a 1.040 OG beer and got 100% real attenuation, the resulting specific gravity would be about 0.991 (corresponding to about 5% alcohol by weight). The apparent attenuation of this beer would be 122%. The apparent attenuation of a yeast strain will vary depending on the types of sugars in the wort that the yeast is fermenting. Thus the number quoted for a particular yeast is an average. For purposes of discussion, apparent attenuation is ranked as low, medium, and high by the following percentages:

- 67-70% = Low
- 71-74% = Medium
- 75-78% = High

Flocculation This term describes how fast or how well a yeast clumps together and settles to the bottom of the fermentor after fermentation is complete. Different yeast strains clump differently and will settle faster or slower. Some yeasts practically "paint" themselves to the bottom of the fermentor while others are ready to swirl up if you so much as sneeze. Highly flocculant yeasts can sometimes settle out before the fermentation is finished, leaving higher than normal levels of diacetyl or even leftover fermentable sugars. Pitching an adequate amount of healthy yeast with adequate aeration is the best solution to this potential problem.

Lag Time This term refers to the amount of time that passes from when the yeast is pitched to when the airlock starts bubbling vigorously on the fermentor. A long lagtime (more than 24 hours) may indicate that the wort was poorly aerated, not enough yeast was pitched and/or that the yeast was initially in poor shape.

Yeast Types

There are two main types of yeast: ale and lager. Ale yeasts are referred to as top-fermenting because much of the fermentation action takes place at the top of the fermentor, while lager yeasts would seem to prefer the bottom. While many of today's strains like to confound this generalization, there is one important difference, and that is temperature. Ale yeasts like warmer temperatures, going dormant below about 55°F (12°C), while lager yeasts will happily work at 40°F. Using certain lager yeasts at ale temperatures 60-70°F (18-20°C) produces a style of beer that is now termed California Common Beer. Anchor Steam Beer™ revived this unique 19th century style.

Yeast Forms

Yeast come in two main product forms, dry and liquid. (There is also another form, available as pure cultures on petri dishes or slants, which is basically liquid yeast with lower cell count.) Dry yeasts are select, hardy strains that have been dehydrated for storability. Dry ale yeast is highly recommended for new brewers.

Dry yeast is convenient because the packets provide a lot of viable yeast cells, they can be stored for extended periods of time and they can be prepared quickly on brewing day. It is common to use one or two packets (7-14 grams) of dried yeast for a typical five gallon batch. This amount of yeast, when properly rehydrated, provides enough active yeast cells to ensure a strong fermentation. Dry yeast can be stored for up to two years (preferably in the refrigerator), but the packets do degrade with time. This is one of the pitfalls with brewing from the no-name yeast packets taped to the top of a can of malt extract. They are probably more than a year old and may not be very viable. It is better to buy another packet or three of a reputable brewer's yeast that has been kept in the refrigerator at the brewshop. Some leading and reliable brands of dry yeast are DCL Yeast, Cooper's, DanStar (produced by Lallemand), Munton & Fison and Edme.

Dry ale yeasts make good beer but the rigor of the dehydration process limits the number of different strains that are available, and in the case of dry lager yeast, eliminates them almost entirely. A few dry lager yeasts do exist, but popular opinion is that they behave more like ale yeasts than lager. DCL Yeast markets two strains of dry lager yeast: S-189 and S-23, though only S-23 is currently available in a homebrewing size. The recommended fermentation temperature is 48-59°F. I would advise you to use two packets per 5 gallon batch to be assured of a good pitching rate. The only thing missing with dry yeast is more variety, which is where liquid yeasts come in. There are more strains of yeast are available in liquid form than in dry.

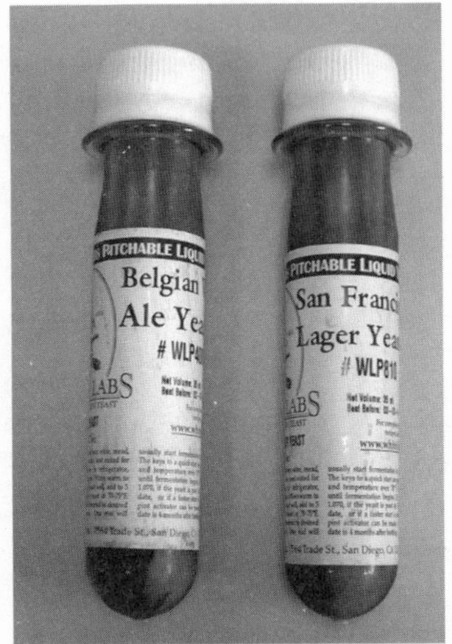

Liquid yeast used to come in 50 ml foil pouches and did not contain as many yeast cells as are in the dry packets. The yeast in those packages needed to be grown in a starter to bring the cell counts up to a more useful level. In the past 2 years, larger 175 ml pouches (Wyeast) and ready-to-pitch tubes (White Labs) have become the most popular forms of liquid yeast packaging and contain enough viable cells to ferment a five gallon batch.

Yeast Strains

There are many different strains of brewer's yeast available nowadays and each strain produces a different flavor profile. Some Belgian strains produce fruity esters that smell like bananas and cherries, some German strains produce phenols that smell strongly of cloves. Those two examples are rather special, most yeasts are not that dominating. But it illustrates how much the choice of yeast can determine the taste of the beer. In fact, one of the main differences between different beer styles is the strain of yeast that is used.

Most major breweries generally have their own strain of yeast. These yeast strains have evolved with the style of beer being made, particularly if that brewery was a founder of a style, such as Anchor Steam™. In fact, yeast readily adapts and evolves to specific brewery conditions, so two breweries producing the same style of beer with the same yeast strain will actually have different yeast cultivars that produce unique beers. Several yeast companies have collected different yeasts from around the world and offer them to home brewers. Some homebrew supply shops have done the same, offering their own brands of many different yeasts.

Dry Yeast Strains

As I mentioned earlier, the dry ale yeast strains tend to be fairly similar, attenuative and clean tasting, performing well for most ale styles. To illustrate with a very broad brush, there are Australian, British and Canadian strains, each producing what can be considered that country's style of pale ale. The Australian type is more woody, the British more fruity, and the Canadian a bit more malty. Fortunately with international interest in homebrewing growing as it is, dry yeast strains and variety are improving. Some of my favorites are Nottingham (DanStar), London Ale (DanStar) and Cooper's Ale.

Here is an incomplete list of popular dry yeast strains and their general characteristics:

Cooper's Ale (Cooper's) All-purpose dry ale yeast. It produces a complex woody, citrus-fruity beer at warm temperatures. More heat tolerant than other strains, 65-75°F; recommended for summer brewing. Medium attenuation and flocculation.

Edme Ale (Edme Ltd.) One of the original dry yeast strains, this produces a soft, bready finish. Medium flocculation and medium attenuation. Fermentation range of 62-70°F.

Munton and Fison Ale (Munton and Fison) An all-purpose ale yeast selected for a long shelf life. A vigorous starter, with neutral flavors. Medium attenuation and high flocculation. Fermentation range of 64-70°F.

London Ale (DanStar) Moderate fruitiness suitable for all pale ale styles. Medium-high attenuation and medium-low flocculation. Fermentation range of 64-70°F.

Nottingham Ale (DanStar) A more neutral ale yeast with lower levels of esters and a crisp, malty finish. Can be used for lager-type beers at lower temperatures. High attenuation and medium-high flocculation. Fermentation range of 57-70°F.

Windsor Ale (DanStar) Produces a full bodied, fruity English ale, but suitable for wheat beers also, including hefe-weizen. Attenuation and flocculation are medium-low. Fermentation range of 64-70°F.

S-04 (DCL Yeast) A well-known commerical English ale yeast selected for its vigorous character and high flocculation. This yeast is recommended for a large range of ale and is especially well adapted to cask-conditioned ales. Recommended temperature range of 64-75°F.

S-23 (DCL Yeast) This lager strain is used by several European commercial breweries. This yeast develops soft estery notes at the recommended temperature range of 48-59°F and more ale-like characteristics at warmer temperatures. From what I have read, I am speculating that this is a Kolsch or Alt-type yeast. This strain of yeast will produce a lager character at 54°F, and homebrewers have reported good results with this yeast. Given the recommended fermentation temperature range, these yeasts may not respond well to lagering (extended secondary fermentation at low temperatures), as described in *Chapter 10*, and *probably* should be maintained at 54°F for the duration of the time in the fermentor, approximately 2-3 weeks. I have not used this yeast myself and cannot say for certain.

Liquid Yeast Strains

There are a lot of liquid yeasts to choose from and in order to keep this simple I will just describe them by general strain. All of the brands of liquid yeast I can think of (Wyeast Labs, White Labs, Yeast Culture Kit Co., and Brew-Tek), are of very good quality, and to describe each companies offering of a particular strain would be redundant. This is not to say that all of the cultivars of a type are the same; within a strain there will be several cultivars that have different characteristics from what is listed here. You will find that each company's offering will be subtly different due to the conditions under which it was sampled, stored, and grown. You may find that you prefer one company's cultivar over another's. Detailed descriptions of each company's cultivar will be available at your brewshop or on the company's website. This is an incomplete list because new strains are being added to the market all the time.

General Purpose Ale Yeasts

American, Californian, or Chico Ale A very "clean" tasting yeast, producing less esters than other types of ale yeast. Good for just about any type of ale. This strain is usually associated with Sierra Nevada Pale Ale. High attenuation, medium flocculation. Suggested fermentation temperature is 68°F.

Australian Ale This all-purpose strain typically comes from Thos. Cooper & Sons of Adelaide, and produces a very complex, woody, and fruity beer. Medium attenuation, medium flocculation. Great for pale ales, brown ales and porters. Suggested fermentation at 68°F.

British Ale This strain typically comes from Whitbread Brewing Co., and ferments crisp, slightly tart, and fruity. More maltiness is evident than with the American ale yeast. Medium attenuation, medium flocculation. Suggested fermentation temperature is 70°F, though it performs well down to 60°F.

Irish Ale The slight residual diacetyl is great for stouts. It is clean, smooth, soft and full bodied. Very nice for any cold-weather ale, at its best in stouts and Scotch ales. Medium flocculation, medium attenuation. Suggested fermentation at 68°F.

Specialty Ale Yeasts

Belgian Ale Lots of fruity esters (banana, spice), and can be tart. Very good for Belgian ales, Dubbels and Tripels. Low flocculation, high attenuation. Suggested fermentation temperature is 70°F.

European Ale This ale yeast typically comes from Wissenschaftliche in Munich. A full bodied complex strain that finishes very malty. Produces a dense rocky head during fermentation. Suggested fermentation at 70°F. High flocculation, low attenuation. It's clean and malty, especially well suited to Altbier. Reportedly a slow starter (longer lag times).

German Altbier Ferments dry and crisp leaving a good balance of sweetness and tartness. Produces an extremely rocky head and ferments well down to 55°F. A good choice for Alt style beers. High flocculation, high attenuation. Suggested fermentation at 62°F.

Kolsch Ale An old German style of beer that is more lager-like in character. Nice maltiness without as much fruit character as other ales. Some sulfur notes that disappear with aging. Low flocculation, high attenuation. Suggested fermentation temperature is 60°F.

London Ale Complex, woody, tart, with strong mineral notes. Could be from one of the several renowned London breweries. Slight diacetyl. High flocculation, low to medium attenuation. Suggested fermentation temperature is 68°F.

Wheat Beer Yeasts

Belgian Wit (White) Beer Mild phenolic character for the classic Belgian Wit beer style. Tart and fruity. Medium flocculation, high attenuation. Suggested fermentation at 70°F.

Weizen Produces the distinctive clove and spice character of wheat beers. The low flocculation of this yeast leaves the beer cloudy (Hefe-Weizen) but it's smooth flavor makes it an integral part of a true unfiltered wheat beer. Low flocculation, medium to high attenuation. Suggested fermentation temperature is 65°F.

Berliner Weisse A tart/sour, fruity and phenolic multi-strain with earthy undertones. Medium flocculation, high attenuation. Suggested fermentation at 68°F.

Lager Yeast

American Lager Very versatile for most lager styles. Gives a clean malt flavor. Some cultivars have an almost green-apple tartness. Medium flocculation, high attenuation. Primary fermentation at 50°F.

Bavarian Lager Lager yeast strain used by many German breweries. Rich flavor, full bodied, malty and clean. This is an excellent general purpose yeast for lager brewing. Medium flocculation, medium attenuation. Primary fermentation at 48°F.

Bohemian Lager Ferments clean and malty, giving a rich residual maltiness in high gravity pilsners. Very suitable for Vienna and Oktoberfest Styles. Medium flocculation, high attenuation. Primary fermentation at 48°F. Probably the most popular lager yeast strain.

California Lager Warm fermenting bottom cropping strain, ferments well to 62°F, having some of the fruitiness of an ale while keeping lager characteristics. Malty profile, highly flocculant, clears brilliantly. This is the yeast that is used for Steam-type beers.

Czech Pils Yeast Classic dry finish with rich maltiness. Good choice for pilsners and bock beers. Sulfur produced during fermentation dissipates with conditioning. Medium flocculation, high attenuation. Primary fermentation at 50°F.

Danish Lager Yeast Rich, yet crisp and dry. Soft, light profile which accentuates hop characteristics. Low flocculation, medium attenuation. Primary fermentation at 48°F.

Munich Lager Yeast One of the first pure yeast strains available to home brewers. Sometimes unstable, but smooth, malty, well rounded and full bodied. Primary fermentation temperature 45°F. It is reported to be prone to producing diacetyl, and accentuates hop flavor. Medium flocculation, high attenuation.

Preparing Yeast and Yeast Starters

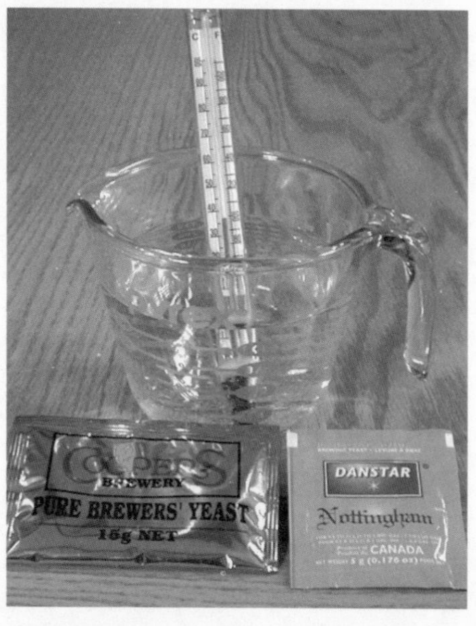

Preparing Dry Yeast

Dry yeast should be rehydrated in water before pitching. Often the concentration of sugars in wort is so high that the yeast can not draw enough water across the cell membranes to restart their metabolism. For best results, rehydrate 2 packets of dry yeast (same kind) in warm water (95-105°F, 35-40°C), and *then* proof the yeast by adding some sugar to see if they are still alive after dehydration and storage.

If it's not showing signs of life (churning, foaming) a half hour after proofing, your yeast may be too old or dead. Unfortunately, this can be a common problem with dry yeast packets, especially if they are the non-name brand packets taped to the top of malt extract beer kits. Using name brand brewers yeasts like those mentioned previously usually prevents this problem. Have a third packet available as back-up.

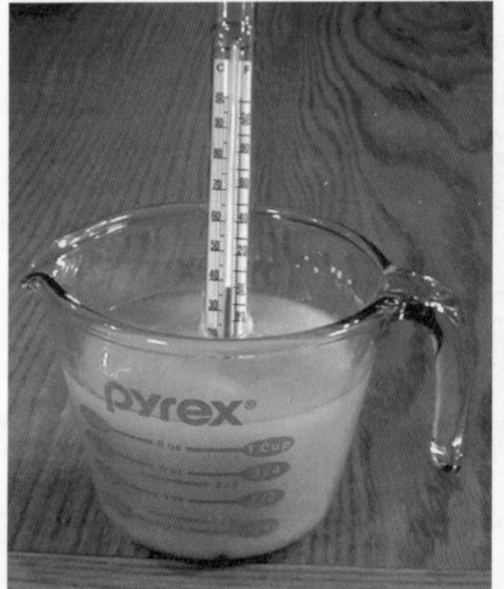

Figure 34 and 35—Dry yeast that has been rehydrated and the same yeast after proofing.

Rehydrating Dry Yeast

1. Put 1 cup of warm (95-105°F, 35-40°C) boiled water into a sanitized jar and stir in the yeast. Cover with plastic wrap and wait 15 minutes.

2. "Proof" the yeast by adding one teaspoon of extract that has been boiled in a small amount of water. Allow the sugar solution to cool before adding it to the jar.

3. Cover and place in a warm area out of direct sunlight.

4. After 30 minutes or so the yeast should be visibly churning and/or foaming, and is ready to pitch.

Note: Lallemand/DanStar does not recommend proofing after rehydration of their yeast because they have optimized its nutrional reserves for quick starting in the main wort. Proofing expends some of those reserves.

Preparing Liquid Yeast

Liquid yeast is generally perceived as being superior to dry yeast because of the greater variety of yeast strains available. Liquid yeast allows for greater tailoring of the beer to a particular style. However, the amount of yeast in a liquid packet is typically much less than the amount in the dry. Liquid yeast usually must be pitched to a starter wort before pitching to the beer in the fermentor. Using a starter gives yeast a head start and increases the population preventing weak fermentations due to under-pitching.

Note: In the six years it has taken to get this book to press, the variety of yeast products has improved dramatically. Today, several companies offer liquid yeasts that are use-by date coded and packaged at higher cell counts so that they do not need to be pitched to a starter. Below I describe how to make a yeast starter, which is meant to build up the cell counts for the 50 ml smack-pack-type yeasts, and yeasts packaged as slants. (A slant is a small tube containing agar or similar growth media and a relatively low number of yeast cells.) Ready-to-pitch yeasts, and the larger 175 ml smack-packs do not need a starter, depending on their freshness, but it never hurts. (Unless your sanitation is poor!)

Making a Liquid Yeast Starter Liquid yeast packets should be stored in the refrigerator to keep the yeast dormant and healthy until they are ready to be used. The 50 ml smack-packs contain an inner bubble of yeast nutrient (i.e., a "smack-pack") that are intended to function as a mini-starter, but are really not adequate for generating enough cells to properly ferment a five gallon batch. They still need to be pitched to a starter wort after activation. The package must be squeezed and warmed to 75-80°F at least two days before brewing. The packet will begin to swell as the yeast wake up and start consuming the nutrients. When the packet has fully swelled, it is time to pitch it to a starter to increase the total cell count to ensure a good fermentation. I prefer to prepare all my liquid yeast packages yeast four days before brewday.

1. If you are going to brew on Saturday, take the yeast packet out of the refrigerator on Tuesday. Let it warm up to room temperature. Place the packet on the countertop and feel for the inner bubble of yeast nutrient. Burst this inner bubble by pressing on it with the heel of your hand. Shake it well. If you are using a slant, proceed directly to Step 3. You will be making two successive starters to take the place of the mini-starter smack pack.

2. Put the packet in a warm place overnight to let it swell. On top of the refrigerator is good. Some brewers, who shall remain nameless, have been known to sleep with their yeast packets to keep them at the right temperature. However, their spouse assured them in no uncertain terms that the presence of the yeast packet did not entitle them to any more of the covers. So, just put the packet somewhere that's about 80°F, like near the water heater.

3. On Wednesday (or Tuesday for slants) you will make up a starter wort. Boil a pint (½ quart) of water and stir in ½ cup of DME. This will produce a starter of about 1.040 OG. Boil this for 10 minutes, adding a little bit of hops if you want to. Put the lid on the pan for the last couple minutes, turn off the stove and let it sit while you prepare for the next step. Adding a quarter teaspoon of yeast nutrient (vitamins, minerals, biotin, and dead yeast cells) to the starter wort is always advisable to ensure good growth. It is available from your brewshop.

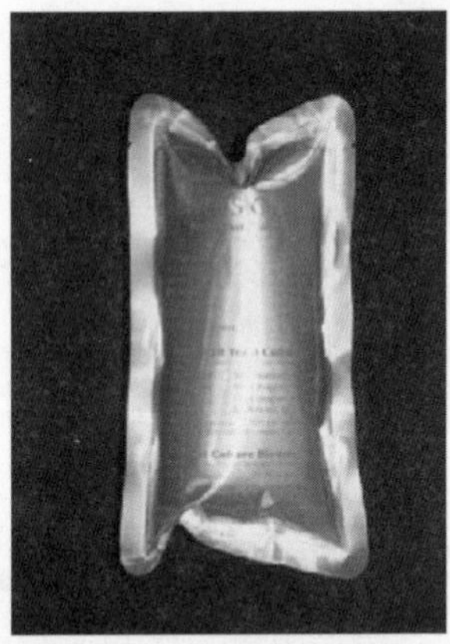

Figure 36—After about 24 hours, the packet has swelled like a balloon. Time to make the starter.

4. Fill the kitchen sink with a couple inches of cold water. Take the covered pot and set it in the water, moving it around to speed the cooling. When the pot feels cool, about 80°F or less, pour the wort into a sanitized glass mason jar or something similar. Pour all of the wort in, even the sediment. This sediment consists of proteins and lipids which are actually beneficial for yeast growth at this stage.

Ideally, the starter wort's temperature should be the same as what you plan the fermentation temperature to be. This allows the yeast to get acclimated to working at that temperature. If the yeast is started warmer and then pitched to a cooler fermentation environment, it may be shocked or stunned by the change in temperature and may take a couple days to regain normal activity.

Step 4—Cool the starter wort.

5. Sanitize the outside of the yeast packet before opening it by swabbing it with isopropyl alcohol. Using sanitized scissors, cut open a corner of the packet and pour the yeast into the jar. Two quart juice or cider bottles work well, and the opening is often the right size to accept an airlock and rubber stopper. Cover the top of the jar or bottle with plastic wrap and the lid.

Shake the starter vigorously to aerate it. Remove and discard the plastic wrap, insert an airlock and put it somewhere out of direct sunlight. If you don't have an airlock that will fit, don't worry. Instead, put a clean piece of plastic wrap over the jar or bottle and secure it loosely with a rubber band. This way the escaping carbon dioxide will be able to vent without exposing the starter to airborne bacteria.

6. On Thursday (or Wednesday for slants) some foaming or an increase in the white yeast layer on the bottom should be evident. These small wort starters can ferment quickly so don't be surprised if you missed the activity. When the starter has cleared and the yeast have settled to the bottom it is ready to pitch to the fermentor, although it will keep for 2-3 days without any problems. However, I recommend that you add another pint or quart of wort to the starter to build up the yeast population even more.

The starter process may be repeated several times to provide more yeast to ensure an even stronger fermentation. In fact, a general rule is that the stronger the beer (more fermentables /higher gravity), the more yeast you should pitch. For strong beers and barleywines, at least 1 cup of yeast slurry or 1 gallon of yeast starter

Step 4—Pour the starter wort into the starter jar.

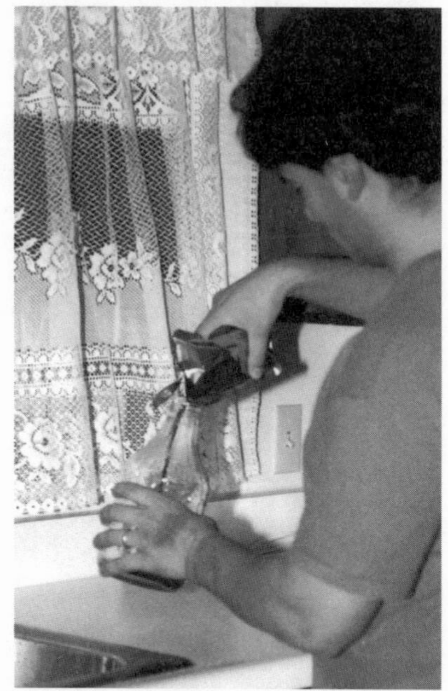

Step 5—Sanitize the pouch and pour the yeast into the jar.

should be pitched to ensure that there will be enough active yeast to finish the fermentation before they are overwhelmed by the rising alcohol level. For more moderate strength beers (1.050 gravity) a 1-1.5 quart starter is sufficient. One recommendation when pitching a large starter is to chill the starter overnight in the refrigerator to flocculate all the yeast. Then the unpleasant tasting starter beer can be poured off so only the yeast slurry will be pitched. This helps prevent the taste of the starter from influencing the taste of the final beer if the starter volume was large, i.e., ½ gallon.

Step 6—This starter has been built up twice and a substantial yeast layer can be seen on the bottom. Most any type of jar can be used for starters—mayonaise, juice, or cider all work well. The top can be covered with plastic wrap or an airlock. Good sanitation is paramount!

When Is My Yeast Starter Ready to Pitch?

A yeast starter is ready to pitch anytime after it has attained high krausen (full activity), and for about a day or two after it has settled out, depending on the temperature. Colder conditions allow the yeast to be stored longer before pitching to a new wort. Yeast starters that have settled out and sat at room temperature for more than a couple days should be fed fresh wort and allowed to attain high krausen before pitching.

A key condition to this recommendation is that the composition of the starter wort and the main wort must be very similar if the starter is pitched at or near peak activity. Why? Because the yeast in the starter wort have produced a specific set of enzymes for that wort's sugar profile. If those yeast are then pitched to a different wort, with a different relative percentage of sugars, the yeast will be impaired and the fermentation may be affected. Kind of like trying to change boats in mid-stream. This is especially true for starter worts made from extract that includes refined sugars. Yeast that has been eating sucrose, glucose, or fructose will quit making the enzyme that allows it to eat maltose–the main sugar of brewer's wort.

If you make your starter using a malt extract that includes refined sugar, it is better to wait until the yeast have finished fermenting and settled out before pitching to the main wort. Why? Because towards the end of fermentation, yeast build up their glycogen and trehalose reserves; kind of like a bear storing fat for the winter. Glycogen and trehalose are two carbohydrates that act as food reserves for the yeast cell. Yeast slowly feed off these reserves when other food is not present, and use this food extensively to fuel the synthesis of essential lipids, sterols, and unsaturated fatty acids when pitched to an oxygenated wort. (Yeast will rapidly deplete their glycogen reserves when exposed to oxygen.) While glycogen can be likened to the fat that a bear stores for winter, the other component, trehalose, acts more like the bear's heavy fur coat. Trehalose seems to get built up on both the inside and outside of the cell membrane, and is generally believed to make the membrane structure more robust and more resistant to environmental stresses. By allowing the yeast starter fermentation to go to completion, these reserves are built up, and upon pitching, the yeast starts out with a ready fuel supply and a clean slate to better adapt it to the new wort. As noted earlier, though, these same reserves are used by the yeast while in hibernation, so if the yeast are left too long before pitching, the reserves may be depleted and should be replenished with a fresh starter wort fermentation before use.

Using Yeast From Commercial Beers

There are many quality microbrewed beers on the market that are bottle conditioned, i.e. naturally carbonated and unfiltered, much the same as homebrewed beers are. The yeast layer from a bottle conditioned beer can be harvested and grown just like the yeast from a liquid yeast packet. This is a common practice among homebrewers because it allows for the use of some special yeast strains in homebrew that would not otherwise be available. This method can be used for cloning some of the specialty styles, such as Belgian Wit, Trappist Ales, or everyone's favorite–Sierra Nevada Pale Ale.

Harvesting yeast from a bottle-conditioned beer is quite simple.

1. After opening the bottle, thoroughly clean the bottle neck and opening with sanitizer to prevent bacterial contamination.
2. Simply pour the beer into a glass as you normally would, leaving the yeast layer on the bottom intact.
3. Swirl up the sediment with the beer remaining in the bottle and pour the yeast sediment into a prepared starter solution as described in the previous section–*Preparing a Liquid Yeast Starter.*

For best results, add the sediment from 2-3 bottles and be sure to use the freshest beer you can find. The starter should behave the same as any other liquid yeast pack starter, though it may take longer to build due to the smaller amount of yeast that you start out with. In fact, you may not notice any activity in the starter for the first couple wort additions until the amount of yeast builds to higher levels. Add more wort as necessary to build the yeast slurry to pitching level.

Support Your Local Micro

In addition, if you have a quality brewpub or microbrewery nearby, the brewers are often happy to provide yeast to homebrewers. A good brewery produces a lot more yeast than they can use and it is usually free of contamination. I keep a spare, sanitized, plastic pint container in the car in case I am visiting a micro and am able to talk to the brewers. (*I know what you are thinking,* "What are the odds that I will be at a brewpub when they are brewing?" *Sometimes it requires several visits a day to even those odds, but that's life.*) If they don't have any yeast available at the moment, they will usually suggest you come back the next day/week when they are transferring, and will give you some then. The advantage to obtaining yeast this way is that you usually get a cup or more of slurry which is more than enough to ferment a 5 gallon batch. You are virtually assured of a vigorous, healthy fermentation, without the fuss of preparing a yeast starter a few days beforehand. The yeast will stay viable for a couple weeks if kept in the refrigerator. But remember, you may want to replenish the yeast's glycogen and trehelose reserves, as described in *When Is My Starter Ready To Pitch,* if the yeast has been stored for a long time.

Simple Yeast Ranching

Each batch of beer you brew is a good source of yeast for a future batch. The best way to obtain yeast is to skim it from the krausen of a currently fermenting beer. To do this, you will need to be using a bucket type fermentor and first skim off the green/brown hop and protein compounds with a sanitized spoon early in the primary phase. As the creamy white krausen builds up, you can skim this fresh yeast off with a sanitized spoon and transfer it to a sanitized jar. Fill the jar with cooled boiled water and place it in the refridgerator. The lack of nutrients in the water will cause the yeast to kind of "hibernate" and it will keep for up to a couple months. You should pitch this yeast to a starter after storage to re-vitalize it.

The only drawback to the above harvesting method is the contamination risk for the current batch. Experienced brewers with good sanitation practices can harvest yeast that way without much risk, but for newer brewers it is probably better to collect the yeast after the fermentation is complete. You can collect yeast from either the bottom of the primary or secondary fermentor. If you obtain yeast from the secondary, it will have only small amounts of trub mixed in and will be easy to seperate. However, you need ot be aware that if you repitch yeast harvested from the secondary several times in succession, you will tend to select the less flocculant cells of the population, and future beers will be slow to clarify. But, if you only repitch once or twice, it is not a big deal. I myself usually harvest yeast from the secondary.

If you harvest yeast from the primary fermentor, you will need to separate the yeast from all the trub that is mixed in. Professional brewers most often do this by "acid washing" the yeast–using acid to lower the pH to about 2.5 so that bacteria is inhibited and using whirlpool methods to seperate the heavier trub from the lighter yeast. But acid washing tends to inhibit the yeast too, and is not strictly necessary. You can simply use chilled boiled* water and two sanitized jars to separate the healthy yeast (white) away from the majority of the trub.

1. After racking the beer, swirl up the yeast layer on the bottom and pour some into a large sanitized jar (such as a mayonnaise jar).
2. Gently pour in some cold, boiled water and swirl it up to get all the yeast and trub in suspension.
3. Let the jar sit for a minute or three to allow most of the trub to settle to the bottom. Gently pour the cloudy water, containing suspended yeast, into another sanitized jar. Discard the dark trub.
4. Add some more water and repeat this procedure until you are left with a substantially light-colored yeast suspension and only a thin brown layer of dead yeast and trub on the bottom of the jar.
5. Store the jar in the refridgerator for up to a couple months. The yeast will turn brown as it ages. Discard it once it turns the color of peanut butter. Eventually the yeast will autolyze and die as its nutritional reserves are used up.

Pitch the yeast to a starter before using to ensure its vitality. If the starter smells wrong–rancid, rubbery, etc., the yeast may be contaminated. The dominant smell of a starter should be a yeasty smell, but sulfur smells are not necessarily bad, especially with lager yeast strains.

***Note:** You want to use boiled water for two reasons:

- For sanitation.
- To avoid exposing the yeast to dissolved oxygen which would cause the yeast to deplete their glycogen reserves before storage.

Yeast Nutritional Needs

From a yeast cells point of view, its purpose in life is to grow, eat, and reproduce. Yeast can do all this with or without oxygen, but using oxygen makes the processes easier for the cell. Yeast use oxygen in the biosynthesis of the compounds that make up their cell membranes that allow them to process sugars for food and grow. Without oxygen, yeast cannot synthesize sterols very well, and reproduction diminishes. Therefore, to ensure a good fermentation, we need to provide the yeast with sufficient oxygen to allow them to grow quickly and reproduce when they are first pitched to the fermentor. Once they have reproduced to sufficient numbers, we can let them get on with turning our wort into beer. The role of oxygen in yeast growth will be discussed more in *Chapter 8-Fermentation.*

MINERALS

Necessary Minerals for Yeast Function

Ion	Concentration
Magnesium	70 ppm
Potassium	120 ppm
Zinc	0.3 ppm
Calcium	180 ppm
Manganese	0.15 ppm
Copper	0.1 ppm

These elements act as catalysts or metabolic co-factors and are absolutely necessary for the health of the yeast cells. The exact requirement of each mineral depends on a variety of factors, including yeast strain and environment. The numbers given are intended to be typical. Note that these numbers are for wort concentration and not brewing water.

Yeast cannot live on sugar alone. Yeast also need minerals, nitrogen, and amino and fatty acids to enable them to live and grow. The primary source for these building blocks are minerals in the water and the free amino nitrogen (FAN), lipids, and minerals from the malted barley. Refined sugars like table sugar, corn sugar or candy sugar do not contain any of these nutrients. And, it is common for extracts (especially kit extracts targeted toward a particular style) to be thinned with refined sugars to lighten the color or reduce the cost of production. An all-malt beer has all the nutrition that the yeast will need for a good fermentation, but all-extract beers may not have sufficient FAN to promote adequate growth. Since malt extract is commonly used for yeast starters, it is always a good idea to add some yeast nutrients to ensure good yeast growth.

If you use ion-exchanged softened water for brewing, the water may not have adequate calcium, magnesium, and zinc for some of the yeast's metabolic paths. Magnesium plays a vital role in cellular metabolism and its function can be inhibited by a preponderance of calcium in the wort.

Brewers adding calcium salts for water chemistry adjustment may want to include magnesium salts as part of the addition if they experience fermentation problems. Usually the wort supplies all the necessary mineral requirements of the yeast, except for zinc which is often deficient or in a non-assimilable form. Additions of zinc can greatly improve the cell count and vigor of the starter, but adding too much will cause the yeast to produce excessive by-products and cause off-flavors. Zinc acts as a catalyst and tends to carry over into the succeeding generation–therefore it is probably better to add it to either the starter or the main wort but not both. The nutrient pouches in the Wyeast smack-packs already contain zinc in addition to other nutrients. For best performance, zinc levels should be between 0.1-0.3 mg/l, with 0.5 mg/l being maximum. If you experience stuck fermentations or low attenuation, and you have eliminated other variables such as: temperature, low pitching rate, poor aeration, poor FAN, age, etc., then lack of necessary minerals may be a significant factor.

Nutritional Supplements

You will see four types of yeast nutrients on the market that can supplement a wort that is high in refined sugars or adjuncts.

Di-ammonium Phosphate–This is strictly a nitrogen supplement that can take the place of a lack of FAN.

Yeast Hulls–This is essentially dead yeast, the carcasses of which act as agglomeration sites and contain some useful residual lipids.

Yeast Nutrient or Energizer–The name can vary, but the intent is a mixture of di-ammonium phosphate, yeast hulls, biotin and vitamins. These mixtures are a more complete dietary supplement for the yeast and what I recommend.

Servomyces™–This product from Lallemand is similar to yeast hulls but differs by having a useful amount of rapidly assimilable zinc, which is an essential enzyme co-factor for yeast health. This product falls within the provisions of the Rheinheitsgebot.

Oxygen

Yeast need oxygen to synthesize sterols and unsaturated fatty acids for cell membrane biosynthesis. Without aeration, fermentations tend to be underattenuated because oxygen availability is a limiting factor for yeast growth–the yeast stop budding when sterol levels become depleted. Higher gravity worts need more yeast for proper fermentation, and thus need more oxygen, but the higher gravity makes it more difficult to dissolve oxygen in

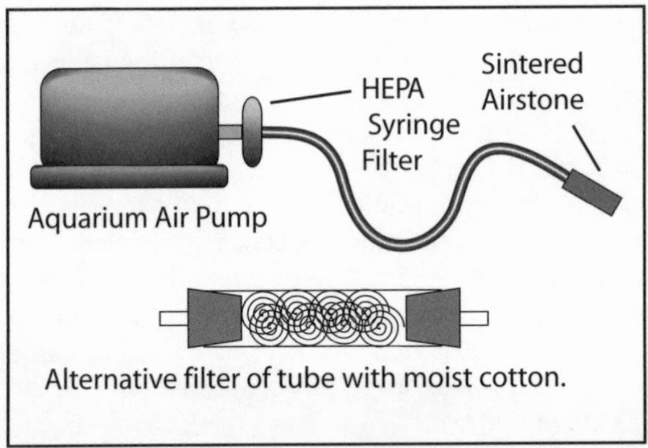

Figure 41—Here is an example of an aquarium air pump using an airstone and a microbial filter for aeration. The filter is a HEPA (medical) syringe filter or alternatively one can be made from a plastic tube, moistened cotton, and rubber stoppers. The moist cotton provides the filtering action and should be thrown away after each use.

the first place. Boiling the wort drives out the dissolved oxygen normally present, so aeration of some sort is needed prior to fermentation. Proper aeration of the wort can be accomplished several ways:

- shaking the container, e.g. the starter jar
- pouring the cooled wort back and forth from the boiling pot into the fermentor
- using a bronze or stainless steel airstone with an aquarium air pump and using it to bubble air into the fermentor for an hour.

For the beginning brewer, I recommend the simplest methods of shaking the starter and pouring the wort. Pouring is also effective if you are doing a partial boil and adding water to the fermentor to make up the total volume. Instead of pouring the wort, you can just pour the water back and forth to another sanitized pot prior to adding the wort.

Using an airpump and airstone to bubble air into the fermentor is very effective and saves you from lifting a heavy fermentor. The only precaution you need to take, other than sanitizing the airstone and hose, is to be sure that the air going into the fermentor is not carrying any mold spores or dust-borne bacteria. To guard against contamination, an in-line filter is used to prevent airborne contamination from reaching the wort. One type is a sterile medical syringe filter and these can be purchased at hospital pharmacies or a your local brewshop. An alternative, build-it-yourself bacterial filter is a tube filled with moist cotton balls. *See Figure 41*. The cotton should be changed after each use.

Aeration is Good, Oxidation is Bad

The yeast is the most significant factor in determining the quality of a fermentation. Oxygen can be the most significant factor in determining the quality of the yeast. Oxygen is both your friend and your enemy. It is important to understand when which is which.

You should not aerate when the wort is hot, or even warm. Aeration of hot wort will cause the oxygen to chemically bind to various wort compounds. Over time, these compounds will break down, freeing atomic oxygen back into the beer where it can oxidize the fatty acids and alcohols, producing off-flavors and aromas like wet cardboard or sherry. The generally accepted temperature cutoff for preventing hot wort oxidation is 80°F.

Oxidation of your wort can happen in several ways. The first is by splashing or aerating the wort while it is hot. This problem is called hot-side aeration or HSA. Older brewing books have advocated pouring the boiling-hot wort into cold water in the fermentor to cool it and add oxygen for the yeast. Unfortunately the wort is still hot enough to be oxidized instead of aerated. Pouring it down the side of the bucket to minimize splashing doesn't really help either since this increases the surface area of the wort exposed to the air. Therefore you must cool the wort first to below 80°F to prevent oxidation, and *then* aerate it to provide the dissolved oxygen that the yeast need. Cooling rapidly between 90-140°F is important because this temperature range is ideal for bacterial growth.

In addition, if oxygen is introduced after primary fermentation has started, it may cause the yeast to produce more of the early fermentation byproducts, like diacetyl. However, some strains of yeast respond very well to "open" fermentations (where the fermentor is open to the air) without producing off-flavors. But even for those yeast strains, aeration after fermentation is complete can lead to staling. When you rack to a secondary fermentor or to the bottling bucket, it is very important to prevent gurgling or splashing. Keep the siphon flowing smoothly by placing the outlet of the siphon hose below the surface of the rising beer. Decrease the difference in height between the two containers when you begin. This will slow the siphon rate at first and prevent turbulence and aeration until the outlet is beneath the surface.

Summary—you want to pitch a sufficient amount of healthy yeast, preferably grown in a starter that matches your intended fermentation conditions. You want to cool the wort to fermentation temperature and then aerate the wort to provide the oxygen that the yeast need to grow and reproduce. Then you want to protect the beer from oxygen after fermentation to prevent oxidation and staling. In the next couple chapters, I will walk you through the practical application of these ideas.

Chapter 7

Boiling and Cooling

First Recipe

Okay, are you ready to take the plunge?
For your first beer, let's make an American pale ale.

> **RECIPE**
>
> **Cincinnati Pale Ale**
>
> Ingredients for a 5 gallon batch
>
> - 3-4 lb. Pale malt extract syrup, unhopped
> - 2 lb. Amber dry malt extract
> - 12 AAU of bittering hops (any variety)
>   For example, 1 oz. of 12% AA Nugget, or 1.5 oz. of 8% AA Northern Brewer
> - 5 AAU of finishing hops (Cascade or other)
>   For example, 1 oz. of 5% Cascade or 1.25 oz. of 4% Liberty
> - 3 packets of dry ale yeast

American pale ale is an adaptation of the classic British pale ale. Most American ale yeast strains are less fruity than comparable English ale yeasts, and thus American pale ale has a cleaner, less fruity taste than its British counterparts. Pale ales vary in color from gold to dark amber and typically have a hint of sweet caramel (from the use of caramel malts) that does not mask the hop finish. We will use amber malt extract for part of our recipe, which contains caramel malt, to achieve this. With the resurgence of interest in ales in the United States, pale ale evolved to reflect a renewed interest in American hop varieties and a higher level of bitterness as microbreweries experimented with craft brewing. The Cascade hop has become a staple of American microbrewing. It has a distinct aroma compared to the European hops and has helped American pale

ale stand shoulder to shoulder with other classic beer styles of the world. Prime examples of this style are Anchor Liberty Ale and Sierra Nevada Pale Ale.

The Finishing hops are often Cascade but can be any other American hop variety like Liberty or Willamette. American pale ale is also commonly dry hopped, so an additional half ounce can be added to the primary fermentor after the bubbling starts to taper off or to the secondary for more hop aroma. Dry hopping does not increase the bitterness of the ale, but it adds a wonderful aroma and flavor.

Beginning the Boil

Figure 42—The brewing water is boiling in the pot, and the malt extract and hops are ready to be added. Warm water for rehydrating the yeast is ready also. Placing a large towel on the floor helps soak up spills and makes clean up much easier later. Four out of five spouses surveyed did not like sticky floors.

1. Boil the brew water. In the brewpot, bring about 3 gallons of water to a boil. Pour this water into the fermentor and leave it to cool. Now bring another 3 gallons of water to boil in the brewpot. You will be boiling the extract in this water and diluting this concentrated wort with the water in the fermentor to make the total 5 gallons. Some water will evaporate during the boil, and some will be lost to the trub. Starting out with something closer to six gallons will ensure that you hit your five gallon recipe volume.

2. Rehydrate the dried yeast. Although many people skip this step with fair results, re-hydrating it assures the best results. While you are waiting for the brew water to boil, rehydrate two packets of dried ale yeast. Put 1 cup of warm (95-105°F, 35-40°C), preboiled water into your sanitized jar and stir in the yeast. Cover with plastic wrap and wait 15 minutes.

If you are using name-brand yeast that was stored well, then proofing is not necessary. See *Chapter 6 - Yeast* for more info.

3. Add malt extract. When the water in the brewpot is boiling, turn off the stove and stir in the malt extract. Be sure the extract is completely dissolved (if your malt extract is the dry variety, make sure there are no clumps; if the extract is syrup, make sure that none is stuck to the bottom of the pot). Next, turn the heat back on and resume the boil. Stir the wort regularly during the boil to be sure that it doesn't scorch.

4. Watch the Pot The next stage is critical. The pot needs to be watched continuously in case it starts to boil over. Return the pot to the heat and bring to a rolling boil, stirring occasionally.

The Hot Break

5. Watch for boilovers. A foam will start to rise and form a smooth surface. This is good. If the foam suddenly billows over the side, this is a boil-over (Bad). If it looks like it is going to boil over, either lower the heat or spray the surface with

water from a spray bottle. Put a few copper pennies into the pot to help prevent boilovers. The foam is caused by proteins in the wort that coagulate due to the rolling action of the boil. The wort will continue to foam until the protein clumps get heavy enough to sink back into the pot. You will see particles floating around in the wort. It may look like Egg Drop Soup. This is called the hot break and may take 5-20 minutes to occur, depending on the amount of protein in your extract. Often the first hop addition triggers a great deal of foaming, especially if hop pellets are used. I recommend waiting until the hot break occurs before doing your first hop addition and timing the hour. The extra boiling time won't hurt.

Covering the pot with the lid can help with heat retention and help you achieve your boil, but it can also lead to trouble. Murphy's Law has its own brewing corollary: "If it can boil over, it will boil over." Covering the pot and turning your back on it is the quickest way to achieve a boilover. If you cover the pot, watch it like a hawk...a hawk and ten buzzards even.

Once you achieve a boil, only partially cover the pot, if at all. Why? Because in wort there are sulfur compounds that evolve and boil off. If they aren't removed during the boil, the can form dimethyl sulfide which contributes a cooked cabbage or corn-like flavor to the beer. If the cover is left on the pot, or left on such that the condensate from the lid can drip back in, then these flavors will have a much greater chance of showing up in the finished beer.

Hop Additions

6. Add hops. Once the Hot break has occurred, add the bittering hops. Stir them in so that they are all wetted. Be careful that the wort doesn't boil over when you add them. These should be boiled for about an hour to extract the alpha acids for bittering. See *Chapter 5–Hops*, for details on how the hop additions affect the beer's flavor.

By the way, have you re-hydrated your yeast yet?

7. Add more hops. Continue the rolling boil for the remainder of the hour. Stir occasionally to prevent scorching. There will probably be a change in color and aroma and there will be clumps of stuff floating in the wort. This is not a concern, its the hot break material i.e. coagulated/precipitated protein. Add half the finishing hops at 30 minutes before the end of the boil, and the last half during the last 15 minutes. These late additions allow less time for the volatile oils to boil away, increasing hop flavor and aroma. If you want to, add a little more during the last five minutes if still more hop aroma is desired. Refer to *Chapter 5–Hops* for more information.

Cooling the Wort

At the end of the boil, it is important to cool the wort quickly. While it is still hot (above 140°F), bacteria and wild yeasts are inhibited. But it is very susceptible to oxidation damage as it cools. There are also the previously mentioned sulfur compounds that evolve from the wort while it is hot. If the wort is cooled slowly, dimethyl sulfide will continue to be produced in the wort without being boiled off; causing off-flavors in the finished beer. The objective is to rapidly cool the wort to below 80°F before oxidation or contamination can occur.

Rapid cooling also forms the "cold break." This is composed of another group of proteins that need to be thermally shocked into precipitating out of the wort. Slow cooling will not affect them. Cold break, or rather the lack of it, is the cause of "chill haze." When a beer is chilled for drinking, these proteins partially precipitate forming a haze. As the beer warms up, the proteins re-dissolve. Only by rapid chilling from near-boiling to room temperature will the cold break proteins permanently precipitate and not cause chill haze. Chill haze is usually regarded as a cosmetic problem. You cannot taste it. However, chill haze indicates that there is an appreciable level of cold-break-type protein in the beer, which has been linked to long-term stability problems. Hazy beer tends to become stale sooner than non-hazy beer. For your first batch, I recommend using a cold water bath to chill the wort, but alternative methods are presented on the next page.

Water Bath

8. Cool It Place the pot in a sink or tub filled with cold/ice water that can be circulated around the hot pot. As mentioned in the previous chapter, it is best to keep the pot lid on, but if you are careful you can speed up the cooling by stirring. Gently stir the wort in a circular manner so the maximum amount of wort is moving against the sides of the pot. Minimize splashing to avoid oxidation. Don't let water from your hands drip inside the pot; this could be a source of contamination. If the cooling water gets warm, replace with colder water. The wort should cool to 80°F in about 30 minutes. When the pot is barely warm to the touch, the temperature is in the right range.

9. Ferment the Wort See the next chapter (*8–Fermentation*) for a discussion of what fermentation is, and the chapter following (*9–Fermenting Your First Batch*) for the rest of the instructions for your first batch.

Ice

People often wonder about adding ice directly to the cooling wort. This idea works well if you remember a couple key points.

- Never use commercial ice. It can harbor dormant bacteria that could spoil your beer.
- Always boil the water before freezing it in an airtight container (like Tupperware). It must be airtight because most freezers also harbor dormant bacteria.
- If the ice will not directly contact the wort, (i.e. you are using a frozen plastic soda bottle or other container in the wort) make sure you sanitize the outside of the bottle first before you put it in the wort.

Copper Wort Chillers

A wort chiller is a coil of copper tubing that is used as a heat exchanger to cool the wort in-place. Wort chillers are not necessary for your first batch of beer, when you are only boiling 2-3 gallons, but this is a good time to make you aware of them. Wort chillers are useful for cooling full volume boils because you can leave the wort on the stove instead of carrying it to a sink or bathtub. Five gallons of boiling hot wort weighs almost 45 pounds and is hazardous to carry.

There are two basic types of wort chillers: immersion and counter-flow. Immersion chillers are the simplest and work by running cold water through the coil. The chiller is immersed in the wort and the water carries the heat away. Counterflow chillers work in an opposite manner. The hot wort is drained from the pot through the copper tubing while cold water flows around the outside of the chiller. Immersion chillers are often sold in homebrew supply shops or can be easily made at home. Instructions for building both types of chiller are given in *Appendix C.*

MURPHY'S LAWS OF BREWING

If it can boil over, it will boilover.

No good beer goes unfinished.

Nature always hides in the hidden flaw.

If you keep messing with it, you will probably screw it up.

If you don't have time to do it right, you will probably end up doing it over.

The race is not always to the swift, nor the battle to the strong, but that's the way to bet.

(i.e., The most conscientious brewer may not win all the ribbons, but he will probably win most of them.)

Did you ever wonder where Murphy's Law came from? Well back at work there was a photocopy of a short article from one of the aerospace trade journals on the wall of my friend's cubicle. It went something like this:

> Captain Murphy was part of an engineering team out at Edward's Air Force Base in California. Their team was investigating the effects of high gravity de-accelerations on jet pilots back in the 1950's. One of their tests involved strapping a test pilot into a rocket chair equipped with strain gages and other sensors to help them quantify the effects of high G stopping. The responsibility for the placement of the various sensors was Capt. Murphy's. Well, the test was run (subjecting the pilot to something like 100 G's of deceleration) and he got pretty banged up.
>
> Only after it was over did the team realize that of all the possible combinations of placing those sensors, Murphy had done it in the one configuration that resulted in useless data. They would have to run the test again. Upon realizing this, Murphy stated, "If there are two or more ways of doing something, and one of them can result in catastrophe, someone will do it that way." Upon hearing this the team leader said, "That's Murphy's Law." The next day at the test de-briefing the team leader shortened it to the now famous, "If anything can go wrong, it will."
>
> Murphy still likes his version better.

Chapter 8

Fermentation

In this chapter, we will discuss fermentation–how the yeast turns wort into beer. As important as the yeast process is to achieving a good batch, it is also the one that is most often taken for granted by beginning brewers. A lot of thought will be given to the recipe: which malts, which hops, but often the yeast choice will be whatever was taped to the top of the kit. Even if some consideration is given to the brand of yeast and the type, very often the conditions to which the yeast is pitched are not planned or controlled. The brewer cools the wort, aerates it a bit, and then pitches his yeast and waits for it to do its thing.

It has been common for brewing texts to over-emphasize a short "lagtime"–the period of time after pitching the yeast before the foamy head appeared in the fermentor. This lagtime was the benchmark that everyone would use to gage the health of their yeast and the vigor of the fermentation. While it is a notable indicator, the lagtime accounts for a combination of pre-fermentation processes that have a great deal to do with the quality of the total fermentation, but that individually are not well represented by time.

A very short lagtime does not guarantee an exemplary fermentation and an outstanding beer. A short lagtime only means that initial conditions were favorable for growth and metabolism. It says nothing about the total amount of nutrients in the wort or how the rest of the fermentation will progress.

The latter stages of fermentation may also appear to finish more quickly when in fact the process was not super-efficient, but rather, incomplete. The point is that speed does not necessarily correlate with quality. Of course, under optimal conditions a fermentation would be more efficient and thus take less time. But it is better to pay attention to the fermentation conditions, and getting the process right, than to a rigid time schedule.

Factors For A Good Fermentation

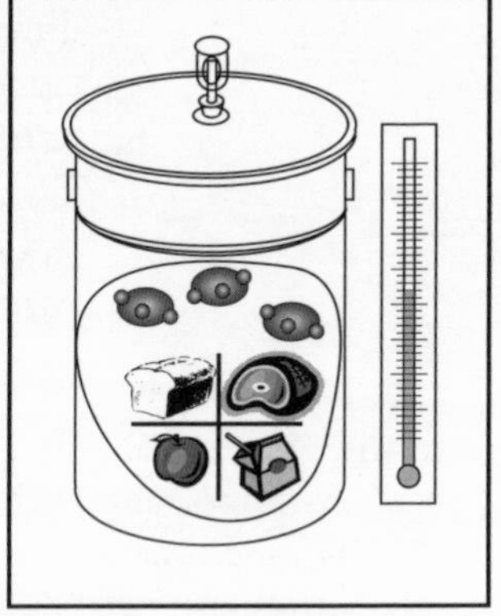

Let's review the preparations from the previous chapters that will help us consistently achieve a good fermentation. There are three principal factors that determine fermentation activity and results: Yeast, Wort Nutrients and Temperature.

Yeast Factors

The first step to achieving a good fermentation is to pitch enough yeast. The yeast can be grown via yeast starters or it can be harvested from previous fermentations. When yeast is harvested from a previous fermentation, it should be taken from the upper layer of the primary yeast cake or from the secondary. This yeast will have the optimum characteristics for re-pitching. In either case, you should plan on pitching at least ⅓ cup (75 ml) of yeast slurry to a typical 5 gallon batch of ale or ⅔ cup of slurry for lagers. For stronger beers, OG > 1.050, more yeast should be pitched to ensure optimum fermentations. For very strong beers like doppelbocks and barleywines, at least 2 cups of slurry should be pitched.

The yeast that is obtained from a healthy starter or recently from a prior fermentation will have good vitality and will readily adapt to the new wort. With good levels of aeration and nutrients, the yeast will quickly multiply to the numbers necessary for an exemplary fermentation.

Wort Factors

There are two considerations that are needed to ensure that the wort has been properly prepared to support a good fermentation. The first is oxygen supplied via aeration. The methods for aerating the wort were covered in *Chapter 6–Yeast*. The role of oxygen in yeast growth will be discussed further in the Adaptation Phase section later in this chapter.

The second consideration is the level of amino acid nutrients in the wort, specifically referred to as Free Amino Nitrogen or FAN. Malted barley normally supplies all of the FAN and nutrients that the yeast need to grow and adapt to the fermentation environment. However, if the recipe incorporates large amounts of adjuncts (e.g. corn, rice, unmalted wheat, unmalted barley), or refined sugars, then the wort may not have the minimum levels of nutrients necessary for the yeast to build strong cells. It is always advisable to add some yeast nutrient powder to worts that are made exclusively from light extracts because these extracts are typically thinned with corn sugar.

In addition, brewers should be aware that in a wort that contains a high percentage of refined sugar (~50%), the yeast will sometimes lose the ability to secrete the enzymes that allow them to ferment maltose. They will adapt themselves right out of a job!

Temperature Factors

The third factor for a good fermentation is temperature. Yeast are greatly affected by temperature–too cold and they go dormant, too hot (more than 10°F above the nominal range) and they indulge in an orgy of fermentation that often cannot be cleaned up by conditioning. High temperatures encourage the production of fusel alcohols–heavier alcohols that can have harsh solvent-like flavors. Many of these fusels esterify during secondary fermentation, but in large amounts these esters can dominate the beer's flavor. Excessively banana-tasting beers are one example of high esters due to high temperature fermentation.

High temperatures can also lead to excessive levels of diacetyl. A common mistake that homebrewers make is pitching the yeast when the wort has not been chilled enough, and is still relatively warm (>80°F). If the wort is warm when the yeast is pitched and slowly cools to room temperature during primary fermentation, more diacetyl will be produced in the early stages than the yeast can reabsorb during the secondary stage. Furthermore, primary fermentation is an exothermic process. The internal temperature of the fermentor can be as much as 10°F above ambient conditions, just due to yeast activity. This is one good reason to keep the fermentor environment in the proper temperature range; so that with a normal vigorous fermentation, the beer turns out as intended, even if it was warmer than the surroundings. But if its mid-summer and you don't have a way to keep the fermentor cool, then you shouldn't bother brewing. The beer will not be very good.

Redefining Fermentation

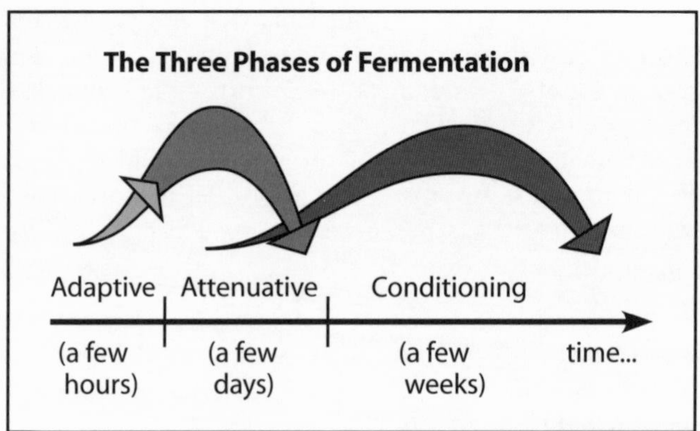

The fermentation of malt sugars into beer is a complicated biochemical process. It is more than just the conversion of sugar to alcohol, which can be regarded as the primary activity. Total fermentation is better defined as three phases, the Adaptation or Lagtime phase, the Primary or Attenuative phase and a Secondary or Conditioning phase. The yeast do not end Phase 2 before beginning Phase 3, the processes occur in parallel, but the conditioning processes occur more slowly. As the majority of simple sugars are consumed, more and more of the yeast will transition to eating the larger, more complex sugars and early yeast by-products. This is why beer (and wine) improves with age to a degree, as long as they are on the yeast. Beer that has been filtered or pasteurized will not benefit from aging.

Lagtime or Adaptation Phase

Immediately after pitching, the yeast start adjusting to the wort conditions and undergo a period of high growth. The yeast use any available oxygen in the wort to facilitate their growth processes. They can use other methods to adapt and grow in the absence of oxygen, but they can do it much more efficiently with oxygen. Under normal conditions, the yeast should proceed through the adaptation phase and begin primary fermentation within 12 hours. If 24 hours pass without apparent activity, then a new batch of yeast should probably be pitched.

At the beginning of the adaptation phase, the yeast take stock of the sugars, FAN and other nutrients present, and figure out what enzymes and other attributes it needs to adapt to the environment. The yeast use their own glycogen reserves, oxygen, and wort lipids to synthesize sterols to build up their cell membranes. The sterols are known to be critical for enabling the cell membrane to be permeable to wort sugars and other wort nutrients. Sterols can also be produced by the yeast under poor oxygen conditions from lipids found in wort trub, but that pathway is much less efficient.

Once the cell walls are permeable, the yeast can start metabolizing the amino nitrogen and sugars in the wort for food. Like every animal, the goal in life for the yeast cell is to reproduce. Yeast reproduce asexually by "budding." Daughter cells split off from the parent cell. The reproduction process takes a lot of energy and aerobic metabolic processes are more efficient than anaerobic. Thus, an oxygen-rich wort shortens the adaptation phase, and allows the yeast to quickly reproduce to levels that will ensure a good fermentation. When the oxygen is used up, the yeast switch metabolic pathways and begin what we consider to be fermentation–the anaerobic metabolism of sugar to alcohol. This pathway is less energy efficient, so the yeast cannot reproduce as proficiently as during the adaptation phase.

The key to a good fermentation is lots of strong healthy yeast–yeast that can get the job done before going dormant due to depleted resources, rising alcohol levels, and old age. As noted, the rate of reproduction is slower in the absence of oxygen. At some point in the fermentation cycle of the beer, the rate of yeast reproduction is going to fall behind the rate of yeast dormancy. By providing optimum conditions for yeast growth and reproduction in the wort initially, we can ensure that this rate transition will not occur until after the beer has become fully attenuated.

Worts that are underpitched or poorly aerated will ferment slowly or incompletely due to lack of viable yeast. Experienced brewers make a big point about aerating the wort and building up a yeast starter because these practices virtually guarantee enough yeast to do the job well.

Primary or Attenuative Phase

The primary or attenuative phase is marked by a time of vigorous fermentation and can last anywhere from 2-6 days for ales, or 4-10 days for lagers, depending on conditions. The majority of the attenuation occurs during the primary phase, when the gravity of the beer drops by ⅔-¾ of the original gravity (OG).

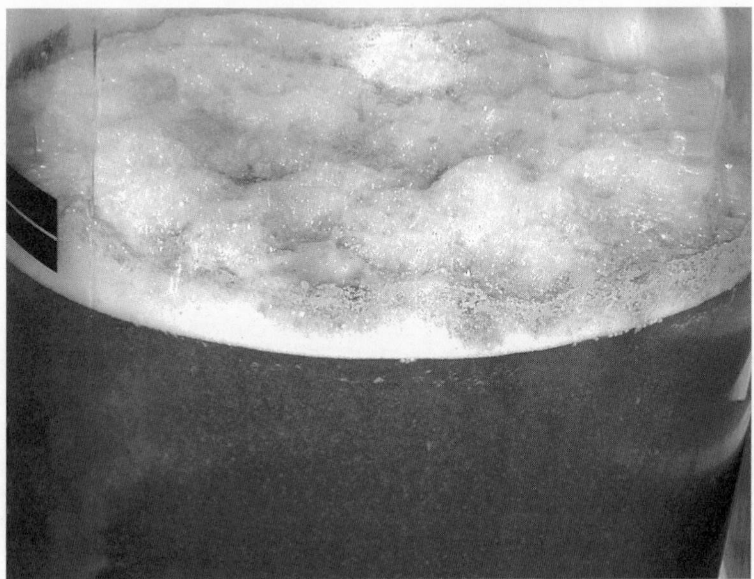

Figure 52—A healthy, creamy, krausen of yeast floats on top during the primary fermentation stage. This is a good time to skim off and harvest some yeast to save for a future batch.

A head of foamy krausen will form on top of the beer. The foam consists of yeast and wort proteins and is a light creamy color, with islands of green-brown gunk that collect and tend to adhere to the sides of the fermentor. The gunk is composed of extraneous wort protein, hop resins, and dead yeast. These compounds are very bitter and if stirred back into the wort, would result in harsh aftertastes. Fortunately these compounds are relatively insoluble and are typically removed by adhering to the sides of the fermentor as the krausen subsides. Aftertastes are rarely, if ever, a problem.

As the primary phase winds down, a majority of the yeast start settling out and the krausen starts to subside. If you are going to transfer the beer off of the trub and primary yeast cake, this is the proper time to do so. Take care to avoid aerating the beer during the transfer. At this point in the fermentation process, any exposure to oxygen will only contribute to staling reactions in the beer, or worse, expose it to contamination.

Many canned kits will advise bottling the beer after one week or after the krausen has subsided. This is not a good idea because the beer has not yet gone through the conditioning phase. At this time the beer would taste a bit rough around the edges (e.g. yeasty flavors, buttery tones, green apple flavors) but that will disappear after a few days or weeks of conditioning, depending on the yeast strain and the fermentation environment.

Figure 53—As the primary stage winds down and the secondary stage takes over, the yeast starts to flocculate and the krausen settles back into the beer.

Secondary or Conditioning Phase

The reactions that take place during the conditioning phase are primarily a function of the yeast. The vigorous primary stage is over, the majority of the wort sugars have been converted to alcohol, and a lot of the yeast cells are going dormant–but some are still active.

The Secondary Phase allows for the slow reduction of the remaining fermentables. The yeast have eaten most all of the easily fermentable sugars and now start to turn their attention elsewhere. The yeast start to work on the heavier sugars like maltotriose. Also, the yeast clean up some of the byproducts they produced during the fast-paced primary phase. But this stage has its dark side too.

Under some conditions, the yeast will also utilize some of the compounds in the trub. The metabolization of these compounds can produce several off-flavors. In addition, the dormant yeast on the bottom of the fermentor begin excreting more amino and fatty acids. Leaving the post-primary beer on the trub and yeast cake for too long (more than about three weeks) will tend to result in soapy flavors becoming evident. Further, after very long times the yeast begin to die and break down–autolysis, which produces rubbery, sulfury tastes and smells. For these reasons, it can be important to get the beer off of the trub and dormant yeast during the conditioning phase.

There has been a lot of controversy within the homebrewing community on the value of racking beers, particularly ales, to secondary fermentors. Many seasoned homebrewers have declared that there is no real taste benefit and that the dangers of contamination and the cost in additional time are not worth what little benefit there may be. And, I will agree that for a new brewer's first, low gravity, pale ale that the risks probably outweigh the benefits. However, I have always argued that through careful transfer, secondary fermentation away from the trub is beneficial to nearly all beer styles. But, for now, I will advise new brewers to only use single stage fermentation until they have gained some experience with racking and sanitation.

Leaving an ale beer in the primary fermentor for a total of 2-3 weeks versus one when using single stage fermentation (i.e. not using a secondary fermentor) will provide time for the conditioning reactions and improve the finished beer. The extra time will also let more sediment settle out before bottling, resulting in a clearer beer and easier pouring.

Conditioning Processes

The conditioning process is a function of the yeast. The vigorous, primary stage is over, the majority of the wort sugars have been converted to alcohol, and a lot of the yeast are going dormant; but there is still yeast activity. During the earlier phases, many different compounds were produced by the yeast in addition to ethanol and CO_2, e.g., acetaldehyde, esters, amino acids, ketones, dimethyl sulfide, etc. Once the easy food is gone, the yeast start re-processing these by-products. Diacetyl and pentanedione are two ketones that have buttery and honey-like flavors. These compounds are considered flaws when present in large amounts and can cause flavor stability problems during storage. Acetaldehyde is an aldehyde that has a pronounced green apple smell and taste. It is an intermediate compound in the production of ethanol. The yeast reduce these compounds during the later stages of fermentation.

The yeast also produce an array of fusel alcohols during primary fermentation in addition to ethanol. Fusels are higher molecular weight alcohols that often give harsh solvent-like tastes to beer. During secondary fermentation, the yeast convert these alcohols to more pleasant, fruity tasting esters. Warmer temperatures encourage ester production.

Towards the end of secondary fermentation, the suspended yeast flocculates (settles out) and the beer clears. This is your indicator for when it is time to bottle. High molecular weight proteins also settle out during this stage. Tannin/phenol compounds will bind with the proteins and also settle out, greatly smoothing the taste of the beer. This process can be helped by chilling the beer, very similar to the lagering process. In the case of ales, this process is referred to as Cold Conditioning, and is a popular practice at most brewpubs and microbreweries. Cold conditioning for a week clears the beer with or without the use of finings. Fining agents, such as isinglass (fish bladders), Polyclar (plastic dust), or gelatin, are added to the fermentor to help speed the flocculation process and promote the settling of haze forming proteins and tannins. While much of the emphasis on using finings is to combat aesthetic chill haze, the real benefit of dropping those compounds is to improve the taste and stability of the beer.

Using Secondary Fermentors

Using a two stage fermentation requires a good understanding of the fermentation process. At any time, racking the beer can adversely affect it because of potential oxygen exposure and contamination risk. It is important to minimize the amount of headspace in the secondary fermentor to minimize the exposure to oxygen until the headspace can be purged by the still-fermenting beer. For this reason, plastic buckets do not make good secondary fermentors unless the beer is transferred just as the primary phase is starting to slow and is still bubbling steadily. Five gallon glass carboys make the best secondary fermentors. Plastic carboys do not work well because they are too oxygen permeable, causing staling.

The following is a general procedure for using a secondary fermentor.

1. Allow the Primary Fermentation stage to wind down. This will be 2-6 days (4-10 days for lagers) after pitching when the bubbling rate drops off dramatically to about 1-5 per minute. The krausen will have started to settle back into the beer.
2. Using a sanitized siphon (no sucking or splashing!), rack the beer off the trub into a another clean fermentor and affix an airlock. The beer should still be fairly cloudy with suspended yeast.

Racking from the primary may be done at any time after primary fermentation has more-or-less completed. (Although if it has been more than 3 weeks, you may as well bottle.) Most brewers will notice a brief increase in activity after racking, but then all activity may cease. This is very normal, it is not additional primary fermentation per se, but just dissolved carbon dioxide coming out of solution due to the disturbance. Fermentation (conditioning) is still taking place, so just leave it alone. A minimum useful time in the secondary fermentor is two weeks. Overly long times in the secondary (for light ales–more than 6 weeks) may require the addition of fresh yeast at bottling time for good carbonation. Always use the same strain as the original. This situation is usually not a concern. See *Chapter 10–What's Different for Lager Beer,* and *Appendix F–Recommended Reading* for related information on lager brewing.

Different beer styles benefit from different lengths of conditioning. Generally, the higher the original gravity, the longer the conditioning time to reach peak flavor. Small beers like 1.035 pale ales will reach peak flavor within a couple weeks of bottling. Stronger/more complex ales, like stouts, may require a month or more. Very strong beers like doppelbocks and barleywines will require 6 months to a year before they condition to their peak flavor. (If oxidation doesn't take its toll first. I have had some pretty awful year-old barleywines.) This conditioning can be done in either the secondary fermentor or the bottle, but the two methods do produce different results. It is up to you to determine how long to give each phase to produce your intended beer. When bottling your first few batches, its always a good idea to set aside a six pack in the corner of the basement and leave it for a time. It is enlightening to taste a homebrewed beer that has had two months to bottle condition and compare it to what the batch initially tasted like.

Secondary Fermentor vs. Bottle Conditioning

Conditioning is a function of the yeast, therefore it is logical that the greater yeast mass in the fermentor is more effective at conditioning than the smaller amount of suspended yeast in the bottle. This is why I recommend that you give your beer more time in the fermentor before bottling. When you add the priming sugar and bottle your beer, the yeast go through the same three stages of fermentation as the main batch, including the production of byproducts. If the beer is bottled early, i.e. 1 week old, then the small amount of yeast in the bottle has to do the double task of conditioning the priming byproducts as well as those from the main ferment. You could very well end up with an off-flavored batch.

Conditioning works better in the fermentor where there is more yeast. Picture this: it is the morning after a big party and everyone pitches in to clean up before going home. After cleaning, everyone gets a cold pizza and a warm six pack of beer to take home with them. Individually, these leftovers (i.e., priming sugar) are easily consumed and cleaned up back home in clean surroundings (the bottles).

The alternative scenario is that the party gets shut down early, and most everyone leaves. The next morning you and a couple guys start cleaning up, but there is leftover pizza and beer to munch on, which makes even more stuff to clean up, and it takes you all day just to get the place looking halfway decent.

Do not be confused, I am not saying that bottle conditioning is bad, but it is different from the conditioning process conditions in the fermentor. Studies have shown that priming and bottle conditioning is a very unique form of fermentation due to the oxygen present in the head space of the bottle–only about 30% of which is used. Additional fermentables have been added to the beer to produce the carbonation, and this results in very different ester profiles than those that are normally produced in the main fermentor. In some styles, like Belgian Strong Ale, bottle conditioning and the resultant flavors are the hallmark of the style. These styles cannot be produced with the same flavors via kegging.

For the best results, the beer should be given time to condition before priming and bottling. And to minimize the risk of off-flavors from sitting on the trub, extended conditioning is best done in a secondary fermentor. Even if the yeast have flocculated and the beer has cleared, there are still active yeast in suspension that will ferment the priming sugar and carbonate the beer.

Summary

Hopefully this chapter has helped you understand what fermentation is and how it works. You need to have sufficient yeast and the right conditions for them to work under to achieve the best possible beer. The next chapter will use this information to walk you through fermenting your first batch.

Chapter 9

Fermenting Your First Batch

So now you have the fruit of your labors cooled in the boiling pot and you feel like celebrating. But don't call in your friends because it's not beer yet. It won't be beer until you have pitched your yeast, and the beer won't be finished until it has completed fermenting which is probably a couple weeks away at least. And then you will still need to bottle it... But have no fear, the hard part is over. What we need to do now is transfer it to your fermentor, make sure the wort has been aerated, pitch the yeast, and find a quiet place to put the fermentor for the next couple weeks.

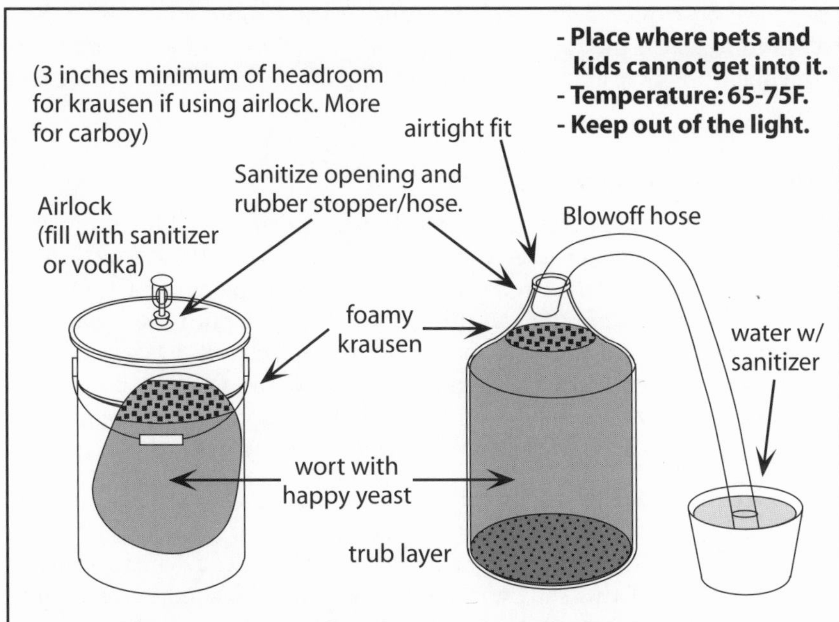

Figure 54—Fermentor Diagrams during primary phase.

Choosing Your Fermentor

Buckets vs. Carboys

There are two types of fermentor commonly available: food grade plastic buckets (bins) and glass carboys. Each type has its own merits. The plastic buckets are less expensive than the glass and much safer to handle. The buckets have the outstanding option of being fitted with spigots, which makes siphoning unnecessary–a real plus. The buckets are typically 6 gallons, leaving 1 gallon of headspace for the fermentation, which is usually sufficient.

The spigot option eliminates siphoning and is practically a necessity at bottling time. A bottling bucket with a spigot allows better distribution of the priming sugar, and greater control of the fill level. In my opinion, this is the only way to bottle.

Although you will need a siphon, glass has the advantage of letting you see your beer and be able to gauge the activity of the fermentation. There are two sizes commonly available, a 6.5 gallon size that is perfect for primary fermentations and a smaller 5 gallon size which is ideal for secondary fermentation. The large size typically has enough headspace to contain the krausen, while the 5 gallon size almost completely eliminates the headspace above the beer, preventing oxidation during the conditioning phase. You will need to shield the carboys from the light, but you can easily tell when fermentation is over and the yeast is settling out.

Airlocks vs. Blowoffs

The decision to use an airlock or blowoff hose is determined by headspace. Usually the buckets and large carboys have enough headspace (at least 3 inches) that the foam does not enter the airlock. If the fermentation is so vigorous that the foam pops the airlock out of the lid, just rinse it out with sanitizer solution and wipe off the lid before replacing it. Contamination is not a big problem during the primary phase. With so much coming out of the fermentor, not much gets in. If the fermentation keeps filling the airlock with crud and popping it out, there is an alternative.

The alternative is called a blowoff hose/tube and it allows foam and hop remnants to be carried out of the fermentor. A blowoff is a necessity if you are using a 5 gallon carboy as your main fermentor. Get a 1 inch diameter plastic hose and fit this snugly inside the mouth in the carboy or enlarge the hole in the bucket lid if necessary. Run the hose down the side and submerge the end in a bucket of sanitizer/water. Always use a large diameter hose to prevent clogging. If the tube gets clogged, the fermentor can get pressurized and blow goo all over the ceiling, or worse–burst.

Transferring the Wort

Your wort should be cool before you pour it into the fermentor. If it is not, refer to *Chapter 7–Boiling and Cooling,* for suggested cooling methods. But before you transfer the wort to the fermentor, you may have been wondering what to do about all the hops and gunk in the bottom of the pot.

There will be a considerable amount of hot break, cold break and hops in the bottom of the boiling pot after cooling. It is a good idea to remove the hot break (or the break in general) from the wort before fermenting. The hot break consists of various proteins and fatty acids which can cause off-flavors, although a moderate amount of hot break can go unnoticed in most beers. The cold break is not considered to be as much of a problem, in fact a small amount of cold break in the fermentor is good because it can provide the yeast with needed nutrients. The hops do not matter at all except that they take up room.

Figure 55—Pouring the wort into the fermentor. Aeration works best if the wort is poured back and forth a few times.

In general however, removal of the break, either by careful pouring from the pot or by racking to another fermentor, is necessary to achieve the cleanest tasting beer. If you are trying to make a very pale beer such as Pilsener style lager, the removal of most of the hot and cold break will make a significant difference.

The most common method for separating the wort from the break is to carefully decant the wort off of it into the fermentor, leaving the break behind. Pouring the wort through a stainless steel strainer can also help with this approach. If you are siphoning the cooled wort from the pot, then attaching a copper scrubby pad to the end of the siphon and whirlpooling can help. Whirlpooling is a means of gathering most of the break and hops into the center of the pot to better enable the siphon to draw off clear wort from the side. Rapidly stir the wort in a circular manner. Continue stirring until all the liquid is moving and a whirlpool forms. Stop stirring and let the whirlpool slow down and settle for 10 minutes or so. The whirlpooling action will form a pile in the center of the pot, leaving the edge relatively clear. The siphon won't clog as quickly now if it draws from the side of the pot.

If you have a vessel to use as a secondary fermentor, you can do either of two things:

a. Siphon First, Pitch Later You can siphon the wort into the first vessel, let it sit for a few hours to let it settle and then rack to your main fermentor to separate it from the trub.

b. Pitch First, Siphon Later The alternative is to pitch your yeast and let it ferment for several days as it undergoes its primary/attenuation phase. (This is the way I do it.) The yeast are much busier eating the more available sugar at this point than scavenging trub, so you can wait until the bubbling of the fermentor slows way down and then rack to a secondary fermentor. Off-flavors associated with sitting on the trub typically take a couple weeks to develop. Although removal of the trub from the fermentation is not critical, it is something to keep in mind as a brewing variable that can be worked-on in your quest for the perfect batch.

Figure 56—Having poured the majority of the wort into the fermenter, I am now attempting to keep most of the trub out. After I throw away the trub, I will pour the wort back and forth to aerate it more.

But let's get back to the job at hand, pouring the wort into the fermentor.

1. Pour the Water Pour the reserved 2.5 gallons of water into the sanitized fermentor. If you are using bottled water, you probably don't need to boil it first, but better safe than sorry. Aeration of the water in the fermentor prior to adding the cooled wort is a good way to provide enough dissolved oxygen for the yeast. It is much easier to aerate this smaller volume of water first, rather than the entire volume later.

2. Pour the Wort Pour the cooled wort into the fermentor, allowing vigorous churning and splashing. This provides more dissolved oxygen that the yeast need. Try to prevent the majority of the hot and cold break from getting into the fermentor. Whole hops help to provide a filter. If some hops and break make it into the fermentor, it is not a big deal.

3. Pour it Back Discard the hops and trub from the brewpot and pour some wort from the fermentor back and forth to the brewpot several times. This will *really* ensure you have enough dissolved oxygen for the yeast. Short of using an airstone and air pump, this is the best way to aerate your wort.

Conducting Your Fermentation

Pitching the Yeast

If your rehydrated and proofed dry yeast is not showing signs of life (churning, foaming) after a half hour, discard it and use the backup yeast, repeating the re-hydration procedure.

4. Pitch No, this doesn't mean to throw the yeast away. It means to throw it in. Pitch (pour) the yeast into the fermentor, making sure to add it all. It is best (for the yeast) if the yeast temperature is the same as the wort temperature you will pitch them to, and it is best for the beer if the wort temperature is the same as the fermentation temperature, when the yeast is pitched. For Ale yeasts, the fermentation temperature range is 65-75°F.

5. Seal Put the fermentor lid in place and seal it. But don't put the airlock in quite yet; if you didn't pour it back and forth earlier, we'll want to shake this up. Place a piece of clean plastic wrap over the hole in the lid and insert the stopper.

6. Shake With the fermentor lid tightly sealed, place it on the floor and rock it back and forth for several minutes to churn it up. This distributes the yeast into the wort and provides more dissolved oxygen that the yeast need to grow. If any wort leaks out, wipe it off with a paper towel that is wet with your sanitizer solution. Place the sanitized airlock and rubber stopper in the lid. The airlock should be filled to the line with sanitizer solution. Many people use vodka or plain boiled water as alternatives. You want something that will not grow mold or contaminate the batch in case it inadvertently gets sucked inside the fermentor.

Fermentation Location

Place the fermentor in a protected area that has a stable temperature between 65-75°F. Good places are closets, basements, or a spare bathroom if you have one. You will probably want to set the fermentor inside a shallow pan or put a towel under it in case any foam escapes through the airlock. Place it in an area that is not exposed to direct sunlight for two reasons. First, to keep it from getting too warm. Secondly, if you are using glass, sunlight will cause a photochemical reaction with the hop compounds and skunk your beer.

Maintain a consistent temperature if possible, because fluctuating temperature stresses the yeast and can impair the fermentation. If the temperature drops overnight and the bubbling stops, don't worry, simply move it to a warmer room and it should pick up again. Temperatures below 55-60°F will cause ale yeast to go into hibernation and slow or stop the fermentation process.

Animals and small children are fascinated by the smell and noises from the airlock, so keep them away. Dogs tend to like beer and will try to sneak samples before its done. Cats hate being left out of the decision-making

during brewing and will attempt to give their inputs at the fermentor later. I remember an acquaintance who was surprised that his fermentation started to take off again after it had previously quieted. When he later opened the fermentor to bottle, he discovered his 3 year old son had been dropping crayons and pencils in through the airlock hole.

Primary Fermentation

Active fermentation should start within 12 hours. It may be longer for liquid yeasts because of lower cell counts, about 24 hours. (Although if you made an adequate starter, it should start every bit as fast as dry.) The airlock will bubble regularly. The fermentation activity can be vigorous or slow; either is fine. The three important factors for a successful fermentation are pitching enough yeast, good wort nutrients, and maintaining a consistent temperature in the correct range. If you do these right, it is common for an ale's primary fermentation to be done in 48 hours. Three days at 65-70°F for primary fermentation is typical for the simple pale ale being described here. Once the bubbling slows down however, do not open the lid to peek. The beer is still susceptible to bacterial infections, particularly anaerobic ones like pediococcus, and lactobacillus–found in your mouth. If you really want to look, peek in through the airlock hole, but keep the lid on.

Figure 59—Decision time—to rack or not to rack...

Secondary Fermentation

Here is where you will need to make a decision. Are you going to use single stage or two stage fermentation for your beer? If you are going to use single stage, i.e. just this one fermentor, then you have nothing further to do but to leave the beer where it is for a total of 2-3 weeks. The conditioning processes will proceed and the beer will clear.

If you are going to rack to a secondary fermentor, I strongly recommend that you use a 5 gallon glass carboy to minimize the headspace and oxygen exposure during conditioning.

Racking

Racking is the term for the process of transferring the beer without disturbing the sediments or exposing it to air. Usually this is done by siphoning. If you have a bucket fermentor with a spigot, then transfer becomes simple. It is imperative to not aerate the wort during transfer after primary fermentation. Any oxygen in the beer at this time will cause staling reactions that will become evident in the flavor of the beer within a couple weeks. Always transfer the beer slowly and keep the outlet tube beneath the surface of the beer as you fill the secondary. Don't let the stream guzzle or spray as you fill. The only way to combat aeration damage is to introduce young beer to the fermentor at bottling time. This process is called "krausening", and is a time-honored method of carbonating beer, but it is an advanced technique that I do not cover. See Siphoning Tips at the end of *Chapter 11–Priming and Bottling* for more info on starting a siphon.

Estimating the Alcohol Content

How much alcohol will there be? This is a common question. While there are various laboratory techniques that can be employed to determine it precisely, there is a simple way to estimate it. The easiest is to use a "triple scale hydrometer" which has a percent alcohol by volume scale right on it. You subtract the respective percentages that correspond to your OG and FG, and there you have it.

If you don't have this type of hydrometer, the following table based on the work of Balling should satisfy your curiosity. Find the intersection of your OG and FG to read your estimated percentage alcohol by volume.

In the next chapter (*10*), we will discuss how the brewing and fermenting of lager beer differs from ales. Then we will prepare to prime, bottle and ultimately consume our beer in *Chapter 11–Priming and Bottling.*

ALCOHOL BY VOLUME

Table 8—Percent Alcohol By Volume (ABV) From OG and FG

	1.030	1.035	1.040	1.045	1.050	1.055	1.060	1.065	1.070	1.075
0.998	4.1	4.8	5.4	6.1	6.8	7.4	8.1	8.7	9.4	10.1
1.000	3.9	4.5	5.2	5.8	6.5	7.1	7.8	8.5	9.1	9.8
1.002	3.6	4.2	4.9	5.6	6.2	6.9	7.5	8.2	8.9	9.5
1.004	3.3	4.0	4.6	5.3	5.9	6.6	7.3	7.9	8.6	9.3
1.006	3.1	3.7	4.4	5.0	5.7	6.3	7.0	7.7	8.3	9.0
1.008	2.8	3.5	4.1	4.8	5.4	6.1	6.7	7.4	8.0	8.7
1.010	2.6	3.2	3.8	4.5	5.1	5.8	6.5	7.1	7.8	8.4
1.012	2.3	2.9	3.6	4.2	4.9	5.5	6.2	6.8	7.5	8.2
1.014	2.0	2.7	3.3	4.0	4.6	5.3	5.9	6.6	7.2	7.9
1.016	1.8	2.4	3.1	3.7	4.4	5.0	5.7	6.3	7.0	7.6
1.018	1.5	2.2	2.8	3.4	4.1	4.7	5.4	6.0	6.7	7.3
1.020	1.3	1.9	2.5	3.2	3.8	4.5	5.1	5.8	6.4	7.1
1.022	1.0	1.6	2.3	2.9	3.6	4.2	4.9	5.5	6.2	6.8
1.024	0.8	1.4	2.0	2.7	3.3	4.0	4.6	5.2	5.9	6.5

Chapter 10

What is Different for Brewing Lager Beer?

What makes lager beer different from ale beer, you ask?

Well, the main difference is temperature. Make that temperature and time. No, there's three: temperature, time and yeast. Let's start with yeast.

Yeast Differences

As discussed in *Chapter 6–Yeast,* lager yeasts like lower fermentation temperatures. Lager yeast produce less fruity esters than ale yeasts but can produce more sulfur compounds during primary fermentation. Many first time lager brewers are astonished by the rotten egg smell coming from their fermentors, sometimes letting it convince them that the batch is infected and causing them to dump it. Don't do it! Fortunately, these compounds continue to vent during the conditioning (lagering) phase and the chemical precursors of other odious compounds are gradually eaten up by the yeast. A previously rank smelling beer that is properly lagered will be sulfur-free and delicious at bottling time. Speaking of Time...

Additional Time

The lower fermentation temperature decreases the rate at which the yeast work and lengthens both the primary and secondary fermentation times. The primary phase for ales is often 2-5 days, but 1-3 weeks is normal for a lager. As mentioned in the previous chapter, the primary and conditioning phases of fermentation happen concurrently, but the conditioning phase takes longer. This is especially true with lager yeasts. The defining character of a lager beer is a clean, malty taste without ale fruitiness. Obviously those rotten egg odors don't belong either. The time that it takes for these compounds to be processed by the yeast can be several weeks to a few months. It depends on the malts used, the yeast strain, and the temperature at which conditioning occurs.

Lower Temperatures

Lager comes from the German word "lagern" which means to store. A lager beer is in cold storage while it ages in the conditioning phase. Temperature influences lagers in two ways. During primary fermentation, the cooler temperature (45-55°F) prevents the formation of fruity esters by the yeast. In addition to producing fewer byproducts during the primary phase, the yeast uses the long conditioning phase to finish residual sugars and metabolize other compounds like diacetyl and acetaldehyde that would otherwise give rise to off-flavors and aromas. Unfortunately, this long time with the beer in contact with the yeast can be a problem. The problem is autolysis, i.e., yeast breakdown, which can produce terrible off-flavors in the beer.

Autolysis

When a yeast cell dies, it ruptures–releasing several off-flavors (sulfur, rubber, etc.) into the beer. When you have a large yeast mass on the bottom of the fermentor, you have a large potential for off-flavors due to autolysis. If this ever happens to you, you will know it. The smell is one you will never forget. It happened to me one time when my wife was making paper as a hobby. She used boiled rice as the glue to hold the shredded paper together. After the rice had been boiled until it became a paste, the paper making was called off that weekend and the pot of rice paste was set aside on the counter top. A wild yeast must have got a hold of it during the next couple days (I remember it bubbling) and the pot was ignored in the days that followed. A busy week went by along with another busy weekend and the unintentional Sake experiment still sat there forgotten. The following weekend, my wife was once again ready to try making paper. I picked up the pot and lifted the lid to see what had happened to it. My knees buckled. My wife turned green and ran to the door coughing and choking. The stench was appalling! It was heinous! The noxious aftermath of a late night of cheap beer and pickled eggs would be refreshing compared to the absolute stench of autolysis. I hope I never have to smell it again.

Luckily, the propensity of yeast to autolyze is decreased by a decrease in activity and a decrease in total yeast mass. What this means to a brewer is that racking to a secondary fermenter to get the beer off the dead yeast and lowering the temperature for the long cold storage allows the beer to condition without much risk of autolysis. At a minimum, a beer that has experienced autolysis will have a strong yeasty taste, or perhaps a burnt rubber smell and taste, and will probably be undrinkable. At worst it will be unapproachable.

As a final note on this subject, I should state that by brewing with healthy yeast in a well-prepared wort, many experienced brewers, myself included, have been able to leave a beer in the primary fermenter for several months without any evidence of autolysis. Autolysis is not inevitable, but it is lurking.

Lager Yeast Pitching and Diacetyl Rests

There are two other items that are significant in brewing a good lager beer and I will describe them briefly. These are yeast pitching and the diacetyl rest. Lager brewing is best described in a book of its own and fortunately someone (Greg Noonan) has done just that. See the Recommended Reading section in the appendices for more information.

Because of the cooler temperatures, the yeast is less active at first. The best way to ensure a strong, healthy lager fermentation is to pitch a much larger yeast starter than you would for an ale. Where you would pitch a one quart starter solution of liquid yeast for an ale, you would use a 2 or 3 quart starter for a lager. This is the equivalent of about ½ to ¾ cup of yeast slurry. In addition, the pitching temperature should be the same as the fermentation temperature to prevent thermally shocking the yeast. In other words, you will need to chill the wort down to 45-55°F before pitching the yeast. The yeast starter should also have been brought down to this temperature range while it was fermenting. A good way to do this is to pitch the yeast packet into a pint of wort at 60°F, let that ferment for a day, cool it 5 degrees to 55°F and add another pint of aerated, cool wort. Let this also ferment for a day, and cool and pitch a third and even fourth time until you have built up 2 quarts or more of yeast starter that is comfortable at 45–55°F. I recommend that you pour off the excess liquid and only pitch the slurry to avoid some off-flavors from that much starter beer.

Some brewers pitch their yeast when the wort is warmer and slowly lower the temperature of the whole fermenter gradually over the course of several days until they have reached the optimum temperature for their yeast strain. This method works, and works well, but tends to produce more diacetyl (a buttery-flavored ketone) than the previous method. As the temperature drops the yeast become less active and are less inclined to consume the diacetyl that they initially produced. The result is a buttery/butterscotch flavor in the lager, which is totally out of style. Some amount of diacetyl is considered good in other styles such as dark ales and stouts, but is considered a flaw in lagers. To remove any diacetyl that may be present after primary fermentation, a diacetyl rest may be used. This rest at the end of primary fermentation consists of raising the temperature of the beer to 55–60°F for 24–48 hours before cooling it down for the lagering period. This makes the yeast more active and allows them to eat up the diacetyl before downshifting into lagering mode. Some yeast strains produce less diacetyl than others; a diacetyl rest is needed only if the pitching or fermentation conditions warrant it.

When to Lager

It takes experience for a brewer to know when primary fermentation is winding down and the beer is ready to be transferred. If you insist on brewing a lager for your very first beer, you are going to be flying blind. You can play it safe by waiting several weeks for the primary phase to completely finish (no more bubbling) and rack then, but you will have missed your opportunity for a diacetyl rest. As discussed in the previous chapter, you should rack to a secondary when the krausen has started to fall back in. The bubbling in the airlock will have slowed dramatically to 1 or 4 bubbles per minute, and a hydrometer reading should indicate that the beer is 3/4 of the way to the terminal gravity. Knowing when to rack takes experience, it's as simple as that.

I like to ferment and lager in glass carboys because the glass allows me to see the activity in the beer. During primary fermentation, there are clumps of yeast and trub rising and falling in the beer and it's bubbling like crazy–it literally looks like there is someone stirring it with a stick. When you see that kind of activity slow down, and things start settling towards the bottom, you know the primary phase is over and it's safe to rack.

The lagering temperature and duration are affected by both the primary fermentation temperature and the yeast strain. These are the four main factors that determine the final character of a lager beer. Some general guidelines for lager fermentation times and temperatures are listed below:

- Check the yeast package information for recommended fermentation temperature(s).
- The temperature difference between the primary phase and the lager phase should be 10-15°F (5-8°C).
- Nominal lagering times are 3-4 weeks at 45°F (7°C), 5-6 weeks at 40°F (4°C), or 7-8 weeks at 35°F (2°C).
- Stronger beers need to be lagered longer.
- Nothing is absolute. Brewing is as much an art as it is science.

A common question is, "If the beer will lager faster at higher temperatures, why would anyone lager at the low temperature?" Two reasons: first, in the days before refrigeration when lager beers were developed, icehouses were the common storage method–it's tradition. Second, the colder lagering temperatures seem to produce a smoother beer than warmer temperatures. This would seem to be due to the additional precipitation and settling of extraneous proteins (like chill haze) and tannins that occur at lower temperatures.

Aagh!! It Froze!!

By the way, what if your beer freezes during lagering?? Horrors!!

Well, it happened to me. Let me tell you about my first lager...

> 'Twas a few weeks before Christmas and all around the house, not an airlock was bubbling, in spite of myself. My Vienna was lagering in the refrigerator out there, with hopes that a truly fine beer, I soon could share.
>
> The Airstat was useless, 32°F couldn't be set, so I turned the 'fridge to Low, to see what I would get. On Monday it was 40°, On Tuesday lower yet, On Wednesday morning I tweaked it, seemed like a good bet.
>
> Later that day when I walked out to the shed, my nose gave me pause, it filled me with dread. In through the door I hurried and dashed, when I tripped on the stoop and fell with a crash. Everything looked ordinary, well what do you know, but just in case, I opened the 'fridge slow.

When what to my wondering eyes should appear, My carboy was FROZEN, I had made Ice beer! My first thought was tragic, I was worried a bit, I sat there and pondered, then muttered, "Aw Sh##!"

More rapid than eagles, my curses they came, and I gestured and shouted and called the fridge bad names. "You Bastard! How could you! You are surely to blame! You're worthless, You're scrap metal, not worth the electric bills I'm paying! To the end of the driveway, with one little call, They will haul you away, haul away, haul away all!"

Unlike dry leaves that before the hurricane fly, when brewers meet adversity, they'll give it another try. So back to the house, wondering just what to do, five gallons of frozen beer, a frozen airlock too. And then in a twinkling, I felt like a goof, the carboy wasn't broken, the beer would probably pull through.

I returned to the shed, after hurrying 'round, gathering cleaning supplies, towels, whatever could be found. I'd changed my clothes, having come home from work, I knew if I stained them, my wife would go berserk. I was loaded with paper towels, I knew just what to do, I had iodophor-ed water and a heating pad too.

The carboy, how it twinkled! I knew to be wary, the bottom wasn't frozen but the ice on top was scary! That darn refridge, it had laid me low, trying to kill my beer under a layer of snow. I cleaned off the top and washed off the sides, picked up a block of ice and threw it outside. I couldn't find the airlock, it was under the shelf, and I laughed when I saw it, in spite of myself.

The work of a half hour out there in the shed, soon gave me to know, I had nothing to dread. The heating pad was working, the ice fell back in, I re-sanitized the airlock, I knew where it had been. Not an Eisbock, but a Vienna I chose, it was the end of the crisis of the lager that froze.

I sprang to my feet, to my wife gave a whistle, and we went off to bed under the down comforter to wrestle. But the 'fridge heard me exclaim as I walked out of sight, "Try that again, you bastard, and you'll be recycled all right!"

Should I Add More Yeast?

When your lager freezes, chances are the yeast has been impaired. If you are towards the beginning of the lagering cycle, then there may not be enough yeast activity after it thaws to properly complete the attenuation and condition the beer. You should probably add new yeast. If you are at the end of the lagering cycle, and were planning on priming and bottle conditioning it, then you should probably add more yeast also. If you are planning on kegging it and force carbonating (like I was), then you don't have to worry about it. I say "probably" because some yeast will survive. Even if the beer freezes completely for a short time, typically 20% of cells will remain active. The questions are: 20% of how many, and just how active? Therefore, you should probably add new yeast.

The yeast you add to the fermenter should be of the same strain as the original yeast. If you are using yeast from a ready-to-pitch package, then that quantity is probably sufficient and you can pour it right in and swirl it around to mix it evenly. Because you are not trying to conduct a primary fermentation and are not concerned about a fast start, you do not need to build up the count any further, nor do you need to acclimate it to the lagering temperature first. The yeast will acclimate over several days and finish the fermentation cycle.

If your yeast came from a small smack-pack or slant, then you may want to build up the cell count by pitching to a starter wort first. And you may want to conduct that starter at your primary fermentation temperature to help the yeast acclimate to the lagering cycle. As noted above, these steps are probably not necessary, but it never hurts to stack the odds in your favor. You can either pitch the starter at full krausen or wait for it to ferment out before adding it. The small amount of primary fermentation byproducts that you add to the beer by pitching at full krausen will not affect the flavor significantly.

Maintaining Lager Temperature

Temperature controllers, like the Airstat, are very handy for maintaining a constant brewing temperature in a spare refrigerator. Controllers work by plugging into the wall outlet and then plugging the fridge into it. A temperature probe is run inside the fridge and it governs the on/off cycling of the compressor to maintain a narrow temperature range. Here in Southern California, I use it to maintain 65°F in the summertime for brewing ales. Check your local homebrew supply shop or some of the larger mail order suppliers for one of the newer controllers. Some controllers will also operate a separate heating circuit (usually in conjunction with a heat lamp) for cold weather brewing conditions.

In my case, my frozen Vienna lagered for 6 weeks at 34°F. I placed blocks of ice next to the carboy instead of relying on the refrigerator for temperature control. In fact, insulated ice boxes are a good way to control temperature for lagering. The blocks of ice will last about 3-4 days. Because of the alcohol present, the beer actually freezes at several degrees below normal. Depending on the time of year and your ambient temperature, an insulated box (like a large picnic cooler) is a very convenient way to lager. My frozen lager went on to take first place in two separate contests in the Vienna/Oktoberfest category.

Bottling

See the next chapter, *Priming and Bottling,* for information on how the bottling and carbonating of lager beers can differ from ale beers.

Brewing American Lager Beer

A lot of people want to know how to brew their favorite American light lager beer, like Bud, Miller, or Coors. First thing I will tell you is that it is difficult to do. *Why?* Because these beers are brewed using all-grain methods that incorporate rice or corn (maize) as about 30% of the fermentables. The rice or corn must be cooked to fully solubilize the starch and then added to the mash so that the enzymes can convert the starches to fermentable sugars. See *Chapters 12–What is Malted Grain,* and *14–How the Mash Works,* for more info.

Second, there is no room in the light body of these beers for any off-flavors to hide–off-flavors stand out. Your sanitation, yeast handling, and fermentation control must be rigorous for this type of beer to turn out right. The professional brewers at Bud, Miller, and Coors are very good at what they do–turning out a light beer, decade after decade, that tastes exactly the same. Though come to think of it, bottled water companies do that too...

Lastly, as an extract brewer, you can really only do rice-type lagers. Rice extract is available in both syrup and powder form, and will produce a decent Heineken or Budweiser clone. Corn syrup and corn sugar have had their corn character stripped away and will not produce a good extract based corn-type lager like Miller or Coors. To brew this type of beer, refer to the recipe in *Chapter 19–Some of My Favorite Beer Styles and Recipes,* for the Classic American Pilsner recipe, *"Your Father's Mustache,"* and reduce the OG and IBUs to the guidelines below. The methods described in the *"YFM"* recipe can be used to brew a typical American lager using flaked corn or corn grits.

Typical American Lager Style Guidelines

Style	OG	FG	IBUs	Color
American Lager	1.035-50	.098-1.012	8-22	2-8

Commercial Example:

American Lager — Budweiser

Typical American Lager Beer

Malts		Gravity Pts.
3.5 lbs. of pale DME		49
1.5 lbs. of dry rice solids (powder)		21
BG for 3 Gallons		1.070
OG for 5 Gallons		1.042
Hops	**Boil Time**	**IBUs**
1 oz of Tettnanger (5%)	60	14
½ oz of Tettnanger (5%)	10	3
Total IBUs		17

Yeast	Fermentation Schedule
American Lager (liquid)	2 weeks at 50°F in primary fermenter rack and lager at 40°F for 4 weeks. Prime and store bottles at room temperature.

Chapter 11

Priming and Bottling

In this chapter we will focus on getting your hard won beer into a bottle and ready for drinking. To bottle your beer you will need: clean bottles, bottle caps, a bottle capper and (I heartily recommend) a bottling bucket. You will also need some sugar to use for priming–that extra bit of fermentable sugar that is added to the beer at bottling time to provide the carbonation.

Many homebrewers get used bottles from restaurants and bars, or buy them new from homebrew shops. Every once in a while you will hear about a guy whose dad or uncle has given him a couple cases of empty swing-top Grolsch™ bottles. He may ask you if he can use them for brewing or something... If this happens, just look him straight in the eye and tell him, "No, those can be quite dangerous, let me dispose of them for you." Be sure to keep a straight face and do your best to sound grim. If you don't think you are up to it, give me a call and I will take care of it. Swing top bottles are great; grab any you can. New rubber gaskets for the stoppers can be purchased at most homebrew shops.

When to Bottle

Ales are usually ready to bottle in 2-3 weeks when fermentation has completely finished. There should be few, if any, bubbles coming through the airlock. If you are fermenting in glass, you will see the beer darken and clear as the yeast flocculates. Although 2-3 weeks may seem like a long time to wait, the flavor won't improve by bottling any earlier. Some books recommend bottling after the bubbling stops, or in about 1 week, but this is usually bad advice. It is not uncommon for fermentation to stop after 3-4 days and begin again a few days later due to a temperature change. If the beer is bottled before fermentation is complete, the beer will become overcarbonated and the pressure may exceed the bottle strength. Exploding bottles are a disaster (and messy to boot).

Bottle Cleaning

As discussed in *Chapter 2,* used bottles need to be cleaned thoroughly before sanitizing. The first time a bottle is used it should be soaked in a cleaning solution (like bleach water), and scrubbed inside and out with a nylon bottle brush. A heavy duty cleaning is needed to ensure that there are no deposits in which bacteria or mold spores can hide. This way the sanitizing solution can reach all areas and you can be assured of sanitized bottles. If you are diligent in rinsing your bottles promptly and thoroughly after each use with your homebrew, only the sanitizing treatment will be necessary before each use in the future. By maintaining clean equipment you will save yourself a lot of work.

After the bottles have been cleaned with a brush, soak them in sanitizing solution or use the dishwasher with the heat cycle on to sanitize them. If you use bleach solution to sanitize, allow the bottles to drain upside down on a rack, or rinse them with boiled water. Do not rinse them out with tap water unless it has been boiled first. Rinsing with unboiled tap water is a

Figure 63—Clean after use, sanitize before use.

number one cause of spoiled batches. Also sanitize the priming container, siphon unit, stirring spoon, and bottle caps. But don't boil or bake the bottle caps, as this may ruin the gaskets.

What Sugar Should I Prime With?

You can prime your beer with any fermentable that you want. Any sugar: white cane sugar, brown sugar, honey, molasses, even maple syrup can be used for priming. The darker sugars can contribute a subtle aftertaste (sometimes desired) and are more appropriate for heavier, darker beers. Simple sugars, like corn or cane sugar, are used most often though many brewers use dry malt extract too. Ounce for ounce, cane sugar generates a bit more carbon dioxide than corn sugar, and both pure sugars carbonate more than malt extract, so you will need to take that into account. Honey is difficult to prime with, because there is no standard for concentration. The gravity of honey is different jar to jar. To use honey, you will need to dilute it and measure its gravity with a hydrometer. For all priming in general, you want to add 2–3 gravity points of sugar per gallon of beer.

Be aware that malt extract will generate break material when boiled, and that the fermentation of malt extract for priming purposes will somtimes (though rarely) generate a krausen/protein ring around the waterline in the bottle, just like it does in your fermenter. Simple sugars don't have this cosmetic problem and the small amount used for priming will not affect the flavor of the beer.

Making the Priming Solution

The best way to prime your beer is to mix your priming sugar into the whole batch prior to bottling. This ensures that all the bottles will be carbonated the same. Some books recommend adding 1 tsp. of sugar directly to the bottle for priming. This is not a good idea because it is time consuming and imprecise. Bottles may carbonate unevenly and explode. Plus there is a greater risk of infection because the sugar has not been boiled. The exception to these rules is to use PrimeTabs™. (More on this product in a minute.)

Here's how to make and add priming solutions:

1. Boil ¾ cup of corn sugar (4 oz by weight), or ⅔ cup of white sugar, or 1 and ¼ cup dry malt extract in 2 cups of water and let it cool. Use the nomograph in *Figure 65* to determine a more precise amount of priming sugar if you wish. You can add the priming solution in either of two ways, depending on your equipment; I prefer the first (2a).

2a. If you have a bottling bucket (see Figure 66) gently pour the priming solution into it. Using a sanitized siphon, transfer the beer into the sanitized bottling bucket. Place the outlet beneath the surface of the priming solution. Do not allow the beer to splash because you don't want to add oxygen to your beer at this point. Keep the intake end of the racking tube an inch off the bottom of the fermenter to leave the yeast and sediment behind.

2b. If you don't have a bottling bucket, open the fermenter and gently pour the priming solution into the beer. Stir the beer gently with a sanitized spoon, trying to mix it in evenly while being careful not to stir up the sediment too much. Wait a half hour for the sediment to settle back down and to allow more diffusion of the priming solution to take place. Use a bottle filler attachment with the siphon to make the filling easier.

Figure 64—Racking to the bottling bucket.

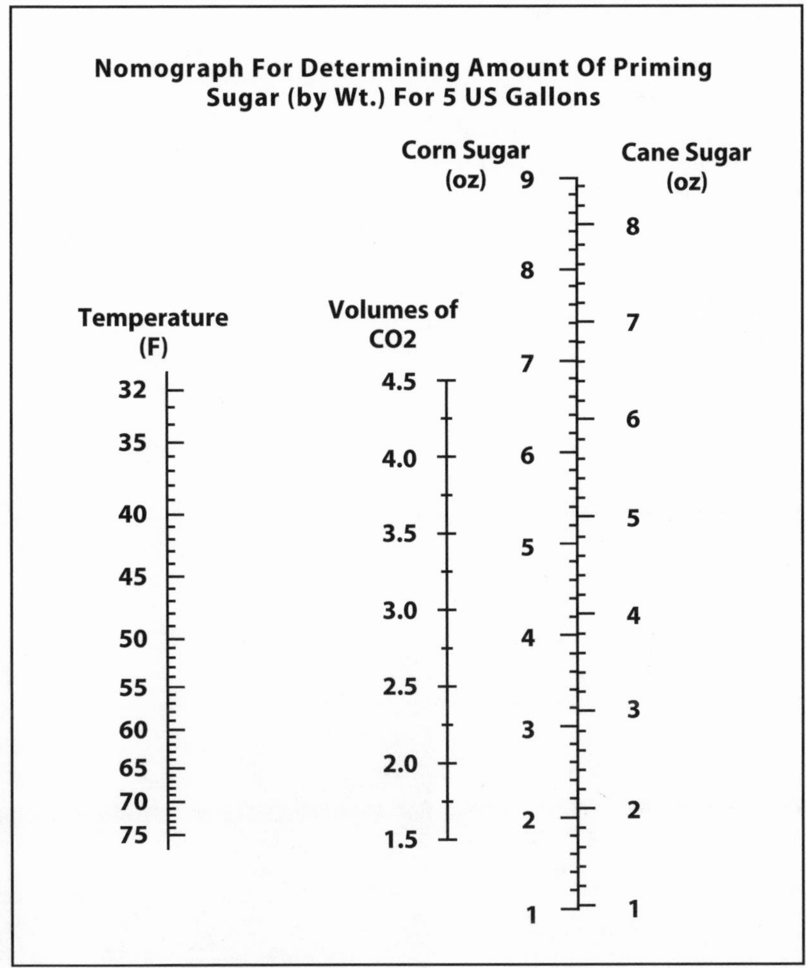

Figure 65—Nomograph for determining more precise amounts of priming sugar. To use the nomograph, draw a line from the temperature of your beer through the Volumes of CO_2 that you want, to the scale for sugar. The intersection of your line and the sugar scale gives the weight of sugar in ounces (either corn or cane) to be added to five gallons of beer to achieve the desired carbonation level. If you are priming more, e.g. six gallons, then the amount of priming sugar can be determined by ratio (e.g. 6/5) to the five gallon amount. Here is a list of typical volumes of CO_2 for various beer styles:

- British ales 1.5-2.0
- Porter, Stout 1.7-2.3
- Belgian ales 1.9-2.4
- American ales 2.2-2.7
- European lagers 2.2-2.7
- Belgian Lambic 2.4-2.8
- American wheat 2.7-3.3
- German wheat 3.3-4.5

Using PrimeTabs™

PrimeTabs (manufactured by Venezia & Company) are high quality, sanitized tablets of corn sugar that you can add directly to your bottles. There is no mixing or boiling required. The tablets are sized such that you can adjust the level of carbonation in your bottles depending on the style and your tastes. For a low carbonation level, typical of a British draught ale, use 2 PrimeTabs per 12 oz. bottle. Use 3 for a more average carbonation level and use 4-5 for a higher carbonation level like that of American lagers. PrimeTabs are sold in packages of 250 tablets, enough for priming an entire 5 gallon batch. By using PrimeTabs, you can eliminate one siphoning step (from the fermenter to the bottling bucket) and reduce the risk of oxidation.

Bottle Filling

The next step is filling the bottles. Place the fill tube of the bottling bucket or bottle filler at the bottom of the bottle. Fill slowly at first to prevent gurgling and keep the fill tube below the waterline to prevent aeration. Fill to about ¾ inch from the top of the bottles. Place a sanitized cap on the bottle and cap. Many people will place the caps on the bottles and then wait to cap several at the same time. After capping, inspect every bottle to make sure the cap is secure.

Age the capped bottles at room temperature for two weeks, out of the light. Aging up to two months can improve the flavor considerably, but one week will often do the job of carbonation for the impatient, it depends on the type and vitality of the yeast.

Figure 66—Bottling using a bottling bucket with filling tube.

Priming and Bottling of Lager Beer

Figure 67—Bottling using a siphon with a bottle filler attachment.

Ninety five percent of the time there is no difference between priming for lager beer and priming ale. But once in a while you will need to add fresh yeast for priming and carbonation purposes. This is most common when the beer is given a long cold lagering for more than two months. If the beer is very clear at bottling time, then the majority of the yeast may have settled out and there may not be enough left to carbonate the beer in the bottle. Prepare some fresh yeast of the same strain and mix it with the priming solution when you rack the beer to the bottling bucket. You will not need as much as you originally pitched to the wort, either one ready-to-pitch package of liquid yeast or about ¼ cup of slurry for 5 gallons.

Since the yeast is being added for carbonation after the lagering phase, there are a couple of differences in procedure from that used to ferment the original wort. Grow the yeast at the temperature you will be carbonating and storing the beer at (usually room temperature) instead of the original pitching temperature. This will produce more esters than the yeast normally would, but the percentage of sugar that is being fermented for carbonation at this stage is so small that the added difference in taste is unnoticeable. The reason for doing it this way is to avoid thermally shocking the yeast and to speed up the carbonation time. It is not necessary to store the beer cold after lagering. The beer can be stored at room temperature without affecting the taste of the beer.

Storage

Two common questions are, "How long will a homebrewed beer keep?" and "Will it spoil?" The answer is that homebrewed beer has a fairly long storage life. Depending on the style and original gravity, the beer will keep for more than a year. I occasionally come across a year-old six pack of pale ale that I had forgotten about and it tastes great! Of course, there are other cases when that year-old six pack has gotten very oxidized in that time, tasting of cardboard or cooking sherry. It really depends on how careful you were with the bottling. Quality in, Quality out.

When cooled prior to serving, some batches will exhibit chill haze. It is caused by proteins left over from those taken out by the cold break. The proteins responsible for chill haze need to be thermally shocked into precipitating out of the wort. Slow cooling will not affect them. When a beer is chilled for drinking, these proteins partially precipitate forming a haze. As the beer warms up, the proteins re-dissolve.

Chill haze is usually regarded as a cosmetic problem. You cannot taste it. However, chill haze indicates that there is an appreciable level of cold-break-type protein in the beer, which has been linked to long-term stability problems. Hazy beer tends to become stale sooner than non-hazy beer.

Finally, it is important to keep the beer out of direct sunlight, especially if you use clear or green bottles. Exposure to sunlight or fluorescent light will cause beer to develop a skunky character. It is the result of a photo-chemical reaction with hop compounds and sulfur compounds. Contrary to popular belief, this is not a character that Heineken, Grolsch, and Molson strive for in their beer. It is simply a result of poor handling by retailers, and storing them under fluorescent lighting. Other beers, like Miller High Life, don't boil hops with the wort but instead use a specially processed hop extract for bittering which lacks the compounds that cause skunking (and flavor). Brown bottles are best unless you make a point of keeping your beer in the dark.

Drinking Your First Homebrew

One final item that nobody ever remembers to tell new brewers until it's too late is: "Don't drink the yeast layer on the bottom of the bottle."

People will say, "My first homebrew was pretty good, but that last swallow was terrible!" or "His homebrew really gave me gas" or "It must have been spoiled, I had to go to the bathroom right away after I drank it."

Welcome to the laxative effects of live yeast!

When you pour your beer from the bottle, pour it slowly so you don't disturb the yeast layer. With a little practice, you will be able to pour out all but the last quarter inch of beer. The yeast layer can really harbor a lot of bitter flavors. It's where the word "dregs" came from. I remember one time my homebrew club was at a popular watering hole for a Belgian beer tasting. The proprietor prided himself on being a connoisseur of all the different beers he sold there. But our entire club just cringed when he poured for us. The whole evening was a battle for the bottle so we could pour our own. Chimay Grande Reserve, Orval, Duvel; all were poured glugging from the bottle, the last glass-worth inevitably being swirled to get all the yeast from the bottom. It was a real crime–not every beer is a hefeweizen. At least I know what their yeast strains taste like now...

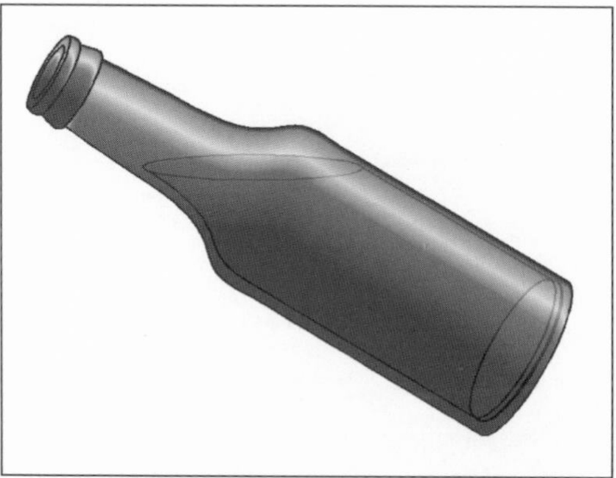

Figure 68—Keep the Yeast Layer in the Bottle! Pour it slowly to avoid disturbing the yeast layer on the bottom. With practice you will leave no more than a quarter inch of beer behind in the bottle.

BREWING TIP

How to Start a Siphon

When racking or bottling, you cannot start a siphon by sucking on it or you will contaminate and sour the batch with bacteria from your mouth.

All parts of the siphon (racking cane, tubing, and cutoff valve or bottle filler) need to be sanitized, especially the inside. After sanitzing, keep the siphon full of solution by plugging the end with your clean-and-sanitized thumb or by using a clamp or valve, and carefully place the racking cane in your beer. Release your thumb/clamp/valve and allow the sanitizer to drain into a jar. As the sanitizer drains, it will draw the beer into the siphon and you can stop and transfer the outlet to your bottling bucket or bottles. Thus you can siphon without risk of contamination.

Section II

Brewing With Extract and Specialty Grain

In this section of the book, I will teach you how to produce some of the wort from the malted grain itself. We will use an intermediate step on the path to all-grain brewing, known as "steeping," along with extract brewing to produce a fresher, more complex tasting wort than can usually be produced from extract alone. The process is not difficult but it takes some additional time and you need to have an understanding of the characters and attributes of the different malts–those that can be steeped versus those needing to be mashed. The steeping of malts will be taught in the next two chapters.

In *Chapter 12–What is Malted Grain?,* I will explain what malt really is and how it is produced. Then I will describe some of the most common malts and their different uses. The last part of the chapter will discuss how we measure the yield and efficiency of an all-grain mash and compare these numbers with what we can obtain by steeping.

Chapter 13–Steeping Specialty Grain, will describe how to improve your extract brewing by using small amounts of specialty grains in an example recipe for a porter. This method does not require any extra equipment (except a sock or grainbag) and gives you a lot more flexibility in producing the wort for your intended style of beer. This chapter will guide you step-by-step through the additions to the brewing process. The additional work is so small and the results so gratifying that you will probably never brew solely with extract again!

Chapter 12

What is Malted Grain?

Defining Malted Grain

The malting process allows the grain to partially germinate, making the seed's resources available to the brewer. During germination enzymes in the aleurone layer (*See Figure 69*) are released, and new enzymes are created, that break down the endosperm's protein/carbohydrate matrix into smaller carbohydrates, amino acids and lipids, and open up the seed's starch reserves. The endosperm is composed of large and small starch granules that are packed like bags of jellybeans in a box. The cell walls (bags) within the matrix holding the starch granules (jellybeans) are primarily composed of beta-glucans (a type of cellulose), some pentosans (gummy polysaccharide) and some protein. The box in this metaphor is the outer husk. The degree to which the enzymes tear open the bags and start unpacking the starch granules (i.e. breakdown the endosperm) for use by the growing plant (or brewers in our case) is referred to as the "modification." One visual indicator that a maltster uses to judge the degree of modification is the length of the acrospire (plant shoot) which grows underneath the husk. The length of the acrospire in a fully modified malt will typically be 75-100% of the seed length.

If germination continued, a plant would grow, and all of the starches that the brewer hoped to use would be used by the plant. So, the maltster gauges the germination carefully and stops the process by drying when he judges he has the proper balance between resources converted by the acrospire and resources consumed by the acrospire.

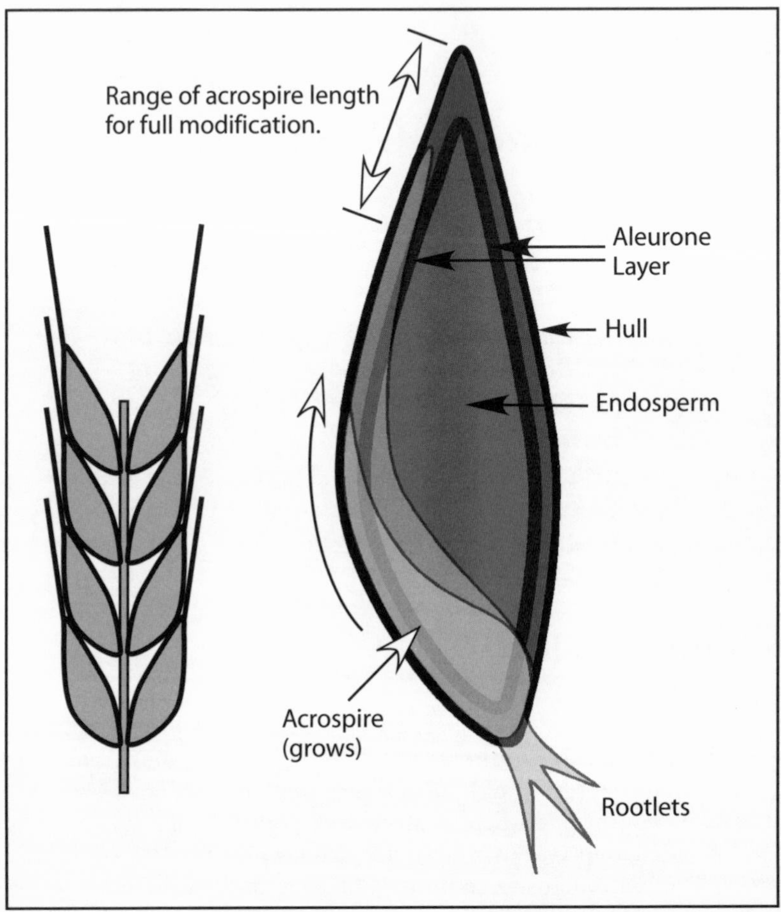

Figure 69—A simplified diagram of a barley kernel during malting, showing a progressive picture of how the acrospire (the plant shoot) grows along one side of the kernel. As it grows, pre-existing enzymes are released and new enzymes are created in the aleurone layer which "modify" the endosperm (the protein/carbohydrate matrix starch reserve) for the acrospire's use.

The purpose of malting is to create these enzymes, break down the matrix surrounding the starch granules, prepare the starches for conversion, and then stop this action until the brewer is ready to utilize the grain. After modification, the grain is dried and the acrospire and rootlets are knocked off by tumbling. The kiln drying of the new malt denatures (destroys) a lot of the different enzymes, but several types remain, including the ones necessary for starch conversion. The amount of enzymatic starch conversion potential that a malt has is referred to as its "diastatic power".

Malted barley is the principal source of the sugars (principally maltose) which are fermented into beer. From a brewer's point of view, there are basically two kinds of malts, those that need to be mashed and those that don't. Mashing is the hot water soaking process that provides the right conditions for the enzymes to convert the grain starches into fermentable sugars. The basic light colored malts such as pale ale malt, pilsener malt and malted wheat need to be mashed to convert the starches into fermentable sugars. These malts make up the bulk of the wort's fermentable sugars. Some of these light malts are kilned or toasted at higher temperatures to lend different tastes e.g., Biscuit, Vienna, Munich, Brown. The toasting destroys some of their diastatic power.

The diastatic power of a particular malt will vary with the type of barley it is made from. There are two basic varieties of barley, two row and six row –referring to the arrangement of the kernels around the shaft. Two row barley is the generally preferred variety, having a bit higher yield per pound, lower protein levels, and claiming a more refined flavor than six row. However, six row has a little higher diastatic power than two row. Historically, the higher protein level of six row barley (which can produce a very heavy bodied beer) drove brewers to thin the wort with unmalted grains like corn and rice. Brewers were able to take advantage of six row barley's higher diastatic power to achieve full conversion of the mash in spite of the non-enzymatic starch sources (adjuncts).

Besides the lighter-colored base and toasted malts, there is another group of malts that don't need to be mashed and these are often referred to as "specialty grain." They are used for flavoring and have no diastatic power whatsoever. These malts have undergone special heating processes in which the starches are converted to sugars by heat and moisture right inside the hull. As a result, these malts contain more complex sugars, some of which do not ferment, leaving a pleasant caramel-like sweetness. These pre-converted malts (called caramel or crystal malts) are available in different roasts or colors (denoted by the color unit Lovibond), each having a different degree of fermentability and characteristic sweetness (e.g., Crystal 40, Crystal 60). Also within the specialty malt group are the roasted malts. These malts have had their sugars charred by roasting at high temperatures, giving them a deep red/brown or black color (e.g. Black Patent malt). The Lovibond color scale ranges from 1 to 600. *See Figure 70.* To put this in perspective, most American mega-brewed light lager beers are less than 5 Lovibond. Guinness Extra Stout on the other hand, is comfortably in the 100s. Specialty malts do not need to be mashed, and can simply be steeped in hot water to release their character. These grains are very useful to the extract brewer, making it easy to increase the complexity of the wort without much effort.

Lastly, there are fermentables not derived from malted barley which are called "adjuncts." Adjuncts include refined sugars, corn, rice, un-malted rye and wheat, and unmalted barley. These are not to be scorned, some adjuncts like wheat and unmalted roasted barley are essential to certain beer styles. Whole brewing traditions like Belgian Lambic, German Weizen, and Irish Stout depend on the use of adjuncts.

Figure 70—Notice the difference in color between the base malt 2L (top), Crystal 60L Malt (below right), and Roasted Unmalted Barley 550L.

Malt Types and Usages

Note: There are a few trademarked products in the following list. I have specified them because they best represent a particular style of malt that is commonly used for a particular flavor or purpose. But this is an incomplete list; every malting house has their specialties and I don't come close to listing every malt. Typical Lovibond color values are listed as *X* L.

Base Malts
(need to be mashed)

Lager Malt 2 L Lager malt can be used to produce ales as well as lagers. The name comes from the fact that pale lagers are the most common style of beer and this is the malt type most commonly used to produce them. Because it tends to be the most available malt, it is used for nearly every other style also. Logically, if you intend to brew a pale lager, you would be best served by using lager malt.

After germination, lager malt is carefully heated in a kiln to 90°F for the first day, withered at 120–140°F for 12-20 hours and then cured at 175-185°F for 4–48 hours depending on the maltster. This produces a malt with fine mild flavor and excellent enzyme potential. It is used as the basis of most of the world's beers along with specialty malts for added flavors.

Pale Ale Malt 3 L This malt type is kilned at higher temperatures than lager malt, giving a slightly toastier malt flavor well suited to Pale Ales.

Wheat Malt 3 L Wheat has been used for brewing beer nearly as long as barley and has equal diastatic power. Malted wheat is used for 5–70% of the mash depending on the style. Wheat has no outer husk and therefore has fewer tannins than barley. It is generally smaller than barley and contributes more protein to the beer, aiding in head retention. But it is much stickier than barley due to the higher protein content and may cause lautering problems if not given a "Protein Rest" during the mash.

Rye Malt 3 L Malted rye is not common but is gaining in popularity. It can be used as 5–10% of the grain bill for a rye "spicy" note. It is even stickier in the mash than wheat and should be handled accordingly.

Kilned Malts
(need to be mashed)

These malts are commonly produced by increasing the curing temperatures used for base malt production, but can also be produced by toasting finished base malts for a period of time in an oven. Suggested times and temperatures for producing these types of malts at home are given in *Chapter 20–Developing Your Own Recipes.*

Biscuit Malt 25 L (DeWolf-Cosyns/Cargill) This fully toasted, lightly roasted malt is used to give the beer a bread and biscuits flavor. It is typically used as 10% of the grainbill. Gives a deep amber color to the beer.

Victory Malt 25 L (Briess) This roasted malt is similar in flavor to Biscuit but gives a more nutty taste to the beer. Victory adds orange highlights to the beer color. Typically used as 10% of the grainbill.

Munich Malt 10 L This malt has an amber color and gives a very malty flavor. This malt has enough diastatic power to convert itself but is usually used in conjunction with a base malt for mashing. This malt is used as 10-60% for Oktoberfests, Bocks, and many others, including pale ales.

Vienna Malt 4 L This malt is lighter and sweeter than Munich malt and is a principal ingredient of light amber beers. Retains enough enzymatic power to convert itself but is often used with a base malt in the mash. Typically used as 10-40% of the grainbill, depending on beer style.

Carapils Malt 3 L (Briess) Also known as Dextrin Malt, this malt is used sparingly and contributes little color but enhances the mouthfeel and perceived body of the beer. A common amount for a five gallon batch is ½ lb. Dextrin malt has no diastatic power. It must be mashed; if steeped it will contribute a lot of unconverted starch and cause starch haze.

Caramel Malts
(may be steeped or mashed)

Caramel Malts (aka. Crystal Malt) have undergone a special heat "stewing" process after the malting which crystallizes the sugars. These sugars are caramelized into longer chains that are not converted into simple sugars by the enzymes during the mash. This results in a more malty, caramel sweet, fuller tasting beer. These malts are used for almost all ale and higher gravity lager styles. Various crystal malts are often added in half pound amounts to a total of 5-25% of the grain bill for a 5 gallon batch.

Caramel 10 10 L This malt adds a light honey-like sweetness and some body to the finished beer.

Caramel 40 40 L The additional color and light caramel sweetness of this malt is perfect for pale ales and amber lagers.

Caramel 60 60 L This is the most commonly used caramel malt, also known as medium crystal. It is well suited for pale ales, English style bitters, porters and stouts. It adds a full caramel taste and body to the beer.

Caramel 80 80 L This malt is used for making reddish colored beers and gives a lightly bittersweet caramel flavor.

Caramel 120 120 L This malt adds a lot of color and bittersweet caramel flavor. Useful in small amounts to add complexity or in greater amounts for old ales, barleywines and doppelbocks.

Special B 220 L (DeWolfe-Cosyns/Cargill) This unique Belgian malt has a roasted nutty-sweet flavor. Used in moderation (¼–½ lb.), it is very good in brown ales, porter, and doppelbocks. Larger amounts, i.e., more than a half pound in a 5 gallon batch, will lend a plum-like flavor (which may be desired in a barleywine in small amounts).

Roasted Malts
(may be steeped or mashed)

These highly roasted malts contribute a coffee or burnt toast flavor to porters and stouts. Obviously these malts should be used in moderation. Some brewers recommend that they be added towards the end of the mash, claiming that this reduces the acrid bite that these malts can contribute. This practice does seem to produce a smoother beer for people brewing with naturally "soft" or low bicarbonate water. These malts are typically used in small amounts and may be ground finely to achieve a better color contribution with a smaller addition.

Chocolate Malt 400L Used in small amounts (½ lb. for 5 gal.) for brown ale and extensively in porters and stouts, this malt has a bittersweet chocolate flavor, pleasant roast character and contributes a deep ruby black color.

Black Patent Malt 580L This is the blackest of the black. It must be used sparingly, generally less than a ¼ lb. per 5 gallons. It contributes a roasted charcoal flavor that can actually be quite unpleasant if used in excess. It is useful for contributing color and/or setting a "limit" on the sweetness of other beer styles using a lot of caramel malt; one or two ounces is useful for this purpose.

Roast Barley 550L This is not actually a malt, but highly roasted plain barley. It has a dry, distinct coffee taste and is the signature flavor of Stouts. It has less of a charcoal bite to it than does Black Patent. Use about ½ lb. per 5 gallons for Stout.

Other Grains and Adjuncts
(need to be mashed)

Oatmeal 1 L Oats are wonderful in a porter or stout. Oatmeal lends a smooth, silky mouthfeel and a creaminess to a stout that must be tasted to be understood. Oats are available whole, steel-cut (i.e. grits), rolled, and flaked. Rolled and flaked oats have had their starches gelatinized (made soluble) by heat and pressure, and are most readily available as "Instant Oatmeal" in the grocery store. Whole oats and "Old Fashioned Rolled Oats" have not had the degree of gelatinization that Instant have had and must be cooked before adding to the mash. "Quick" oatmeal has had a degree of gelatinization but does benefit from being cooked before adding to the mash. Cook according to the directions on the box (but add more water) to ensure that the starches will be fully utilized. Use 0.5-1.5 lb. per 5 gal batch. Oats need to be mashed with barley malt (and its enzymes) for conversion.

Flaked Corn (Maize) Flaked corn is a common adjunct in British bitters and milds and used to be used extensively in American light lager (although today corn grits are more common). Properly used, corn will lighten the color and body of the beer without overpowering the flavor. Use 0.5-2 lb. per 5 gal batch. Corn must be mashed with base malt.

Flaked Barley Flaked unmalted barley is often used in Stouts to provide protein for head retention and body. It can also be used in other strong ale styles. Use 0.5-1 lb. per 5 gal batch. Flaked barley must be mashed with base malt.

Flaked Wheat Unmalted wheat is a common ingredient in wheat beers, including: American Wheat, Bavarian Weisse, and is essential to Belgian Lambic and Wit. It adds starch haze and high levels of protein. Flaked wheat adds more wheat flavor "sharpness" than malted wheat. Use 0.5-2 lb. per 5 gal batch. Must be mashed with base malt.

Flaked Rice Rice is the other principal adjunct used in American and Japanese light lagers. Rice has very little flavor and makes for a drier tasting beer than corn. Use 0.5-2 lb. per 5 gal batch. It must be mashed with base malt.

Oat and Rice Hulls Not an adjunct per se, the hulls of oats and rice are not fermentable, but they can be useful in the mash. The hulls provide bulk and help prevent the mash from settling and becoming stuck during the sparge. This can be very helpful when making wheat or rye beers with a low percentage of barley malt and barley husks. Use 2-4 quarts of oat or rice hulls for 6-10 lbs. of wheat if doing an all-wheat beer. Rinse thoroughly before using.

Extraction and Maximum Yield

All of these grains can be used to produce the fermentable sugars that make up the wort. But to brew the same beer recipe consistently, we need to be able to quantify how much yield we can expect from each type of grain. Under laboratory conditions, each grain will yield a typical amount of fermentable and non-fermentable sugars that is referred to as its percent extraction or maximum yield. The maximum yield is usually listed on malt lot analysis sheet as dry basis fine grind (DBFG). This weight percentage of soluble extract typically ranges from 50–82%, with some wheat malts hitting as high as 85%. This means that 80% (for example) of the malt's weight is soluble in the laboratory mash. (The other 20% represents the husk, and insoluble proteins and starches.) In the real world, we brewers will never hit this target, but it is useful as a basis for comparison.

The reference for comparison is pure sugar (sucrose) because it yields 100% of its weight as soluble extract when dissolved in water. (One pound of sugar will yield a specific gravity of 1.046 when dissolved in 1 gallon of water.) To calculate the maximum yield for the malts and other adjuncts, the DBFG percentage for each is multiplied by the reference number for sucrose–46 points/pound/gallon (PPG).

The rest of the world uses the metric system (SI units) and the maximum yield is listed as hot water extract (HWE). The concept is exactly the same as PPG, but with conversions for pounds and gallons to liters and kilograms i.e., liter degrees per kilogram. The baseline for sucrose becomes 384 L°/kg, and the DBFG percentage is applied to it. The combined conversion factor for converting PPG to HWE is 8.345.

For example, let's look at a typical pilsner base malt. Most light base malts have a maximum yield (DBFG) of about 80% by weight of soluble materials. So, if we know that sugar will yield 100% of its weight as soluble sugar and that it raises the gravity of the wort by 46 PPG, then the maximum increase in gravity we can expect from pilsner base malt, at 80% solubility, is 80% of 46 or 37 PPG. The HWE value would be 309 L°/kg.

The maximum yields for the malts are listed in *Table 9*. You may be wondering how useful the maximum yield number of a malt can be if you can never expect to hit it. The answer is to apply a scaling factor to the maximum yield and derive a number we will usually achieve–a typical yield.

Extraction Efficiency and Typical Yield

The maximum yield is just that, a value you might get if all the mash variables (e.g. pH, temperature, time, viscosity, grind, phase of the moon, etc.) lined up and 100% of the starches where converted to sugars. But most brewers, even commercial brewers, don't get that value in their mashes. Most brewers will approach 80-90% of the maximum yield (i.e. 90% of the maximum 80%). This percentage is referred to as a brewer's extraction efficiency and the resulting yield is the typical yield from our brewing system. The extraction efficiency is dependent on the mash conditions and the lautering system. These extraction details will be discussed further in the chapters to follow: *Chapter 14–What is Mashing?, Chapter 16–The Methods of Mashing,* and *Chapter 17–Getting the Wort Out.*

For the purposes of our discussion of the typical yields for the various malts and adjuncts, we will assume an extract efficiency of 85%, which is considered to be very good for homebrewers. A few points less yield (i.e. 80 or 75% extraction efficiency), is still considered to be good extraction. A large commercial brewery would see the 10% reduction as significant because they are using thousands of pounds of grain a day. For a homebrewer, adding 10% more grain per batch to make up for the difference in extraction is a pittance.

Table 9—Typical Malt Yields in Points/Pound/Gallon

Malt Type	DBFG (Max.% Yield)	Maximum PPG	Typical PPG (85%)	PPG Steep
2 Row Lager Malt	80	37	31	—
6 Row Base Malt	76	35	30	—
2 Row Pale Ale Malt	81	38	32	—
Biscuit/Victory Malt	75	35	30	—
Vienna Malt	75	35	30	—
Munich Malt	75	35	30	—
Brown Malt	70	32	28	8*
Dextrin Malt	70	32	28	4*
Light Crystal (10-15L)	75	35	30	14*
Pale Crystal (25-40L)	74	34	29	22
Medium Crystal (60-75L)	74	34	29	18
Dark Crystal (120L)	72	33	28	16
Special B	68	31	27	16
Chocolate Malt	60	28	24	15
Roast Barley	55	25	22	21
Black Patent Malt	55	25	22	21
Wheat Malt	79	37	31	—
Rye Malt	63	29	25	—
Oatmeal (Flaked)	70	32	28	—
Corn (Flaked)	84	39	33	—
Barley (Flaked)	70	32	28	—
Wheat (Flaked)	77	36	30	—
Rice (Flaked)	82	38	32	—
Malto-Dextrin Powder	100	40	(40)	(40)
Sugar (Corn, Cane)	100	46	(46)	(46)

Malt % Yield data obtained and averaged from several sources.
Steeping data is experimental and was obtained by steeping 1 lb. in 1 gal at 160°F for 30 minutes. All malts were crushed in a 2 roller mill at the same setting.

*The low extraction from steeping is attributed to unconverted starches as revealed by an iodine test.

Calculating Your Efficiency

There are two different gravities that matter to a brewer: one is the extraction or boil gravity (BG), and the other is the post-boil or pitching gravity (OG). And, ninety percent of the time, the pitching OG is what people are referring to because it determines the strength of the beer. When brewers plan recipes, they think in terms of the pitching OG, which assumes that the wort volume is the final size of the batch, e.g., 5 gallons.

But, when it comes to the efficiency of the mash and lauter, we want to think in terms of the boil gravity. The Extraction Efficiency section and Table 9 gave us the maximum malt yields that allows us to evaluate our mashing and lautering processes.

When all-grain homebrewers get together to brag about their brewing prowess or equipment and they say something like, "I got 30 PPG from my mash schedule", they are referring to the overall yield from their mash in terms of the amount of wort they collected.

It is important to realize that the total amount of sugar is constant, but the concentration (i.e. gravity) changes depending on the volume. To understand this, let's look at the unit of points/pound/gallon. This is a unit of concentration, so the unit is always expressed in reference to 1 gallon ("per gallon"). In mashing, you are collecting "x" number of gallons of wort that has a gravity of "1.0yy" that was produced from "z" pounds of malt. To calculate your extraction in terms of PPG, you need to multiply the number of gallons of wort you collected by its gravity and divide that by the amount of malt that was used. This will give you the gravity (points per gallon) per pound of malt used. Let's look at an example using the recipe for Palmer's Short Stout.

For our example batch, we will assume that 8.5 pounds of malt was mashed and lautered to produce 6 gallons of wort that yielded a BG of 1.038. The brewer's total sugar extraction for this batch would be 6 gallons multiplied by 38 points per gallon = 230 points. Dividing the total points by the pounds of malt

RECIPE

Palmer's Short Stout

OG = 1.050 for 5 Gallons

- 6.5 lbs of 2 row base malt
- 1/2 lb. of Chocolate malt
- 1/2 lb. of Crystal 120 malt
- 1/2 lb. of Dextrin malt
- 1/2 lb. of Roast Barley

  (8.5 lbs. total)
- 1 oz. EK Goldings (6%) 60 min
- 1 oz. EK Goldings (6%) 15 min

  35 IBUs

Irish Ale Yeast

gives us our mash extraction in points/pound e.g. 230/8.5 = 27 PPG. This value is good, if not great–30 PPG is basically what everyone shoots for. Comparing these numbers to lager malt's 37 PPG maximum gives us a good approximation of our extraction efficiency: 27/37 = 73%, while 30/37 = 81%. When compared in this way, our efficiency looks a bit low, but you need to remember that the there are lower-yielding malts in the recipe. If we look at the maximum PPG numbers from *Table 9* for each of the recipe's malts, we can calculate our actual extraction efficiency:

Malts	OG based on max. PPG
6.5 lbs. of 2 Row	37 x 6.5 / 6 = 40.1
0.5 lb. of Chocolate Malt	28 x .5 / 6 = 2.3
0.5 lb. of Crystal 60	34 x .5 / 6 = 2.8
0.5 lb. of Dextrin Malt	32 x .5 / 6 = 2.6
0.5 lb. of Roast Barley	25 x .5 / 6 = 2.1
8.5 lbs. total	49.9 points total

In this case, our boil gravity of 1.038 means our extraction efficiency was 38/49.9 = 76%. Usually I think you will find that your efficiency will be closer to 80%.

For the metric folks, in terms of HWE, it would look like:

Malts	OG based on max. L°/kg
2.95 kg of 2 Row	309 x 2.95 / 22.7 = 40.1
0.227 kg of Chocolate Malt	234 x .227 / 22.7 = 2.3
0.227 kg of Crystal 60	284 x .227 / 22.7 = 2.8
0.227 kg of Dextrin Malt	267 x .227 / 22.7 = 2.6
0.227 kg of Roast Barley	209 x .227 / 22.7 = 2.1
3.86 kg total	49.9 points total

Planning Malt Quantities for a Recipe

We can use the efficiency concept in reverse when designing a recipe to achieve a targeted OG. Let's go back to our Short Stout example.

To produce a 1.050 wort, how much malt will we need?

1. First, we need to determine/guess an anticipated yield or extraction efficiency for the recipe. For this example, we will choose 30 PPG or 85%.

2. Then we multiply the target gravity (50) by the recipe volume (e.g. 5 gal) to get the total amount of sugar. 5 x 50 = 250 pts.

3. Dividing the total points by our anticipated yield (30 PPG) gives the pounds of malt required. 250 / 30 = 8.3 lbs.
(I generally round up to the nearest half pound, i.e., 8.5)

4. So, 8.5 lbs. of malt will give us our target OG in 5 gallons. Using the malt values for 85% Efficiency in *Table 9*, we can figure out how much of each malt to use to make up our recipe. (If you had chosen a different efficiency for your system, e.g. 80%, then you would apply that percentage to all the DBFG numbers in *Table 9*.)

Malts	OG based on Typical PPG (85%)
6.5 lbs. of 2 Row	31 x 6.5 / 6 = 40.1
0.5 lb. of Chocolate Malt	24 x .5 / 6 = 2.3
0.5 lb. of Crystal 60	29 x .5 / 6 = 2.8
0.5 lb. of Dextrin Malt	28 x .5 / 6 = 2.6
0.5 lb. of Roast Barley	22 x .5 / 6 = 2.1
8.5 lbs. total	50.6 points total

Remember though that this is the post-boil gravity. When you are collecting your wort and are wondering if you have enough, you need to ratio the measured gravity by the amount of wort you have collected to see if you will hit your target after the boil. For instance, to have 5 gallons of 1.050 wort after boiling, you would need (at least):

6 gallons of 1.042 (250 pts/6 gal)

or 7 gallons of 1.036 (250 pts/7 gal)

So, when brewing with grain, you need to plan how much malt to use if you are going to collect 6-7 gallons of wort that will boil down to 5 gallons at a target OG. (Actually you need 5.5 gallons post-boil if you want to plan for fermentation losses from the hops and trub.) I hate not having enough wort for a batch, so I always plan for a little extra. I mention these considerations again in *Chapter 19–Some of My Favorite Beer Styles and Recipes.*

Chapter 13

Steeping Specialty Grains

One of the best things that a new brewer can do to get a feel for using grain is to steep specialty grains in hot water and use this wort for an extract-based recipe. Using specialty grain allows the brewer to increase the complexity of the wort from what is available commercially as extract-alone. Steeping grain also adds freshness to an extract brew. Often, the extract you buy may be more than a year old and the resulting beer may have a dull, soapy character due to oxidation. Creating some new wort by steeping crushed grain adds back the fresh malt character that is often missing from all extract recipes.

Historically, brewers had to settle for light, amber, or dark extract. Nowadays, there is a great deal more variety in brewing kits and some extract producers take to the time to produce a kit that incorporates several malts and real individuality. But generally, if a brewer wants complexity, then they have to achieve it themselves.

Just about every beer style may be made by using pale malt extract and steeping the specialty grains listed below. Brown Ales, Bitters, India Pale Ales, Stouts, Bocks, Pilseners; all can be made using this method. And the resulting beer flavor will be superior than what can be made using extracts alone. Award winning beers can be made solely from extract, but freshness of the extract is often an issue and using grain can make up the difference between a good beer and an outstanding one.

And its fun to experiment, right?

The Grain

As was discussed in the previous chapter, there are basically two kinds of malts: those that need to be mashed and those that don't. Mashing is the hot water soaking process that provides the right conditions for the enzymes to convert the grain starches into fermentable sugars. Specialty malts like caramel and roasted malts do not need to be mashed. These malts have undergone a special kilning process in which the starches are converted to sugars by heat right inside the hull. As a result, these malts contain more complex sugars, some of which do not ferment, leaving a pleasant caramel-like sweetness. Caramel malts are available in different lovibond ratings (color), each having a different degree of fermentability and characteristic sweetness. Roasted malts have had their sugars charred by roasting at high temperatures, giving them a deep red/brown or black color and bittersweet, dark chocolate, or coffee-like flavors.

Mechanics of Steeping

To use the caramel and roasted specialty malts, the grain must be crushed to expose the sugars to the water. While the grain is soaking, the hot water is leaching the sugars out of the grain and dissolving them into the wort. The factors that influence how well the sugars are extracted are the steeping time, temperature and the particle size. Obviously, the finer you crush the malt the more completely you can extract the sugars. However, most supply shops have their mills adjusted for mashing and lautering purposes and if the particle size where much smaller, it would be difficult to contain within the grain-bag.

TYPICAL STEEPING YIELD

Table 10—Typical Malt Steeping Yields in Points/Pound/Gallon

Malt Type	PPG Steep
2 Row Base Malt	—
6 Row Base Malt	—
2 Row British Pale Malt	—
Biscuit/Victory Malt	—
Vienna Malt	—
Munich Malt	—
Brown Malt	8*
Dextrin Malt	4*
Light Crystal (10-15L)	14*
Pale Crystal (25-40L)	22
Medium Crystal (60-75L)	18
Dark Crystal (120L)	16
Special B	16
Chocolate Malt	15
Roast Barley	21
Black Patent Malt	21
Wheat Malt	—
Rye Malt	—
Oatmeal (Flaked)	—
Corn (Flaked)	—
Barley (Flaked)	—
Wheat (Flaked)	—
Rice (Flaked)	—
Malto-Dextrin Powder	(40)
Sugar (Corn, Cane)	(46)

Steeping data is experimental and was obtained by steeping 1 lb. in 1 gal at 160°F for 30 minutes. All malts were crushed in a 2 roller mill at the same setting.

* The low extraction from steeping is attributed to unconverted starches as revealed by an iodine test.

Steeping specialty grain is like making tea. The crushed grain is soaked in hot water (150-170°F) for 30 minutes. Even though a color change will be noticeable early on, steep for the entire 30 minutes to get as much of the available sugar dissolved into the wort as possible. The grain is removed from the water and that water (now a wort) is then used to dissolve the extract for the boil.

The one sticky part is the phrase, "The grain is removed from the water..." How? Well, the best way is to buy a grainbag. These bags are made of nylon or muslin and have a drawstring closure. They will hold a couple pounds of crushed specialty grain, making in essence a giant tea bag. Most homebrew supply shops have pre-packaged specialty grains in 0.5-1 pound amounts for just this purpose.

The analogy to a tea bag is a good one in that if the grain is steeped too long (hours), astringent tannin compounds (a.k.a. phenols) can be extracted from the grain husks. The compounds give the wort a dry puckering taste, much like a black teabag that has been steeped too long. The extraction of tannins is especially prevalent if the water is too hot–above 170°F. Previous practices for steeping specialty grains had the brewer putting the grain in the pot and bringing it to a boil before removal. That method often resulted in tannin extraction.

Water chemistry also plays a role in tannin extraction. Steeping the heavily roasted malts in low alklinity water (i.e. low bicarbonate levels) will produce conditions that are too acidic and harsh flavors will result. Likewise, steeping the lightest crystal malts in highly alkaline water could produce conditions that are too alkaline and tannin extraction would be a problem again. For best results, the ratio of steeping water to grain should be less than 1 gallon per pound. For more information on water chemistry for steeping and mashing, see *Chapter 15–Understanding the Mash pH*.

Steeping differs from mashing in that there is no enzyme activity taking place to convert grain or adjunct starches to sugars. Steeping specialty grains is entirely a leaching and dissolution process of sugars into the wort. If grain with enzyme diastatic potential is steeped, that's a mash. See the following chapters for more detail on that process.

Example Batch

As an example, I will outline the procedure for making a Porter (one of my favorite styles). A Porter is an ale style with a dark color, very malty flavor, and a bit of a roasted finish. A Porter differs from a Brown Ale by being less hoppy, darker, and more full bodied, but with less of a roasted malt flavor than a Stout.

Port O' Palmer Porter

Malts		Gravity Pts.
6 lbs. of Pale Malt Extract (LME)		72
½ lb. of Chocolate Malt		3
½ lb. of Crystal 60L Malt		3
¼ lb. of Black Patent Malt		1
BG for 3 Gallons		1.079
OG for 5 Gallons		1.048
Hops	**Boil Time**	**IBUs**
1 oz of Nugget (10%)	60	26
¾ oz of Willamette (5%)	40	9
½ oz of Willamette (5%)	20	4
Total IBUs		39

Yeast	Fermentation Schedule
American Ale (liquid)	Primary ferment at 65°F for 2 weeks. Or 1 week primary and 2 weeks secondary.

Procedure The procedure is identical to that for extract brewing. However, the specialty grains will be steeped in the pot before the extract is added. For best results, the ratio of steeping water to grain should be less than 1 gallon per pound.

1. The water in the boiling pot is heated until it reaches 160°F ± 10°.
2. The grain bag is immersed in the pot for 30 minutes. The grain bag may be dunked and swirled like a tea bag during this time to make sure that all of the grain is wetted. Agitation will help to improve the yield.
3. After 30 minutes, remove the grain bag from the pot, giving it a squeeze to drain the excess wort and avoid dripping on the stove.
4. Now the brewer has a preliminary wort to which the extract is added. More water may be added at this time to bring the wort up to boiling volume.
5. The wort is brought to a boil and the brewing proceeds exactly as for extract brewing described in the previous chapters.

Figure 73—Joe Brewer checks the temperature of the water for steeping the specialty grain. The temperature should be between 150°F-170°F.

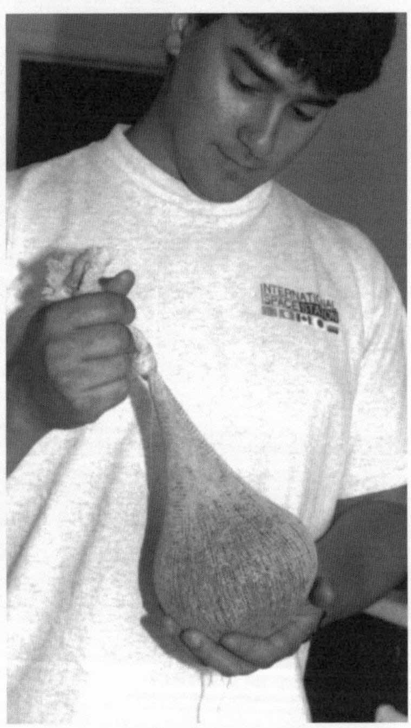

Figure 74—The grainbag contains 1.25 pounds of crushed specialty grain.

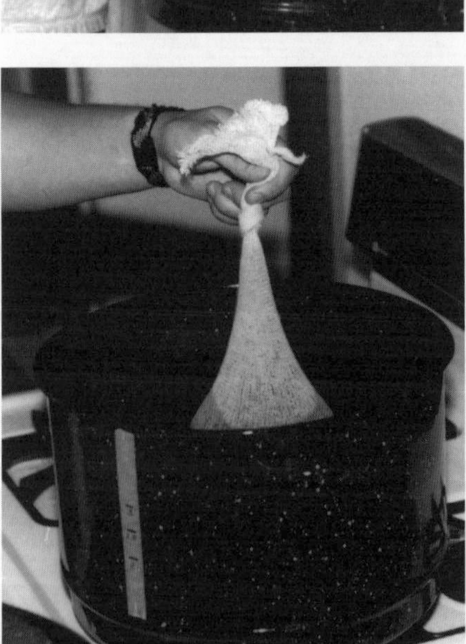

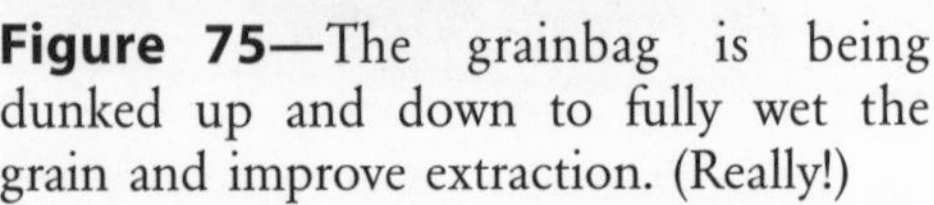

Figure 75—The grainbag is being dunked up and down to fully wet the grain and improve extraction. (Really!)

Figure 76—Okay, the specialty grains have steeped for 30 minutes and are ready to come out. The bag is drained and the grain is discarded.

Figure 77—Joe Brewer stirs in the malt extract and the boil is off and running. Brewing proceeds exactly as previously described in Chapter 7

Section III

All-Grain Brewing

Welcome to the third section of *How To Brew.* Here is where we remove the training wheels and do everything from scratch. All of the world's classic beers are produced using malted grain and the methods which I am now going to teach you. The all-grain brewing method allows you the most flexibility in designing and producing an individual wort. Once you have mastered these basic techniques, you will be able to walk into any beer store or pub, select any beer (with the possible exception of the Belgian Lambics–which rely on natural fermentation via airborne wild yeast and bacteria of the Lambic Valley), and say with confidence, "I can brew this." The fundamental techniques and related science will be explained in the following chapters.

Using all-grain brewing can be like driving a car. You can get in, turn the key and off you go; using it to go from point A to point B without much thought about it. Or you can know what's under the hood–knowing that by checking the oil, changing the spark plugs and listening for clanking noises that there are things you can do to make that car work more efficiently for you. Without getting into internal combustion theory, I am going to teach you what is under the hood of your mash. You may not use all of this information (Lord knows I haven't changed my oil in over a year), but at least you will have a good understanding of what is available to you.

In *Chapter 14–How the Mash Works,* I will explain how different temperatures activate different malt enzymes and how these enzymes convert the malt starches into fermentable sugars. Each temperature rest and its related enzyme groups will be described with respect to the effects on the composition of the wort.

The difference between a good brewer and a great brewer is their ability to control the brewing process. The pH of the mash affects enzyme activity as well as the flavor of the wort. In *Chapter 15–Understanding the Mash pH,* we will discuss how the malts and the brewing water combine to determine the pH of the mash. Water chemistry will be explained by looking at a city water report and showing you how to use the report's information to customize your mash. The chemistry of the brewing water can be adjusted through the use of brewing salts to insure proper mash conditions for best performance of the enzymes discussed in the preceding chapter.

In *Chapter 16–The Methods of Mashing,* we get down to brass tacks: I describe how to actually make the mash. There are two principal methods–infusion and decoction. Infusion is the simpler and I will discuss how to use it to brew your first all-grain beer. In *Chapter 17–Getting the Wort Out,* the mechanics of lautering will be discussed so that you will have a better idea of how to conduct the lauter for the best extraction. Finally, in *Chapter 18–Your First All-Grain Batch,* we do it–step by step. Sound interesting? Let's go!

Chapter 14

How the Mash Works

An Allegory

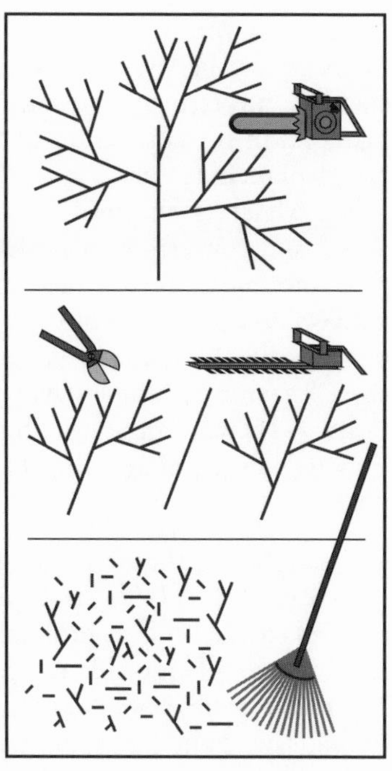

Picture this: There has been a big windstorm that has blown down a big tree and a lot of other branches in the backyard. Your dad decides that some yardwork will build character–yours. Your task is to cut as much of it as you can into two inch lengths and haul it out to the road. You have two tools to do this with: a hedge trimmer and a pair of hand-held clippers. The hedge trimmer is in the garage, but the last time anyone saw the clippers, they had been left outside in the grass, which has since grown knee high. Plus, there are a lot of brambles growing around the tree which will make access and hauling it away difficult. Fortunately your dad has decided that your older brother and sister should take part in this too, and will send them out there with the weed whacker and lawn mower right now. Likewise, he will do you a favor and cut off a few of the big limbs at the joints with the chainsaw before you start. He won't cut many because the football game is starting soon. As soon as the grass is cut, you can find your clippers and get to work.

Your tools are rather limited for the amount of work you have to do. The hedge trimmer will be really useful for cutting all of the end twigs off, but will quit working once you get back towards the branches. The clippers will be useful then–they will be able to cut the middles of all the branches, but aren't strong enough to cut through the joints. When you are done, there will be a lot of odd branched pieces left over in addition to your little pieces. Your success will be measured by how many little pieces make it out to the road. The rake won't handle anything much larger than 12 inches. A large part of your success is going to depend on how well your dad, brother, and sister do in making the tree accessible to you. If you leave a lot of the tree behind, and if the stuff you get out to the road consists of a lot of medium sized pieces, instead of the small pieces your dad wanted, then you won't have done the job correctly. You had better plan your activity carefully...

Defining the Mash

Mashing is the brewer's term for the hot water steeping process which hydrates the barley, activates the malt enzymes, and converts the grain starches into fermentable sugars. There are several key enzyme groups that take part in the conversion of the grain starches to sugars. During malting, the debranching (chainsaw), beta-glucanase (lawnmower) and proteolytic (weed whacker) enzymes do their work, preparing the starches for easy access and conversion to sugars. During the mash, a limited amount of further modification can be accomplished, but the main event is the conversion of starch molecules into fermentable sugars and unfermentable dextrins by the diastatic enzymes (clippers and hedge trimmer). Each of these enzyme groups is favored by different temperature and pH conditions. A brewer can adjust the mash temperature to favor each successive enzyme's function and thereby customize the wort to their taste and purpose.

The starches in the mash are about 90% soluble at 130 °F and approach 99% solubility at 149°F. Both malted and unmalted grains have their starch reserves locked in a protein/carbohydrate matrix which prevents the enzymes from being able to physically contact the starches for conversion. Unmalted grain starch is more locked-up than malted is. Crushing or rolling the grain helps to hydrate the starches during the mash. Once hydrated, the starches can be gelatinized (made soluble) by heat alone or by a combination of heat and enzyme action. Either way, an enzymatic mash is needed to convert the soluble starches to fermentable sugars.

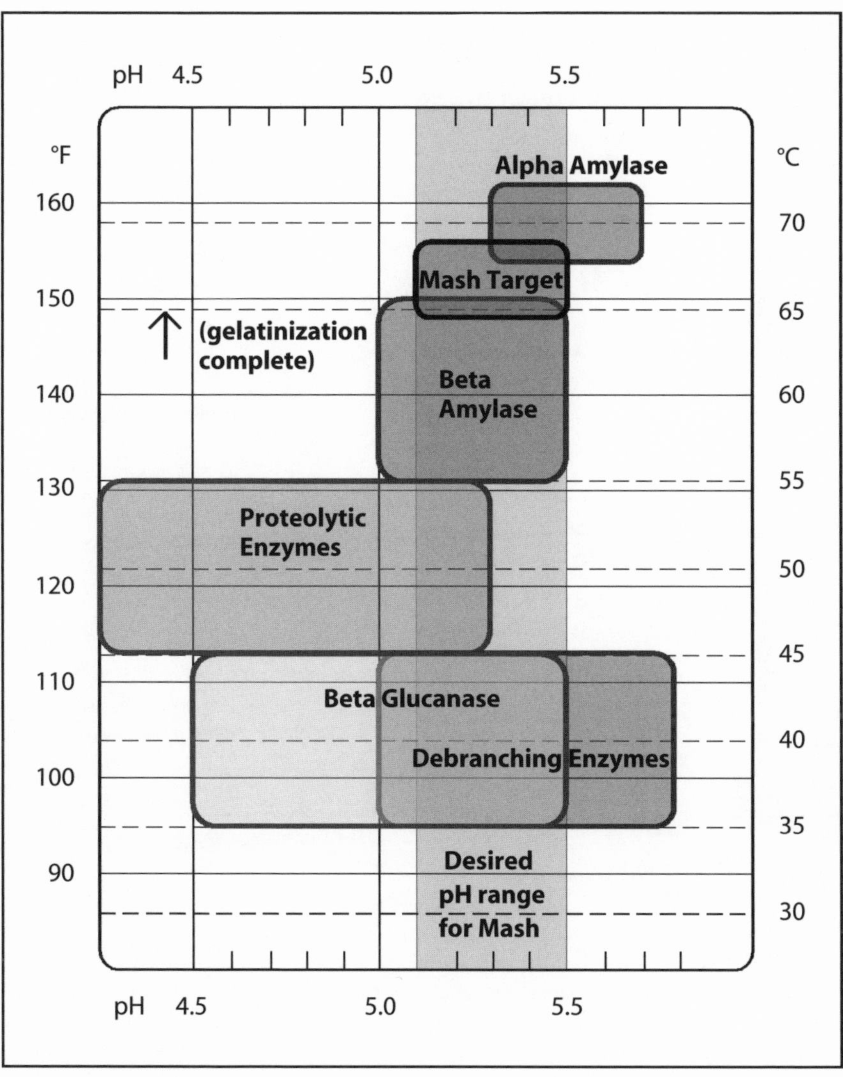

Figure 79—Typical enzyme temperature and pH ranges in the mash. From the numbers given in Table 11.

MASH ENZYMES

Table 11—Major Enzyme Groups and Functions

Enzyme	Optimum Temperature Range	Working pH Range	Function
Phytase	86-126°F	5.0-5.5	Lowers the mash pH. No longer utilized.
Debranching (var.)	95-113°F	5.0-5.8	Solubilization of starches.
Beta Glucanase	95-113°F	4.5-5.5	Best gum breaking rest.
Peptidase	113-131°F	4.6-5.3	Produces Free Amino Nitrogen (FAN).
Protease	113-131°F	4.6-5.3	Breaks up large proteins that form haze.
Beta Amylase	131-150°F	5.0-5.5	Produces maltose.
Alpha Amylase	154-162°F	5.3-5.7	Produces a variety of sugars, including maltose.

Note: The above numbers were averaged from several sources and should be interpreted as typical optimum activity ranges. The enzymes will be active outside the indicated ranges but will be destroyed as the temperature increases above each range.

The Acid Rest

Before the turn of the (last) century, when the interaction of malt and water chemistry was not well understood, brewers in Pilsen used the temperature range of 86-126°F to help the enzyme phytase acidify their mash when using only pale malts. The water in the area is so pure and devoid of minerals that the mash would not reach the proper pH range without this Acid Rest. Most other brewing areas of the world did not have this problem.

Malted barley is rich in phytin, an organic phosphate containing calcium and magnesium. Phytase breaks down phytin into insoluble calcium and magnesium phosphates and myo-inositol–a vitamin. The process lowers the pH by removing the phosphate ion buffers and producing weak acids. The acid rest is not used nowadays because it can take several hours for this enzyme to lower the mash pH to the desired 5.1-5.5 range. Today, through knowledge of water chemistry and appropriate mineral additions, proper mash pH ranges can be achieved from the outset without needing an acid rest.

Doughing-In

To the best of my knowledge, the temperature rest (holding period) for phytase is no longer used for lowering the mash pH by any commercial brewery. However, this regime (95-113°F) is sometimes used by brewers for "Doughing In"–mixing the grist with the water to allow time for the malt starches to soak up water and time for the enzymes to be distributed. The debranching enzymes, e.g. limit dextrinase, are still active in this regime and break up a small percentage of dextrins at this early stage of the mash, although but they are quickly denatured at temperatures over 122°F. The vast majority of debranching occurs during malting as a part of the modification process. Only a small percentage of the debranching enzymes survive the drying and kilning processes after malting, so not much more debranching can be expected. With all of that being said, the use of a 20 minute rest at temperatures near 104°F (40°C) has been shown to be beneficial to improving the yield from all enzymatic malts. This step is considered optional but can improve the total yield by a couple of points.

The Protein Rest and Modification

Modification is the term that describes the degree of breakdown during malting of the protein-starch matrix (endosperm) that comprises the bulk of the seed. Moderately-modified malts benefit from a protein rest to break down any remnant large proteins into smaller proteins and amino acids as well as to further release the starches from the endosperm. Fully-modified malts have already made use of these enzymes and do not benefit from more time spent in the protein rest regime. In fact, using a protein rest on fully modified malts tends to remove most of the body of a beer, leaving it thin and watery. Most base malt in use in the world today is fully modified. Moderately-modified malts are often available from German maltsters. Brewers have reported fuller, maltier flavors from malts that are less modified and make use of this rest in decoction mashing.

Malted barley also contains a lot of amino acid chains which form the simple proteins needed by the germinating plant. In the wort, these proteins are instead utilized by the yeast for their growth and development. Most wort proteins, including some enzymes like the amylases, are not soluble until the mash reaches temperatures associated with the protein rest (113-131°F). The two main proteolytic enzymes responsible are peptidase and protease. Peptidase works to provide the wort with amino acid nutrients that will be used by the yeast. Protease works to break up the larger proteins which enhances the head retention of beer and reduces haze. In fully modified malts, these enzymes have done their work during the malting process.

The temperature and pH ranges for these two proteolytic enzymes overlap. The optimum pH range is 4.2-5.3 and both enzymes are active enough between 113–131°F that talking about an optimum range for each is not relevant. This optimum pH range is a bit low with respect to most mashes, but the typical mash pH of 5.3 is not out of the ballpark. There is no need to attempt to lower the mash pH to facilitate the use of these enzymes. The typical Protein Rest at 120 -130°F is used to break up proteins which might otherwise cause chill haze and can improve the head retention. This rest should only be used when using moderately-modified malts, or when using fully modified malts with a large proportion (>25%) of unmalted grain, e.g. flaked barley, wheat, rye, or oatmeal. Using this rest in a mash consisting mainly of fully modified malts would break up the proteins responsible for body and head retention and result in a thin, watery beer. The standard time for a protein rest is 20-30 minutes.

The other enzymes in this temperature regime are the beta-glucanases/cytases–part of the cellulose enzyme family, and are used to break up the beta glucans in (un)malted wheat, rye, oatmeal and unmalted barley. These glucan hemi-celluloses (i.e. brambles) are responsible for the gumminess of dough and if not broken down will cause the mash to turn into a bowl of porridge that even Papa Bear can't swallow. Fortunately, the optimum temperature range for the beta glucanase enzyme is below that for the proteolytics. This allows the brewer to rest the mash at 98-113°F for 20 minutes to break down the gums without affecting the proteins responsible for head retention and body. The use of this rest is only necessary for brewers incorporating a large amount (>25%) of unmalted or flaked wheat, rye or oatmeal in the mash. Sticky mashes and lauters from lesser amounts can usually be handled by increasing the temperature at lautering time (mashout). See *Chapter 17–Getting the Wort Out (Lautering)*, for further discussion.

Starch Conversion/Saccharification Rest

Finally we come to the main event: making sugar from the starch reserves. In this regime the diastatic enzymes start acting on the starches, breaking them up into sugars (hence the term saccharification). The amylases are enzymes that work by hydrolyzing the straight chain bonds between the individual glucose molecules that make up the starch chain. A single straight chain starch is called an amylose. A branched starch chain (which can be considered as being built from amylose chains) is called an amylopectin. These starches are polar molecules and have different ends. (Think of a line of batteries.) An amylopectin differs from an amylose (besides being branched) by having a different type of molecular bond at the branch point, which is not affected by the diastatic enzymes. (Or, theoretically, feebly at best.)

Let's go back to our yardwork allegory. You have two tools to make sugars with: a pair of clippers (alpha amylase) and a hedge trimmer (beta amylase). While beta is pre-existing, alpha is created via protein modification in the aleurone layer during malting. In other words, the hedge trimmer is in the garage, but the clippers are out in the grass and brambles somewhere. Neither amylase will become soluble and useable until the mash reaches protein rest temperatures, and in the case of moderately-modified malts, alpha amylase may have a bit of genesis to complete.

BREWING TIP

Conversion Check

You can use iodine (or iodophor) to check a sample of the wort to see whether the starches have been completely converted to sugars. As you may remember from high school chemistry, iodine causes starch to turn black. If the mash enzymes converted all of the starches, there should be no color change when a couple drops of iodine are added to a wort sample. Wort that is high in dextrins will turn a strong reddish color when iodine is added.

The wort sample should not have any grain particles in it. The iodine will only add a slight tan or reddish color as opposed to a flash of heavy black color if starch is present.

Beta amylase works by hydrolyzing the straight chain bonds, but it can only work on "twig" ends of the chain, not the "root" end. It can only remove one (maltose) sugar unit at a time, so on amylose, it works sequentially. (A maltose unit is composed of two glucose units, by the way.) On an amylopectin, there are many ends available, and it can remove a lot of maltose very efficaciously (like a hedge trimmer). However, probably due to its size/structure, beta cannot get close to the branch joints. It will stop working about 3 glucoses away from a branch joint, leaving behind a "beta amylase limit dextrin."

Alpha amylase also works by hydrolyzing the straight chain bonds, but it can attack them randomly, much as you can with a pair of clippers. Alpha amylase is instrumental in breaking up large amylopectins into smaller amylopectins and amyloses, creating more ends for beta amylase to work on. Alpha is able to get within one glucose unit of a amylopectin branch and it leaves behind an "alpha amylase limit dextrin."

The temperature most often quoted for mashing is about 153°F. This is a compromise between the two temperatures that the two enzymes favor. Alpha works best at 154-162°F, while beta is denatured (the molecule falls apart) at that temperature, working best between 131-150°F. Beta amylase has a life of 40-60 minutes at 150°F.

What do these two enzymes and temperatures mean to the brewer? The practical application of this knowledge allows the brewer to customize the wort in terms of its fermentability. A lower mash temperature, less than or equal to 150°F, yields a thinner bodied, more attenuable beer. A higher mash temperature, greater than or equal to 156°F, yields a less fermentable, sweeter beer. This is where a brewer can really fine tune a wort to best produce a particular style of beer.

Manipulating the Starch Conversion Rest

There are three other factors besides temperature that affect the amylase enzyme activity. These are the grist/water ratio, pH, and time. Beta amylase is favored by a low wort pH, about 5.0. Alpha is favored by a higher pH, about 5.7. However, a beta-optimum wort is not a very fermentable wort, leaving a lot of amylopectin starch unconverted; alpha amylase is needed to break up the larger chains so beta can work on them. Likewise, an alpha-optimum wort will not have a high percentage of maltose but instead will have a random distribution of sugars of varying complexity. Therefore, a compromise is made between the two enzyme optimums.

Brewing salts can be used to raise or lower the mash pH but these salts can only be used to a limited extent because they also affect the flavor. Water treatment is an involved topic and will be discussed in more detail in the next chapter. For the beginning masher, it is often better to let the pH do what it will and work the other variables around it, as long as your water is not extremely soft or hard. Malt selection can do as much or more to influence the pH as using salts in most situations. The pH of the mash or wort runnings can be checked with pH test papers sold at brewshops, and swimming pool supply stores.

The grist/water ratio is another factor influencing the performance of the mash. A thinner mash of more than 2 quarts of water per pound of grain dilutes the relative concentration of the enzymes, slowing the conversion, but ultimately leads to a more fermentable mash because the enzymes are not inhibited by a high concentration of sugars. A stiff mash of less than 1.25 quarts of water per pound is better for protein breakdown, and results in a faster overall starch conversion, but the resultant sugars are less fermentable and will result in a sweeter, maltier beer. A thicker mash is more gentle to the enzymes because of the lower heat capacity of grain compared to water. A thick mash is better for multirest mashes because the enzymes are not denatured as quickly by a rise in temperature.

As always, time changes everything; it is the final factor in the mash. Starch conversion may be complete in only 30 minutes, so that during the remainder of a 60 minute mash, the brewer is working the mash conditions to produce the desired profile of wort sugars. Depending on the mash pH, water ratio and temperature, the time required to complete the mash can vary from under 30 minutes to over 90. At a higher temperature, a stiffer mash and a higher pH, the alpha amylase is favored and starch conversion will be complete in 30 minutes or less. Longer times at these conditions will allow the beta amylase time to breakdown more of the longer sugars into shorter ones, resulting in a more fermentable wort, but these alpha-favoring conditions are deactivating the beta; such a mash is self-limiting.

Lower temperatures, a thinner mash, and lower pH will slow the conversion, but given enough time it will produce a more attenuable wort. Alpha amylase works slowly under these conditions, but it does work.

Summary A compromise of all factors yields the standard mash conditions for most homebrewers: a mash ratio of about 1.5 quarts of water per pound grain, pH of 5.3, temperature of 150–155°F and a time of about one hour. These conditions yield a wort with a nice maltiness and good fermentability.

Chapter 15

Understanding the Mash pH

What Kind of Water Do I Need?

"What kind of water do I need for all-grain brewing?" (you ask)

Usually, the water should be of moderate hardness and low-to-moderate alkalinity, but it depends...

"What do these terms mean? Depends on What?"
"Where can I get this kind of water?"
"What is my own water like?"

This chapter is all about answering those questions. The answers will depend on what type of beer you want to brew and the mineral character of the water that you have to start with.

The term "hardness" refers to the amount of calcium and magnesium ions in the water. Hard water commonly causes scale on pipes. Water hardness is balanced to a large degree by water alkalinity. Alkaline water is high in bicarbonates. Water that has high alkalinity causes the mash pH to be higher than it would be normally. Using dark roasted malts in the mash can balance alkaline water to achieve the proper mash pH, and this concept will be explored later in this chapter.

Reading A Water Report

To understand your water, you need to get a copy of your area's annual water analysis. Call the Public Works department at City Hall and ask for a copy, they will usually send you one free-of-charge. An example for Los Angeles is shown in *Table 12*. Water quality reports are primarily oriented to the safe drinking water laws regarding contaminants like pesticides, bacteria and toxic metals. As brewers, we are interested in the Secondary or Aesthetic Standards that have to do with taste and pH.

There are several important ions to consider when evaluating brewing water. The principal ions are Calcium (Ca^{+2}), Magnesium (Mg^{+2}), Bicarbonate (HCO_3^{-1}) and Sulfate (SO_4^{-2}). Sodium (Na^{+1}), Chloride (Cl^{-1}) and Sulfate (SO_4^{-2}) can influence the taste of the water and beer, but do not affect the mash pH like the others. Ion concentrations in water are usually discussed as parts per million (ppm), which is equivalent to a milligram of a substance per liter of water (mg/l). Descriptions of these ions follow.

Calcium (Ca^{+2})

Atomic Weight = 40.0
Equivalent Weight = 20.0
Brewing Range = 50-150 ppm.

Calcium is the principal ion that determines water hardness and has a $^{+2}$ charge. As it is in our own bodies, calcium is instrumental to many yeast, enzyme, and protein reactions, both in the mash and in the boil. It promotes clarity, flavor, and stability in the finished beer. Calcium additions may be necessary to assure sufficient enzyme activity for some mashes in water that is low in calcium. Calcium that is matched by bicarbonates in water is referred to as "temporary hardness". Temporary hardness can be removed by boiling (see Bicarbonate). Calcium that is left behind after the temporary hardness has been removed is called "permanent hardness".

Magnesium (Mg^{+2})

Atomic Weight = 24.3
Equivalent Weight = 12.1
Brewing Range = 10-30 ppm.

This ion behaves very similarly to Calcium in water, but is less efficacious. It also contributes to water hardness. Magnesium is an important yeast nutrient in small amounts (10–30 ppm), but amounts greater than 50 ppm tend to give a sour-bitter taste to the beer. Levels higher than 125 ppm have a laxative and diuretic affect.

WATER REPORT EXAMPLE

Table 12—Los Angeles Metropolitan Water District Quality Report (1996 data)

Parameter	State Maximum Level (mg/L)	Delivered Average (mg/L)
Primary Standards		
Clarity	.5	.08
Microbiological		
Total Coliform	5%	.12%
Fecal Coliform	(detection)	0
Organic Chemicals		
Pesticides/PCBs	*(various—JP)*	ND
Semi-Volatile Organics	*(various—JP)*	ND
Volatile Organics	*(various—JP)*	ND
Inorganic Chemicals *(list edited—JP)*		
Arsenic	.05	.002
Cadmium	.005	ND
Copper	(zero goal)	ND
Fluoride	1.4-2.4	.22
Lead	(zero goal)	ND
Mercury	.002	ND
Nitrate	10	.21
Nitrite	1	ND
Secondary Standards—Aesthetic		
Chloride	*250	91
Color	15	3
Foaming Agents	.5	ND
Iron	.3	ND
Manganese	.05	ND
pH	NS	8.04
Silver	.1	ND
Sulfate	*250	244
Total Dissolved Solids	*500	611
Zinc	5	ND
Additional Parameters		
Alkalinity as CaCO3	NS	114
Calcium	NS	68
Hardness as CaCO3	NS	283
Magnesium	NS	27.5
Potassium	NS	4.5
Sodium	NS	96

* = Recommended Level
NS = No Standard ND = Not Detected

Bicarbonate (HCO_3^{-1})

Molecular Weight = 61.0
Equivalent Weight = 61.0
Brewing Range = 0-50 ppm for pale, base-malt only beers.
50-150 ppm for amber colored, toasted malt beers.
150-250 ppm for dark, roasted malt beers.

The carbonate family of ions are the big players in determining brewing water chemistry. Carbonate (CO_3^{-2}), is an alkaline ion, raising the pH, and neutralizing dark malt acidity. Its cousin, bicarbonate (HCO_3^{-1}), has half the buffering capability but actually dominates the chemistry of most brewing water supplies because it is the principal form for carbonates in water with a pH less than 8.4. Carbonate itself typically exists as less than 1% of the total carbonate/bicarbonate/carbonic acid species until the pH exceeds 8.4. There are two methods the homebrewer can use to bring the bicarbonate level down to the nominal 50-150 ppm range for most pale ales, or even lower for light lagers such as Pilsener. These methods are boiling and dilution.

Carbonate can be precipitated (ppt) out as Calcium Carbonate ($CaCO_3$) by aeration and boiling according to the following reaction:

$$2HCO_3^{-1} + Ca^{+2} + O_2 \text{ gas} \rightarrow CaCO_3 \text{ (ppt)} + H_2O + CO_2 \text{ gas}$$

where oxygen from aeration acts as a catalyst and the heat of boiling prevents the carbon dioxide from dissolving back into the water to create carbonic acid.

Dilution is the easiest method of producing low carbonate water. Use distilled water from the grocery store (often referred to as Purified Water for use in steam irons) in a 1:1 ratio, and you will effectively cut your bicarbonate levels in half, although there will be a minor difference due to buffering reactions. Bottom Line–if you want to make soft water from hard water (e.g. to brew a Pilsener), dilution with distilled water is the best route.

Sulfate (SO_4^{-2})

Molecular Weight = 96.0
Equivalent Weight = 48.0
Brewing Range = 50-150 ppm for normally bitter beers.
150-350 ppm for very bitter beers

The sulfate ion also combines with Ca and Mg to contribute to permanent hardness. It accentuates hop bitterness, making the bitterness seem drier, more crisp. At concentrations over 400 ppm however, the resulting bitterness can become astringent and unpleasant, and at concentrations over 750 ppm, it can cause diarrhea. Sulfate is only weakly alkaline and does not contribute to the overall alkalinity of water.

Sodium (Na^{+1})

Atomic Weight = 22.9
Equivalent Weight = 22.9
Brewing Range = 0-150 ppm.

Sodium can occur in very high levels, particularly if you use a salt-based (i.e. ion exchange) water softener at home. In general, you should never use softened water for mashing. You probably needed the calcium it replaced and you definitely don't need the high sodium levels. At levels of 70-150 ppm it rounds out the beer flavors, accentuating the sweetness of the malt. But above 200 ppm the beer will start to taste salty. The combination of sodium with a high concentration of sulfate ions will generate a very harsh bitterness. Therefore keep at least one or the other as low as possible, preferably the sodium.

Chloride (Cl^{-1})

Atomic Weight = 35.4
Equivalent Weight = 35.4
Brewing Range = 0-250 ppm.

The chloride ion also accentuates the flavor and fullness of beer. Concentrations above 300 ppm (from heavily chlorinated water or residual bleach sanitizer) can lead to mediciney flavors due to chlorophenol compounds.

Water Hardness, Alkalinity, and milliEquivalents

Hardness and Alkalinity of water are often expressed "as $CaCO_3$". Hardness-as referring to the cation concentration, and alkalinity-as referring to the anions i.e. bicarbonate. If your local water analysis does not list the bicarbonate ion concentration (ppm), nor "Alkalinity as $CaCO_3$", to give you an idea of the water's buffering power to the mash pH, then you will need to call the water department and ask to speak to one of the engineers. They will have that information.

Calcium, and to a lesser extent magnesium, combine with bicarbonate to form chalk which is only slightly soluble in neutral pH (7.0) water. The total concentration of these two ions in water is termed "hardness" and is most noticeable as carbonate scale on plumbing. Water Hardness is often listed on municipal water data sheets as "Hardness as $CaCO_3$" and is equal to the sum of the Ca and Mg concentrations in milliequivalents per liter (mEq/l) multiplied by 50 (the "equivalent weight" of $CaCO_3$). An "equivalent" is a mole of an ion with a charge, + or –, of 1. The equivalent weight of Ca^{+2} is half of its atomic weight of 40, i.e. 20. Therefore if you divide the concentration in ppm or mg/l of Ca^{+2} by 20, you have the number of milliequivalents per liter of Ca^{+2}. Adding the number of milliequivalents of calcium and magnesium together and multiplying by 50 gives the hardness as milliequivalents per liter of $CaCO_3$.

$$(Ca\ (ppm)/20 + Mg\ (ppm)/12.1) \times 50 = \text{Total Hardness as } CaCO_3$$

These operations are summarized in *Table 13*.

Water pH

You would think that the pH of the water is important but actually it is not. It is the pH of the mash that is important, and that number is dependent on all of the ions we have been discussing. In fact, the ion concentrations are not relevant by themselves and it is not until the water is combined with a specific grain bill that the mash pH is determined, and it is *that* pH which affects the activity of the mash enzymes and the propensity for the extraction of astringent tannins from the grain husks.

Many brewers have made the mistake of trying to change the pH of their water with salts or acids to bring it to the mash pH range before adding the malts. You can do it that way if you have enough experience with a particular recipe to know what the mash pH will turn out to be; but it is like putting the cart before the horse. It is better to start the mash, check the pH with test paper and then make any additions you feel are necessary to bring the pH to the proper range. Most of the time adjustment won't be needed due to the natural acidity of the malts.

However, most people don't like to trust to luck or go through the trial and error of testing the mash pH with pH paper and adding salts to get the right pH. There is a way to estimate your mash pH before you start and this method is discussed in a section to follow, but first, let's look at how the grain bill affects the mash pH.

Balancing the Malts and Minerals

Let me state the goal right up front: *for best results, the mash pH should be 5.1-5.5 when measured at mash temperature, and 5.4-5.8 when measured at room temperature*. (At mash temperature the pH will measure about 0.3 lower due to greater dissociation of the hydrogen ions.) When you mash 100% base malt grist with distilled water, you will usually get a mash pH between 5.7-5.8 (measured at room temperature). The natural acidity of roasted specialty malt additions (e.g. caramel, chocolate, black) to the mash can have a large effect on the pH. Using a dark crystal or roasted malt as 20% of the grainbill will often bring the pH down by half a unit (.5 pH).

CONCENTRATION CONVERSION TABLE

Table 13—Conversion Factors for Ion Concentrations

To Get	From	Do This
Ca (mEq/l)	Ca (ppm)	Divide by 20
Mg (mEq/l)	Mg (ppm)	Divide by 12.1
HCO_3 (mEq/l)	HCO_3 (ppm)	Divide by 61
$CaCO_3$ (mEq/l)	$CaCO_3$ (ppm)	Divide by 50
Ca (ppm)	Ca (mEq/l)	Multiply by 20
Ca (ppm)	Total Hardness as $CaCO_3$	You Can't
Ca (ppm)	Ca Hardness as $CaCO_3$	Divide by 50 and multiply by 20
Mg (ppm)	Mg (mEq/l)	Multiply by 12.1
Mg (ppm)	Total Hardness as $CaCO_3$	You Can't
Mg (ppm)	Mg Hardness as $CaCO_3$	Divide by 50 and multiply by 12.1
HCO3 (ppm)	Alkalinity as $CaCO_3$	Divide by 50 and multiply by 61
Ca Hardness as $CaCO_3$	Ca (ppm)	Divide by 20 and multiply by 50
Mg Hardness as $CaCO_3$	Mg (ppm)	Divide by 12.1 and multiply by 50
Total Hardness as $CaCO_3$	Ca as $CaCO_3$ and Mg as $CaCO_3$	Add them.
Alkalinity as $CaCO_3$	HCO_3 (ppm)	Divide by 61 and multiply by 50

In distilled water, 100% caramel malt would typically yield a mash pH of 4.5-4.8, chocolate malt 4.3-4.5, and black malt 4.0-4.2. The chemistry of the water determines how much of an effect each malt addition has.

The best way to explain this is to describe two of the world's most famous beers and their brewing waters. *See Table 14.* The Pilsen region of the Czech Republic was the birthplace of the Pilsener style of beer. A Pils is a soft, golden clear lager with a very clean hoppy taste. The water of Pilsen is very soft, free of most minerals and very low in bicarbonates.

The Pilsen brewers used an acid rest with this water to bring the pH down to the target mash range of 5.1-5.5 using only the pale lager malts.

The other beer to consider is Guinness, the famous stout from Ireland. The water of Ireland is high in bicarbonates (HCO_3^{-1}), and has a fair amount of calcium but not enough to balance the bicarbonate. This results in hard, alkaline water with a lot of buffering power. The high alkalinity of the water makes it difficult to produce light pale beers that are not harsh tasting. The water does not allow the pH of a 100% base malt mash to hit the target range, it remains higher (>pH 6) and this extracts phenolic and tannin compounds from the grain husks. The lower pH of an optimum mash (5.1-5.5) normally prevents these compounds from appearing in the beer. But why is this region of the world renowned for producing outstanding dark beers? The reason is the dark malt itself. The highly roasted black malts used in making Guinness Stout add acidity to the mash. The natural acidity of these malts counteracts the alkalinity of the carbonates in the water, lowering the mash pH into the target range.

The fact of the matter is that dark beer cannot be brewed in Pilsen, and light lagers can't be brewed in Dublin without adding the proper type and amount of buffering salts. Before you brew your first all-grain beer, you should get a water analysis from your local water utility and look at the mineral profile to establish which styles of beer you can best produce. The use of roasted malts such as Caramel, Chocolate, Black Patent, and the toasted malts such as Munich and Vienna, can be used successfully in areas where the water is alkaline (i.e., a pH greater than 7.5 and a carbonate level of more than 200 parts per million) to produce good mash conditions. If you live in an area where the water is very soft (like Pilsen), then you can add brewing salts to the mash and sparge water to help achieve the target pH. The next two sections of this chapter, *Residual Alkalinity and Mash pH*, and *Using Salts for Brewing Water Adjustment*, discuss how to do this.

Table 14 lists examples of classic beer styles and the mineral profile of the city that developed them. By looking at the city and its resulting style of beer, you will gain an appreciation for how malt chemistry and water chemistry interrelate. Descriptions of the region's beer styles follow.

Pilsen The very low hardness and alkalinity allow the proper mash pH to be reached with only base malts, achieving the soft rich flavor of fresh bread. The lack of sulfate provides for a mellow hop bitterness that does not overpower the soft maltiness; noble hop aroma is emphasized.

Dublin Famous for its stout, Dublin has the highest bicarbonate concentration of the cities of the British Isles, and Ireland embraces it with the darkest, maltiest beer in the world. The low levels of sodium, chloride and sulfate create an unobtrusive hop bitterness to properly balance all of the malt.

FAMOUS BREWING WATERS

Table 14—Water Profiles From Notable Brewing Cities

City/Style	Ca^{+2}	Mg^{+2}	HCO_3^{-1}	SO_4^{-2}	Na^{+1}	Cl^{-1}
Pilsen Pilsener	10	3	3	4	3	4
Dublin Dry Stout	118	4	319	54	12	19
Dortmund Export Lager	225	40	220	120	60	60
Vienna Vienna Lager	200	60	120	125	8	12
Munich Oktoberfest	76	18	152	10	?	2
London British Bitter	52	32	104	32	86	34
Edinburgh Scottish Ale	125	25	225	140	55	65
Burton India Pale Ale	352	24	320	820	54	16

Numbers are given in parts per million (ppm).

Sources

Burton—"Malting and Brewing Science Vol. 1"
Dortmund—Noonen, G.,"New Brewing Lager Beer"
Dublin— "The Practical Brewer",
Edinburgh—Noonen, G.,"New Brewing Lager Beer"
London—Westermann and Huige,"Fermentation Technology",
Munich—"Malting and Brewing Science Vol. 1"
Pilsen—Wahl-Henius,"American Handy Book"
Vienna—Noonen, G.,"New Brewing Lager Beer"

Dortmund Another city famous for pale lagers, Dortmund Export has less hop character than a Pilsner, with a more assertive malt character due to the higher levels of all minerals. The balance of the minerals is very similar to Vienna, but the beer is bolder, drier, and lighter in color.

Vienna The water of this city is similar to Dortmund, but lacks the level of calcium to balance the carbonates, and lacks as well the sodium and chloride for flavor. Attempts to imitate Dortmund Export failed miserably until a percentage of toasted malt was added to balance the mash, and Vienna's famous red-amber lagers were born.

Munich Although moderate in most minerals, alkalinity from carbonates is high. The smooth flavors of the dunkels, bocks and oktoberfests of the region show the success of using dark malts to balance the carbonates and acidify the mash. The relatively low sulfate content provides for a mellow hop bitterness that lets the malt flavor dominate.

London The higher carbonate level dictated the use of toasted and dark malts to balance the mash, but the chloride and high sodium content also smoothed the flavors out, resulting in the well known ruby-dark porters and copper-colored pale ales.

Edinburgh Think of misty Scottish evenings and you think of Strong Scotch ale–dark ruby highlights, a sweet malty beer with a mellow hop finish. The water is similar to London's but with a bit more bicarbonate and sulfate, making a beer that can embrace a heavier malt body while using less hops to achieve balance.

Burton-on-Trent Compared to London, the calcium and sulfate are remarkably high, but the hardness and alkalinity are balanced to nearly the degree of Pilsen. The high level of sulfate and low level of sodium produce an assertive, clean hop bitterness. Compared to the ales of London, Burton ales are paler, but much more bitter, although the bitterness is balanced by the higher alcohol and body of these ales.

Residual Alkalinity and Mash pH

Before you conduct your first mash, you probably want to be assured that it will probably work. Many people want to brew a dark stout or a light pilsener for their first all-grain beer, but these very dark and very light styles need the proper brewing water to achieve the desired mash pH. While there is not any surefire way to predict the exact pH, there are empirical methods and calculations that can put you in the ballpark, just like for hop IBU calculations. To estimate your probable mash pH, you will need the calcium, magnesium and alkalinity ion concentrations from your local water utility report.

Background:

In 1953, Gernan brewing scientist Paulas Kohlbach determined that 3.5 equivalents (Eq) of calcium reacts with malt phytin to release 1 equivalent of hydrogen ions which can "neutralize" 1 equivalent of water alkalinity. Magnesium, the other water hardness ion, also works but to a lesser extent, needing 7 equivalents to neutralize 1 equivalent of alkalinity. This chemical reaction does not require enzyme activity or an acid rest. Alkalinity which is not neutralized is termed "residual alkalinity" (abbreviated RA).

On a per volume basis, this can be expressed as:

mEq/L RA = mEq/L Alkalinity - [(mEq/L Ca)/3.5 + (mEq/L Mg)/7]
where mEq/L is defined as milliequivalents per liter.

This residual alkalinity will cause an all-base-malt mash to have a higher pH than is desirable, resulting in tannin extraction, etc. To counteract the RA, brewers in alkaline water areas like Dublin added dark roasted malts which have a natural acidity that brings the mash pH back into the right range. To help you determine what your RA is, and what your mash pH will probably be for a 100% base malt mash, I have put together a nomograph (*Figure 80, on the inside back cover*) that allows you to read the pH after marking-off your water's calcium, magnesium and alkalinity levels. To use the chart, you mark off the calcium and magnesium levels to determine an "effective" hardness (EH), then draw a line from that value through your alkalinity value to point to the RA and the approximate pH.

After determining your probable pH, the chart offers you two options:

a) You can plan to brew a style of beer that approximately matches the color guide above the pH scale

b) You can estimate an amount of calcium, magnesium, or bicarbonate to add to the brewing water to hit a targeted pH.

I will show you how this works in the following examples.

Determining the Beer Styles That Best Suit Your Water

1. A water report for Los Angeles, CA, states that the three ion concentrations are:

Ca (ppm) = 70

Mg (ppm) = 30

Alkalinity = 120 ppm as $CaCO_3$

2. Mark these values on the appropriate scales. (Indicated by circles and triangle on Figure 81.)

3. Draw a line between the Ca and Mg values to determine the Effective Hardness. (Middle circle.)

4. From the value for EH, draw a line through the Alkalinity value to intersect the RA/pH scale. This is your estimated mash pH (5.8).

5. Looking directly above the pH scale (*Figure 80*), the color guide shows a medium-light shade which corresponds to most amber, red and brown ales and lagers. Most Pale Ale, Brown Ale and Porter recipes can be brewed with confidence.

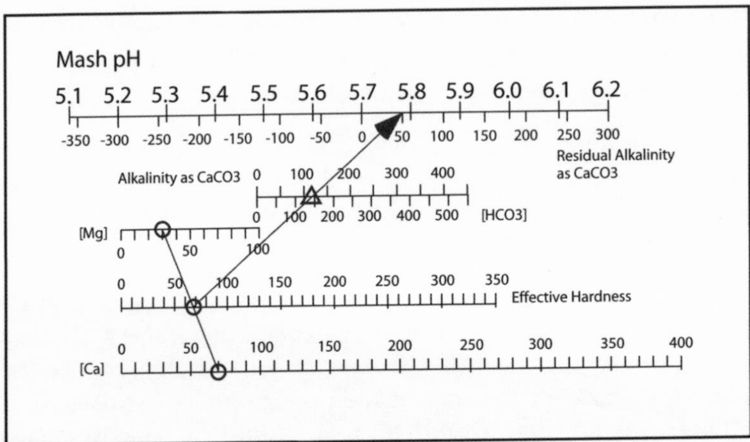

Figure 81—Estimating mash pH for Los Angeles.

Determining Calcium Additions to Lower the Mash pH

But what if you want to brew a much paler beer, like a Pilsener or a Helles? Then you will need to add more calcium to balance the alkalinity that your malt selection cannot.

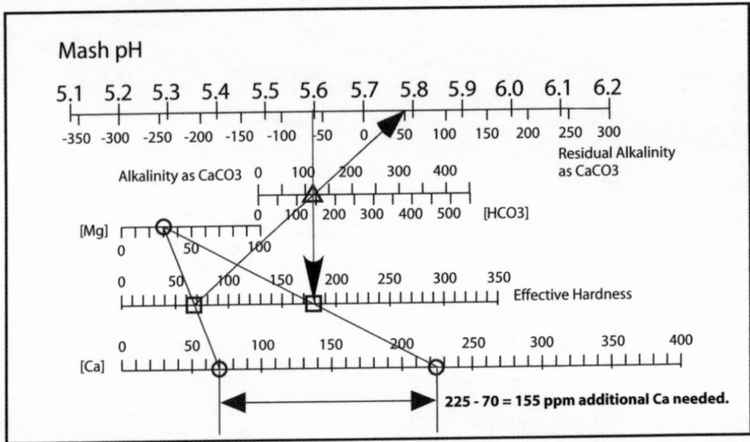

Figure 82—Using nomograph to determine calcium addition.

1. Go back to the nomograph and pick a point on the pH scale that is within the desired color range. In this example, I picked a value of about pH 5.6.

2. Draw a line from this pH value back through your Alkalinity value (from the water report), and determine your new EH value.

3. From the original Mg value from the report, draw a line through the new EH value and determine the new Ca value needed to produce this effective hardness.

4. Subtract the original Ca value from the new Ca value to determine how much calcium (per gallon) needs to be added. In this example, 145 ppm/gal. of additional calcium is needed.

5. The source for the calcium can be either calcium chloride or calcium sulfate (gypsum). See the following section for guidelines on just how much of these salts to add.

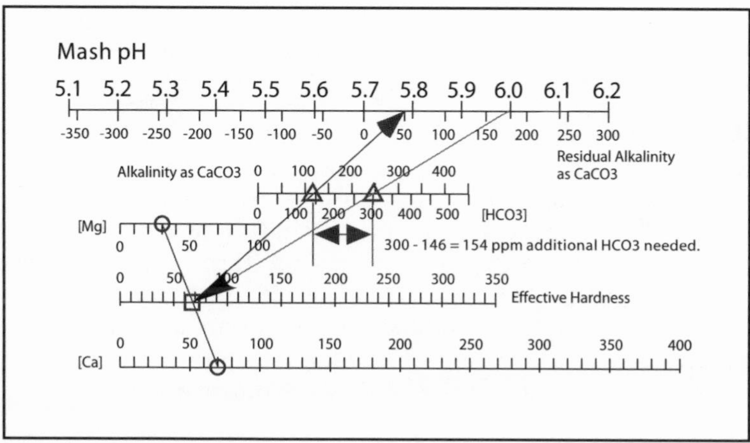

Figure 83—Using nomograph to determine bicarbonate addition.

Determining Bicarbonate Additions to Raise the Mash pH

Likewise, you can determine how much additional alkalinity (HCO_3) is needed to brew a dark stout if you have water with low alkalinity.

1. You determine your initial mash pH from your water report, and then determine your desired pH for the style you want to brew. In this example, I have selected pH 6, which corresponds to a dark beer on the color guideline.

2. The difference is that this time you draw a line from the desired pH to the original EH, passing through a new Alkalinity.

3. Subtract the original alkalinity from the new alkalinity to determine the additional bicarbonate needed. The additional bicarbonate can be added by either using sodium bicarbonate (baking soda) or calcium carbonate. Using calcium carbonate additions would also affect the EH, causing you to re-evaluate the whole system, while using baking soda would also contribute high levels of sodium, which can contribute harsh flavors at high levels. You will probably want to add some of each to achieve the right bicarbonate level without adding too much sodium or calcium.

Using Salts for Brewing Water Adjustment

Brewing water can be adjusted (to a degree) by the addition of brewing salts. Unfortunately, the addition of salts to water is not a matter of 2+2=4, it tends to be 3.9 or 4.1, depending. Water chemistry can be complicated; the rules contain exceptions and thresholds where other rules and exceptions take over.

Fortunately for most practical applications, you do not have to be that rigorous. You can add needed ions to your water with easily obtainable salts. To calculate how much to add, use the nomograph or another water chart to figure out what concentration is desired and then subtract your water's ion concentration to determine the difference. Next, consult *Table 15–Brewing Salts (page 190)* to see how much of an ion a particular salt can be expected to add. Don't forget to multiply the difference in concentration by the total volume of water you are working with.

Let's look back at the nomograph example where we determined that we needed 145 ppm of additional calcium ion. Let's say that 4 gallons of water are used in the mash.

1. Choose a salt to use to add the needed calcium. Let's use gypsum.

2. From Table 15, gypsum adds 61.5 ppm of Ca per gram of gypsum added to 1 gallon of water.

3. Divide the 145 ppm by 61.5 to determine the number of grams of gypsum needed per gallon to make the desired concentration. 145/61.5 = 2.4 grams

4. Next, multiply the number of grams per gallon by the number of gallons in the mash (4). 2.4 x 4 = 9.6 grams, which can be rounded to 10 grams.

5. Unless you have a gram scale handy, you will want to convert that to teaspoons which is more convenient. There are about 4 grams of gypsum per teaspoon, which gives us 10/4 = 2.5 teaspoons of gypsum to be added to the mash.

6. Lastly, you need to realize how much sulfate this addition has made. 2.5 grams per gallon equals 368 ppm of sulfate added to the mash, which is a lot. In this case, it would probably be a good idea to use calcium chloride for half of the addition.

Table 15 provides information on the use and results of each salt's addition. Brewing salts should be used sparingly to make up for gross deficiencies or overabundance of ions. The concentrations given are for 1 gram dissolved in 1 gallon of distilled water. Dissolution of 1 gram of a salt in your water will probably result in a slightly different value due to your water's specific mineral content and pH. However, the results should be reasonably close.

There are several brewing software programs that are very handy for these types of water calculations as well as all types of mashing and recipe calculations. Two examples are *Promash* at *www.promash.com*, and *Strangebrew* at *www.strangebrew.com*. The functionality of these brewing applications have been thoroughly reviewed and I can assure you that they are comprehensive and easy to use.

My final advice on water treatment is that if you want to brew a pale beer and have water that is very high in carbonates and low in calcium, then your best bet is to use bottled water* from the store or to dilute your water with distilled water and add gypsum or calcium chloride to make up the calcium deficit. Watch your sulfate and chloride counts though. Mineral dilution with water is not as straightforward as it is with wort dilution, due to the various ion buffering effects, but it will be reasonably close.

Good Luck!

* *You should be able to get an analysis of the bottled water by calling the manufacturer. I have done this with a couple of different brands.*

BREWING SALTS

Table 15—Brewing Salts for Water Adjustment

Brewing Salts for Raising Mash pH

Brewing Salt (formula) Common Name	Conc. at 1 gram/gal.	Grams per level teaspoon	Comments
Calcium Carbonate ($CaCO3$) a.k.a. Chalk	105 ppm Ca^{+2} 158 ppm CO_3^{-2}	1.8	Because of its limited solubility it is only effective when added directly to the mash. Use for making dark beers in areas of soft water. Use nomograph and monitor the mash pH with pH test papers to determine how much to add.
Sodium Bicarbonate ($NaHCO3$) a.k.a. Baking Soda	75 ppm Na^{+1} 191 ppm HCO_3^{-1}	4.4	Raises pH by adding alkalinity If your mash pH is too low or your water has low residual alkalinity, then you can use this in the same way as calcium carbonate.

Brewing Salts for Lowering Mash pH

Brewing Salt (formula) Common Name	Conc. at 1 gram/gal.	Grams per level teaspoon	Comments
Calcium Sulfate ($CaSO4$ *2 $H2O$) a.k.a. Gypsum	61.5 ppm Ca^{+2} 147.4 ppm SO_4^{-2}	4.0	Useful for adding calcium if the water is low in sulfate. Can be used to add sulfate "crispness" to the hop bitterness.
Calcium Chloride ($CaCl2$ *2 $H2O$)	72 ppm Ca^{+2} 127 ppm Cl^{-1}	3.4	Useful for adding calcium if the water is low in chlorides.
Magnesium Sulfate ($MgSO4$ *7 $H2O$) a.k.a. Epsom Salt	26 ppm Mg^{+2} 103 ppm SO_4^{-2}	4.5	Lowers pH by a small amount Used to add sulfate "crispness" to the hop bitterness.

Chapter 16

The Methods of Mashing

In chapters 14 and 15 you learned about the chemistry going on in the mash tun. In this chapter we will discuss how to physically manipulate the mash to create a desired character in the wort and the beer. There are two basic schemes for mashing: Single Temperature–a compromise temperature for all the mash enzymes, and Multi-Rest–where two or more temperatures are used to favor different enzyme groups. You can heat the mash in two ways also, by the addition of hot water (Infusion) or by heating the mash tun directly. There is also a combination method, called Decoction Mashing, where part of the mash is heated on the stove and added back to the main mash to raise the temperature. All of these mashing schemes are designed to achieve saccharification (convert starches to fermentable sugars). But the route taken to that goal can have a considerable influence on the overall wort character. Certain beer styles need a particular mash scheme to arrive at the right wort for the style.

Single Temperature Infusion

This method is the simplest, and does the job for most beer styles. All of the crushed malt is mixed (infused) with hot water to achieve a mash temperature of 150–158°F, depending on the style of beer being made. The infusion water temperature varies with the water-to-grain ratio being used for the mash, but generally the initial "strike water" temperature is 10–15°F above the target mash temperature. The equation is listed below in the section, "Calculations for Infusions." The mash should be held at the saccharification temperature for about an hour, hopefully losing no more than a couple degrees. The mash temperature can be maintained by placing the mash tun in a warm oven, an insulated box or by adding heat from the stove. The goal is to achieve a steady temperature.

One of the best ways to maintain the mash temperature is to use an ice chest or picnic cooler as the mash tun. This is the method I recommend throughout the rest of this section of the book. Instructions for building a picnic cooler mash/lauter tun are given in Appendix D.

If the initial infusion of water does not achieve the desired temperature, you can add more hot water according to the infusion calculations.

Multi-Rest Mashing

A popular multi-rest mash schedule is the 40°C-60°C-70°C (104-140-158°F) mash, using a half hour rest at each temperature, first advocated for homebrewers by George Fix. This mash schedule produces high yields and good fermentability. The time at 40°C improves the liquefaction of the mash and promotes enzyme activity. As can be seen in *Figure 79–Enzyme Ranges,* several enzymes are at work, liquefying the mash and breaking down the starchy endosperm so the starches can dissolve. As mentioned in the previous chapter in the section on the Acid Rest, resting the mash at this temperature has been show to improve the yield, regardless of the malts used. Varying the times spent at the 60 and 70°C rests allows you to adjust the fermentable sugar profiles. For example, a 20 minute rest at 60°C, combined with a 40 minute rest at 70°C produces a sweet, heavy, dextrinous beer; while switching the times at those temperatures would produce a drier, lighter bodied, more alcoholic beer from the same grain bill.

If you use less modified malts, such as a German Pils malt, a multi-rest mash will produce maltier tasting beers although they need a protein rest to fully realize their potential. In this case the mash schedule suggested by Fix is 50-60-70°C, again with half hour rests. The rest at 50°C takes the place of the liquefaction rest at 40°C and provides the necessary protein rest. This schedule is well suited for producing continental lager beers. These schedules are provided as guidelines. You, as the brewer, have complete control over what you can choose to do. Play with the times and temperatures and have fun.

Multi-rest mashes require you to add heat to the mash to achieve the various temperature rests. You can add the heat in a couple of ways, either by infusions or by direct heat. If you are using a kettle as a mash tun, you can heat it directly using the stove or a stand-alone hotplate. (See Figure 84) The first temperature rest is achieved by infusion as in the Single Temperature mash described above. The subsequent rest(s) are achieved by carefully adding heat from the stove and constant stirring to keep the mash from developing hotspots and scorching. The mash can be placed in a prewarmed oven (125-150°F) to keep the mash from losing heat during the rests. After the conversion, the mash is carefully poured or ladled from the mash tun into the lauter tun and lautered. The hot mash and wort is susceptible to oxidation from hot side aeration (HSA) due to splashing at this stage, which can lead to long term flavor stability problems.

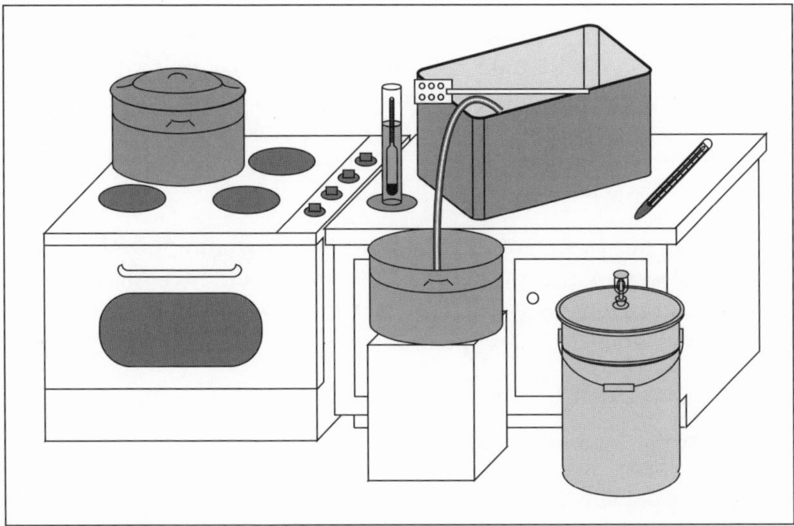

Figure 84—Mashing on the Stove- The grist is added to a pot of hot water on the stove for the first temperature rest. The mash is then placed in the oven (warm) to help maintain the temperature for the desired time. Then the mash pot is returned to the stovetop to be heated to the next rest. After mashing the mash is transferred to the lauter tun and lautered into the boiling pot. The mash tun (first pot) is then used to heat water for the sparge.

If you are using a picnic cooler for your mash tun, multi-rest mashes are a bit trickier. You need to start out with a stiff mash (e.g. .75-1 quarts per pound of grain), to leave yourself enough room in the tun for the additional water. Usually only 2 temperature rests are possible with this method because the amount of heat necessary to change the temperature of the mash increases with each addition. Reaching a third rest is possible if the change in temperature is only a few degrees. For example, raising the mash temperature for 8 lbs. of grain from 150°F to 158°F at a mash ratio of 2 quarts per pound would require approximately 2.7 quarts of boiling water.

Infusion Calculations

These calculations allow you to estimate the amount of heat provided by a volume of hot water so you can predict how much that heat will change the temperature of the mash. This method makes a few simplifications, one of which is the assumption that no heat will be lost to the surroundings, but we can minimize this error by pre-heating the tun with some boiling hot water.

Most of the thermodynamic constants used in the following equations have been rounded to single digits to make the math easier. The difference in the results is at most a cup of hot water and less than 1°F. Experience has shown the equation to be fairly reliable and consistent batch-to-batch, as long as you pre-heat the tun.

When mixing hot water with dry grain for the initial infusion, the equation is algebraically simplified so that the amount of grain does not matter, only your initial grain temperature, the target mash temperature, and the ratio (r) of water to grain in quarts per pound.

Initial Infusion Equation

Strike Water Temperature $Tw = (.2/r)(T2 - T1) + T2$

Mash Infusion Equation

$Wa = (T2 - T1)(.2G + Wm)/(Tw - T2)$

where:

r = The ratio of water to grain in quarts per pound.

Wa = The amount of boiling water added (in quarts).

Wm = The total amount of water in the mash (in quarts).

T1 = The initial temperature (°F) of the mash.

T2 = The target temperature (°F) of the mash.

Tw = The actual temperature (°F) of the infusion water.

G = The amount of grain in the mash (in pounds).

The infusion water does not have to be boiling, a common choice is to use the sparge water at 170°F. Then Tw becomes 170°F and more water (Wa) will be needed to make up the additional quantity of heat.

Multiple Rest Infusion Example:

This example will push the envelope with three rests. We are going to mash 8 lbs. of grain through a 104 °F, 140 °F, and 158 °F (40, 60, and 70 °C) multi-rest mash schedule. For the purposes of this example, we will assume that the temperature of the dry grain is 70 °F (21 °C). The first infusion will need to take the temperature of the mash from 70 °F to 104 °F.

1. We will start with an initial water ratio of 1 qt/lb. Using the initial infusion equation, the strike water temperature is:

   Tw = (.2/r)(T2-T1) + T2

   = (.2/1)(104 - 70) +104 = 110.8 or 111°F

2. For the second infusion, to bring the temperature to 140 °F, we need to use the mash infusion equation. At 1 qt/lb, Wm is 8 qt. We will assume that our boiling water for the infusions has cooled somewhat to 210 °F.

   Wa = (T2 - T1) X (0.2G + Wm) ÷ (Tw - T2)

   Wa = (140 - 104) X (1.6 + 8) ÷ (210 - 140)

   Wa = 36 X 9.6 ÷ 70 = 4.9 qt

3. For the third infusion, the total water volume is now 8 + 4.9 = 12.9 qt.

   Wa = (158 - 140) X (1.6 + 12.9) ÷ (210 - 158)

   Wa = 18 X 15.1 ÷ 52 = 5.2 qt

   The total volume of water required to perform this schedule is:

   8 + 4.9 + 5.2 = 18.1 qt, or 4.5 gallons.

   The final water-to-grain ratio has increased to 2.26 qt/lb (18.1 ÷ 8).

Decoction Mashing

Decoction mashing is a way to conduct multi-step mashes without adding additional water or applying heat to the mash tun. It involves removing about a third of the mash to another pot where it is heated to conversion temperature, rested, then boiled and returned to the mash tun. The portion removed should be pretty stiff, no free water should be showing above the top of the grain.

This procedure accomplishes three things. First, the addition of boiling hot gruel to the main mash raises the temperature of the mash to the next rest. Second, the boiling process breaks up the starch molecules of the unconverted grist and produces a higher degree of extraction from the less modified continental malts. Lastly, it makes it possible to achieve the full, rich maltiness characteristic of German Oktoberfest and other continental lagers. For more information on decoction mashing, see the *Recommended Reading Section* in *Appendix F*.

Summary

When all is said and done though, single rest infusion mashing is the easiest method for producing an all-grain wort. The most common homebrewing mash schedule consists of a water-to-grain ratio of 1.5-2 quarts per pound, and holding the mash between 150-155°F for 1 hour. Probably 90% of the beer styles in the world today can be produced with this method.

BREWING TIP

Use Decoctions to Fix Infusions

Let's suppose your infusions didn't quite work—the mash temperature is too low. If you have added all the hot water the mash tun can take, and/or you are over 3 quarts per pound ratio, you can use a small decoction to add heat without adding any more water!

Simply take a 2 quart sauce pan and dip it into the mash. Pull out a thick portion (mostly grain) and heat it to the conversion temperature of 155°F, hold it there for about 10 minutes, and then boil it for about 5 minutes. Return this hot decoction to the mash tun and stir it in evenly to raise the mash temperature without creating hotspots.

Check your mash temperature. If it is still low, the decoction process can be repeated.

Chapter 17

Getting the Wort Out (Lautering)

Okay, let's see where we are: we have discussed the different types of grain and how they can be used, we have talked about the mash enzymes and how they are affected by temperature and pH, and we have learned how the brewing water and grainbill combine to determine the mash pH and how we can manipulate it. In the last chapter, we moved from the chemical aspects of the mash to the physical. We learned about the several basic methods of conducting a mash and producing the wort. In this chapter, we are going to discuss how we separate the malt sugars from the grain.

Aspects of Lautering

Lautering is the method most brewers use to separate the sweet wort from the mash. A lauter tun consists of a large vessel to hold the mash and a false bottom or manifold to allow the wort to drain out and leave the grain behind. Lautering can be conducted several ways, but it usually consists of three steps. These are: mashout, recirculation, and sparging.

What is Mashout?

Before the sweet wort is drained from the mash and the grain is rinsed (sparged) of the residual sugars, many brewers perform a mashout. Mashout is the term for raising the temperature of the mash to 170°F prior to lautering. This step stops all of the enzyme action (preserving your fermentable sugar profile) and makes the grainbed and wort more fluid. For most mashes with a ratio of 1.5-2 quarts of water per pound of grain, the mashout is not needed. The grainbed will be loose enough to flow well. For a thicker mash, or a mash composed of more than 25% of wheat or oats, a mashout may be needed to prevent a set mash/stuck sparge. This is when the grain bed plugs up and no liquid will flow through it. A mashout helps prevent this by making the sugars more fluid; like the difference between warm and cold honey. The mashout step can be done using external heat or by adding hot water according to the multi-rest infusion calculations. *(See Chapter 16.)* A lot of homebrewers tend to skip the mashout step for most mashes with no consequences.

What is Recirculation?

After the grain bed has settled and is ready to be lautered, the first few quarts of wort are drawn out through the drain of the lauter tun and poured back in on top of the grainbed. The first few quarts are almost always cloudy with proteins and grain debris and this step filters out the undesired material from getting in your boiling pot. The wort should clear fairly quickly. After the worts starts running clear (it will still be dark and a little bit cloudy), you are ready to collect the wort and sparge the grainbed. Re-circulation may be necessary anytime the grain bed is disturbed and bits of grain and husk appear in the runoff, though if your grainbed has good depth, disturbing it is unlikely.

What is Sparging?

Sparging is the rinsing of the grain bed to extract as much of the sugars from the grain as possible without extracting mouth-puckering tannins from the grain husks. Typically, 1.5 times as much water is used for sparging as for mashing (e.g., 8 lbs. malt at 2 qt./lb. = 4 gallon mash, so up to 6 gallons of sparge water). The temperature of the sparge water is important. The water should be no more than 170°F, as husk tannins become more soluble above this temperature, depending on wort pH. This could lead to astringency in the beer.

The wort should be drained slowly to obtain the best extraction. Sparge time varies (.5-2.5 hours) depending on the amount of grain and the type of lautering system. Sparging means "to sprinkle" and this explains why you may have seen or heard discussion of "sparge arms" or sprinklers over the grain bed for lautering (continuous method). If you properly maintain an inch of free water over the grainbed to assure fluidity, there is no real reason to use one, except that they are nifty. There are three main methods of sparging: English, batch and continuous.

English Method In the English method of sparging, the wort is completely drained from the grain bed before more water is added for a second mash and drained again. The first and second runnings are often used to make separate beers. The second running is lighter in gravity and was traditionally used for making a Small Beer, a lighter bodied, low alcohol beer suitable for high volume quaffing at mealtimes.

Batch Sparging This method is a U.S. homebrewing practice where large volumes of sparge water are added to the mash all-at-once, instead of gradually, and is more often used with the larger rectangular chest coolers. The grain bed is allowed to settle, re-circulated for clarity, and then the wort is drained off. Usually two or sometimes three sparges are combined to create the wort. It is less efficient than continuous sparging (you will use 10-15% more grain than a standard recipe), but it is convenient. This method differs from the English method in that the different runnings are combined to produce a single beer. Batch and no-sparge brewing will be described fully at the end of *Chapter 18–Brewing Your First All-Grain Beer*.

Continuous Sparging This method usually results in better extractions. The wort is re-circulated and drained until about an inch of wort remains above the grain bed. The sparge water is gently added, as necessary, to keep the fluid at least at that level. The goal is to gradually replace the wort with the water, stopping the sparge when the gravity is ≤1.008, or when enough wort has been collected, whichever comes first. This method demands more attention by the brewer, but can produce a higher yield.

Figure 85—A well crushed grist with a good mix of large and small particles and unshredded husk.

A Good Crush Means Good Lautering

There is a trade-off between particle size and extraction efficiency when mashing crushed grain. Fine particles are more readily converted by the enzymes and yield a better extraction. However, if all the grain were finely ground you would end up with porridge which could not be lautered. Coarse particles allow for good fluid flow and lautering but are not converted as well by the enzymes. A good crush has a range of particle sizes that allows for a compromise between extraction and lautering.

A good crush is essential for getting the best mash efficiency and extraction. There are two basic kinds of grain mill commercially available today. The Corona corn mill uses two counter-rotating disks to grind the malt. This often results in finely ground flour and shredded husks, which is not good for lautering purposes. Setting the crush too fine often leads to stuck sparges. This type of grain mill can produce a good crush without too much husk damage if the spacing is set properly (.035-.042 inch). It is the least expensive kind of grain mill, usually selling at about $50.00.

The other type of grain mill crushes the malt between two rollers like a clothes wringer. There is much less damage to the husks this way which helps keep the grainbed from compacting during the sparge. Two roller mills are more expensive than the Corona mill, about $100-150.00, but are often adjustable, and will give a better, more consistent crush to the grain with less husk damage. Examples of this type of mill are the MaltMill–Jack Schmidling Productions, Marengo, IL, the Philmill 2–Listermann Mfg. Inc, Cincinnati, OH, the Valley Mill–Valley Brewing Equipment, Ottawa, ON, and the Brewtek Mill–Brewer's Resource, Lake Forest, CA.

There is also a single roller mill which uses one roller against a fixed plate to crush the grain. It is the (original) PhilMill–Listermann Mfg. Inc, Cincinnati, OH, and also produces a good crush, like the two roller mills. It sells for about $80.

The insoluble grain husks are important for a good lauter. The grainbed forms its own filter from the husk and grain material. The husks prevent the grainbed from completely settling and allow water to flow through the bed, extracting the sugar. It is important to keep the grainbed fully saturated with water so it doesn't get compacted and impermeable. The wort is drawn out through the bottom of the bed by means of a false bottom or manifold which has openings that allow the wort to be drawn off, but prevent the grain from being sucked in as well. Usually these openings are narrow slots, or holes up to an eighth of an inch in diameter. See *Appendix D* for details on lauter tun design.

Getting the Most From the Grainbed

The grainbed can be a few inches to a couple feet deep, but the optimum depth depends on the overall tun geometry and the total amount of grain being mashed. If the grainbed is very shallow, from lautering too little grain in too large a tun, then the filter bed will be inadequate, the wort won't clear, and you will probably get hazy beer. A minimum useful depth is probably about 4 inches but a depth of 8–18 inches is preferable. In general, deeper is better, but if it is too deep, then the grainbed is more easily compacted and may not let any wort through, making lautering nearly impossible.

Recalling *Chapter 12*, extraction efficiency is determined by measuring the amount of sugar extracted from the grain after lautering and comparing it to the theoretical maximum yield. In an optimum mash, all the available starch is converted to sugar. This amount varies depending on the malt, but it is generally 37-ish points per pound per gallon for a 2 row barley base malt. This means that if 1 pound of this malt is crushed and mashed in 1 gallon of water, the wort would have a specific gravity of 1.037. Most brewers would get something closer to 1.030. This difference represents an extraction efficiency of 80%, and the difference could be attributed to poor conversion in the mash, but it can also be caused by lautering inefficiency.

Let's think about the grainbed–it is composed of grain particles, sugars and insoluble grain husks. Ideally, the particles should all be small with an equal spacing between them and all particles would be equally well rinsed. Of course, this isn't the case. The grain particles vary quite a bit in size and this variation leads to regions of greater density within the grainbed. Since fluids always follow the path of least resistance, this leads to a problem of preferential flow through the grainbed causing some regions of grain to be completely rinsed and other regions to not be rinsed at all. Non-uniform flow is a major cause of poor extraction.

Our goal in the lautering process is to rinse all the grain particles in the tun of all the sugar, despite all of the non-ideal conditions. To do this we need to focus on two things:

- Keep the grainbed completely saturated with water.
- Make sure that the fluid flow through the grainbed to the drain is slow and uniform.

By keeping the grainbed covered with at least an inch of water, the grainbed is in a fluid state and not subject to compaction by gravity. Each particle is free to move and the liquid is free to move around it. Settling of the grainbed due to loss of fluidity leads to preferential flow (a major cause of poor extraction) and can result in a stuck sparge.

The more uniformly the water moves through the grainbed, the more sugar it can extract from the grain. This results in better extraction efficiency. Fluid flow through the grainbed is complex and depends greatly on the design of your lauter tun.

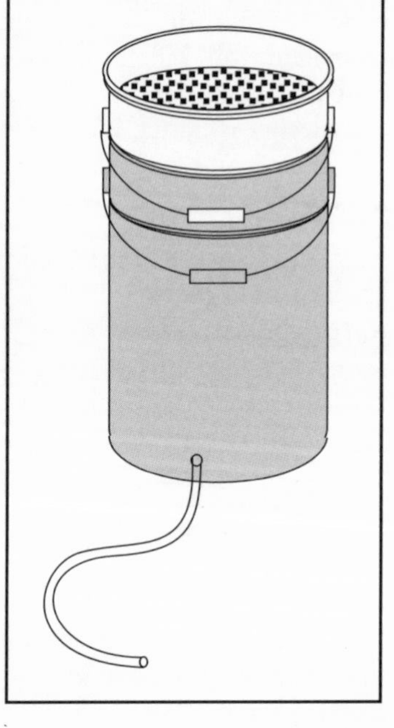

The original (at least the most popularized) home lautering system was probably the bucket-in-a-bucket false bottom championed by Charlie Papazian in *The Complete Joy of Homebrewing (1984)*. This setup is fairly effective and very cheap to assemble. Using two food-grade 5-gallon buckets, the inner bucket is drilled with lots of small holes to form a false bottom that holds the grain and allows the liquid to run off; the sweet wort passes into the outer bucket and is drawn off through a hole in the side. False bottom systems usually rinse the grainbed uniformly, but there are two drawbacks that need to be considered. The first is that false bottoms have the potential to flow too fast because of the very large drainage area available and can compact the grainbed as a result. Stuck sparges from draining too fast are a common problem for homebrewers using false bottoms for the first time. Secondly, false bottoms need to fit/seal well around the edges to prevent flow from bypassing the grainbed.

Picnic coolers offer a few advantages not available with buckets, adding both simplicity and efficiency. A cooler's built-in insulation provides better mash temperature stability than a bucket can provide. Their size also allows mashing and lautering in the same vessel. Thus it's as simple as pouring the grain into the cooler, adding hot water, waiting the hour, and then draining the sweet wort.

Coolers offer two options for lautering: they can accommodate traditional false bottoms or use a simple slotted-pipe "manifold" system. Ready-made false bottoms (e.g., Phil's Phalse Bottom–Listermann Mfg., and the Fermentap false bottom) are available for round coolers, but you can also build a slotted pipe manifold for just a few dollars. They can be built to fit whatever type and size of cooler you have. The total investment for the cooler, manifold and all the parts required to convert it into a mash/lauter tun is usually less than $40. Everything you need to build one of these tuns is readily available at a hardware store.

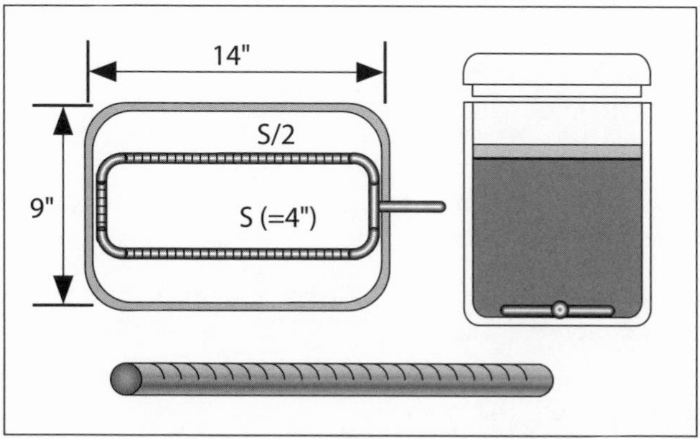

Figure 88—Rectangular Cooler Mash/Lauter Tun showing top and end views of the cooler along with a detail of the slotted manifold pipe. (The other thing is the lid.)

Manifolds are less likely to compact the mash and cause a stuck sparge at high flow rates during lautering, due to having less open drain area. But overall, their efficiency is only a few percent less than a false bottom. This brings us to the question–*what is the optimum outflow rate?* There is a trade-off: if you lauter too quickly you will collect a lot of wort but have a low extraction, if you lauter too slowly you will have great extraction but you will take all day to do it. Most homebrewers use the rule of thumb of 1 quart per minute. If your extraction is low, i.e. less than 28 points/pound/gallon, you should try a lower flow rate. The best way to control your flow rate by using a ball valve or stopcock on the outflow.

Another extraction efficiency problem that needs to be considered when designing your tun is preferential flow down the walls. The smooth space between the grainbed and the wall of the tun can be the path of least resistance to the drain. To minimize this short circuiting, false bottoms should fit tightly and manifold pipes should be spaced so that the distance from the outer pipes to the wall of the tun is half of the inter pipe spacing *(see Figure 88)*. For example, a manifold with a pipe spacing of 4 inches should have 2 inches of space between the manifold and the adjacent walls. Preferential flow is more of a concern in false-bottom systems because a loose fitting false bottom with a gap at the wall presents an unobstructed flow path to the drain.

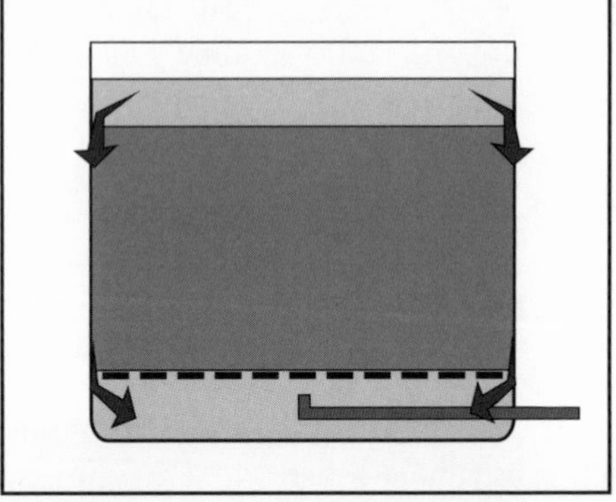

Figure 89—Preferential flow along the walls and around the edge of the false bottom.

It may be difficult to visualize how all of these guidelines combine to help you lauter efficiently, so let's summarize:

- Maintain an inch of water over the grainbed during the lauter to assure fluidity and free flow.
- Regulate the flow with a valve to assure the best extraction and prevent compacting the grainbed.
- When designing your lauter tun for more uniform flow, either:
  - Make sure the false bottom fits well.
  - Space the manifold pipes away from the walls.

Complete instructions and design details for building a mash/lauter tun from a cooler are given in *Appendix D–Building a Mash/Lauter Tun.* I also elaborate on how to design the manifold for the most uniform flow through the grainbed.

In the next chapter we will get your feet wet (probably literally). I am going to walk you through your first all-grain mash from start to finish. I will describe some extra equipment you will probably need and then we will get started.

Chapter 18

Your First All-Grain Batch

One of the comments you will most often hear from first time all-grainers is, "I didn't realize it would be so easy!" Making beer from scratch is really very easy, it just takes some preparation. So far, you have seen the various steps and delved into the details in a few areas, but the best way to learn is by doing. Hopefully you have done several extract batches and a couple extract-and-specialty grain batches by now. You should know to have your ingredients and brewing water ready, with everything clean and sanitized. Unless you have purchased a grain mill, have the grain crushed for you at the brew shop. Crushed grain will stay fresh for about two weeks if kept cool and dry.

Additional Equipment

- Mash/Lauter Tun
- Sparge Water Pot (5 gallon minimum size)
- Wort Boiling Pot (8 gallon size preferred)
- Hydrometer

Mash/Lauter Tun The easiest way to brew all-grain beer is to use a picnic cooler mash/lauter tun. I described how they can aid mashing and lautering in the last chapter, and instructions for building one are given in *Appendix D*. A 24 quart rectangular cooler or 5 gallon round beverage cooler are probably the best choices for 5 gallon batches. The illustrations that follow in this chapter show the 24 quart rectangular cooler.

Sparge Water Pot You will need a large pot to heat your mash water and your sparge water. You can use your old 5 gallon brewpot for this, or you can purchase a larger 8 gallon pot. You will probably use 3 gallons of water for a typical mash, and you will need about 4-6 gallons of water for a typical sparge, so be forewarned.

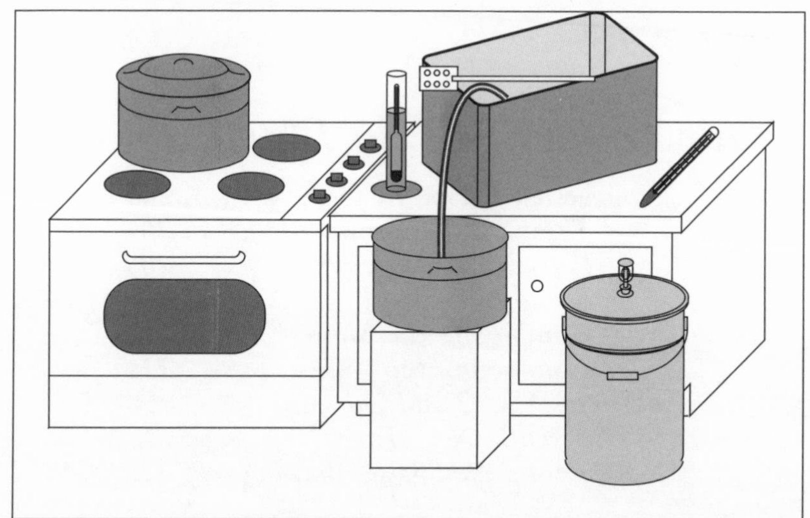

Figure 90—Common Mashing Setup. This picture depicts what is probably the most common home mashing setup. The Mash/Lauter Tun sits on the counter near the stove and two large pots are used: one to prepare the sparge water and the other to receive and boil the wort.

Wort Boiling Pot You will need to get a new brewpot because you are going to be boiling the whole batch. You need a pot that can comfortably hold 6 gallons without boiling over. An enamelware 8 gallon pot is the most economical choice at about $40.

Hydrometer You will want to purchase a hydrometer if you don't have one already. A hydrometer allows you to monitor the extraction process and its use is explained in *Appendix A.*

Suggested Recipe

For this beer, we will make a Brown Ale, using three malts and a single temperature infusion mash. I will take you through the entire grain brewing procedure and then go back and discuss some options for various steps. Of course, if there is another beer style that you prefer, you are welcome to use one of the other recipes from *Chapter 19*. Be sure to adjust your hopping schedule to take the full volume boil and lower boil gravity into account.

Tittabawassee Brown Ale

Malts		Gravity Pts.
7 lbs. of 2 row base malt		35
1 lb. of Crystal 60L malt		5
¼ lb. of Chocolate malt		1
BG for 6 Gallons		1.041
OG for 5 Gallons		1.049

Hops	Boil Time	IBUs
¾ oz of Nugget (10%)	60	28
1 oz of Willamette (5%)	15	9
Total IBUs		37

Yeast	Fermentation Schedule
British Ale (liquid)	Primary ferment at 65°F for 2 weeks. Or 1 week primary and 2 weeks secondary.

Options	
Partial Mash	3 lbs. of 2 row base malt 1 lb. of Crystal 60L Malt ¼ lb. of Chocolate Malt
(Add to Boil)	3 lbs. of Pale DME

Mash Schedule–Single Temperature Infusion

Rest Type	Temperature	Duration
Conversion	152°F	60 min

Mash Schedule:

- Single infusion of 165°F Strike Water at a ratio of 1.5 quarts/pound grain (~12.5 quarts).
- Target Mash temperature of 154°F. Mash time of 1 hour. No Mashout.
- Lauter to collect 6-7 gallons of wort total. (Or 3-4 gallons if Partial Mashing.)
- Target gravity of 1.049 for 5 gallons (or 1.041 for 6 gallons of wort before boiling.)
- Adjust the amount of Chocolate Malt (¼-½ lb.)depending on how brown you want it.

Partial Mash Option

An option for beginning all-grainers is to take the transition only half-way. Use a small mash to provide wort complexity and freshness, but use a can of extract to provide the bulk of the fermentables. This option is particularly attractive for brewers living in small apartments with not much room in the kitchen for large pieces of equipment. Using a partial mash was how I first started using grain and I was extremely pleased with the results.

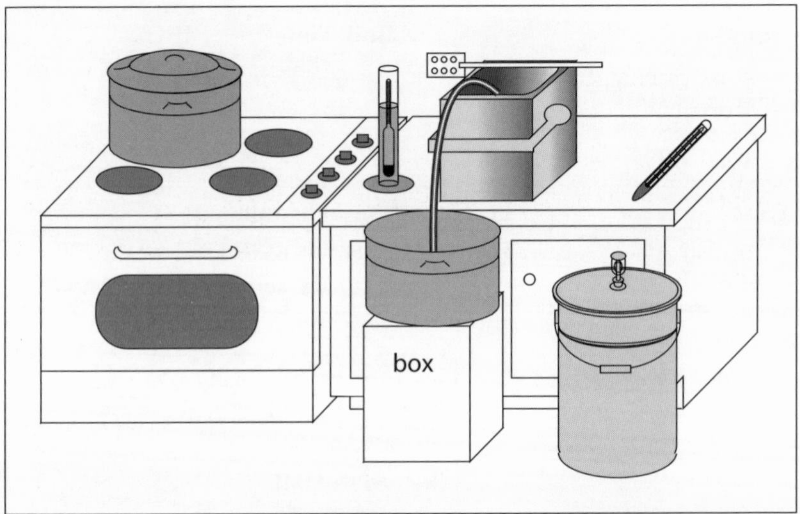

A partial mash is carried out just like a full scale mash, but the volume of wort collected is only the 3-4 gallons that you would normally boil when brewing with extract. The procedure is also similar to using extract & steeped specialty grain, the extract is added to the grain-based wort and the boil proceeds as usual. You can mash in either a pot on the stove or buy a smaller cooler (3-4 gal.) and build a small manifold. You probably have a small beverage cooler already that would work well with a drop-in manifold like that shown with the rectangular cooler in *Figures 92 & 93.* One advantage to using a manifold, versus pouring the mash into a strainer, is that you avoid aerating the wort while it is hot. As was discussed in *Chapter 6–Yeast,* and *Chapter 8–Fermentation,* oxidation of hot wort at any time will lead to flavor stability problems in the beer later.

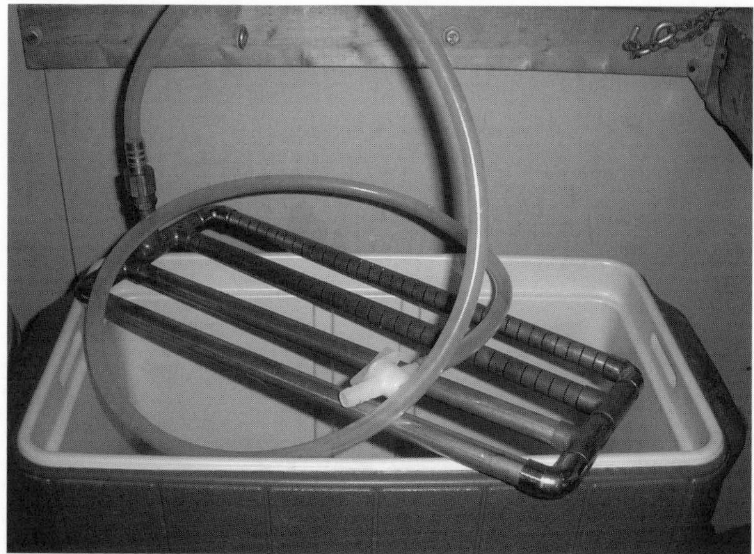

Figure 92—This view shows the slots cut in two of the pipes of copper manifold. The slots should face down. The design of copper manifolds is discussed in Appendix D.

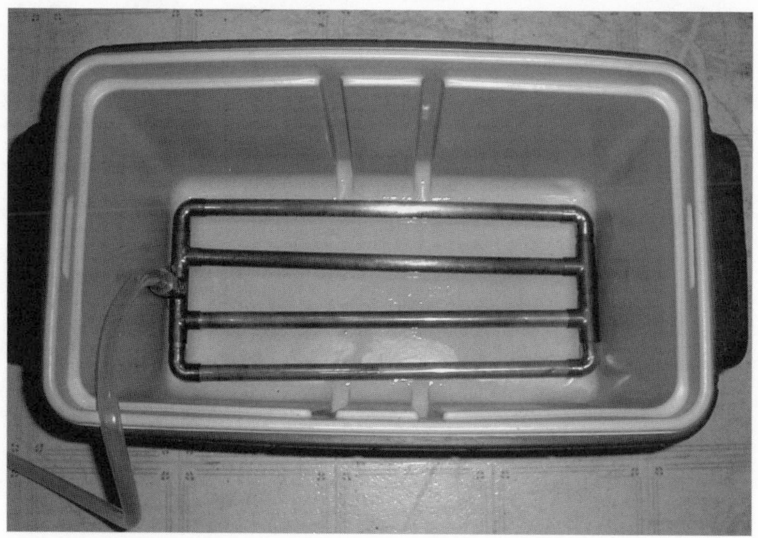

Figure 93—The lautering manifold is now installed in the bottom of the cooler. Designs will vary depending on what you have to work with. (According to my kids, the pipes are supposed to be perfectly parallel...)

Figures 94 & 95—These two types of mash/lauter tun coolers are part of a three tier, gravity fed brewing system. A three tier setup is not required when using a cooler, it just happens to be the way I do it. More often brewers use the cooler in the kitchen, and boil in other pots. I used to do it that way before my wife decided she wanted my hobby out of her kitchen.

Figure 96—This is my hot water tank that feeds the sparge. It is a converted stainless steel beer keg with the top cut out and fittings installed. A thermometer is shown in front and the sight tube along the left side shows how much water is being used. The keg sits on top of a propane burner which is very handy when heating 6+ gallons of water. Another propane burner fires the boiling kettle. Full volume boils for a 5 gallon batch can be difficult on a kitchen stove; propane is an economical alternative. Propane burners are a necessity when brewing 10 gallon batches.
You can also fill another cooler with your sparge water and drain it to your lauter tun. Many homebrewers do it this way.

Starting the Mash

1. Heat Brewing Water Heat up enough water to conduct the mash. At a water-to-grain ratio of 1.5:1 qt./lb., the amount would be 12.5 quarts or about 3 gallons. Always make more, you will often need it. Heat up 4 gallons if you can. At a ratio of 1.5:1, the initial infusion temperature should be 163°F to create a mash temperature of 152°F. (See *Chapter 16–The Methods of Mashing,* for the infusion calculations.)

2. Preheat the Tun Preheat the cooler with some hot water, about a gallon. Swirl it around to heat up the cooler and then pour it back to your sparge water pot. Preheating will prevent initial heat loss from the mash to the tun, which can throw off your infusion calculations.

3. Dough-in First pour in about 1 gallon of your strike water into the Mash Tun and stir in the crushed grain. This is the doughing-in stage. Then gradually mix all the water and grist together to avoid shocking the enzymes. Stir it to make sure all the grain is fully wetted, but don't splash. Hot side aeration can occur anytime the wort is hotter than 80°F. Oxidation of wort compounds will not be affected by the subsequent boil, and will cause flavor stability problems later. *See Figure 97.*

4. Check the Temperature Check the temperature of the mash to see if it has stabilized in the target temperature range of 150-155°F. If the temperature is too low, ex. 145 °F, add some more hot water. If it is too high, ex. 160°F, then add cold water to bring it down. 155°F is the highest we would want for this recipe. It will yield a sweet, medium bodied wort with good attenuation. *See Figure 98.*

Figure 97—Doughing-in. The mash water is added slowly while stirring to ensure full wetting and avoid thermally shocking the enzymes

5. Adjust the Temperature Okay, the mash temperature came out a little low (148°F) so I am adding 2.5 quarts of hot water to bring it up to 152°F. *See Figures 98 and 99.*

Conducting the Mash

6. Monitor Stir the mash every 15-20 minutes to prevent cold spots and help ensure a uniform conversion. Monitor the temperature each time you stir. If the temperature drops by less than 5 degrees over the hour, nothing further needs to be done. Cover the mash tun with the cooler lid between stirrings and let it sit for a total of an hour.

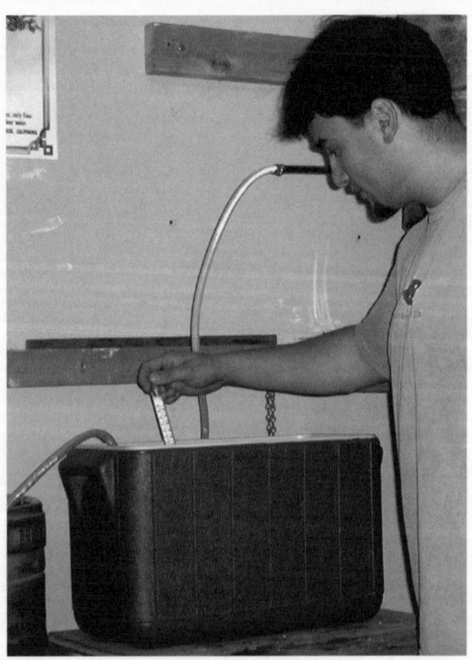

Figure 98—Check the temperature of the mash after the infusion.

Figure 99—Adding 2.5 quarts of hot water to raise the mash temperature another 4°F, to 152°F. Don't forget to put the lid back on! If you notice that the temperature drops below 145°within a half hour, you can add more water to bring the temperature back up.

Figure 100—A picture of the mash at t=30 minutes. Some of the larger particles are floating around, as are some husks. Notice it has cleared; it is no longer cloudy with starch, and it smells great.

7. Heat the Sparge Water Meanwhile, heat up your sparge water. You will need 1.5-2 times as much sparge water as you used for the mash. The water temperature should be less than boiling, preferably 165-175°F. If the sparge water is too hot, the probability of tannin extraction from the grain husks increases substantially.

Conducting the Lauter

Okay, the hour has gone by and the mash should look a little bit different. It should be less viscous and smell great. If you grainbed is shallow (<6"), place a plastic coffee can lid on top of the grainbed. This is what you will pour your sparge water onto to keep from stirring up the grainbed too much.

8. Recirculate Drain off the first runnings into a quart pitcher. The wort will be cloudy with bits of grain. Slowly pour the wort back into the grainbed, recirculating the wort. Repeat this procedure until the wort exiting the tun is pretty clear (like unfiltered apple cider). It will be dark amber colored, hazy, but not cloudy. It should only take a couple quarts.

9. Lauter Once the wort has cleared, drain the wort carefully into your boiling pot. Fill the pot slowly at first and allow the level to cover the outlet tube. Be sure to have a long enough tube so that the wort enters below the surface and does not splash. The splashing of hot wort before the boil can cause long term oxidation damage to the flavor of the beer.

10. Add the Sparge Watch the outflow of wort, you do not want to lauter too fast, as this could compact the grainbed and you would get a stuck sparge. A rate of 1 quart/minute is recommended. Allow the wort level in the tun to drop until it is about an inch above the level of the grain. Now start adding the sparge water, either from the hot water tun or by pouring in a couple quarts at a time, onto the coffee can lid, maintaining at least an inch of free water above the grainbed.

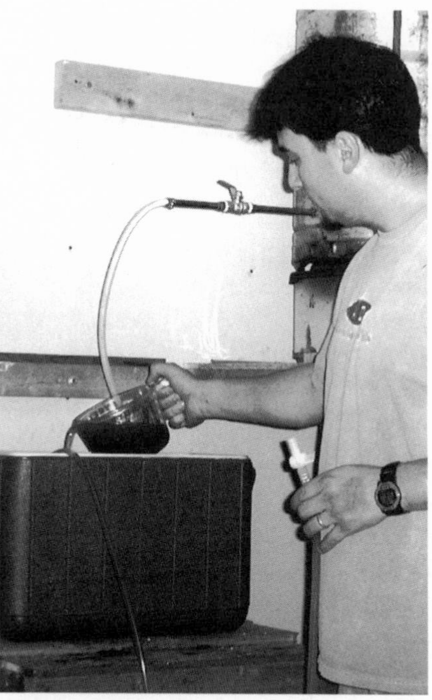

Figure 102—Pouring the recirculation wort back into the mash tun. Repeat until it is as clear as apple cider.

Figure 103—You are sparging! Woo-Hoo!

11. Stuck Sparge? If the wort stops flowing, even with water above the grainbed, then you have a stuck sparge. There are 2 ways to fix it: (a) Blow back into the outlet hose to clear any obstruction of the manifold; or (b) Close the valve and add more water, stirring to re-suspend the mash. You will need to re-circulate again. Stuck sparges are an annoyance, but usually not a major problem.

12. Keep Lautering Continue adding sparge water and draining the wort into your pot. At no time should you attempt to lift the pot with only one hand, especially if you are attempting to grab a stool with the other. The wort will spill.

13. Gauge Your Progress An advantage to brewing a dark beer is that you can see the color of the wort change as you lauter. It will get a lot ligher when most of the sugars are extracted. If you over-sparge, the mash pH will rise abruptly and tannin extraction is likely. You will usually collect more than enough wort before this happens. In any event, you should stop lautering when the gravity of the runoff falls below 1.008. If you have lautered too fast, you will not rinse the grains effectively, and you will get poor extraction. So, watch your wort volume, runoff color, and check the runoff gravity with your hydrometer towards the end of the lauter.

14. Calculate Efficiency Measure the gravity in the boiling pot (stir it first) and multiply the points by the number of gallons you collected. Then divide by the number of pounds of grain you used. The result should be somewhere around 30. 27 is okay, 29 is good, and over 30 is great. If it is 25 or below, you are lautering too fast or you are not getting good conversion in the mash, which could be caused by having too coarse a grist, the wrong temperature, not enough time, or a pH factor, et cetera.

Okay, throw the spent grain on the compost pile and you are done! You have produced your first all-grain wort! All-grain brewing produces more break material than extract brewing, so you will probably want to add irish moss during the last 15 minutes of the boil to help coagulation and clarity. Rehydrate it in warm water before use for best results. Don't overboil or its effects will be lost back into the wort.

Figure 104—The wort is brought to a boil and the hops are added. Pretty easy, eh?

Figure 105—Now the boil is over and its time to chill the wort. Joe Brewer uses a large Binford immersion wort chiller made from 50 feet of 1/2 inch diameter copper tubing wrapped in a continuous double coil to chill the 6 gallons of wort. (insert Tim Allen soundtrack)

Immerse the chiller during the last few minutes of the boil to sanitize it before you turn off the heat and start chilling.

Figure 106—A view of the chilling wort. Hops are visible floating around the edges of the chiller coils. Move it around and stir for better cooling.

Things You Could Do Differently Next Time

The procedure is nearly the same for other styles of beer. If you are making a Stout or perhaps a mellow dark ale or lager, one thing you can do to take some of the bite out of the dark grains is to add them later in the mash. Add the Black Patent or Roasted Barley during the last 10 minutes before you sparge. This is one means of coping with low alkalinity water when making dark beers. Saving the acidic malts until the end will reduce their acidifying effect on the mash.

Figure 108—The fermenter is sanitized and ready to receive the wort. Some Star San foam is still visible in the neck of the carboy—that's fine, it won't affect the fermentation at all.

Another change you can make is to do a two or three step mash. The yield can be improved by doughing in at a low temperature (105°F) with a thick mash (.75:1 or 1:1) and letting that rest for 15-20 minutes. Then you add more hot water to get the mash to saccharification rest temperature. Or you can use the pot-on-the-stove method to heat the mash. Use the usual ratio of 1.5 quarts per lb. and use the stove to heat the mash to the different target temperatures. It is very important to stir the bottom of the tun while heating to prevent scorching. After the mash is complete, carefully transfer the mash to the lauter tun (cooler with manifold), and sparge.

You could also use a decoction mash to do the rests. This method is most applicable when you are attempting to brew a drier, continental lager-style beer using less-modified malts.

If you feel that your extraction is too low while you are lautering, you can stir and start over if you want to. Simply close the runoff valve, add a little more water, stir the mash thoroughly and let it settle. You will need to repeat the re-circulating step, but this will often make a big difference if you were getting poor extraction from lautering too fast or channeling. In fact, most commercial breweries practice a technique called "raking" during the lauter, where they stir the grainbed with rakes a few inches above the manifold or false bottom. As long as you have a deep enough grainbed that you won't disturb the grain forming the filter around the collection device, you won't get any cloudiness coming through, and you will improve your extraction. Or you can just add another ½ pound of malt to the recipe. Grain is cheap.

Well, that was pretty easy, wasn't it? Not too much spillage I hope. A little practice and you will be able to do it in your sleep.

Figure 109—This picture shows the aquarium air pump aeration of the wort. Aeration is very important for a healthy fermentation.

Figure 110: The yeast has been pitched to the wort and now, 8 hours later, a krausen has started to form on top. A blow-off tube is usually not needed for a 5 gallon batch fermenting in a 6.5 gallon carboy.

Batch and No-Sparge Brewing

In between the first and second editions of this book, I finally got on the bandwagon with a couple of methods that several of my friends have been using for years: batch sparge and no-sparge brewing. These mashing and lautering methods use 10-25% more grain than a standard recipe (continuous sparge) to produce a larger mash that does not have to be closely monitored during the lauter.

Towards the end of the continuous sparging process, as the gravity of the runnings falls to 1.008, the mash pH rises to about 6 as the sugars are extracted and the buffering effect of the malt/wort is replaced by water. This rise in mash pH tends to extract greater proportions of tannins, polyphenols, and silicates into the wort which have a dulling effect on the taste. Batch sparging with a standard recipe grainbill can exacerbate this effect because the majority of the buffering capability is drained away before adding the second sparge volume. Therefore the grainbills for batch sparge and no-sparge brewing need to be scaled up to make up for inefficiencies that might otherwise lead to a rise in pH and off-flavors. These methods can produce a richer, smoother tasting wort with the same gravity as a standard recipe, but use a simpler lautering process that is more robust and pH stable.

So why doesn't everyone use these methods if they're so great? Because continuous sparging methods are more economical for commercial breweries and usually work just fine for homebrewing as well. Everyone learns about continuous sparging first and most all-grain recipes you will see (such as those in brewing magazines) are based on the efficiency of this method. That's why I used it for your first all-grain batch–better to start with the basics, then build from there. Using the batch or no-sparge method uses more grain and increases the size of the mash tun you need.

For example, here is a comparison of the standard 5 gallon recipe (continuous sparging) and the batch sparge and no-sparge recipes for the Tittabawassee Brown Ale you brewed for your first all-grain batch:

Grainbill	Standard	Batch	No-sparge
pale ale malt	7 lbs.	7.6 lbs.	8.5 lbs.
crystal 60 malt	1 lbs.	1.1 lbs.	1.25 lbs.
chocolate malt	.25 lbs.	.3 lbs.	.5 lbs.
Total weight	8.25 lbs	9.0 lbs.	10.25 lbs.
Total mash volume	3.75 gal	4.9 gal.	8 gal.

Each method produces the same 6 gallons of 1.041 wort. The obvious difference is the size of the mash: 4.9 for batch sparge and 8 gallons for no-sparge, versus 3.75 gallons for the continuous sparge. You will probably need a bigger mash tun for these methods.

Batch Sparge Recipe Calculations:

Batch sparging works best when two sparge volumes of the same size are combined to create the wort. To keep the process simple, we want the first sparge volume to be what we get when we simply drain the mash. To do this, we need to calculate the optimum mash ratio that will give us that volume, including the water that will be absorbed by the grain. Then the batch sparge brewing process becomes as easy as conducting the mash, draining the first runnings to the boiling kettle, adding an equal volume of sparge water back to the mash, draining again, and boiling!

First, let's define the terms in the equations:

Inputs:

- OG: Standard recipe original gravity (just the points part i.e. 1.0<u>49</u>).
- Gr: Standard recipe grainbill (total pounds).
- Vr: Standard recipe batch size (e.g., 5 gallons).
- Vb: Standard recipe boil volume (e.g., 6 gallons).

Calculation Coefficients:

- k: Water-retention coefficient (0.5 quart per pound)

Outputs:

- W: Batch sparge water volume (quarts).
- Rb: Batch sparge mash ratio (quarts/lb.).
- S: Scale-up factor for grainbill.
- Gb: Batch sparge grainbill (total pounds).
- Vm: Volume of water for the mash (quarts).
- BG: Boil gravity (points).
- BG_1: Gravity of the first runnings (points).
- BG_2: Gravity of the second runnings (points).
- Vt: Total volume of the mash (quarts).

1. Decide how many gallons of wort you will boil to achieve your recipe volume and thus your sparge volume (e.g. Vb = 6 gallons).
$W = Vb/2$ *(3 gallons i.e., 12 quarts)*

2. Calculate the optimum batch sparge mash ratio.
$Rb = (Vb + (Vb^2 + 2k \cdot Vb \cdot Gr)^{1/2})/Gr$ *(1.85 qts/lb.)*

3. Calculate the scale-up factor.

$S = 1/(1 - k^2/Rb^2)$ *(1.08)*

4. Calculate the batch sparge grainbill.

$Gb = S \cdot Gr$ *(8.9 or ~9.0 lbs.)*

5. Calculate the volume of water for the mash.

$Vm = Rb \cdot Gb = W + k \cdot Gb$ *(16.6 quarts)*

6. Calculate the gravity of the first runnings.

$BG_1 = 4 \cdot S \cdot Vr \cdot OG/Vm$ *(1.0$\underline{64}$)*

7. Calculate the gravity of the second runnings.

$BG_2 = 4 \cdot Vr \cdot OG \cdot (k/Rb) \cdot (1 - (k/Rb))/(Gr \cdot (Rb - k))$ *(1.0$\underline{17}$)*

8. Verify the combined boil gravity and recipe gravity.

$BG = (BG_1 + BG_2)/2$ and $OG = BG \cdot Vb/Vr$ *(1.0$\underline{40}$ and 1.0$\underline{49}$)*

9. Calculate the total batch sparge mash volume (quarts). The volume of 1 pound of dry grain, when mashed at 1 quart per pound, has a volume of 42 fluid ounces (1.3125 quarts or .328 gallons). Higher ratios only add the additional water volume.

$Vt = Gb(1.3125 + (Rb - 1))$ *(19.5 qts. i.e., 4.9 gallons)*

No-Sparge Recipe Calculations:

Here is how to calculate a no-sparge version from a standard recipe, such as those given in *Chapter 19.* These calculations combine the scaling-up of the grainbill with a three step infusion mash method that makes the whole process more manageable.

Inputs:

- OG: Standard recipe original gravity (just the points part i.e. 1.0$\underline{49}$).
- Gr: Standard recipe grainbill (total pounds).
- Vr: Standard recipe batch size (e.g. 5 gallons).
- Vb: Standard recipe boil volume (e.g. 6 gallons).

Calculation Coefficients:

- k: Water-retention coefficient (0.5 quart per pound)
- Rr: Standard recipe conversion rest mash ratio (e.g., 2 quarts/lb.)

Outputs:

- S: Scale-up factor for grainbill.
- Gn: No-sparge grainbill (total pounds).
- BG: No-sparge boil gravity (points).

Outputs *con't*:

Rn: No-sparge final mash ratio (quarts/lb.).

Wn: No-sparge total water volume (quarts).

Wmo: Mashout water volume (quarts).

Vt: No-sparge total mash volume. (quarts).

1. Decide how many gallons of wort you will boil to achieve your recipe volume (e.g., Vb = 6 gallons).

2. Calculate the scale-up factor.

$S = 4 \cdot Vb/(4 \cdot Vb - k \cdot Gr)$ *(1.2)*

3. Calculate the no-sparge grainbill.

$Gn = S \cdot Gr$ *(9.96 lbs.† See Below)*

4. Calculate the no-sparge boil gravity.

$BG = OG \cdot Vr/Vb$ *(1.041)*

5. Calculate the no-sparge mash ratio.

$Rn = (4 \cdot Vb + k \cdot Gn)/Gn$ *(2.84 (qts/lb)*

6. Calculate the total no-sparge water volume (quarts).

$Wn = Gn \cdot Rn = 4 \cdot Vb + k \cdot Gn$ *(29.1 qts.)*

7. Calculate the volume of water you will use for mashout (quarts).

$Wmo = Gn(Rn-Rr)$ or Wn – infusions *(8.6 qts.)*

8. Calculate the total no-sparge mash volume (quarts).

$Vt = Gn(1.3125 + (Rn - 1))$ *(32.3 qts i.e., 8 gallons)*

No-Sparge Multiple Infusion Mash Procedure

1. From the no-sparge recipe equations, we have determined that the scale-up factor for the Tittabawassee Brown Ale is 1.2. Applying the scale-up factor to each malt gives us:

Grainbill	Standard	No-sparge
pale ale malt	7 lbs.	8.5 lbs.†
crystal 60 malt	1 lbs.	1.25 lbs.†
chocolate malt	.25 lbs.	.5 lbs.†
Total weight	8.25 lbs	10.25 lbs.
Total mash volume	3.75 gal	8 gal.

†When scaling up the individual malts, you can round up to the nearest quarter pound to make weighing easier.

2. From Chapter 16, we can calculate the infusions for dough-in and conversion, based on the new grainbill of 10.25 lbs.

Dough-in Infusion

Target temperature:	104°F
Dough-in infusion ratio:	1 quart/lb.
Infusion water temperature	111°F
Infusion volume:	10.25 quarts

Conversion Infusion

Water volume of mash is:	10.25 quarts
Target temperature:	154°F
Infusion water temperature:	210°F
Infusion volume:	10 quarts
Total water volume	20.25 quarts

3. At this point we have a rather ordinary mash of 10.25 lbs in 20.25 quarts of water, i.e., a mash ratio of about 2 qts/lb. The total volume of this mash is about 6 gallons. Now we will calculate how much water we need to add to make up the total no-sparge water volume (Wn) and use it for a mashout infusion.

   $Wn = 4(Vb + kGn) = 29.125$ quarts

   $Wmo = Wn - \text{infusions} = 29.125 - 20.25 = 8.875$ or 9 quarts

4. At first glance, you might say "just add 9 more quarts and call it good" but we really don't want to push the mashout temperature over 170°F. So, we want to calculate the infusion temperature that will give us a final mash temperature of 170°F (max). From Chapter 16, we can re-arrange the infusion equation to find the infusion temperature.

   $Tw = (T2 - T1)(.2G + Wm)/Wa + T2$

   $Tw = (170 - 154)(.2 \cdot 10.25 + 20.25)/9 + 170 = 209.6$ or 210°F

   In this case, using our usual infusion water temperature of 210°F, we don't need to worry about increasing the potential for tannin extraction. However, if we were going to collect 7 gallons instead of 6, which would mean infusing 13 quarts instead of 9, the temperature of the infusion would need to be reduced to 198°F.

5. Yes, there are a few calculations involved and it's a lot bigger mash, but it does simplify things to add all the water to the mash, recirculate, and drain it to start your boil. No worrying about the pH and gravity of the final runnings, no worrying about whether you will hit your target gravity–this process is robust. And if you want to simplify the calculations aspect, then putting the equations into a spreadsheet or using a brewing software program like Promash or Strangebrew will make it easy.

Section IV

Recipes, Experimentation, and Troubleshooting

In this section, we learn how to design, improvise, experiment, and troubleshoot. In *Chapter 19–Some of My Favorite Styles and Recipes,* I attempt to convey a "big picture" of the world of brewing and give you a couple options for brewing some of my favorite beer styles. Unfortunately, I am one of those people who cook by adding a pinch of this and a handful of that, so this chapter was difficult to write. In fact, the next chapter, *Chapter 20–Developing Your Own Recipes,* was even harder to write, because I had a hard time explaining how to proceed on intuition. But that is the intent of the chapter–to encourage you to try new things and tweak the things you are currently doing.

It naturally follows that the final chapter is called *Is My Beer Ruined?* This is a frequent cry for help on the internet brewing forums. In this chapter I will try to coach you through some of the most common problems by examining the most common symptoms and their possible causes. Hopefully this chapter will be very useful, but rarely needed. Right?

Chapter 19

Some of My Favorite Beer Styles and Recipes

Style Descriptions

There are so many styles of beer; its hard to know where to begin. There is a lot more to a style than just whether its light or dark. Each beer style has a characteristic taste, imparted by either the yeast, the malts, the hops, the water, or all four. A style is best defined by naming all the ingredients, and the fermentation particulars. Change any one item, and you have probably hopped into another style category (no pun intended). Each country, each geographic region, even each town, can have its own style of beer. In fact, you may be starting to realize by now that many beer styles originate from local brewing conditions. Access to ingredients, the local water profile, the climate–all of these elements combine to dictate the character of the best beer that the brewer can produce. To a certain extent, your success and satisfaction as a homebrewer is going to depend on understanding what style(s) your local conditions will allow you to best produce.

The place to start when defining a style is the yeast. Is it an ale or a lager strain that is used? What is the temperature profile of the fermentation?

The next important aspect is the malt. Each of the malts and grains listed in *Chapter 12* has a unique taste that it contributes to the beer. As an example, stouts are defined in part by the flavor of roasted unmalted barley.

The hop variety plays a part too. The difference between English pale ale and American pale ale is predominantly due to the differences in flavor between English and American hops. Even the same variety of hop, grown in different regions, will have a different character.

Both ales and lagers are brewed in a wide variety of styles from strong and rich (barleywine and dopplebock) to crisp and hoppy (IPA and pilsner). The main difference between the two comes from the type of yeast used and the fermentation process. Ales are fermented at room temperature and typically have a noticeable amount of fruity-smelling esters due to this warm fermentation. The fruitiness can be subdued–as in a dry stout or dominating–as in a barleywine.

Lagers on the other hand, lack any fruity character and may be crisp and hoppy like a pilsner or sweet and malty like a dopplebock. Both ales and lagers are malty, but this character can vary from a minimal light toast/biscuit note to a thick and chewy symphony. *Figure 111* attempts to visually represent the similarities and differences between beer styles.

Coming up with a common set of descriptors for beer styles is more difficult than it sounds since there are so many styles to compare, each with a different character. One way to do it is to describe ranges for physical attributes like Original and Final Gravity, IBUs and Color, but this is really only half the story. To try and give you the other half, I illustrate each description with a commercial example and a baseline recipe. In each recipe, I identify the appropriate malt extracts and specialty grains, hop varieties, yeast strain, and fermentation conditions. I have grouped the styles by Ale and Lager according to the yeast; and sorted them on the basis of color and body to progress from lighter beers to heavier.

For each of the styles presented, I have listed the style/substyle guidelines from the Beer Judge Certification Program–a national organization that seeks to advance the appreciation of beer through common standards of evaluation and the education of its member judges (www.bjcp.org). Included in these style guidelines is the color range for the beer in SRM. The unit is taken from the acronym for the Standard Reference Method used by the American Society of Brewing Chemists (ASBC). SRM units are equivalent to Lovibond units when comparing beer color. Personally, I feel that the color value is the least important target when trying to brew to a style; if you get the malt flavor right, the color should be right too.

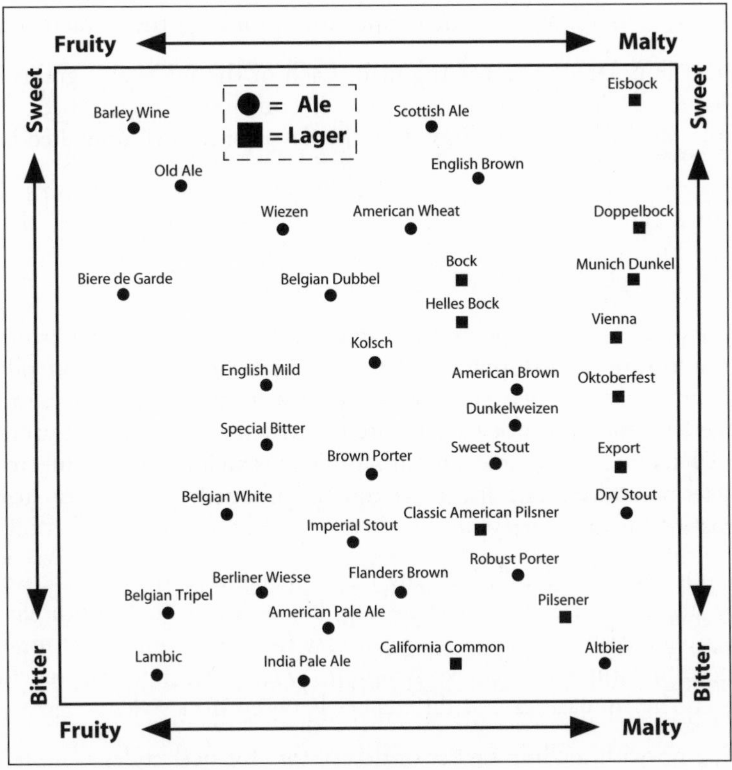

Figure 111—Relative Flavors of Beer Styles This chart is not to any scale but is a subjective attempt to describe how different beer styles taste relative to one another. As an over-simplification, a beer may be Malty–Sweet, Malty–Bitter, Fruity–Sweet, or Fruity–Bitter. Each beer style was placed on the chart via a great deal of "arm waving". The flavors often overlap between styles, and the variation within a single style can often bridge the positions of the styles next to it. This chart also fails to describe a beer's intensity. Some beer styles like Imperial Stout and Barleywine can literally cover half the chart in their complexity. A beer like Coors Light™ would be smack-dab in the middle (and probably on another plane behind the chart). As I said above, this is my oversimplified attempt to give you a first glance at how a lot of the beer styles relate to one another.

Notes on Recipes: The recipes use both extract and specialty grain because this provides the most insight into the beer style for the beginning brewer. If you do not have access to a particular specialty grain, then substitute an equivalent amount of an extract that contains that grain. For example: Amber malt extract instead of Pale extract with Crystal 60 malt or Dark malt extract instead of Pale extract with Chocolate malt.

All recipe calculations for OG and IBUs assume the use of a 3 gallon high gravity boil for a 5 gallon batch. Depending on the type of extract used, the actual boil volume could be as high as 4 gallons. You may want to recalculate your gravity and hop additions for your own equipment. All-grain versions of the same recipes assume an extract efficiency of 85% (*see Table 9*) and 6 gallons of wort being collected and boiled to produce the same 5 gallon batch. Depending on your equipment and extract efficiency, you may want to bump up the recipe amounts by 10% to get better yield. Hop boil utilization will increase when all-grain brewing because of the full volume boil and lower boiling gravity, so be sure to use the calculations presented in *Chapter 5–Hops,* to adjust your hop amounts accordingly. It would probably be more realistic to state all amounts in terms of an actual batch size of 5.5 gallons to account for wort lost to the trub and hops. Plus, depending on your extract efficiency, and the vigor of your boil, you may need to collect 7 gallons of wort in order to have 5 gallons of beer at bottling time. But those considerations depend on your own methods and equipment, so I have chosen to teach you how to do these calculations yourself, and give you easy numbers to work with. Onward!

(The main recipe section starts on the page 232.)

Bonus Recipe!–Stuck here because it was better than a blank page in the middle of the chapter, due to a layout conflict.

This porter recipe uses Brown Malt which has a roasted edge to it. See page 243 for more info on porters. The first time I brewed it, I thought I had a failure on my hands until I attempted to use it in a tasting as an example of an astringent beer. About 3 months had gone by from the last time I had tasted it, and when my dad said, "Oh yes, this is really good!" I thought I had the wrong keg; I was amazed at how good it was.

San Gabriel Porter (All-Grain Recipe)

Malts	Gravity Pts.
8 lbs. of Pale Ale Malt	42
1 lb. of Crystal 80L malt	5
1 lb. of Brown malt	5
½ lb. of Chocolate malt	2
½ lb. of Special B malt	2
BG for 6 Gallons	1.056
OG for 5 Gallons	1.067

Hops	Boil Time	IBUs
1 oz of Galena (11%)	60	36
½ oz of EK Goldings (5%)	40	7
½ oz of EK Goldings (5%)	20	5
Total IBUs		48

Yeast	Fermentation Schedule
Irish Ale (liquid)	1 week at 65°F in primary ferment. 3 weeks in secondary. Allow to bottle condition for 1 month.

Mash Schedule–Single Temperature Infusion

Rest Type	Temperature	Duration
Beta Amylase	145°F	30 min
Alpha Amylase	158°F	30 min

Remember to let this age a couple months to get smooth. It's really good.

Three Weisse Guys–American Wheat Beer

Malts	Gravity Pts.
6 lbs. of Wheat Malt Extract (LME) (60% Wheat, 40% Barley)	72
BG for 3 Gallons	1.072
OG for 5 Gallons	1.043

Hops	Boil Time	IBUs
1.5 oz of Liberty (4%)	60	17
1 oz of Liberty (4%)	30	9
Total IBUs		26

Yeast	Fermentation Schedule
American Ale (liquid)	10 days at 65°F in primary fermenter

Options

All-Extract	(same)
All-Grain	5 lbs. of 2 row base malt 3 lbs of flaked wheat

Mash Schedule–Multi-Rest Infusion

Rest Type	Temperature	Duration
Beta Glucan	110°F	15 minutes
Protein Rest	125°F	15 minutes
Conversion	154°F	60 min

Wheat Beer Style Guidelines

Substyle	OG	FG	IBUs	Color
American Wheat	1.035-55	1.008-15	10-30	2-8
Bavarian Weizen	1.040-56	1.010-14	10-20	2-9
Bavarian Dunkleweizen	1.040-56	1.010-14	10-20	10-23
Berliner Weisse	1.026-36	1.006-09	3-8	2-4
Weizenbock	1.066-80	1.015-22	15-30	7-25
Belgian Wit	1.042-55	1.008-12	15-22	2-4

The Ale Styles

Wheat

You may not realize it, but wheat beer used to be one of the most popular styles in America a century ago. Wheat was abundant and after a hot hard day working in the fields, a light, tart wheat beer is very refreshing. The most popular style of wheat beer at the time was patterned after the tart Berliner Weiss beers of Germany. Berliner Weiss is brewed using three parts wheat malt to one part barley malt and fermented with a combination of ale yeast and lactic acid bacteria. After fermentation it is dosed with a substantial quantity of young, fermenting beer (kraus-ened), and bottled. American weissbier used similar yeast cultures, but the common practice was to use unmalted wheat in the form of grits; only about 30% of the grist was wheat. The excess of proteins in wheat cause most wheat beers to be hazy, if not downright cloudy. Hefeweizens go a step further with the beer being cloudy with suspended yeast. The thought of drinking that much yeast is appalling in a pale ale, but it really works with hefeweizens; they are quite tasty. Hefeweizen is not tart like Berliner Weiss because it are not fermented with lactic acid cultures.

Wheat beer became extinct with Prohibition in the United States, and has only been revived in the last decade. Today's American wheat beer is loosely modeled after weizen but are made with a standard, flocculant ale yeast and not the specialized German weizenbier yeasts with their spicy, clove-like character. The Noble-type hops are most appropriate for the light body and spicy character of wheats. Wheat beers are usually light, but dunkles (darks), bocks (strong) and dunkles weizenbock are common variations. Spices are often used with wheat beers; Belgian Wit uses Coriander and dried Curacua orange peel with some lactic acid sourness to produce a truly unique beer.

<u>Commerical Examples:</u>

American Wheat	Sierra Nevada Wheat
Bavarian Weizen	Ayinger, Erdinger
Berliner Weisse	Schultheiss Berliner Weisse
Belgian Wit	Celis White

Lord Crouchback's Special Bitter–English Pale Ale

Malts	Gravity Pts.
6 lbs. of Pale Malt Extract (LME)	72
½ lb. of Crystal 60 malt	3
BG for 3 Gallons	1.075
OG for 5 Gallons	1.045

Hops	Boil Time	IBUs
1 oz of Target (9%)	60	25
¾ oz of EK Goldings (5%)	30	8
¾ oz of EK Goldings (5%)	15	5
Total IBUs		38

Yeast	Fermentation Schedule
Whitbread English Ale (dry)	10 days at 65°F in primary fermenter

Options

All-Extract	4 lbs. of pale LME 2 lbs of amber DME
All-Grain	7 lbs. of British Pale Ale malt ½ lbs of Crystal 60L

Mash Schedule–Single Temperature Infusion

Rest Type	Temperature	Duration
Conversion	152°F	60 min

British Pale Ale Style Guidelines

Substyle	OG	FG	IBUs	Color
Ordinary Bitter	1.030-38	1.008-13	20-40	6-14
Special Bitter	1.039-45	1.009-14	20-45	6-14
Burton Ale	1.046-65	1.011-20	30-65	6-14

Commercial Examples:

Ordinary Bitter	Fuller's Chiswick Bitter
Special Bitter	Young's Special Bitter
Burton Ale	Bass Worthington White Shield

Pale Ales

There is a lot of variety in the Pale Ale family. Pale is a relative term and was originally applied as pale-as-compared-to-Stout. Pale ales can range from golden to deep amber, depending on the amount of Crystal malts used. Crystal malts are the defining ingredient to the malt character of a Pale ale, giving it a honey or caramel-like sweetness. The top fermenting ale yeast and warm fermentation temperature give pale ales a subtle fruitiness. Pale ales are best served cool, about 55 °F, to allow the fruit and caramel notes to emerge.

There are several varieties of Pale Ale–nearly every country has their own version–which is more than I will attempt to cover here. I will provide a description and recipe for my three favorite types: English, India, and American.

English Special Bitter

There are several substyles of British pale ale, these include the bitter, special bitter and India pale ale. These styles share many characteristics. All are brewed from water high in sulfates for a crisp hop finish to balance the ester and malt flavors. Many examples of the style have a hint of butterscotch from the presence of diacetyl. These beers usually have what is considered a low level of carbonation. Drinkers in the United States would probably describe them as flat. The beer is brewed to a low final gravity yielding a dry finish with only a low level of residual sweetness that does not mask the hop finish. In particular, the English Special Bitter is a marvelous beer. There is a supporting depth of malt flavor with fruity overtones that adds warmth, but the hop bitterness is the distinguishing characteristic of the flavor and lingers in the finish.

Victory and Chaos–India Pale Ale

Malts	**Gravity Pts.**
8 lbs. of Pale Malt Extract (LME)	96
½ lb. of Crystal 20L malt	5
BG for 3 Gallons	1.101
OG for 5 Gallons	1.062

Hops	**Boil Time**	**IBUs**
2 oz of Galena (11%)	60	48
2 oz of EK Goldings (5%)	15	11
1 oz of EK Goldings (5%)	5	2
Total IBUs		61

Yeast	**Fermentation Schedule**
Whitbread English Ale (dry)	2 weeks at 65°F in primary fermenter or 1 wk primary and 3 wk secondary with 1 oz EKG dry hopped.

Options	
All-Extract	7 lbs. of pale LME 2 lbs of amber DME
All-Grain	10 lbs. of British Pale Ale malt 1/2 lbs of Crystal 20L

Mash Schedule–Single Temperature Infusion

Rest Type	Temperature	Duration
Conversion	152°F	60 min

India Pale Ale

This ale was originally just a stronger version of the Burton pale ale, but the style has evolved a bit to today's version, which does not use as much Crystal malt. The IPA style arose from the months-long sea journey to India, during which the beer conditioned with hops in the barrel. Extra hops were added to help prevent spoilage during the long voyage. This conditioning time mellowed the hop bitterness to a degree and imparted a wealth of hop aroma to the beer. Homebrewed IPA should also be given a long conditioning time either in the bottle or in a secondary fermentor. If a secondary fermentor is used the beer should be dry hopped with an ounce of British aroma hops like East Kent Goldings. Conditioning time should be 4–6 weeks depending on OG and IBU levels. Stronger = Longer. It is also worth noting that there are English and American versions of IPA, depending on the hop varieties you use. I prefer the softer English hop varieties for this amount of hoppiness.

India Pale Ale Style Guidelines

Style	OG	FG	IBUs	Color
India Pale Ale	1.050-75	1.012-16	40-60+	8-14

Commercial Example:

India Pale Ale — Anchor Liberty Ale, Victory Hop Devil

Lady Liberty Ale–American Pale Ale

Malts	**Gravity Pts.**
6 lbs. of Pale Malt Extract (LME)	72
½ lb. of Crystal 60L malt	5
BG for 3 Gallons	1.077
OG for 5 Gallons	1.046

Hops	**Boil Time**	**IBUs**
¾ oz of Northern Brewer (9%)	60	18
¾ oz of Cascade (7%)	30	11
¾ oz of Cascade (7%)	15	7
Total IBUs		36

Yeast	**Fermentation Schedule**
American Ale (liquid)	10 days at 65°F in primary fermenter <u>or</u> 1 wk primary and 2 wk secondary with 1/2 oz Cascade dry hopped.

Options

All-Extract	4 lbs. of pale LME 2 lbs of amber DME
All-Grain	7 lbs. of British Pale Ale malt ½ lbs of Crystal 60L

Mash Schedule–Single Temperature Infusion

Rest Type	Temperature	Duration
Conversion	155°F	60 min

American Pale Ale

Lady Liberty Ale

American pale ale is an adaptation of classic British pale ale. The American Ale yeast strain produces less esters than comparable ale yeasts, and thus American pale ale has a less fruity taste than its British counterpart. American pale ales vary in color from gold to dark amber and typically have a hint of sweet caramel from the use of crystal malt that does not mask the hop finish. With the resurgence of interest in ales in the United States, American pale ale evolved from a renewed interest in American hop varieties and a higher level of bitterness as microbreweries experimented with craft brewing. The Cascade hop has become a staple of American microbrewing and is the signature hop for American pale ales. It has a distinctive citrusy aroma compared to European hops and has enabled American pale ale to stand shoulder to shoulder with other classic beer styles.

American Pale Ale Style Guidelines

Substyle	OG	FG	IBUs	Color
American Pale Ale	1.045-56	1.010-15	20-40	4-11
American Amber Ale	1.045-56	1.010-15	20-40	11-18

Commercial Examples:

American Pale Ale	Sierra Nevada Pale Ale
American Amber Ale	Humboldt Red Nector

Tittabawassee Brown Ale–American Brown Ale

Malts	**Gravity Pts.**
6 lbs. of pale malt extract (DME)	80
1 lb. of Crystal 60L malt	6
¼ lb. of Chocolate malt	1
BG for 3 Gallons	1.091
OG for 5 Gallons	1.055

Hops	**Boil Time**	**IBUs**
¾ oz of Nugget (10%)	60	18
1 oz of Willamette (5%)	30	11
1 oz of Willamette (5%)	15	6
Total IBUs		33

Yeast	**Fermentation Schedule**
Nottingham Ale (Dry)	10 days at 65°F in primary fermenter <u>or</u> 1 wk primary and 2 wk secondary

Options

All-Extract	4 lbs. of pale LME 2.5 lbs of amber DME .25 lbs. dark DME
All-Grain	7 lbs. of 2 row base malt 1 lbs of Crystal 60L ¼ lb. of Chocolate malt

Mash Schedule–Single Temperature Infusion

Rest Type	Temperature	Duration
Conversion	154°F	60 min

Brown Ales

There are several kinds of brown ale, but we will only describe three variations: sweet, nutty, and hoppy. The sweet brown ales of England are made with a lot of Crystal malt and a low hopping rate. Low gravity/bitterness brown ales are called Milds. The nutty brown ales, also of England, are made with Crystal malt plus a percentage of toasted malts (e.g. Biscuit or Victory) but still a low hopping rate. The hoppy brown ales, which can be nutty also, arose from the US homebrew scene when hop-crazy homebrewers decided that most brown ales were just too wimpy. Beauty is on the palate of the beholder, I suppose. Brown Ales as a class have grown to bridge the gap between Pale Ales and Porters. I will present a basic American brown ale and include a nutty option. Contrary to popular myth there are no nuts or nut extracts in classic brown ales; toasted malts give the beer a nut-like flavor and nut brown color. You can add 1/2 lb. of home toasted base malt, Victory malt, or Biscuit malt to the recipe to give the beer a more nutty character. For the best results, this malt addition should be mashed with with at least an equal amount of base malt. See Chapter 20-Experiment! for a description of how to make your own toasted malt at home.

Brown Ale Style Guidelines

Substyle	OG	FG	IBUs	Color
Mild	1.030-38	1.008-13	10-20	10-25
Northern Brown Ale	1.040-50	1.010-13	15-30	12-30
Southern Brown Ale	1.040-50	1.011-14	15-24	20-35
American Brown Ale	1.040-60	1.010-17	25-60	15-22

Commercial Example:	
Mild	Highgate Mild (UK)
Northern Brown Ale	Newcastle Brown Ale
Southern Brown Ale	Mann's Brown Ale
American Brown Ale	Pete's Wicked Ale, Lost Coast Downtown Brown

Port O' Palmer–Porter

Malts	Gravity Pts.
6 lbs. of Pale Malt Extract (LME)	72
½ lb. of Chocolate Malt	3
½ lb. of Crystal 60L Malt	3
¼ lb. of Black Patent Malt	1
BG for 3 Gallons	1.079
OG for 5 Gallons	1.048

Hops	Boil Time	IBUs
1 oz of Nugget (10%)	60	26
¾ oz of Willamette (5%)	40	9
½ oz of Willamette (5%)	20	4
Total IBUs		39

Yeast	Fermentation Schedule
American Ale (liquid)	2 weeks at 65°F in primary ferment. Or 1 week primary and 2 weeks secondary.

Options

All-Extract	4 lbs. of Pale LME 2 lbs. of Amber DME 1 lb. of Dark DME
All-Grain	7.5 lbs. of 2 row base malt or British Pale Ale malt ½ lb. of Chocolate Malt ½ lb. of Crystal 60L Malt ¼ lb. of Black Patent Malt

Mash Schedule–Single Temperature Infusion

Rest Type	Temperature	Duration
Conversion	156°F	60 min

Porter Style Guidelines

Substyle	OG	FG	IBUs	Color
Brown Porter	1.040-50	1.008-14	20-30	20-35
Robust Porter	1.050-65	1.012-16	25-45	30+

Porter

A porter is a dark ale with a very malty flavor and a bit of a roasted finish. A porter differs from a brown ale by being darker, stronger, more full bodied, and having a roastier malt finish than a brown, but less so than a stout. Porters should be fairly well attenuated (dry), though sweet porters are not uncommon. Compared to stout, a porter should be lighter in both body and color. When held up to the light, a porter should have a deep ruby red glow.

Historically, porters preceded stouts and had a much different character than today. This difference can be described as a tartness or sourness imparted by both the yeast and the malt. Porter used to be brewed and stored in wooden barrels that harbored a yeast called Brettanomyces which imparts a secondary fermentation characteristic commonly described as "horse sweat". Another one of those acquired tastes. The other dominant note was from the use of Brown Malt, which was used as the base malt. The beer was then aged for about 6 months before serving. The aging time was necessary for the rough flavors of the brown malt to mellow. My San Gabriel Porter, an all-grain recipe on page 231 due to lack of symmetry, uses brown malt and does indeed benefit from 4 months of conditioning time. What starts out as harshly bitter-malt beer turns into a sweeter, smooth elixir. It is a very good beer if you are careful to not to oxidize it during the brewing and let it age for several months before drinking.

For Porters and Stouts, British and Irish yeast strains are good choices for more of the tart character that is part of these styles. Any of the dry yeasts like Nottingham or Windsor would also be good. The Port 'O Palmer recipe uses American Ale yeast since it is intended to mimic Sierra Nevada Porter.

Commercial Examples:

Brown Porter	Yuengling Porter
Robust Porter	Sierra Nevada Porter

Mill Run Stout

Malts	Gravity Pts.
6 lbs. of pale malt extract (DME)	84
½ lb. of Crystal 60L malt	3
½ lb. of roast barley	3
BG for 3 Gallons	1.090
OG for 5 Gallons	1.054

Hops	Boil Time	IBUs
1 oz of Galena (11%)	60	27
1 oz of Chinook (11%)	30	20
Total IBUs		47

Yeast	Fermentation Schedule
Irish Ale (Liquid)	10 days at 65°F in primary fermenter or 1 wk primary and 3 wk secondary

Options

All-Extract	6 lbs. of dark DME
All-Grain	8 lbs. of Pale Ale malt ½ lb of Crystal 60L ½ lb. of Roast Barley ½ lb. of flaked barley

Mash Schedule–Single Temperature Infusion

Rest Type	Temperature	Duration
Conversion	154°F	60 min

Grain Option: Add a half pound of Chocolate Malt in place of, or in addition to the other grains.

Oatmeal Stout: Oatmeal Stout Extract is now available from some of the larger mail-order homebrew suppliers. Use in place of the Dark DME. The all-grain brewer can add a pound of Instant Oats to the mash with a 20 minute Beta Glucan Rest at 110°F to make lautering easier.

Coffee Stout: This is an easy variation to any Stout recipe. Simply add up to a quart of fresh, moderately-strong, drip-brewed coffee to the fermentor. If the coffee is boiled with the wort it degrades the aroma and flavor. (It's why coffee percolators quickly went out of style after Mr. Coffee came along.)

Stout

Arguably one of the most popular styles among homebrewers, stouts vary a lot in flavor, degree of roastiness, and body. There are dry stouts, sweet stouts, export stouts, oatmeal stouts, coffee stouts and more besides. The one defining characteristic of a stout is the use of highly roasted malts and/or unmalted roast barley. The most popular, Guinness Extra Stout, is the defining example of Irish dry stout and uses only pale malt, unmalted roast barley and flaked barley; no crystal malt is used. English stouts tend to be of the sweet stout style and will include chocolate and crystal malts. Some English stouts do not use any black malt or roast barley at all. Export stouts are brewed to a very high gravity, 1.075-1.100 with a huge complexity of flavors, sweet and tarry, fruity and quite bitter. Oatmeal stouts are my favorite, being a sweet stout with the smooth silkiness of oatmeal added in. Coffee stouts are another homebrew favorite, the taste of coffee perfectly complements the roast character of a stout.

Stout Style Guidelines

Substyle	OG	FG	IBUs	Color
Dry Stout	1.035-50	1.007-11	30-50	35+
Sweet Stout	1.035-66	1.010-22	20-40	35+
Oatmeal Stout	1.035-60	1.010-18	20-50	35+
Foreign Extra Stout	1.050-75	1.010-17	35-70	35+
Russian Imperial Stout	1.075-95+	1.018-30+	50-90+	20-40

Commercial Examples:

Dry Stout	Guinness Draught
Sweet Stout	Mackeson Stout
Oatmeal Stout	Anderson Valley Oatmeal Stout
Foreign Extra Stout	Guiness Foreign Extra Stout
Russian Imperial Stout	John Smith Imperial Russian Stout

Fightin' Urak-Hai Barleywine

Malts	Gravity Pts.
5 lbs. of wheat malt extract (LME)	45
8 lbs. of pale malt extract (DME)	84
½ lb. of Special B malt	2
½ lb. of Chocolate Malt	2
BG for 4 Gallons	1.133
OG for 5 Gallons	1.106

Hops	Boil Time	IBUs
3 oz of Columbus (10%)	60	49
3 oz of Nugget (12%)	30	45
1 oz of Columbus (10%)	15	8
Total IBUs		102

Yeast	Fermentation Schedule
English Ale (Liquid)	Pitch the entire yeastcake from a previous batch of beer, preferably from the secondary fermenter. Be sure to use a blowoff tube in a 6.5 gallon fermenter–this will be messy. 2-3 weeks at 65°F in the primary fermenter and 1-3 months in the secondary. Bottle and condition for an additional month before drinking.

Options

All-Extract	Substitute 1.5 lbs. of dark DME for the specialty grains.
All-Grain	5 lbs. of Wheat malt 12 lbs. of Pale Ale malt ½ lb of Special B ½ lb. of Chocolate Malt

Mash Schedule–Multi-Rest Infusion

Rest Type	Temperature	Duration
Beta Rest	140°F	30 min.
Alpha Rest	158°F	30 min.

Commercial Examples:

English Barleywine	Young's Old Nick
American Barleywine	Anchor's Old Foghorn

Barleywine

Barleywine is the drink of the gods, the intellectual ones anyway. Few beverages can equal the complexity of flavors that a properly aged barleywine has: malt, fruit, spice, and warmth from the high level of alcohol (9-14%). Barleywine has been around for several hundred years. It was known as Strong Ale in medieval times and was probably brewed long before the introduction of hops. Recipes for barleywines vary greatly, but can be loosely organized into 3 categories. There are strong barleywines with more emphasis on the malt and sweetness than on the hop character. There are more balanced strong barleywines which strive to keep the hop bitterness and flavor on equal footing with malt. Finally there are the lightweights of the barleywine world, often the ones that are most available commercially, that make use of various brewing sugars to lighten the body while keeping the alcohol content high. The hop levels are usually balanced in these lighter barleywines.

Barleywines tend to require the use of malt extracts to help achieve the high gravities that are their hallmark. Barleywines usually consist primarily of pale and crystal malts to avoid masking the flavor with roasted malts. The color of barleywine ranges from deep gold to ruby red. Wheat and rye malts are popular additions for "accent", counterbalancing the heavy maltiness of the barley. A barleywine is meant to be sipped in front of the fire on a cold winter's night, providing the fuel for philosophical thoughts on science and the wonders of metallurgy.

Barleywines are consumed in small amounts so it best to use 12 oz or smaller bottles. The amount of priming sugar should be reduced to 1/2 cup per 5 gallons because the beer will continue to ferment for months in the bottle. The normal amount of priming sugar plus this residual fermentation would cause the bottles to overcarbonate.

Barleywine Style Guidelines

Substyle	OG	FG	IBUs	Color
English Barleywine	1.080-120+	1.020-30+	50-100	10-22
American Barleywine	1.080-120+	1.020-30+	50-100	10-22

Zatec Pils–Pilsener Lager

Malts	Gravity Pts.
6.5 lbs. of Alexander's Pale LME	78
BG for 3 Gallons	1.078
OG for 5 Gallons	1.047

Hops	Boil Time	IBUs
1 oz of Perle (7%)	60	19
1.25 oz of Saaz (4%)	30	10
1 oz of Saaz (4%)	15	5
Total IBUs		34

Yeast	Fermentation Schedule
Bohemian Lager (liquid)	2 weeks at 50°F in primary fermenter rack and lager at 40°F for 5 weeks. Prime and store bottles at room temperature.

Options

All-Extract	(same)
All-Grain	8 lbs. of 2 row base malt or German Pils malt*

Mash Schedule–Multi-Rest Infusion or Decoction*

Rest Type	Temperature	Duration
Protein*	125°F	20 min.
Beta Rest	140°F	30 min.
Alpha Rest	158°F	30 min.

*If you use a less modified German or Czech Pils malt, then decoction mashing and a protein rest are recommended. The protein rest is not advised for fully modified malt.

The Lager Styles

Pilsner

Beer as the world knew it changed dramatically in 1842 when the brewery in the town of Pilsen (today part of the Czech Republic) produced the first light golden lager. Until that time, beers had been rather dark, varying from amber ("pale"), to deep brown or black. Today Pilsner Urquell™ is that same beer, "the Original of Pilsen." The original Pilsner beer is a hoppy, dry beer of 1.045 OG. The Pilsner style is imitated more than any other and interpretations run from the light flowery lagers of Germany to the maltier, more herbal versions of the Netherlands, to the increasingly tasteless varieties of Light and Dry from the United States and Japan. Most of these are broadly in the Pilsner style but lack the assertive noble hop bitterness and flavor of the original.

Brewing a true pilsner can be fairly difficult, especially from an all-grain point of view. Pilsen has very soft water, the next closest thing to distilled water and the malt flavors are very clean and fresh. There is no place for an off-flavor to hide. The use of only base malt makes maintaining a proper mash pH difficult, especially during lautering, for brewers using moderately hard water. Water that is high in carbonates has too much buffering capacity for the meager amount of acidity provided by the malt. When brewing an all-grain pilsner, it is often best to use a large proportion of distilled or de-ionized water to provide the right mash conditions and prevent tannin astringency.

Pilsner Style Guidelines

Substyle	OG	FG	IBUs	Color
Northern German Pilsner	1.044-50	1.008-13	25-45	2-4
Bohemian Pilsner	1.044-56	1.013-17	35-45	3-5

Commercial Example:

Northern German Pilsner	Bitburger Pils
Bohemian Pilsner	Pilsner Urquell

Your Father's Mustache–Classic American Pilsner

Malts	Gravity Pts.
7 lbs. of 6 row (or 2 row) base malt	37
1.75 lbs. of flaked maize or 2 lbs of corn grits or polenta*	10
BG for 6 Gallons	1.047
OG for 5 Gallons	1.056

Hops	Boil Time	IBUs
¾ oz of Saaz (4%)	FWH	
1 oz of Cluster (7.5%)	60	27
½ oz of Tettnanger (5%)	10	2
¼ oz of Tettnanger (5%)	0	0
Total IBUs		29

Yeast	Fermentation Schedule
Bavarian Lager (liquid)	2 weeks at 48°F in primary fermenter rack and lager at 32°F for 6-7 weeks. Prime and store bottles at room temperature.

Mash Schedule–Multi-rest infusion for use with grits.

Rest Type	Temperature	Duration
Dough-in	119°F	20 min.
Beta Rest	145°F	30 min.
Alpha Rest	158°F	30 min.
Mashout	170°F	10 min.

* If you are using corn grits or polenta, you need to cook this cereal first. Here's the whole show:

1. In a kitchen pot, combine the grits and about 10 oz. of crushed malt and heat to 153°F. Hold temperature in a warm (150°F) oven for 20 minutes.
2. Meanwhile, dough-in main mash at 119°F for 20 minutes.
3. Bring cereal mash to a boil, and simmer for 30 minutes.
4. Raise the main mash to the 145°F Beta Rest for 30 minutes.
5. Add the cereal mash to the main mash and bring the temperature to the Alpha Rest and hold for 30 minutes.
6. Mashout at 170°F and hold for 10 minutes.
7. Lauter and add FWH to brewpot.

Recipe contributed by Jeff Renner

Classic American Pilsner

Around the turn of the century in the United States, the Pilsner style was very popular but with a typically American difference. That difference was corn (maize). Its only natural that in the largest corn growing region in the world that some would wind up in beer as a fermentable. In addition, 6 row barley was the most common variety available but its higher protein levels made it difficult to brew with. Adding corn (with almost no protein) to the mash helped dilute the total protein levels and added some flavor complexity as well. Unfortunately, Prohibition and higher brewing costs afterward helped to increase the use of corn and rice in American Pilsner-style beers to the point of blandness.

The beer of our grandfathers was a delicious, malty sweet beer with a balanced hoppiness. The brewing water should be low in sulfates. No commercially produced beer today adequately represents this beer that started the lager revolution in the United States. The strength of this beer used to fall in the mid 50s with a hopping of 25–40 IBUs. The style had become lighter by the time of Prohibition and afterwards tended to have an average gravity in the mid 40s with a correspondingly lower hopping rate of 20–30 IBUs. This beer can only be brewed using all-grain techniques due to the use of flaked maize or cooked corn grits which must be mashed. Refined corn sugar just doesn't cut it. Flaked maize allows the beer to be made with a single temperature infusion mash, while the grits have to be cooked first. Grits give a more authentic flavor and a detailed procedure is given with the recipe. (And it's more fun.)

Classic American Pilsner Style Guidelines

Style	OG	FG	IBUs	Color
Classic American Pilsner	1.044-60	1.010-15	25-40	3-6

Commercial Example:
(none)

No. 4 Shay Steam–California Common Beer

Malts	**Gravity Pts.**
6 lbs. of pale malt extract (LME)	72
¾ lb. of Crystal 40L malt	5
¼ lb. of malto-dextrin powder	3
BG for 3 Gallons	1.080
OG for 5 Gallons	1.048

Hops	**Boil Time**	**IBUs**
1.5 oz of Northern Brewer (7.5%)	60	30
.5 oz of Northern Brewer (7.5%)	15	5
Total IBUs		35

Yeast	**Fermentation Schedule**
California Lager (Liquid)	2 weeks at 60°F in primary fermenter

Options

All-Extract	6 lbs. of pale LME ½ lb. of amber DME ¼ lb of malto-dextrin powder
All-Grain	7 lbs. of 2 row base malt ¾ lb of Crystal 40L ½ lb. of Dextrin malt

Mash Schedule–Single Temperature Infusion

Rest Type	Temperature	Duration
Conversion	153°F	60 min.

California Common (Steam-type)

This is the most well-known historic American beer style; it was developed in the San Francisco Bay area in the mid-1800s. The Steam appellation most likely refers to the high degree of carbonation that the beers were reportedly served with, as well as its then high-tech sound. San Francisco has a moderate climate year-round, typically cool, cloudy and about 60°F in the winter months. The new bottom cropping (lager) yeasts did not behave like the ale yeasts brewers were used to working with. So, they hit on using wide shallow vessels, normally used for cooling after boiling, for fermentation which allowed the wort to stay cooler during fermentation and provided for faster settling of the yeast after fermentation. Using lager yeast at these relatively high temperatures caused the beer to develop some of the fruity notes of ales while retaining the clean crisp taste of lager beers. American grown hops, like Cluster, were used to the tune of 20–40 IBUs. The hop profile of Steam-type beer is predominantly from higher alpha acid hops with a more herbal character. The present day incarnation of California Common Beer, Anchor Steam™ beer, uses American grown Northern Brewer exclusively. The beer should be highly carbonated with a medium body and a light caramel color.

[The name of this beer comes from a Shay Steam Locomotive (Engine No. 4) that I tended one summer at Cass Scenic Railroad in Cass, WV.]

California Common Beer Style Guidelines

Style	OG	FG	IBUs	Color
California Common	1.044-55	1.011-14	35-45	8-14

Commercial Example:	
California Common	Anchor Steam

Einbock–Bock

Malts	Gravity Pts.
7 lbs. of pale malt extract (LME)	96
1.5 lbs. of Crystal 15L malt	7
1.5 lb. of Munich malt	~4
BG for 3 Gallons	1.107
OG for 5 Gallons	1.064

Hops	Boil Time	IBUs
1.5 oz of Perle (9%)	60	28
¾ oz of Tettnanger (4%)	10	2
Total IBUs		30

Yeast	Fermentation Schedule
Bavarian Lager (Liquid)	2 weeks at 50°F in primary fermenter Lager for 6 weeks at 35°F

Options

All-Extract	8 lbs. of pale LME 2 lbs. of amber DME ¼ lb of malto-dextrin powder
All-Grain	5 lbs. of 2 row base malt 5 lbs of Munich malt 1 lb. of Crystal 15L malt

Mash Schedule–Single Temperature Infusion

Rest Type	Temperature	Duration
Dough-in	104°F	20 min.
Beta Rest	140°F	30 min.
Alpha Rest	158°F	30 min.

Doppelbock Option: Increase the extract to 9 lbs. and change the Crystal Malt from Crystal 15 to Crystal 80. Increase the hop amounts to maintain about 30 IBUs for the batch. Also, use a larger starter, about 1 gallon's worth, but only pitch the slurry.

Bock

Bock beer is an old style, most likely introduced in Munich about 1638. The style grew out of the then world-famous beer of Einbeck. It was a strong beer brewed from 1/3 wheat and 2/3 barley with a pale color, crisp taste, and a hint of acidity. (The acidity was a carryover from the sour wheat beers of the day.) It was brewed as an ale, but was stored cold for extended periods. Einbecker beer was widely exported and was the envy of the region.

For years, the nobles of Munich tried to imitate the strong northern beer in their breweries with limited success. Finally in 1612, the brewmaster of Einbeck was persuaded to go south and work on producing a strong beer for Munich. The beer was released in 1638, a strong beer interpretation of the Munich Braunbier, a rich malty brown ale. The classic Munich Bock beer is a lager with an assertive malt character, a warmth from the higher alcohol level and only enough hop bitterness to just balance the sweetness of the malt. Bock and its big monastic brother, Doppelbock, should not have any fusel alcohol character nor any of the fruitiness of ales.

Doppelbock is a descendent of the heavy, rich beers of the Paulener Monks, who brewed this beer as liquid bread for their fasts at Lent and Advent. They named their beer, "Salvator" and many breweries brewing in this style have appended -ator to their beer's names. Today, Doppelbock has a higher contribution of roasted malt, yielding hints of chocolate or vanilla. These beers are fermented cold to force the yeast to take their time in consuming the high gravity worts. The beer is lagered for a long period to encourage the yeast to reduce any off flavors that would detract from the malt taste.

Bock Style Guidelines

Style	OG	FG	IBUs	Color
Traditional Bock	1.064-72	1.013-20	20-35	14-30
Doppelbock	1.073-120	1.018-30	20-40	12-30

Commercial Example:	
Traditional Bock	Einbecker Mai Ur-Bock
Doppelbock	Paulener Salvator

Cold But Not Baroque–Vienna

Malts	Gravity Pts.
7 lbs. of pale malt extract (LME)	84
¼ lbs. of Crystal 30L malt	2
¼ lbs. of Crystal 80L malt	1
¼ lbs. of Crystal 120L malt	1
<¼ lb. of Black Patent malt	0
BG for 3 Gallons	1.088
OG for 5 Gallons	1.053

Hops	Boil Time	IBUs
1 oz of Liberty (4%)	45	9
2 oz of Liberty (4%)	30	15
1 oz of Liberty (4%)	15	5
Total IBUs		29

Yeast	Fermentation Schedule
Bohemian Lager (Liquid)	2 weeks at 45°F in primary fermenter Lager for 6 weeks at 35°F

Options

All-Extract	6 lbs. of pale LME 1 lbs. of amber DME ½ lb of dark DME
All-Grain	7.5 lbs. of 2 row base malt ¼ lb. of Crystal 30L malt ¼ lb. of Crystal 80L malt ¼ lb. of Crystal 120L malt <¼ lb. of Black Patent malt

Mash Schedule–Multi-Rest Infusion

Rest Type	Temperature	Duration
Dough-in	104°F	20 min.
Beta Rest	140°F	20 min.
Alpha Rest	158°F	40 min.

Vienna

The Vienna style of lager was developed in the mid-1800s in the town of Vienna, naturally. It grew from the Marzen/Oktoberfest styles of Bavaria, but was influenced by the rise of the Pilsener style of Bohemia. Attempts to imitate the Pilsen style had resulted in harsh beers, due to the differences in brewing water between the two regions. The water of Bavaria (Germany) is higher in carbonates than that of Bohemia (Czech Republic). As discussed in *Chapter 15,* the use of pale malts in alkaline water results in too high a mash pH that extracts tannins from the grain husks. Of course, they didn't know this back then. They did know that they could brew darker beers that didn't have the astringency problems. The sweet amber lager now known as Vienna was the result of their efforts to produce a lighter beer. It became immensely popular and was copied in other brewing countries.

There was a lot of immigration from Central Europe to Texas and Mexico at that time, and of course the people brought their beer and brewing techniques with them. The hot climate were abysmal for lager brewing though, and commercial offerings were poorly regarded. Fortunately by the late 1800s, refrigeration became commercially viable and variations of Old World style lagers became very popular. The principle variation of the Vienna style in the New World is the Graf-Style Vienna, named after the Mexican brewer (Santiago Graf) who developed it. It incorporated a small percentage of heavily roast malt to compensate for the more alkaline water of the region, giving it a deep amber color with hints of red.

Vienna Style Guidelines

Style	OG	FG	IBUs	Color
Vienna	1.046-52	1.010-14	18-30	8-12

Commercial Example:	
Vienna	Ambier, Negra Modelo

Denkenfreudenburgerbrau–Oktoberfest

Malts	Gravity Pts.
7 lbs. of pale malt extract (LME)	84
½ lbs. of Caramunich malt	4
½ lbs. of Crystal 80L malt	3
½ lbs. of Crystal 120L malt	3
½ lb. of Munich malt	3
BG for 3 Gallons	1.097
OG for 5 Gallons	1.058

Hops	Boil Time	IBUs
2 oz of Liberty (4%)	45	17
1 oz of Liberty (4%)	30	7
1 oz of Liberty (4%)	15	5
Total IBUs		29

Yeast	Fermentation Schedule
Bavarian Lager (Liquid)	2 weeks at 45°F in primary fermenter Lager for 6 weeks at 35°F

Options

All-Extract	6 lbs. of pale LME 2 lbs. of amber DME
All-Grain	7 lbs. of 2 row base malt ½ lb. of Caramunich malt ½ lb. of Crystal 80L malt ½ lb. of Crystal 120L malt ½ lb. of Munich malt

Mash Schedule–Multi-Rest Infusion

Rest Type	Temperature	Duration
Dough-in	104°F	20 min.
Beta Rest	140°F	30 min.
Alpha Rest	158°F	30 min.

Oktoberfest

The Marzen and Festival beer were part of the basis of the Vienna style. Whereas the Vienna was intended to be the everyday premium drinking beer, the Oktoberfest was made for festivals. The original festival was a royal wedding sometime around 1500, and they have been celebrating ever since. (Some beers are worth it.) This rich amber style incorporates quite a bit of variation, from being soft and malty, malty and dry, to malty and balanced, and malty/bitter. Be that as it may, the hallmark of the Oktoberfest/Marzen style is the maltiness and a drier finish to make it less filling. If you plan to Polka for 12 hours straight, then this is your beer.

Oktoberfest Style Guidelines

Style	OG	FG	IBUs	Color
Oktoberfest/Maerzen	1.050-64	1.012-16	20-30	7-14

Commercial Example:	
Oktoberfest/Maerzen	Spaten Ur-Maerzen

Chapter Summary

So there you have it–the Reader's Digest version of some of the classic beer styles of the world. There are many, many more. If all this talk of different malts and tastes has made you thirsty, zip on down to your local GoodBeer Store, and bring back some samples for research and development. Don't be shy–how else can you decide what your want to brew next?

Chapter 20

Developing Your Own Recipes

Now it's time to drop the training wheels and strike out on your own. You have read about the various beer styles of the world and you should now have a better idea of the kind of beer you like best and want to brew. Homebrewing is all about brewing your own beer. Recipes are a convenient starting point until you have honed your brewing skills and gained familiarity with the ingredients. Do you need a recipe to make a sandwich? 'Course not! You may start out by buying a particular kind of sandwich at a sandwich shop, but soon you will be buying the meat and cheese at the store, cutting back on the mayo a little, giving it a shot of Tabasco, using real mustard instead of that yellow stuff and voila'–you have made your own sandwich just the way you like it! Brewing your own beer is the same process.

This chapter will present more guidelines for using ingredients to attain a desired characteristic. You want more body, more maltiness, a different hop profile, less alcohol? Each of these can be accomplished and this chapter will show you how.

Developing Your Own Recipes

Recipe design is easy and can be a lot of fun. Pull together the information on yeast strains, hops, and malts, and start defining the kinds of tastes and character you are looking for in a beer. Make sure you understand the signature flavors of your chosen beer style before you starting adding lots of stuff–otherwise you will probably end up with a beer that just tastes weird. Choose a style that is close to your dream beer and decide what you want to change about it. Change just one or two things at a time so you will better understand the result.

To help get your creative juices flowing, here is a rough approximation of basic recipes for the common ale styles:

Pale Ale—base malt plus a half pound of caramel malt,
Amber Ale—pale ale plus a half pound of dark caramel malt,
Brown Ale—pale ale plus a half pound of chocolate malt
Porter—amber ale plus a half pound of chocolate malt,
Stout—porter plus a half pound of roast barley.

Yes, those recipes are pretty crude, but I want you to realize how little effort it takes to produce a different beer. When adding a new malt to a recipe, start out with a half pound or less for a five gallon batch. Brew the recipe and then adjust up or down depending on your tastes. Try commercial beers in each of the styles and use the recipes and guidelines in this book to develop a feel for the flavors the different ingredients contribute.

Read recipes listed in brewing magazines, even if they are all-grain and you are not a grain brewer. By reading an all-grain recipe and the descriptions of the malts they are using, you will gain a feel for what that beer would taste like. You will get an idea of the proportions to use. For example, if you look at five different recipes for amber ale, you will probably notice that no one uses more than 1 lb. of any one crystal malt–all things are good in moderation. If you see an all-grain recipe that sounds good, but aren't ready to brew all-grain, use the principles given in Chapter 12 to duplicate the recipe using extract and the specialty grains. You may need to use a partial mash for some recipes, but most can be reasonably duplicated without.

The choice of yeast strain is your number one determinant for flavor. Take any ale recipe and change the ale yeast strain to a lager strain and you have a lager recipe. Look at yeast strain information and determine what flavors different strains would give to the recipe. Use the calculations in Chapters 5 and 12 to estimate the IBUs and the gravity of the beer. Plan a final gravity for the beer and decide what factors you would use to achieve it, i.e., extract brand, mash schedule, yeast strain, fermentation temperature, etc. You as the brewer have almost infinite control over the end result. Don't be afraid to experiment.

Increasing the Body

Very often brewers say that they like a beer but wish it had more body. What exactly is "more body"? Is it a physically heavier, more dense beer? More flavor? More viscosity? It can mean all those things. In many cases it means a higher final gravity (FG), but not at the expense of incomplete fermentation. On a basic level, adding unfermentables is the only way to increase the FG and increase the body/weight/mouthfeel of the beer. There are two types of unfermentables that can be added: unfermentable sugars and proteins.

Unfermentable sugars are highly caramelized sugars, like those in crystal malts, and long chain sugars referred to as dextrins. Dextrin malt and malto-dextrin powder have already been discussed in the ingredients chapters. Dextrins are tasteless carbohydrates that hang around, adding some weight and viscosity to the beer. The effect is fairly limited and some brewers suspect that dextrins are a leading cause of "beer farts," which result when these unfermentable carbohydrates are finally broken down in the intestines.

Dark caramel and roasted malts like Crystal 80, Crystal 120, Special B, Chocolate Malt, and Roast Barley have a high proportion of unfermentable sugars due to the high degree of caramelization (or charring). The total soluble extract (percent by weight) of these malts is close to that of base malt, but just because it's soluble does not mean it is fermentable. These sugars are only partially fermentable and contribute both a residual sweetness and higher FG to the finished beer. These types of sugars do not share dextrin's digestive problems and the added flavor and color make for a more interesting beer. The contribution of unfermentable sugars from enzymatic and caramel malts can be increased by mashing at a higher temperature (i.e. 158°F) where the beta amylase enzyme is deactivated. Without this enzyme, the alpha amylase can only produce large sugars (including dextrins) from the starches and the wort is not as fermentable. The result is a higher final gravity and more body.

Proteins are also unfermentable and are the main contributor to the mouthfeel of a beer. Compare an oatmeal stout to a regular stout and you will immediately notice the difference. These mouthfeel-enhancing proteins are commonly referred to as "medium-sized proteins." During the protein rest, peptidase breaks large proteins into medium proteins and protease breaks medium proteins into small proteins. In a typical well-modified malt, a majority of the large proteins have already been broken down into medium and small proteins. A protein rest is not necessary for further protein breakdown, and in fact, would degrade the beer's mouthfeel. A protein rest to produce medium-sized proteins for increased body is only practical when brewing with moderately-modified malts, or wheat and oatmeal—which are loaded with large proteins.

To add more body to an extract-based beer, add some caramel malt or malto-dextrin powder. You can also increase the total amount of fermentables in the recipe which will raise both the OG and FG, and give you a corresponding increase in alcohol too.

Grain brewers can add dextrin malt, caramel malt, unmalted barley or oatmeal in addition to using the methods above. Grain brewing lends more flexibility in fine tuning the wort than extract brewing.

Changing Flavors

What if you want a maltier tasting beer? A bigger, more robust malt flavor is usually achieved by adding more malt or malt extract to the recipe. A 1.050 OG beer is maltier than a 1.035 OG beer. If you add more extract, be sure to increase the bittering hops a bit to keep it balanced. This brings up another way to enhance the maltiness of a beer and that is to cut back on the flavor and aroma hop additions. You can keep the total hop bitterness and balance the same by adding more bittering hops at the beginning of the boil, but by cutting back on the middle and late hop additions, the malt flavors and aromas will be more dominant.

But what if you don't want the increased alcohol level that comes with an increase in gravity? The solution will depend on what flavor profile you are trying to achieve. If you want a stronger or crisper malt flavor, use a small amount of one of the toasted malts (e.g. vienna, munich, biscuit, etc.) in place of some of the base malt to help produce the malty aromas of German Bocks and Oktoberfests. If you want a richer, sweeter flavor, then use the next higher lovibond level of caramel malt to give a higher proportion of unfermentable sugars than the preceding caramel malt. If the flavor of the beer is too caramel sweet, then do the opposite. You can add Carastan or Crystal 15 or 25 malt to produce a lighter, honey-like sweetness instead of the caramel of Crystal 60 and 80 or the bittersweet of Crystal 120 and Special B.

If the flavor profile tastes a bit flat or you want to add some complexity to the beer, then substitute small amounts of different specialty malts for a larger single malt addition, while keeping the same OG. For instance, if a recipe calls for a half pound of Crystal 60L malt, try using a quarter pound each of Crystal 40L and Crystal 80. Or if a recipe calls for a half pound of Chocolate malt, try using just a quarter pound of Chocolate and adding a quarter pound of toasted malt or caramunich. For the same strength beer, you will have more flavors.

Using Honey

I have not mentioned honey until now because I don't use it often. Fermented honey is called mead, and a combination of beer and mead is called braggot. Many brewers like to use a bit of honey in their beer to add a bit of a kick and lighten the body. Some brewers like to use it as a priming sugar. But estimating the fermentability of honey can be tricky. The water content of honey varies from batch to batch so it is hard to know how much extract (i.e., ppg) is represented by a given weight or volume. The only recourse is to dilute it with a known amount of water and measure it with a hydrometer. Also, honey does not contain any of the amino acids that yeast need for nutrition. Therefore when you are brewing with honey and especially when you are making mead, you need to add yeast nutrient to the batch. Honey can impart a strong aroma and sharp sweet flavor that can be overpowering if more than a couple pounds are used in the batch. Start out with one pound and see how you like it; it can be added to any beer style. But be forewarned, honey based alcohol also tends to give nasty hangovers...

Toasting Your Own Malt

As a homebrewer, you should feel free to experiment in your kitchen with malts. Oven toasted base malt adds nutty and toasty flavors to the beer, which is a nice addition for brown ales, porters, bocks, and oktoberfests. Toasting-your-own is easy to do and the toasted grain can be used by both steeping and mashing. If steeped, the malt will contribute a high proportion of unconverted starch to the wort and the beer will be hazy, but a nice nutty, toasted flavor will be evident in the final beer. There are several com-

TOASTING YOUR OWN

Table 17—Grain Toasting Times and Temperatures

Temp.	Dry/Wet	Time	Flavors
275 °F	Dry	1 hour	Light nutty taste and aroma.
350 °F	Dry	15 minutes	Light nutty taste and aroma.
350 °F	Dry	30 minutes	Toasty, Grape-Nuts cereal flavor.
350 °F	Dry	1 hour	More roasted flavor, very similar to commercial Brown Malt.
350 °F	Wet	1 hour	Light sweet Toasty flavor.
350 °F	Wet	1.5 hours	Toasted Malty, slightly sweet.
350 °F	Wet	2 hours	Strong Toast/Roast flavor similar to Brown Malt, but slightly sweet.

binations of time and temperature that can be used in producing these special malts, so I will explain a couple of the factors that influence the flavor and describe the two methods I use.

The principal reaction that takes place when you toast malt is the browning of starches and proteins, known as the Maillard Reaction. As the starches and proteins brown, various flavor and color compounds are produced. The color compounds are called "melanoidins" and can improve the stability of beer by slowing oxidation and staling reactions as the beer ages.

Since the browning reactions are influenced by the wetness of the grain, water can be used in conjunction with the toasting process to produce different flavors in the malt. Soaking the uncrushed malt in water for an hour will provide the water necessary to optimize the Maillard browning reactions. Toasting wet malt will produce more of a caramel flavor due to partial starch conversion taking place from the heat. Toasting dry grain will produce more of a toast or Grape-Nuts™ cereal flavor which is perfect for nut-brown ales.

The malt should be stored in a paper bag for 2 weeks prior to use. This will allow time for the harsher aromatics to escape. Commercial toasted malts are often aged for 6 weeks before sale. This aging is more important for the highly toasted malts–toasted for more than a half hour (dry) or 1 hour (wet).

Discretion Is the Better Part of Flavor

There comes a time in every home brewer's development when they look at an item (e.g. maple syrup, molasses, Cheerios, chile peppers, potatoes, pumpkins, loquats, ginger root, spruce tips, heather, licorice, stale bread, mis-matched socks) and say, "Hey, I could ferment that!" While many of the mentioned items will indeed work in the fermenter (socks work well for dry-hopping), it is easy to get carried away and make something that no one really wants to drink a second glass of. I thought I would like spiced holiday beer–I didn't. I thought I would like a molasses porter–I didn't. I thought I would like loquat wheat beer–4 hours peeling and seeding 3 bags of those little bastards for something I couldn't even taste!

Experimentation is fine and dandy but be forewarned that you may not like the result. Refined sugars like molasses, candy sugar, honey, and maple syrup can taste wonderful in the right proportion–as an accent to a beer. But keep firmly in mind that you are brewing beer and not a liqueur. Refined sugars often generate fusel alcohols which can have solvent-like flavors. If you want to try a new fermentable or two in a recipe, go ahead but use a small amount so that it doesn't dominate the flavor. I feel hypocritical telling you to hold back after first saying to spread your wings and develop your own recipes. But I don't want you to spend a lot of time making a batch that is undrinkable. Just because it *can* be done, doesn't mean it *should* be done. Okay, enough said.

In the next chapter I will lead you through common problems and their causes and define some of the most common off-flavors.

Chapter 21

Is My Beer Ruined?

"Is My Beer Ruined?!"

This phrase has got to be the most frequently asked question by new brewers, and usually the answer is "No." Depending on the cause, it might end up with an odd flavor or aroma, but you will still be able to drink it and chalk it up as another lesson on the way to brewing that perfect beer. Although a lot can potentially go wrong with a batch, most problems arise from just a couple of root causes. If the recipe was good and you used quality ingredients, there are three common culprits: poor sanitation, bad yeast, or the wrong temperature. Most problems become noticeable once the beer is in the fermentor and nothing (or something weird) is happening. Let's examine some common symptoms and their possible causes.

Common Problems

Symptom:
I added the yeast 2 days ago and nothing is happening.

Cause 1: Leaky Bucket Lack of fermentation can be due to several things. If the airlock is not bubbling, it may be due to a poor seal between the lid and the bucket. Fermentation may be taking place but the CO2 is not coming out through the airlock.

Cure: This is not a real problem; it probably won't affect the batch. Fix the seal or get a new lid next time.

Cause 2: Bad Yeast When a batch is not fermenting , the most common problem is with the yeast. If dry yeast has been properly packaged and stored, it should be fully viable for up to two years. However, if you are using a yeast package that came taped to the top of a dusty can of malt extract, then the yeast may be too old or may have been subjected to poor storage conditions, and will not work for you.

Yeast need to be treated with care and be given the proper growing conditions. Dry yeast are de-hydrated–they're parched, they're in no condition to start work. They need some nice warm water to get re-hydrated in, some time to do some stretching, maybe an appetizer, and then they will be ready to tackle a full wort. If the dry yeast is just sprinkled onto the surface of the wort, some of the yeast will be up to the challenge, but most won't.

Cure: Re-hydration of yeast in plain water is strongly recommended because of the principles of osmosis. In a wort with a high concentration of dissolved sugar, the water that the yeast needs cannot be drawn across the cell membrane to wet it. The water is instead locked up in the wort, hydrating the sugars. A friend of mine, who insists on remaining nameless, was misled by the term, "pitching", and for his first batch attempted to forcibly throw each granule of dried yeast into the wort so that it would be wetted. That batch didn't turn out very well.

Likewise, liquid yeast cultures also need their breakfast routine. They have been kept in a refrigerator and need to be warmed and fed before there will be enough active yeast to do the job properly. There are a lot more yeast cells in a dry yeast packet than in a liquid packet. The liquid packet needs to be grown in a starter to produce enough cells to take on the job of a full five gallon wort. Both liquid and dry yeast cultures will have a lag time from when they are pitched until they start fermenting in earnest. Aeration, the process of dissolving oxygen into the wort, provides the yeast with the oxygen they need to greatly boost their growth rate and make enough yeast cells to do the job properly.

Cause 3: Too Cold The fermentation conditions may be too cold for an otherwise healthy yeast population. Ale yeast tend to go dormant below 60°F. If the yeast were re-hydrated in really warm water (105°F) and then pitched to a much cooler wort (65°F), the large difference in temperature can thermally shock the yeast and cause a longer lag time as they adjust. Or in some cases, that otherwise normal ale fermentation temperature could cause those warm-acclimated yeast to call it quits.

Cure: Try warming the fermentor by 5°F; it may make all the difference.

Cause 4: Improper Sanitation Sanitation can be carried too far some times. When you were preparing the warm water for rehydrating or boiling your yeast starter, did you cool it to the proper temperature range? If the water is too cold (below 80°F) the yeast will be sluggish and have a hard time getting rehydrated. If it is too hot (above 105°F) then the yeast are going to get scalded, and refuse to have anything to do with you and your wort. Also, if you added the yeast to the Starter wort and then boiled it, well, they're dead.

Cure: Pitch new yeast.

Symptom:
I added the yeast yesterday and it bubbled all day but it's slowing down/stopped today.

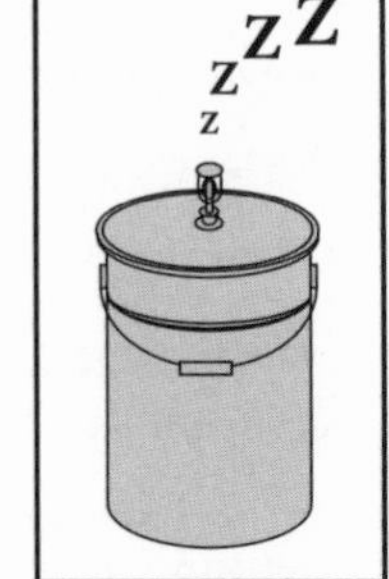

Cause 1: Lack of Preparation As I stated on the previous page, yeast that are improperly prepared, whether from lack of re-hydration, lack of numbers (i.e. lack of Starter), or lack of aeration, will often fail to finish the job.

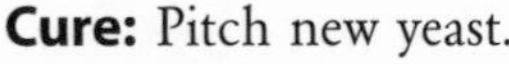

Cure: Pitch new yeast.

Cause 2: Too Cold Temperature can also be a major factor for fermentation performance. If the temperature of the room where the fermentor is cools down, even by only 5°F overnight, then the yeast can be slowed dramatically.

Cure: Always strive to keep the fermentation temperature constant, the yeast will thank you for it.

Cause 3: Too Warm The flip side of the coin could be that the temperature was warm, e.g. 75°F, and the yeast got the job done ahead of schedule. This often happens when a lot of yeast is pitched, the primary fermentation can be complete within 48 hours. This is not necessarily a good thing, as ferments above 70°F tend to produce a lot of esters and phenolics that just don't taste right. The beer will still be good, just not as good as it could have been. It will depend on your tastes and the yeast strain.

Cure: Always strive to keep the fermentation temperature within the recommended range, the yeast will thank you for it.

Symptom: The last batch (did that) but this batch is (doing this).

Cause 1: Different Conditions Different yeast strains behave differently and different ingredients can cause the same yeast to behave differently. Different temperatures can cause the same yeast working on the same ingredients to behave differently. Different yeasts working on different ingredients at different temperatures will produce different beers. Profound, eh?

Cure: Be patient; don't jump to conclusions. Go watch TV.

Cause 2: Yeast Health If you are brewing identical recipes at the identical temperatures then a difference in fermentation vigor or length may be due to yeast health, aeration or other factors. Only if something like odor or taste is severely different should you worry.

Cure: Wait and see.

Symptom: The airlock is clogged with gunk.

Cause: Vigorous Fermentation Sometimes ferments are so vigorous that the krausen is forced into the airlock. Pressure can build up in the fermentor if the airlock gets plugged and you may end up spraying brown yeast and hop resins on the ceiling.

Cure: The best solution to this problem is to switch to a blow-off hose. Fit a large diameter hose (e.g. 1 inch) into the opening of the bucket or carboy and run it down to a bucket of water.

Symptom: White stuff/brown stuff/green stuff is floating/growing/moving.

Cause 1: Normal Fermentation The first time you look inside your fermentor, you will be treated to an amazing sight. There will be whitish yellow-brown foam on top of the wort, containing greenish areas of hops and resins. This is perfectly normal. Even if it appears slightly slimy, it is probably normal. Only if something hairy starts growing on top of the wort should you be concerned. I remember one guy reporting a dead bat floating in his fermentor...That was definitely cause for alarm.

Cure: Get a new bat.

Cause 2: Mold A simple case of mold.

Cure: Mold can often be just skimmed off with no lasting effect on the beer's flavor. Withdraw a sample of the wort with a siphon or turkey baster and taste it. If it tastes foul then its not worth keeping. Otherwise the beer was probably not harmed. Infections in beer caused by molds are not dangerous. Be meticulous in your sanitation and you should not have any problems.

Symptom: It smells like rotten eggs.

Cause 1: Yeast Strain Rotten egg odors (hydrogen sulfide) can have two common causes: the yeast strain and bacteria. Many lager yeast strains produce noticeable amounts of hydrogen sulfide during fermentation. The smell and any sulfur taste will dissipate during lagering.

Cure: Let the beer condition or lager for a few weeks after primary fermentation.

Cause 2: Bacteria Bacterial infections can also produce sulfury odors and if you are not brewing a lager beer, then this is a good sign that you have an infection.

Cure: Let the fermentation complete and then taste it before bottling to see if it is infected. Toss it if it is.

Symptom:
It smells like vinegar.

Cause 1: Bacteria In this case, it probably is. Aceto bacteria (vinegar producing) and Lacto bacteria (lactic acid producing) are common contaminates in breweries. Sometimes the infection will produce sweet smells like malt vinegar, other times they will produce cidery smells. It will depend on which bug is living in your wort. Aceto bacteria often produce ropy strands of jelly which can be a good visual indicator, as can excessive cloudiness, after several weeks in the fermentor (although some cloudiness is not unusual, especially in all-grain beers).

Cure: If you don't like the taste, then pour it out. Lactic infections are desired in some beer styles. Be more meticulous with your sanitation, and don't suck to start siphons.

Cause 2: Wild Yeast and Bacteria Two other bugs are also common, Brettanomyces and Pediococcus. Brettanomyces is supposed to smell like horse sweat or a horse blanket. Raise your hand if you know what a horse smells like. From sweat, I mean. Anyone? I think Brett smells like leather, myself. Pediococcus can produce diacetyl and acidic aromas and flavors.

One man's garbage can be another man's gold, though. These two cultures and Lacto bacteria are actually essential to the Belgian Lambic beer styles. Under any other circumstances, beers that taste like Lambics would be discarded instead of being carefully nurtured and blended over a two year period. Lambic beers have a pronounced tartness with fruity overtones. This type of beer is very refreshing and is excellent with heavy food.

Cure: Be meticulous in your sanitation, or investigate Lambic brewing.

Symptom:
It won't stop bubbling.

Cause 1: Cool Temperatures A beer that has been continually fermenting (bubbling) for a long time (more than a week for ales, more than 3 weeks for lagers) may not have something wrong with it. It is often due to the fermentation being a bit too cool and the yeast are working slower than normal.

Cure: This condition is not a problem.

Cause 2: Gusher Infection However, the sustained bubbling is often due to "gusher type" infections. These infections can occur at any time and are due to wild yeasts or bacteria that eat the normally-unfermentable sugars, like dextrins. The result in the fermentor is a beer that keeps bubbling until all of the carbohydrates are fermented, leaving a beer that has no body and very little taste. If it occurs at bottling time, the beer will overcarbonate and will fizz like soda pop, fountaining out of the bottle.

Cure: Improve your sanitation next time.

If the beer seems to be bubbling too long, check the gravity with a hydrometer. Use a siphon or turkey baster to withdraw a sample from the fermentor and check the gravity. If the gravity is still high, in the teens or twenties, then it is probably due to lower than optimum temperature or sluggish yeast. If it is below 10 and still bubbling at several per minute, then a bug has gotten hold. The beer will not be worth drinking due to the lack of flavor.

Symptom: The fermentation seems to have stopped but the hydrometer says 1.025.

Cause 1: Too Cool This situation is commonly referred to as a "stuck fermentation" and can have a couple causes. The simplest cause and probably the most common is temperature. As previously discussed, a significant drop in temperature can cause the yeast to go dormant and settle to the bottom.

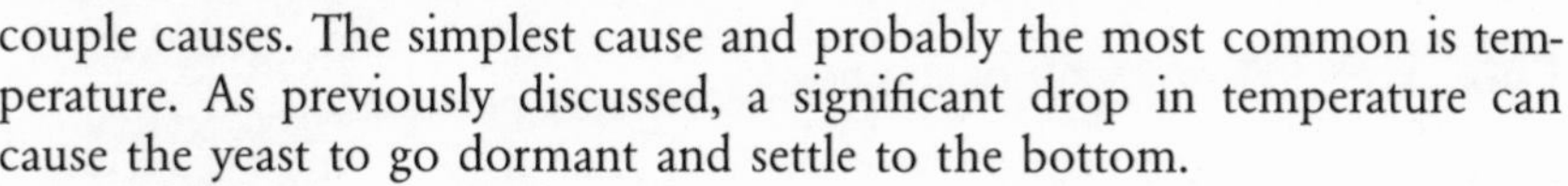

Cure: Moving the fermentor to a warmer room and swirling the fermentor to stir up the yeast and get them back into suspension will often fix the problem.

Cause 2: Weak Yeast / Underpitched The other most common cause is weak yeast. Referring back to previous discussions of yeast preparation, weak yeast or low volumes of healthy yeast will often not be up to the task of fermenting a high gravity wort. This problem is most common with higher gravity beers, OGs greater than 1.048.

Cure: Add more yeast.

Cause 3: Low Attenuating Extracts Another common cause for extract kit brewers is the use of extracts high in dextrins. Two brands are known to be high in unfermentables, Laaglanders Dry Malt Extract (Netherlands) and John Bull Liquid Malt Extract (UK). These are not bad extracts, in fact they are high quality, but their use is better suited to heavier bodied beers like strong ales, porters and stouts, where a high finishing gravity is desired.

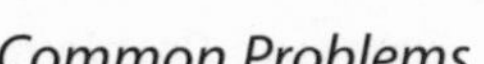

Symptom:
It won't carbonate.

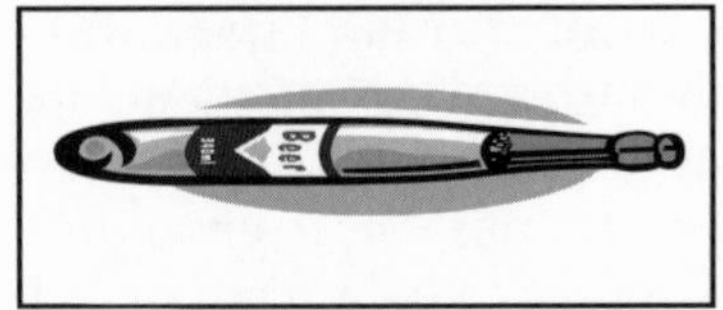

Causes: Need More Time Time, temperature and yeast strain all combine to form a government committee with the charter to determine a range of times when they can expect to be 90% finished with the Carbonation/Residual Attenuation Project. This committee works best without distractions– the meetings should be held in quiet, low light areas in a warm room. If the committee was given enough budget (priming sugar), then they should arrive at a consensus in about 2 weeks. If they don't get their act together within a month, then it's time to rattle their cages and shake things up a bit.

Cure: The yeast may have settled out prematurely and the bottles need to be shaken to get the yeast back into suspension. Likewise if the temperature is too cool in the room, moving the bottles to a warmer room may do the trick.

Symptom:
The bottles are overcarbonated.

Cause 1: Too much sugar You used too much priming sugar.

Cure: Vent and re-cap all of the bottles.

Cause 2: Bottled too soon You bottled before fermentation was complete.

Cure: Vent and re-cap all of the bottles.

Cause 3: Wild yeast A "gusher bug" has gotten into the beer. Gusher bugs (i.e., pediococcus and/or wild yeasts) are a real problem as they will keep on fermenting the beer until there is nothing left but fizzy bitter alcoholic water. The real danger with overcarbonation is exploding bottles. Bottle grenades can be very dangerous both from flying glass and from glass slivers left in the carpet.

Cures: Refrigerate the bottles and drink them while there is still some flavor left.

I recall one story I read on the rec.crafts.brewing newsgroup where a brewer recounted how both he and his partner had each added 3/4 cup of priming sugar to the batch, thinking that the other one had not. By venting and recapping all the remaining bottles after the initial explosions, they thought they had saved the batch. Then a massive storm front swept through and the corresponding drop in barometric pressure caused the rest of the bottles to explode. Be careful!

Symptom: The (finished) beer is hazy/cloudy.

Cause 1: Chill haze This is the number one cause of cloudy homebrew. It is caused by an insufficient cold break during cooling after the boil.

Cure: Use a wort chiller.

Cause 2: Starch If you made an all-grain beer and had incomplete conversion, or added/steeped a malt that needed to be mashed to an extract batch, then you can have residual starches in the beer that will cause cloudiness.

Cure: Check your malts to be sure if they need to be steeped or mashed. Watch the mash temperature and perhaps mash longer next time.

Cause 3: Yeast Yeast strains that have low flocculation, such as German Hefeweizen, will cause the beer to be cloudy.

Cure: Use a different yeast strain if you want a clearer beer.

In all cases, cloudiness can be combated by adding fining agents (e.g. isinglass, gelatin, Polyclar, bentonite) after fermentation. When all-grain brewing, the clarity can be enhanced by adding Irish Moss towards the end of the boil.

Common Off-Flavors

There are many flavors that contribute to the overall character of a beer. Some of these flavors have been previously described as malty, fruity, or bitter. When it comes time to figure out why a beer tastes bad though, we need to get more specific. In this section we will discuss several different flavors that can be perceived and what could cause each.

Acetaldehyde

A flavor of green apples or freshly cut pumpkin; it is an intermediate compound in the formation of alcohol. Some yeast strains produce more than others, but generally it's presence indicates that the beer is too young and needs more time to condition.

Alcoholic

A sharp flavor that can be mild and pleasant or hot and bothersome. When an alcohol taste detracts from a beer's flavor it can usually be traced to one of two causes. The first problem is often hot fermentation temperatures. At temperatures above 80°F, yeast can produce too much of the higher weight fusel alcohols which have lower taste thresholds than ethanol. These alcohols taste harsh to the tongue, not as bad as cheap tequila, but bad nonetheless.

Fusel alcohols can be produced by excessive amounts of yeast, or when the yeast sits too long on the trub. This is one reason to move the beer off of the hot and cold break when the beer is going to be spending a lot of time in the fermentor.

Astringent

Astringency differs from bitterness by having a puckering quality, like sucking on a tea bag. It is dry, kind of powdery, and is often the result of steeping grains too long or when the mash pH exceeds about 6. Oversparging the mash or using water that is too hot are common causes for extracting tannins. It can also be caused by over-hopping during either the bittering or finishing stages. Bacterial infections can also cause astringency, i.e. vinegar tones from aceto bacteria.

The brown scum that forms during fermentation and clings to the side of the fermentor is intensely bitter and if it is stirred back into the beer could cause very astringent tastes. The scum should be removed from the beer, either by letting it cling undisturbed to the sides of an oversize fermentor, or by skimming it off the krausen, or blowing off the krausen itself from a 5 gallon carboy. I have never had any problems by simply letting it cling to the sides of the fermentor.

Cidery

Cidery flavors can have several causes but are often the result of adding too much cane or corn sugar to a recipe. One component of a cidery flavor is acetaldehyde which has a green-apple character. It is a common fermentation byproduct and different yeasts will produce different levels of it depending on the recipe and temperature. Cidery flavors are encouraged by warmer than normal temperatures and can be decreased by lagering.

If it is caused by aceto bacteria, then there is nothing to be done about it. Keep the fruit flies away from the fermentor next time.

Diacetyl

Diacetyl is most often described as a butter or butterscotch flavor. Smell an unpopped bag of butter flavor microwave popcorn for a good example. It is desired to a degree in many ales, but in some styles (mainly lagers) and circumstances it is unwanted and may even take on rancid overtones. Diacetyl can be the result of the normal fermentation process or the result of a bacterial infection (i.e., pediococcus). Diacetyl is produced early in the fermentation cycle by the yeast and is gradually reassimilated towards the end of the fermentation. A brew that experiences a long lag time due to weak yeast or insufficient aeration will produce a lot of diacetyl before the main fermentation begins. In this case there is often more diacetyl than the yeast can consume at the end of fermentation and it can dominate the flavor of the beer.

Dimethyl Sulfides (DMS)/ Cooked Vegetable Flavors

Like diacetyl in ales, DMS is common in many light lagers and is considered to be part of the character. DMS is produced in the wort during the boil by the reduction of another compound, S-methyl-methionine (SMM), which is itself produced during malting. When a malt is roasted or toasted, the SMM is reduced beforehand and does not manifest as DMS in the wort, which explains why it is more prevalent in pale lagers. In other styles, DMS is a common off-flavor, and can be caused by poor brewing practices or bacterial infections.

DMS is continuously produced in the wort while it is hot and is usually removed by vaporization during the boil. If the wort is cooled slowly these compounds will not be removed from the wort and will dissolve back in. Thus it is important to not completely cover the brewpot during the boil or allow condensate to drip back into the pot from the lid. The wort should also be cooled quickly after the boil, either by immersing in an ice bath or using a wort chiller.

When caused by bacterial infection, DMS has a more rancid character, more liked cooked cabbage than corn. It is usually the result of poor sanitation. Repitching the yeast from an infected batch of beer will perpetuate the problem.

Estery / Fruity

Ales are supposed to be slightly fruity, and Belgian and German wheat beers are expected to have minor banana flavor components, but sometimes a beer comes along that could flag down a troop of monkeys. Esters are produced by the yeast and different yeast strains will produce different amounts and types. In general, higher fermentation temperatures produce more esters. Next batch, contrive to lower the fermentation temperature by a few degrees.

Grassy

Flavors reminiscent of chlorophyll and fresh cut grass occasionally occur and are most often linked to poorly stored ingredients. Poorly stored malt can pick up moisture and develop musty smells. Aldehydes can form in old malt and can contribute green grass flavors. Hops are another source of these green flavors. If the hops are poorly stored or not properly dried prior to storage, the chlorophyll compounds will become evident in the beer.

Husky / Grainy

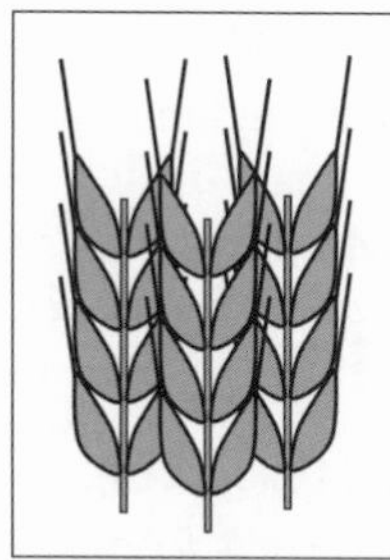

These flavors are akin to the astringent flavors produced from the grain husks. These flavors are more evident in all-grain beers due to poor grain crushing or sparging practices. If the grain husks are shredded during crushing by the use of a Corona grain mill for instance, these husk flavors are more likely to be extracted during the sparge. Follow the same procedures recommended to prevent astringency to correct the problem.

Grainy flavors can also be contributed by highly toasted malts. If you are making your own toasted malts, allow them to age at least two weeks after crushing so the harsher aromatic compounds can dissipate. Cold conditioning the beer for a month or two will often cause these harsh compounds to settle out with the yeast.

Medicinal

These flavors are often described as medicinay, Band-Aid™ like, or can be spicy, like cloves. The cause are various phenols which are initially produced by the yeast. Chlorophenols result from the reaction of chlorine-based sanitizers (bleach) with phenol compounds and have very low taste thresholds. Rinsing with boiled water after sanitizing is the best way to prevent these flavors.

Metallic

Metallic flavors are usually caused by unprotected metals dissolving into the wort but can also be caused by the hydrolysis of lipids in poorly stored malts. Iron and aluminum can cause metallic flavors leaching into the wort during the boil. The small amount could be considered to be nutritional if it weren't for the bad taste. Nicks and cracks ceramic coated steel pots are a common cause, as are high iron levels in well water.

Stainless steel pots will not contribute any metallic flavors. Aluminum pots usually won't cause metallic flavors unless the brewing water is alkaline with a pH level greater than 9. Shiny new aluminum pots will sometimes turn black when boiling water due to chlorine and carbonates in the water.

The protective (grayish) oxides of aluminum can be enhanced by heating the clean pot in a dry oven at 250°F for about 6 hours.

Moldy

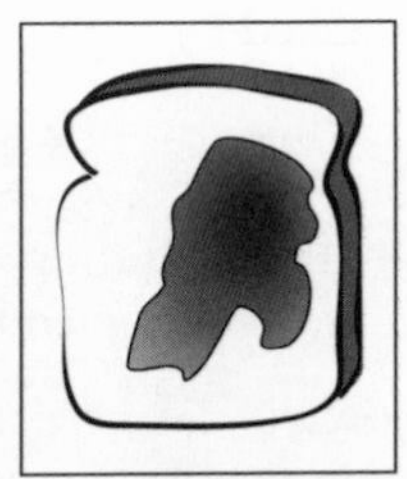

Molds are quickly recognized by their smell and taste. Black bread molds and mildew can grow in both wort and beer. Contamination is likely if the wort or beer is exposed to musty or damp areas during fermentation. If the infection is caught early enough, it can often be removed by skimming or cleaning of the surface before it significantly contaminates the batch. Chances are though that the spores have contaminated the batch and it could crop up again.

Oxidized

Oxidation is probably the most common problem with beer including commercial beers. If the wort is exposed to oxygen at temperatures above 80°F, the beer will sooner or later develop wet cardboard or sherry-like flavors, depending on which compounds were oxidized. See the discussion of oxygen and the wort in *Chapter 6–Yeast*.

Soapy

Soapy flavors can be caused by not washing your glass very well, but they can also be produced by the fermentation conditions. If you leave the beer in the primary fermentor for a relatively long period of time after primary fermentation is over ("long" depends on the style and other fermentation factors), soapy flavors can result from the breakdown of fatty acids in the trub. Soap is, by definition, the salt of a fatty acid; so you are literally tasting soap.

Solvent-like

This group of flavors is very similar to the alcohol and ester flavors, but are harsher to the tongue. These flavors often result from a combination of high fermentation temperatures and oxidation. They can also be leached from cheap plastic brewing equipment or if PVC tubing is used as a lautering manifold material. The solvents in some plastics like PVC can be leached by high temperatures.

Skunky

Skunky or cat-musk aromas in beer are caused by photochemical reactions of the isomerized hop compounds. The wavelengths of light that cause the skunky smell are the blue wavelengths and the ultraviolet. Brown glass bottles effectively screen out these wavelengths, but green bottles do not. Skunkiness will result in beers if the beer is left in direct sunlight or stored under fluorescent lights, as in supermarkets. Beers which use pre-isomerized hop extract and/or very little flavoring hop additions will be fairly immune to damage from ultraviolet light.

Yeasty

The cause of this flavor is pretty easy to understand. If the beer is green, is too young, and the yeast has not had time to settle out, it will have a yeasty taste. Watch your pouring method too, keep the yeast layer on the bottom of the bottle.

If the yeast is unhealthy and begins autolyzing it will release compounds that initially may be described as yeasty, although later the smell will turn rubbery.

Section V

Appendices

This final section is the closet–a place I could put extensive details and how-to's. *Appendix A–Hydrometers,* discusses the use and temperature correction of hydrometers. You don't really need one when you are just starting out, but once you start making your own recipes and start using grain, they become indespensible.

Appendix B–Brewing Metallurgy, is everything you never wanted to know about metals cleaning, corrosion, and joining. I am a metallurgist–I like this stuff. As my wife says, "Don't get him started!" But, a lot of homebrewers build their own equipment and this information can come in handy.

Appendix C–Building Wort Chillers, explains how to go about building one of these things for yourself. A wort chiller is one of the most useful things ever invented by mankind. Chillers can also be purchased at most homebrewing shops if you don't want to make your own.

Appendix D–Building a Mash/Lauter Tun, takes the mystery out of mashing. Lauter tuns are very easy to construct from an ice chest or picnic cooler. As usual, I am probably giving you more information than you need, but my intention is to help you build it right the first time.

Appendix E–Conversion Factors, contains tables for various metric conversions as well as brewer's units like hot water extract and °Plato.

Appendix F–Recommended Reading, lists other books by various authors that should be useful to you. Often these are books that I used as reference material, or books by authors who explore a particular topic well.

Appendix A

Using Hydrometers

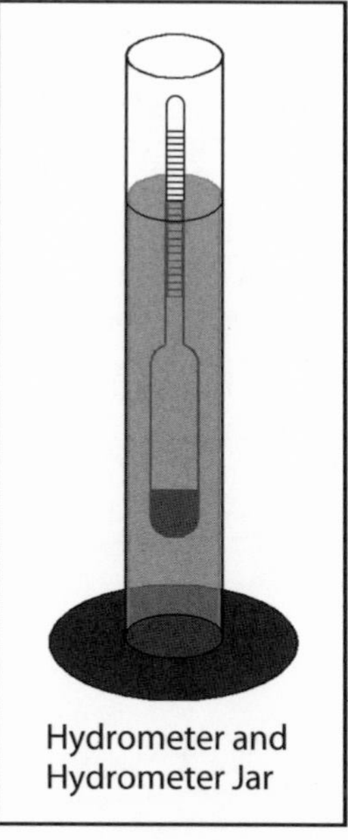
Hydrometer and Hydrometer Jar

A hydrometer measures the difference in gravity (density) between pure water and water with sugar dissolved in it, by flotation. A hydrometer is used to gauge the progress of fermentation by measuring one aspect of it–attenuation. Attenuation is the degree of conversion of sugar to ethanol by the yeast. Water has a specific gravity of 1.000. Beers typically have a final gravity between 1.015 and 1.005. Champagnes and meads can have gravities less than 1.000, because of the large percentage of ethyl alcohol, which has a specific gravity of less than 1. Hydrometer readings are standardized to 59°F (15°C). Liquid gravity (density) is dependent on temperature, and so hydrometer readings are adjusted to reflect the gravity of the liquid at this standard temperature.

A hydrometer is a useful tool in the hands of a brewer who knows what wort gravity is and why he wants to measure it. Beer recipes often list the Original and/or Final Gravities (OG and FG) to better describe the beer to the reader. For an average beer yeast, a rule of thumb is that the FG should be about ¼ to ⅕ of the OG. For example, a typical beer OG of 1.040 should finish about 1.010 (or lower). A couple of points either way is not unusual.

It needs to be emphasized that the stated FG of a recipe is not the goal. The goal is to make a good tasting beer. The hydrometer should be regarded as only one tool available to the brewer as a means to gauge the fermentation progress. The brewer should only be concerned about a high hydrometer reading when primary fermentation has apparently ended and the reading is about one half of the OG, instead of the nominal one forth. Proper yeast preparation should prevent this problem.

Beginning brewers often make the mistake of checking the gravity too frequently. Every time you open the fermenter, you are risking infection from airborne microbes. Check the gravity when you are ready to pitch the yeast, then leave it alone until the bubbling in the airlock stops. Checking the gravity in-between will not change anything except to possibly contaminate it. Also, always remove a sample of the wort to test it. Don't stick the hydrometer into the whole batch. Use a sanitized siphon or wine thief (turkey baster) to withdraw a sample of the wort to a hydrometer jar (tall, narrow jar) and float the hydrometer in that. There is less chance of infection and you can drink the sample to see how the fermentation is coming along. It should taste like beer even though it may taste a bit yeasty.

The hydrometer temperature correction table is shown at right. Hydrometer readings are standardized to 15°C (59°F). When discussing specific gravities of worts and beers with other brewers, always quote the standardized value. Measure the specific gravity of your wort, take the temperature, and add the correction value (delta G) given in the table. The correction number is added to the specific gravity number, 1.0XX.

Example: If the wort temperature is 108°F, and the measured gravity of the sample is 1.042, the delta G value would be between .0077 and .0081. Rounding it off to the third decimal place gives us .008, which is added to 1.042, yielding 1.050 as the standardized reading.

HYDROMETER CORRECTION TABLE

Table 18—Hydrometer Temperature Corrections

°C	delta G	°F	°C	delta G	°F
0	–0.0007	32.0	25	0.0021	77.0
1	–0.0008	33.8	26	0.0023	78.8
2	–0.0008	35.6	27	0.0026	80.6
3	–0.0009	37.4	28	0.0029	82.4
4	–0.0009	39.2	29	0.0032	84.2
5	–0.0009	41.0	30	0.0035	86.0
6	–0.0008	42.8	31	0.0038	87.8
7	–0.0008	44.6	32	0.0041	89.6
8	–0.0007	46.4	33	0.0044	91.4
9	–0.0007	48.2	34	0.0047	93.2
10	–0.0006	50.0	35	0.0051	95.0
11	–0.0005	51.8	36	0.0054	96.8
12	–0.0004	53.6	37	0.0058	98.6
13	–0.0003	55.4	38	0.0061	100.4
14	–0.0001	57.2	39	0.0065	102.2
15	0	59.0	40	0.0069	104.0
16	0.0002	60.8	41	0.0073	105.8
17	0.0003	62.6	42	0.0077	107.6
18	0.0005	64.4	43	0.0081	109.4
19	0.0007	66.2	44	0.0085	111.2
20	0.0009	68.0	45	0.0089	113.0
21	0.0011	69.8	46	0.0093	114.8
22	0.0013	71.6	47	0.0097	116.6
23	0.0016	73.4	48	0.0102	118.4
24	0.0018	75.2	49	0.0106	120.2

Appendix B

Brewing Metallurgy

This appendix may contain a lot more detail than most brewers need, but being a metallurgist, I frequently get asked about metals usage in brewing, so I thought my book would be a good place to write it all down for reference. The three main topics are: cleaning, corrosion, and joining. I will discuss how to best clean the various metals and how the different metals corrode. Homebrewers make a lot of their own equipment from off-the-shelf parts at the hardware store, but you should be aware how building an item from dissimilar metals can accelerate corrosion. Likewise, the joining of metals can present a challenge, so I will provide tips for soldering, brazing and welding.

Information on corrosion protection and welding is helpful of course, but the primary concern in brewing is flavor. We want to taste beer, not the materials or processes used in production. While some metals like aluminum, iron, and carbon steel will merely taste bad, other metals can be toxic if the concentrations are high enough. The last section of this appendix lists toxicity information for the metals commonly found in brewing and plumbing.

General Information and Cleaning

Aluminum

Aluminum is a good choice for brewpots and actively-heated mash/lauter tuns. It has high heat conductivity which helps prevent hot spots and scorching of the wort or mash, and is less expensive than stainless steel. The aluminum alloys most commonly used for cookware are alloys 3003 and 3004, which have very high corrosion resistance. Under the conditions of temperature and pH (4-8.5) normally encountered in brewing, aluminum (by itself) will not corrode and should not contribute any metallic flavor to your beer. However, when using aluminum for a brewing pot, do not clean the metal shiny bright between uses or you may get a metallic off-flavor. Like all metals, aluminum depends on a passive surface oxide for corrosion resistance, and scouring the metal shiny bright will remove the passive film. Allow it to grow dull and gray with use. To encourage a passive film in a brand new pot–wash it thoroughly, dry it thoroughly, and then put it in your oven (dry) at 350°F for about 10 minutes. This will help the anhydrous oxide layer to thicken. To clean aluminum, I recommend percarbonate-based cleaners like Straight A and PBW, or unscented dishwashing detergent like Ivory. Do not use bleach because it can cause pitting of the aluminum.

Aluminum will corrode if placed adjacent to another metal like copper in wort or beer, but even this most aggressive situation is usually insignificant in home brewing. I will discuss this in the galvanic corrosion section later.

Copper

Copper has a long history in brewing. It has high heat conductivity, is easy to form, and was traditionally used for making the brewing kettles or "coppers." These days professional brewers typically choose stainless steel because it is stronger, more inert, and easier to maintain. But for the homebrewer, copper and brass are still the cheapest and best choices for wort chillers and fittings. Copper is relatively inert to both wort and beer. With regular use, it will build up a stable oxide layer (dull copper color) that will protect it from any further interaction with the wort.

You should be aware that copper can develop a toxic blue-green oxide called verdigris. Verdigris includes several chemical compounds–cupric acetate, copper sulfate, cupric chloride, etc.–and these blue-green compounds should not be allowed to contaminate your beer or any other food item. To clean heavy oxidation, including verdigris, use vinegar or oxalic acid-based cleansers like Revereware Copper and Stainless Steel cleaner.

For regular cleaning of copper and brass, unscented dish detergent or sodium percarbonate-based cleaners are preferred. Cleaning and sanitizing copper wort chillers with bleach solutions is not recommended. Copper is attacked by oxidizers like bleach and hydrogen peroxide. These cleaning agents will quickly cause copper and brass to blacken as oxides form. These black oxides do not protect the surface from further corrosion, and since they are formed under alkaline conditions, are quickly dissolved by the acidic wort. If a wort chiller is cleaned or sanitized with bleach, the yeast will be exposed to potentially harmful levels of dissolved copper. No off-flavors are associated with copper, almost all of it is removed from solution by the yeast.

Brass

Brass is a group of alloys made from copper and zinc with some lead thrown in for machinability. The lead percentage varies, but for the alloys used in plumbing fittings it is 3% or less. Lead does not alloy or mix with the copper and zinc in brass, but instead exists as tiny globules. (Like bananas in Jell-O.) These globules act as a lubricant during machining and result in a micro-thin film of lead being smeared over the machined surface. It is this lead that can be dissolved off by the wort. While this teeny, tiny amount of lead is not a health concern, most people would be happier if wasn't there at all.

Fortunately, this surface lead is very easy to remove by soaking the parts in a solution of vinegar and hydrogen peroxide. You can get these at the grocery store or drug store. You can use white distilled vinegar or cider vinegar, just check the label to be sure it is 5% acid by volume. The hydrogen peroxide should be 3% by volume. To make the solution mix them at a 2-to-1 volume ratio of vinegar to peroxide. Simply immerse the parts in the solution and watch for the color of the parts to change. The process takes about 5 minutes to clean and brighten the surface. The color of the brass will change to buttery yellow-gold when the process is finished. If the solution starts to turn blue or green and/or the parts start darkening, it means that the parts have been soaking too long, the peroxide is used up, and the copper is dissolving which will expose more lead. Make up a fresh solution and soak the parts again.

While zinc in an important nutrient for yeast, it can be too much of a good thing. Corrosion of brass can cause soapy or goaty flavors plus increased acetaldehyde and fusel alcohol production when zinc concentrations exceed 5 ppm. But like copper, brass is usually stable in wort and will turn dull with regular use as it builds up a passive oxide layer. Brass should be treated like copper for normal cleaning.

Carbon Steel

Carbon steel is predominantly iron, alloyed with carbon and other trace elements. In homebrewing it is commonly used for porcelain-enamel cookware and as rollers in grain mills. Many homebrewers get started in the hobby with a speckled, black brewpot because of their low cost. The drawback with these pots is that the porcelain can become cracked or chipped with use, exposing the steel to the wort. While a little extra iron/rust in your diet won't hurt you, it will taste bad. There is no practical way to fix these flaws in the porcelain, and the steel will rust between uses. A rusty pot will cause metallic, blood-like off-flavors in the wort.

Many brewers like to build their own roller mills for crushing grain. Carbon steel is not stainless steel and needs to be protected against rusting by oiling or plating. If the roller steel is kept clean and dry between crushes, then it usually won't rust. It can be cleaned with a nylon or brass wire brush to remove any light rusting that may occur. Cleaning with steel wool or a steel wire brush will actually promote corrosion.

You can improve the corrosion resistance of carbon steel slightly by rubbing it with vegetable oil and buffing it off like car wax. By doing this you protect the surface oxides from hydration, producing a black oxide rather than rust. The black oxide is more adherent and will eventually cover the entire surface inhibiting further corrosion. The oil will become more wax-like too as the volatile components vaporize over time. This oxide/wax coating has limited corrosion resistance and direct contact with water will usually induce red rust. The rust can be cleaned away as described above to restore the more passive surface.

Stainless Steel

Stainless steels are iron alloys containing chromium and nickel. The most common type of stainless steels used in the food and beverage industry are the 300 series–typically containing 18% chromium and 8% nickel. The specific alloys that are most often used are AISI 304 and 316, which are very corrosion resistant and are basically inert to beer. The presence of chromium and its oxides inhibit rust and corrosion. Stainless steel is referred to as being "passivated" when the protective chromium oxide surface layer is unbroken. If this oxide layer is breached by iron (from a wire brush or drill bit) or dissolved by chemical action (like bleach) or compositionally altered by heat (brazing or welding) it will rust. The problem with stainless steel corrosion is usually not an off-flavor, but more often a hole in a valuable piece of equipment.

If the protective oxide layer is compromised, stainless steel can be repassivated by thorough cleaning to remove the contamination. Usually this cleaning involves dipping the steel in nitric or citric acid to dissolve free-iron or heavy oxides. But before you head out to buy acid, let me emphasize that you do not need it to passivate your stainless steel. The key to achieving a passive surface is getting the steel clean and free of contaminants. The easiest way to do this at home is to use a kitchen cleanser made for cleaning stainless steel cookware. Three examples are Bar Keepers Friend, Kleen King, and Revereware Stainless Steel cleanser. The active ingredient in these cleansers is oxalic acid, and it serves the same cleaning purpose as nitric acid. Once the surface has been cleaned to bare metal, the passive oxide layer will reform almost immediately. These cleansers also work very well for cleaning copper.

What this means is that you can perform cutting, grinding, soldering, or welding on your stainless steel and with just a few minutes of work with cleanser and a green scrubby, it will be passive again. Be sure to rinse thoroughly with clean water afterward so you don't leave any acid behind. Do not use steel wool or even a stainless steel scrubby, they will cause rust.

As you may be realizing, stainless steel is not invulnerable. Unfortunately, people tend to assume it is and then are shocked when it does corrode. Stainless steel has an Achilles heel, and that weakness is chlorine, which is common in cleaning products. Chlorine can dissolve the protective oxides, exposing the metal surface to the environment. Let's suppose you are sanitizing a corny keg with bleach. If there is a scratch, or a rubber gasket against the steel creates a crevice, then these secluded areas can lose their passivation. Inside the crevice, on a microscopic scale, the chlorides can combine with the oxygen from the oxide to form chlorite ions. That crevice becomes a tiny, highly active site compare to the more passive stainless steel around it, so it corrodes. This mechanism is known as crevice corrosion.

The same thing can happen at the water's surface if the keg is only half full. In this case, the steel above the waterline is in air and the passive oxide layer is stable. Beneath the surface, the oxide layer is less stable due to the chloride ions, but it is uniform. With a stable area above, and a less stable but very large area below, the waterline becomes the "crevice." Usually this type of corrosion will manifest as pitting or pinholes. The mechanism described is accelerated by localization so a pit is most often the result and can cause pinholes in kegs within a few hours.

Bio-fouling (trub deposits) and beerstone scale (calcium oxylate) can cause corrosion by a similar mechanism. The metal underneath the deposit can become oxygen depleted via biological or chemical action. When this happens, it will lose passivation and become pitted. This is why the removal of beerstone from stainless steel storage or serving tanks is important. The dairy industry has the same problem with calcium oxylate and uses phosphoric acid to dissolve the buildup. Phosphoric acid is a good choice as it does not attack the steel. Do not use swimming pool (muriatic) acid to dissolve beerstone or clean stainless steel. The acid used for swimming pools is actually hydrochloric acid, which is very corrosive to stainless steel.

A second way that chlorides can cause corrosion of stainless is by concentration. This mode is very similar to the crevice mode described above. By allowing chlorinated tap water to evaporate and dry on a steel surface, the chlorides become concentrated. The next time the surface is wetted, dissolution of the oxides at that spot will occur quickly, creating a shallow pit. The next time the keg is allowed to dry, that pit will probably be one of the last sites to dry, causing chloride concentration again. At some point in the life of the keg, that site will become deep enough for crevice corrosion to take over and the pit will corrode through.

To prevent the stainless steel from being attacked and pitted by the use of chlorinated cleaning products like bleach, follow these three simple guidelines:

- Do not allow the stainless steel vessel to sit for extended periods of time (hours, days) filled with bleach water or another chlorinated cleaning solution.
- If you use bleach for cleaning, rinse the vessel thoroughly with water and dry it to prevent evaporation concentration.
- Use percarbonate-based cleaning products like PBW, Straight A, B-Brite and One-Step, which won't attack the protective oxide layer.

Galvanic Corrosion

All corrosion is basically galvanic (an over-generalization). The electrochemical difference between two metals in an electrolyte causes an electric current to flow and causes one of the metals to ionize. These ions combine with oxygen or other elements to create corrosion products. Cleaning off the corrosion products will not solve the problem. The cause of the corrosion is usually the environment (electrolyte) and the metals themselves. Think back to your high school chemistry class and I will explain. An electrolyte can be defined as any liquid containing dissolved ions or salts, like tap water or sea water. Metals will corrode faster in strong electrolytes (sea water) than in weak electrolytes (tap water). Sticking a copper wire and a nail in a potato will give a different voltage (and therefore a different corrosion rate), than putting them in a glass of beer. And the ratio of the surface areas directly affects the corrosion rate too.

Because the galvanic corrosion potential of two metals depends on several factors, including electrolyte and surface area, the standard electrolyte for comparing galvanic potential is seawater. A galvanic series lists the corrosion potential of different metals from most active to most passive. When two metals are placed in contact with one another in the electrolyte, the most active metal of the pair will corrode. The separation of the two metals in the series gives an indication of the aggressiveness of the corrosion, all other factors being equal.

The surface area factor works like this: if you have an active metal coupled to a passive metal, and the passive metal has a larger surface area than the active metal, the corrosion of the active metal will be increased. If the active metal area is larger than the area of the passive metal, the corrosion of the active metal will decrease significantly. In either case, most of the corrosion will take place at the interface of the two metals.

GALVANIC SERIES

Table 19—Galvanic Series in Sea Water

Most Active
Magnesium
Zinc
Galvanized Steel
Aluminum (3003, 3004, pure)
Cadmium
Carbon Steel and Cast Iron
Un-passivated Stainless Steels
Lead-Tin Solder
Lead
Tin
Brass
Copper
Bronze
Passivated Stainless Steels
Silver Solder
Silver
Titanium
Graphite
Gold
Platinum
Most Passive

This means is that if you have small area of aluminum in contact with a large area of brass, the aluminum will corrode quickly. But, if you mount a small brass fitting on an aluminum pot, very little corrosion of the aluminum will take place because of the large difference in surface areas. Brass, copper, stainless steel, and silver solder are close enough together on the galvanic series that there is not much potential for corrosion between them. In my own experience, I've had brass and copper fittings mounted or soldered to my stainless steel converted kegs for the past 6 years and have not seen any corrosion to speak of.

This brings up the deciding factor in galvanic corrosion situations–exposure time. As homebrewers, our equipment is not operated 7 days a week. The equipment is only exposed to an electrolyte for a few hours at time, every couple of weeks or so. This is not much exposure compared to a professional brewery or other industrial corrosion situations. So, even if we design and build equipment with galvanic couples, the useful life of our equipment is pretty long.

Soldering, Brazing, and Welding

Soldering Soldering is the only non-mechanical joining process you need 90% of the time when you are building homebrewing equipment. The other 10% usually consists of welding a stainless steel nipple onto a converted stainless steel keg (more on this later). Soldering with silver plumbing solder allows you to join any of the metals we've discussed–although I would not advise soldering brass or copper to aluminum because of the increased galvanic affect.

The most common difficulty encountered when trying to solder to stainless steel is lack-of-wetting–the solder just balls up and sits there. This is caused by not having the proper flux. The surface oxides that protect stainless steel also make it difficult for the solder to wet it. Look for a flux that contains hydrochloric acid or zinc chloride. The second most common difficulty is getting the parts hot enough. Most of the time a propane torch is sufficient, but sometimes a methylacetylene-propadiene (MPS) type gas (e.g., MAPP gas) is needed if the parts are very large. MPS gas burns hotter than propane, but not as hot as acetylene and does not need special equipment. A good strategy is to "tin" one of the parts with solder beforehand to create a pre-wetted surface. Flux is then applied to the other parts and the joint is fitted together and heated. In this way, the surfaces are protected from oxidation until the solder can melt and make the joint. Once hot, more solder can be fed into the joint to finish it.

Brazing Brazing is exactly like soldering except the filler metals are stronger and melt at higher temperatures. Unless you are going to butt braze a nipple onto the side of a keg, there is no real reason to use brazing instead of soldering. Brazing provides for a stronger joint, but usually the strength of soldering is more than adequate. A problem with brazing stainless steel is that the temperatures used are right in an embrittling temperature range of 800-1600°F (425-870°C). These temperatures allow the chromium to diffuse away from the grain boundaries to form chromium carbides, depleting that area of chromium and creating un-stainless steel. In other words, it will crack and rust. Steel that has been exposed to these temperatures are referred to as being "sensitized." This situation soon leads to localized corrosion and rapid cracking of the grain boundaries. All exposure to these temperatures is cumulative and the resulting chromium diffusion cannot be corrected in any practical manner for homebrewers. It is much better to just avoid these temperatures and prevent it from occurring.

Welding If you need a really strong joint in stainless steel, the best method is welding, and the best welding method for adding nipples to converted kegs or pots is gas tungsten arc welding (GTAW), also known as TIG welding. TIG welding has the advantage of a small weld head, lower heat input is required, and filler metal is optional. The other common welding methods for stainless steel: gas metal arc welding (GMAW) also known as MIG, and shielded metal arc welding (SMAW) or "Stick Arc." These processes are not as well suited for welding thin sections. Although MIG is probably the most common process for welding stainless steel, the large weld head must be held close to the work and this decreases its effectiveness in tight areas.

It is pretty easy to check the *Yellow Pages* under *Welding* and find a local stainless steel welder to do the job for you. You will most likely not exceed their one hour minimum charge. In fact, when I had nipples put on 3 kegs a few years ago, I was only charged $25 dollars for the bunch. One thing to keep in mind after welding though is that the blue-ish or straw colored area around the weld joint is no longer passivated. The heat has created different oxides that can corrode, so you will need to use the stainless steel cleansers mentioned earlier to clean the discoloration away to bare metal so it can repassivate itself.

Hopefully this appendix has given you the information you need to help choose your materials and processes for gadget building. The points to remember are:

- Metals depend on passive surface oxides for corrosion protection
- Cleaning metals shiny bright may lead to off-flavors
- Soldering will usually do the job, and if not, welding is easily hired out.

Toxicity of Metals

While many people are aware of the general toxicity of lead and cadmium, most people don't know *how* they are toxic. In all cases of acute heavy metal poisoning by ingestion, the symptoms are nausea and vomiting. Chronic (long term) poisoning symptoms are more varied, but often involve skin discoloration, weakness, and anemia. The following information comes from two books on industrial hygiene and much of the data is from standard FDA animal testing. The notation "LD50" means that half of the (mice) in the test were killed.

Aluminum

Usage: Cookware and tubing. Galvanically active.

There was concern in the last ten years that the use of aluminum in cooking and the ingestion of aluminum contributed to Alzheimer's Disease. The medical study that generated the controversy was later found to have been flawed due to contamination of the test samples. An independent experiment conducted by Jeff Donaghue and reported in Brewing Techniques, Vol. 3, No. 1, showed that in side-by-side, aluminum vs. stainless steel, boils of wort from a single mash, there was no detectable difference in the amount of aluminum between the samples either before or after fermentation. The amount of aluminum in the wort boiled in the aluminum pot was less than the detection limit for the test–.4 mg/l or .4 ppm. If you drank twenty liters (5 gal.) of that beer, you would only ingest 20 milligrams of aluminum, about the same amount as a single buffered aspirin tablet, and half of what you would get from a single antacid tablet.

Acute Toxicity: Aluminum chloride–770 mg/kg body weight LD50

Chronic Toxicity: No data.

Cadmium

Usage: Cadmium is an ingredient in some solders and brazing alloys, none of which are approved for use with food. Also used as an industrial protective coating for steel, like galvanizing but with a more golden color. Galavanically active.

Acute Toxicity: Symptoms are exhibited upon ingestion of 14.5 mg, which causes nausea and vomiting. A case where a 180 lb man ingested 326 mg was not fatal. The presence of copper or zinc at the time of ingestion will lesson the absorption of cadmium into the body, and reduce the toxic effects.

Chronic Toxicity: A study with rats found a 50% reduction in hemoglobin over 3 months when rats drank water containing 50 ppm. Other rats drinking water with .1 to 10 ppm for 1 year showed no change in hemoglobin levels.

Chromium

Usage: Secondary constituent of stainless steel. Used as electroplated coating for carbon steel. Galvanically passive.

The Chromium 6 ion, which has received so much publicity lately, is not encountered in homebrewing. Chromium 6 is generated in solution during chromium electroplating and is a waste water contaminant. Chromium 6 is not generated by water sitting in contact with electroplated chromium, nor by the galvanic corrosion of stainless steel.

Acute Toxicity: Soluble chromates are of very low toxicity when ingested, 1500 mg/kg body weight before symptoms are seen. Chromium is most toxic when inhaled as fumes or dust.

Chronic Toxicity: No documented evidence of long term toxicity from soluble chromates.

Copper

Usage: Rigid and flexible tubing for plumbing and refrigeration systems. Galvanically passive.

Copper is an essential nutrient and the average daily intake is 2-5 milligrams. Ninety nine percent is excreted from the body in the feces.

Acute Toxicity: 200 mg/kg body weight of copper salts is the lowest lethal dose.

Chronic Toxicity: While dosages are not recorded, chronic poisoning symptoms include: headache, fever, nausea, sweating and exhaustion. Sometimes hair, fingernails, skin, and bones will turn green.

Iron

Usage: Primary constituent of carbon steel and stainless steel. Galvanically active.

While iron is an essential nutrient, overdoses of iron supplements are very dangerous.

Acute Toxicity: Ferric Chloride–400 mg/kg LD50. Symptoms of iron toxicity include: headache, nausea, vomiting, anorexia/ weight loss and shortness of breath. Skin might turn gray.

Chronic Toxicity: No data on dose. 10mg per day is the USRDA for men, 12mg per day for women.

Lead

Usage: Tertiary constituent of brass; used in plumbing fixtures, fittings, and non-food grade solders.

Acute Toxicity: The oral dose of soluble lead needed to kill a guinea pig is 1330 mg/kg body weight.

Chronic Toxicity: Lead slowly accumulates in the body. Normal intake from environmental sources averages .3 mg a day. Ninety two percent is excreted. Blood tests are a good indicator of lead exposure. Normal blood lead levels in adults are between 3-12 micrograms per 100 grams of whole blood. Adverse affects are not seen until a person has a blood lead level of over 20 micrograms/100 grams whole blood for several years. The more serious symptoms are not seen until blood levels test over 50 micrograms for a period of 20 years, or from a single massive dose. The symptoms of lead poisoning range from loss of appetite, metallic taste in the mouth, to anxiety, nausea, weakness, headache, to tremors, dizziness, hyperactivity, to seizures, coma and death from cardiorespiratory failure. Men will also suffer from impotence and sterility.

Zinc

Usage: Zinc is a secondary constituent of brass. It is an essential nutrient and the USRDA is 15 mg.

Acute Toxicity: Mass poisonings have been repeatedly reported from drinking acidic beverages from galvanized containers. (e.g. Wine punch in trash cans) Fever, nausea, stomach cramps, vomiting and diarrhea occurred 3-12 hours after ingestion. The lowest lethal dose in guinea pigs is 250 mg/kg.

Chronic Toxicity: No apparent injury in rats from .5 to 34 mg of ZnO for periods of 1 month up to 1 year.

References:

"Casarett and Doull's Toxicology," 2nd Edition, MacMillan Publishing Co., New York, 1980.

"Patty's Industrial Hygiene and Toxicology," 3rd Edition, Vol. 2A, John Wiley and Sons Inc., New York, 1981.

Owen, Charles, A., "Copper Deficiency and Toxicity," Noyes Publications, Park Ridge, New Jersey, 1981.

My thanks to Mike Maag–Industrial Hygienist with the Virginia Dept of Labor and Industry for helping me track down this information.

Appendix C

Building Wort Chillers

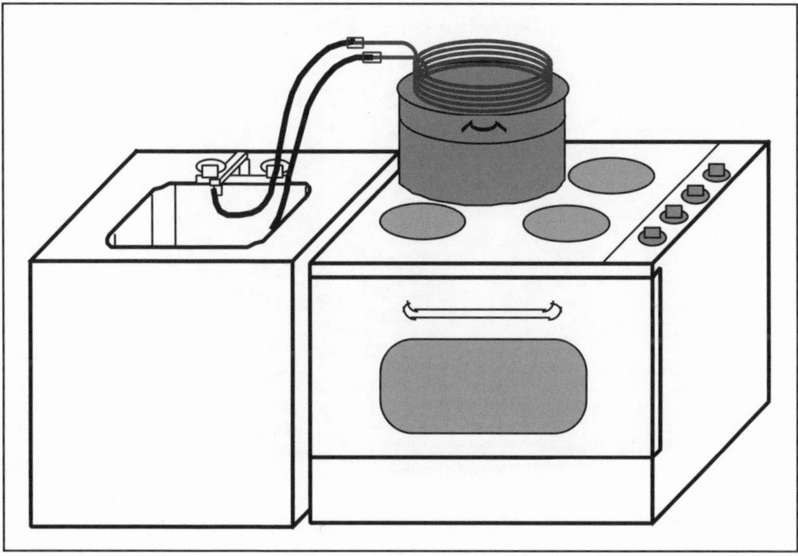

Figure 157—Immersion chilling on the stove.

Wort chillers are copper heat exchangers that help cool the wort quickly after the boil. There are two basic types: Immersion and Counterflow. The first works by circulating cold water through the tubing and submersing the cooling coil in the hot wort. The counterflow version works by running the hot wort through the tubing while cold water runs outside in the opposite direction. The basic material for both types is 3/8 inch diameter soft copper tubing. Half inch dia. tubing also works well, especially for large scale immersion chilling, but 3/8" is the most common. Do not use less than 3/8" because the restricted water flow impairs cooling efficiency.

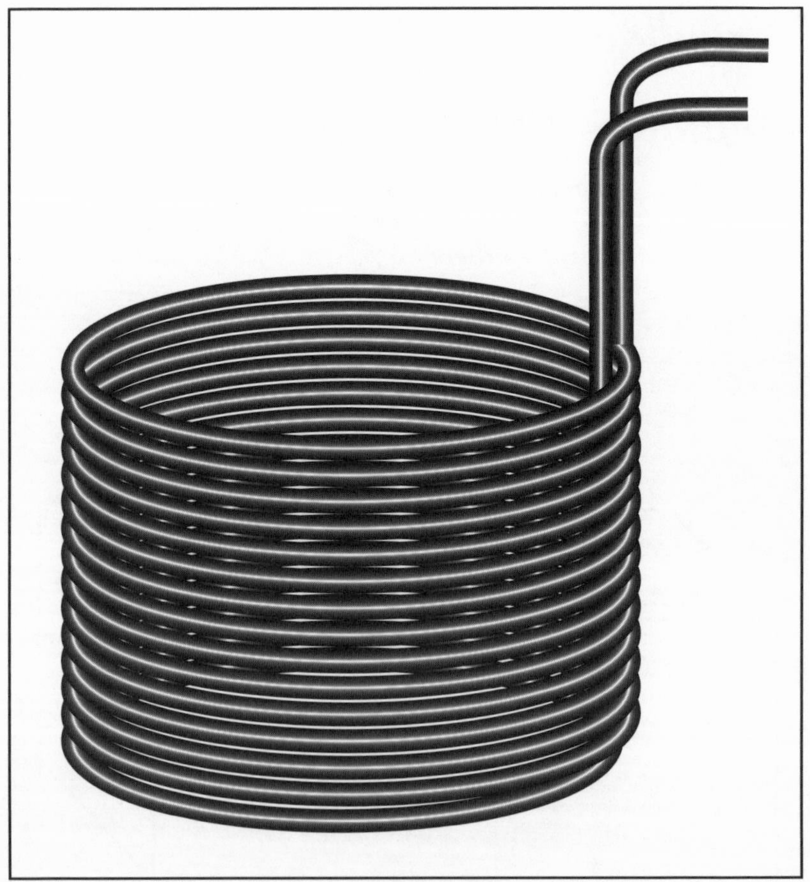

Figure 158—Immersion Wort Chiller.

Immersion Chillers

Immersion chillers are the simplest to build and work very well for small boils done on the stove in the kitchen. An immersion chiller is easy to construct. Simply coil about 30-50 feet of soft copper tubing around a pot or other cylindrical form. Spring-like tube benders can be used to prevent kinks from forming during bending. Be sure to bring both ends of the tube up high enough to clear the top of your boiling pot. Attach compression-to-pipe-thread fittings to the tubing ends. Then attach a pipe-thread-to-standard garden hose fitting. This is the easiest way to run water through the chiller without leaking. The cold water IN fitting should connect to the top coil and the hot water OUT should be coming from the bottom coil for best chilling performance. An illustration of a immersion chiller is shown at left and in *Figure 105* on page 217.

The advantages of an immersion chiller are that it is easily sanitized by placing it in the boil and will cool the wort before it is poured into the fermenter. This allows you to separate the wort from the cold break. Make sure the chiller is clean before you put it into the wort. Place it in the boiling wort the last few minutes before the heat is turned off and it will be thoroughly sanitized. Working with cool wort is much safer than hot wort. The cool wort can be poured into the fermenter with vigorous splashing for aeration without having to worry about oxidation damage. The wort can also be poured through a strainer to keep the spent hops and much of the break material out of the fermenter.

Counterflow Chillers

Counterflow Chillers are a bit more difficult to build but cool the wort a bit better. Counterflow chillers use more water to cool a smaller volume of wort faster than an immersion chiller so you get a better cold break and clearer beer. The drawbacks are that the cold break is carried into the fermentor with the wort, keeping the inside of the chiller clean between batches, and preventing hops and hot break material in the kettle from clogging the intake. A copper pot scrubby can be attached to the end of the racking cane to help filter out hop particles.

The increased efficiency of a counterflow chiller lets you use a shorter length of tubing to achieve the same amount of wort cooling. The tube-within-a-tube chiller can be coiled into a convenient roll. The hot side of the chiller, the racking tube intake, needs to be copper or another heat resistant material. Plastic racking canes tend to melt from the heat of the pot when the hot wort is siphoned into the chiller. Counterflow chillers are best used when there is a spigot mounted on the side of the pot negating the need to siphon the wort.

More details on next page.

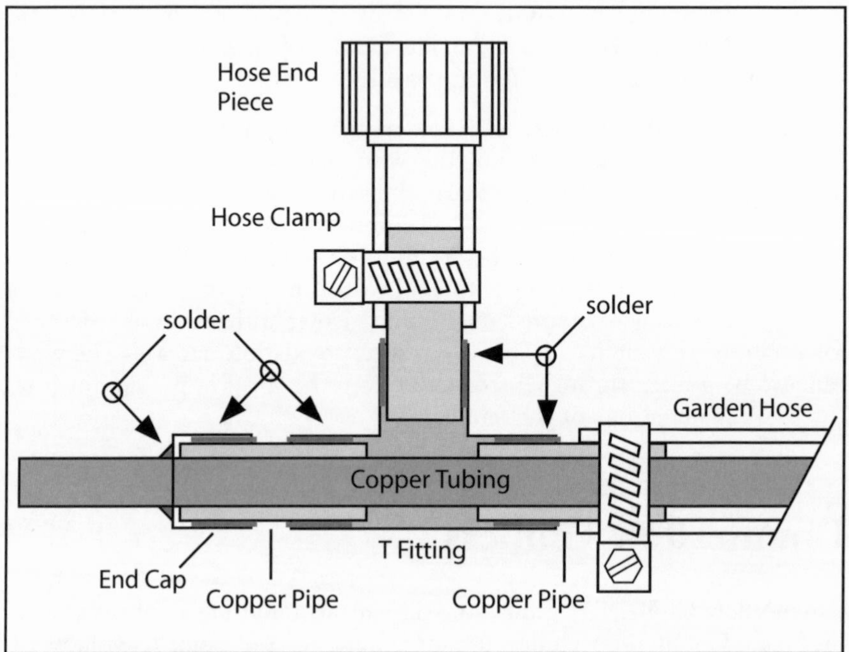

Figure 159—Suggested Counterflow Wort Chiller Design

Figure 159 shows one example for building the counterflow fittings and assembling the copper tubing inside the garden hose. The parts are common 1/2 inch ID rigid copper tube, an end cap and T sweat-type fittings. The parts are soldered together using lead-free silver solder and a propane torch. The ends of the garden hose are cut off and reattached via the tube clamps to the T's. The 3/8 inch diameter soft copper tubing that the wort travels thru exits the end cap thru a 3/8 inch diameter hole. The opening for the tubing is sealed with a fillet joint soldered around the hole.

There is a company that manufactures fittings exclusively for building counterflow chillers. These fittings are known as Phil's Phittings from the Listermann Mfg Co (www. listermann.com). The fittings make building a counterflow chiller very easy.

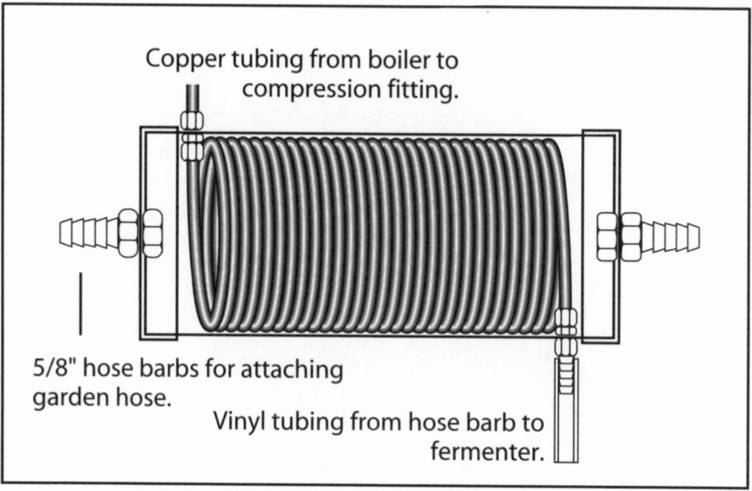

Figure 160—Hybrid chiller inside a PVC pipe.

Hybrid Chillers

There is a third type of chiller that is a hybrid of the previous two types. This chiller has the hot wort flow through the copper tubing like a counterflow, but the cooling water bathes the coil similar to an immersion chiller. This type of chiller is very popular and can be built for about the same cost as a counterflow. The basic materials are 2 feet of 6 inch diameter PVC pipe, and 20-30 ft. of 3/8" copper tubing. Brass or plastic hose barbs can be used for the water fittings but brass compression fittings should be used to attach the copper tubing to the hot side of the chiller. To obtain a good seal, a rubber washer and the "flat" of the compression/NPT fitting should be on the inside of the PVC pipe. With this type of chiller, it is important to have good water throughput to get a good chill. One option is to place a smaller diameter closed PVC pipe inside the copper coil to increase the flow of cooling water along the coils, rather than through the middle of the chiller body.

Appendix D

Building a Mash/Lauter Tun

In this appendix I will describe how to build a mash/lauter tun out of a common picnic cooler. Building one is inexpensive and the easiest way to start all-grain brewing. You may use either a rectangular chest cooler or a cylindrical beverage cooler fitted with a false bottom or manifold. Manifolds can be made from either rigid copper tubing with slip fittings or soft copper tubing with compression fittings. Everything you need to build one of these tuns is readily available at a hardware store.

False Bottom or Pipe Manifold?

The first step in building a mash/lauter tun is not to buy a cooler; the first step is to decide whether you will use a false bottom or a pipe manifold to collect the wort. The reason is that each lautering system works best with a different type of cooler. For the best performance you need to choose a cooler and lautering system that complement each other. Here is a list of pros and cons for each:

False Bottoms

Pros:

- False bottoms are always more efficient than manifolds–near 100%.
- False bottoms will lauter 96-98% of the grain in the grainbed uniformly.
- The efficiency of false bottoms hardly varies with grainbed depth.
- Pre-fabricated false bottoms for round beverage coolers are readily available from Listermann Mfg., Fermentap, and other suppliers.

Cons:

- False bottoms are tedious to fabricate yourself and difficult to fit to rectangular coolers. They should fit closely around the edges of the tun to prevent gaps that can allow sparge water to bypass the grainbed and reduce the yield.
- False bottoms are more prone to stuck sparges when the lauter flow is too fast.

Manifolds

Pros:

- Copper pipe manifolds are easy to build and fit to any size cooler.
- Efficiency can range from 88-98% depending on configuration, but highly efficient configurations are easily built.
- Properly designed, manifolds will lauter 90-95% of the grain in the grainbed uniformly.
- A center-to-center pipe spacing of 2 inches is optimum, although a larger spacing of up to 3 inches is still highly efficient, regardless of other variables.
- Stuck sparges are rare with manifolds.

Cons:

- The efficiency of manifolds varies with the pipe spacing and the grainbed depth.
- The grainbed is not lautered below the manifold, so the pipe slots should face down and be as close to the bottom of the tun as possible.
- Deeper grainbeds (8-12 inches) are more efficient.

The next few sections will discuss the science behind lauter tun flow and explain how these conclusions were derived. While these discussions are interesting, you may want to skip it and proceed directly to Choosing Your Cooler, if you have already decided which lautering system you will use.

Fluid Mechanics

To extract the wort from all regions of the grainbed, there must be fluid flow from all regions to the drain. In a perfect world, the wort would separate easily from the grain and we could simply drain the grainbed and be done. But it is not a perfect world, and we must rinse or sparge the grainbed to get most of the sugars, and some sugar is still left behind.

If some regions of the grainbed are far from the drain, and experience only 50% of the sparge flow, then only 50% of the wort from those regions will make it to the drain. Fluid mechanics allows us to model the flow rates for all regions of the grainbed and determine how well a grainbed is rinsed. These differences can be quantified, enabling us to compare different lauter tun configurations.

To illustrate, let's look at a cross section of a 10"W x 8"D lauter tun using a single pipe manifold. *See Figure 161a.* For every unit volume of water that rinses the grainbed, grain at the top of the grainbed will experience "unit" or 100% flow. As the flow moves deeper into the grainbed, it must converge to the single drain. This means that the region immediately above the drain can experience ten times the unit flow, while a region off to the side will only experience a tenth of unit flow. A vector flow plot for two pipes in *Figure 161b* demonstrates the same behavior, although the convergence affect is less. *Figure 162* shows the flow rate distribution for the single pipe manifold. For purposes of illustration, unit flow (the big white upper area) is drawn within the bounds of ±10% of actual unit flow, and lines for 50%, 90%, 110%, and 200% of unit flow are shown. *Figures 161* and *162* convey the same idea, but *Figure 162* lets us quantify the percentages of flow for this grainbed. A histogram (*Figure 163*) can be constructed from this data that summarizes the flow distribution and we can use the histogram to measure two aspects of lautering performance–efficiency and uniformity. *Figures 164* and *165* illustrate how these flows and histogram compare to a false bottom. The differences will be explored more fully in the next couple sections as we look at the concepts of lauter efficiency and unifomity.

FLUID MECHANICS

For fluid flow through porous material, Darcy's Law states that flow velocity is proportional to pressure variations and inversely proportional to the flow resistance. The resistance (or, inversely, the permeability) to flow is determined by the media—in our case, the grist. By combining this velocity/pressure relationship with a statement that water is conserved (i.e., water is not created or destroyed), we can form a numerical model which describes the fluid flow throughout the tun.

Darcy's Law: $\boldsymbol{u} = -K/\mu \ \nabla \ p$

where p is the pressure (actually the velocity potential), μ is the absolute (or shear) viscosity, K is the permeability, and ***u*** is the Darcean velocity (bulk flow velocity).

Conservation of water: $\nabla \bullet \boldsymbol{u} = 0$

Combination: $\nabla^2 \ p = 0$ (Laplace's equation)

Assuming K and μ are constant everywhere, this equation holds true everywhere except the top of the tun, where water is added, and the pipe slot, where liquor flows out of the tun. The tun walls are rigid (they can support any pressure), and nothing flows through the walls.

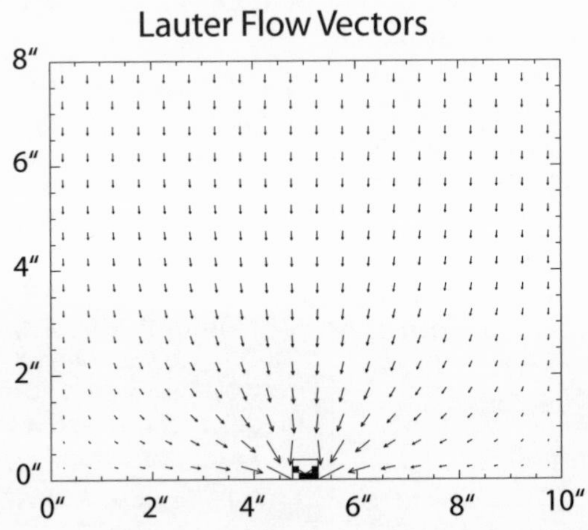

Figure 161—These pictures show the flow vectors in a lauter tun consisting of a single pipe and double pipes. The size of the arrows indicate the relative speed of the flow. Note how the flows converge to the pipes, leaving low flow areas in the corners. This same behavior has been observed when flowing food coloring dye through a grainbed in a glass aquarium.

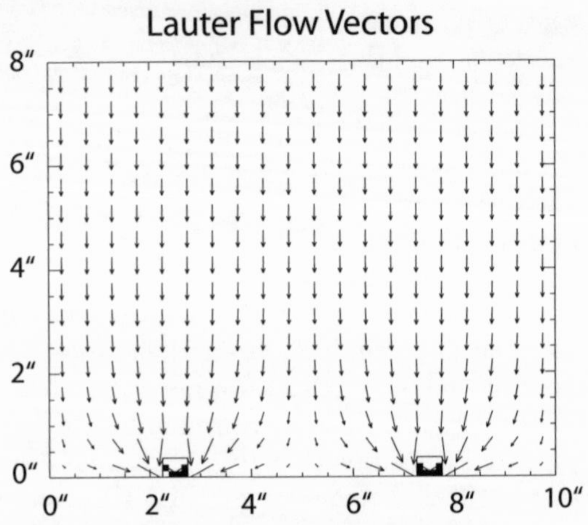

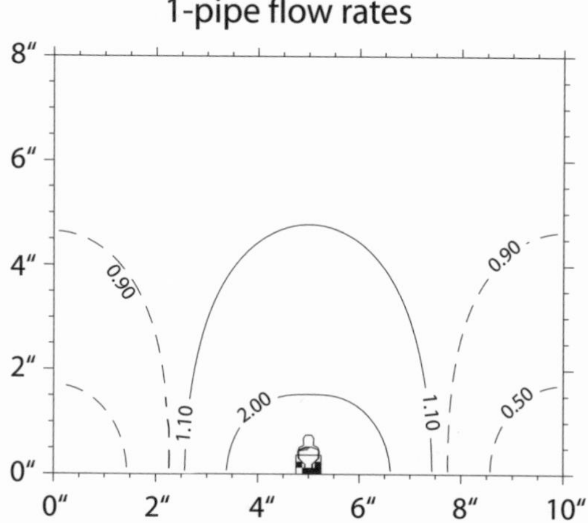

Figure 162—Darcy's Law allows us to quantify the flow velocity at any point within the lauter tun. The lines show the boundaries for 50, 90, 110, and 200% of unit flow velocity. The area above the flow lines is a region of uniform flow.

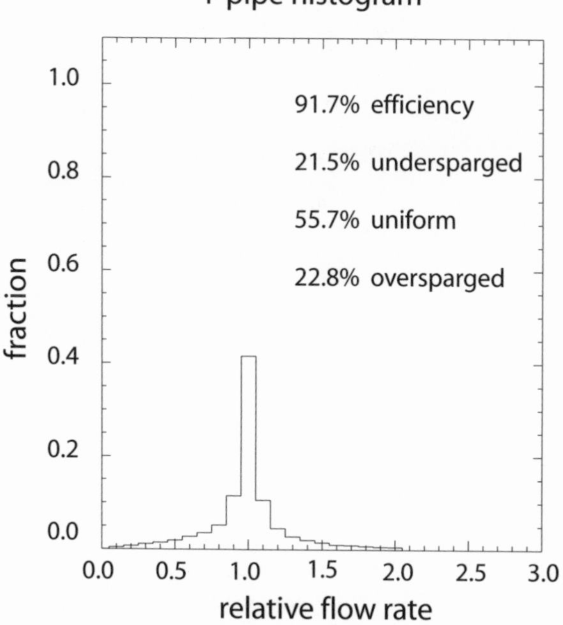

Figure 163—Histogram showing the relative amounts of different percentages of unit flow as described by Figure 162.

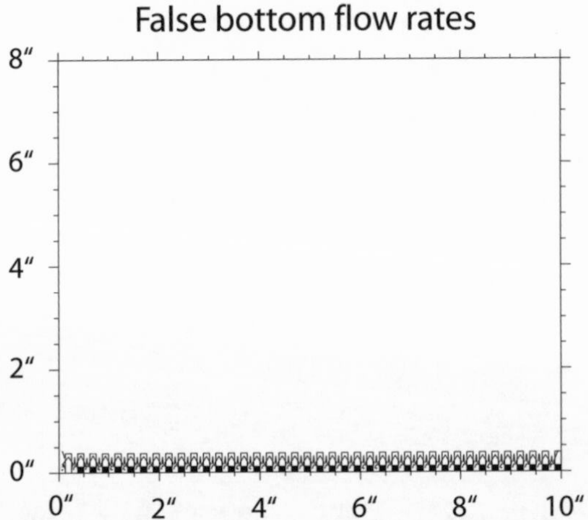

Figure 164—As in Figure 162, the lines for 50, 90, 110, and 200% on unit flow are shown, but the convergence zone is so small that you can't pick them out. This false bottom model represents 1/8″ holes on 1/4″ centers.

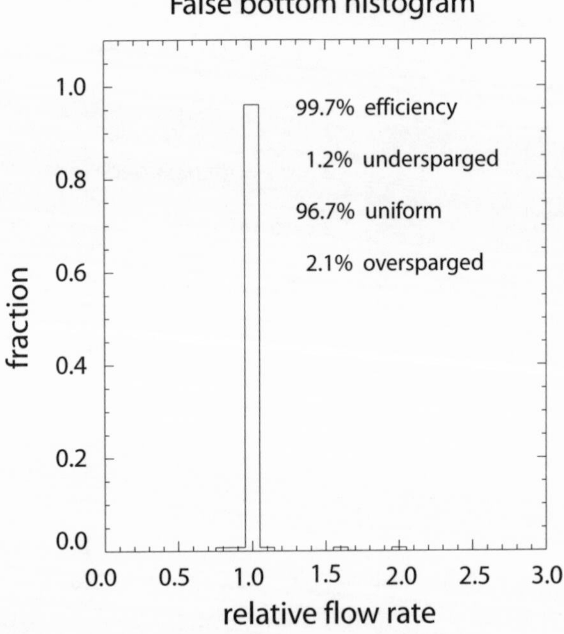

Figure 165—As expected, the histogram shows that the vast majority of the grainbed lies within the big white uniform region above the convergence zone.

Efficiency

Earlier we stated that 50% of the unit flow rate would only extract 50% of the sugar. However, we cannot say that a 200% flow rate will extract 200% of the sugar. If we assume that 100% of the unit flow rate extracts 100% of the sugar, then there is no more sugar to extract, and higher flow rates do not extract anything further, except possibly tannins. If we add up all the extraction from the different flow regions of the grainbed we can determine the efficiency percentage for that configuration.

For example, if a single pipe manifold system lautered 5% of the grainbed at 40% of unit flow, 10% at 60% flow, 15% at 80% flow, and 70% of the grainbed at 100% of unit flow or greater, the efficiency of that tun would be calculated as 90%

(5 x 40 + 10 x 60 + 15 x 80 + 70 x 100 = 90%).

A "perfect" false bottom would lauter the entire grainbed with 100% of unit flow, because every region would have equal access to the drain, and would be 100% Efficient. The computer model estimates a real false bottom (eighth inch holes on quarter inch centers) to be 99.7% efficient. *(See Figure 165)*

Uniformity

While efficiency gives a measure of the extract quantity, the uniformity gives a measure of its quality. To discuss uniformity, we look at three percentages of flow: flow less than 90%, flow between 90-110%, and flow greater than 110%. With these three percentages, we can compare different configurations that have similar efficiency, and determine if one configuration is more uniform than another. Flow values between 90-110% are considered "uniformly sparged," with values less than 90% being undersparged and values over 110% oversparged. Generally, the percentage of oversparging is roughly the same as the percentage of undersparging for any one configuration.

Returning to our single pipe manifold example, let's look at the histogram in Figure 163. From the histogram we can determine that only 56% of the grainbed is uniformly sparged, with 21% being undersparged and 23% over. This means 23% of the grainbed is subject to tannin extraction. But these percentages can be adjusted dramatically by tweaking a few variables.

The following four plots summarize the analysis of all the numerical models for pipe spacing, wall spacing, and depth, for half inch dia. pipes. Each plot shows the behavior of the stated quantity as a function of center-to-center pipe spacing, and as a function of grainbed depth. The relationships are nearly linear except at close pipe spacings and shallow grainbed depths.

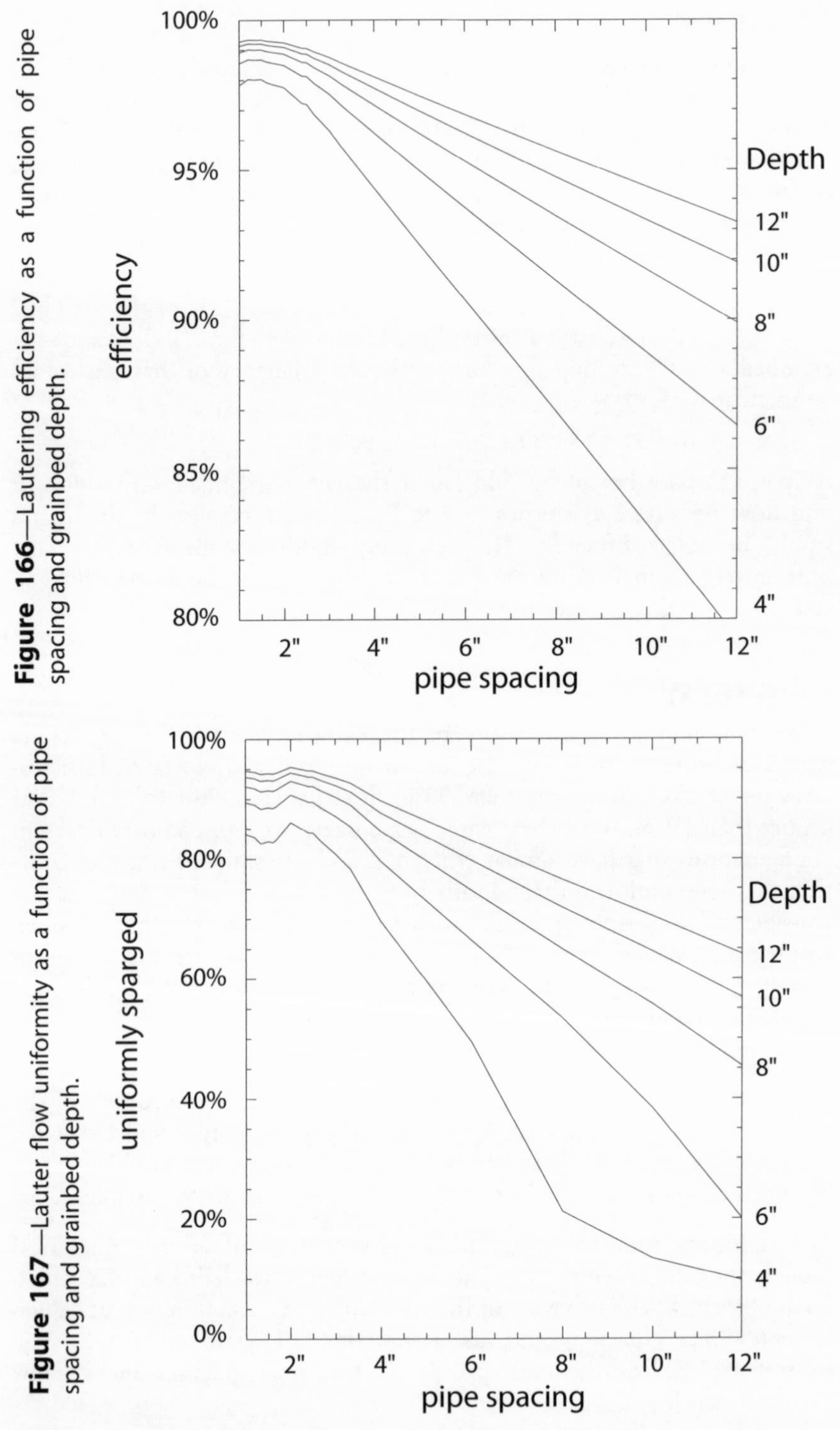

Figure 166—Lautering efficiency as a function of pipe spacing and grainbed depth.

Figure 167—Lauter flow uniformity as a function of pipe spacing and grainbed depth.

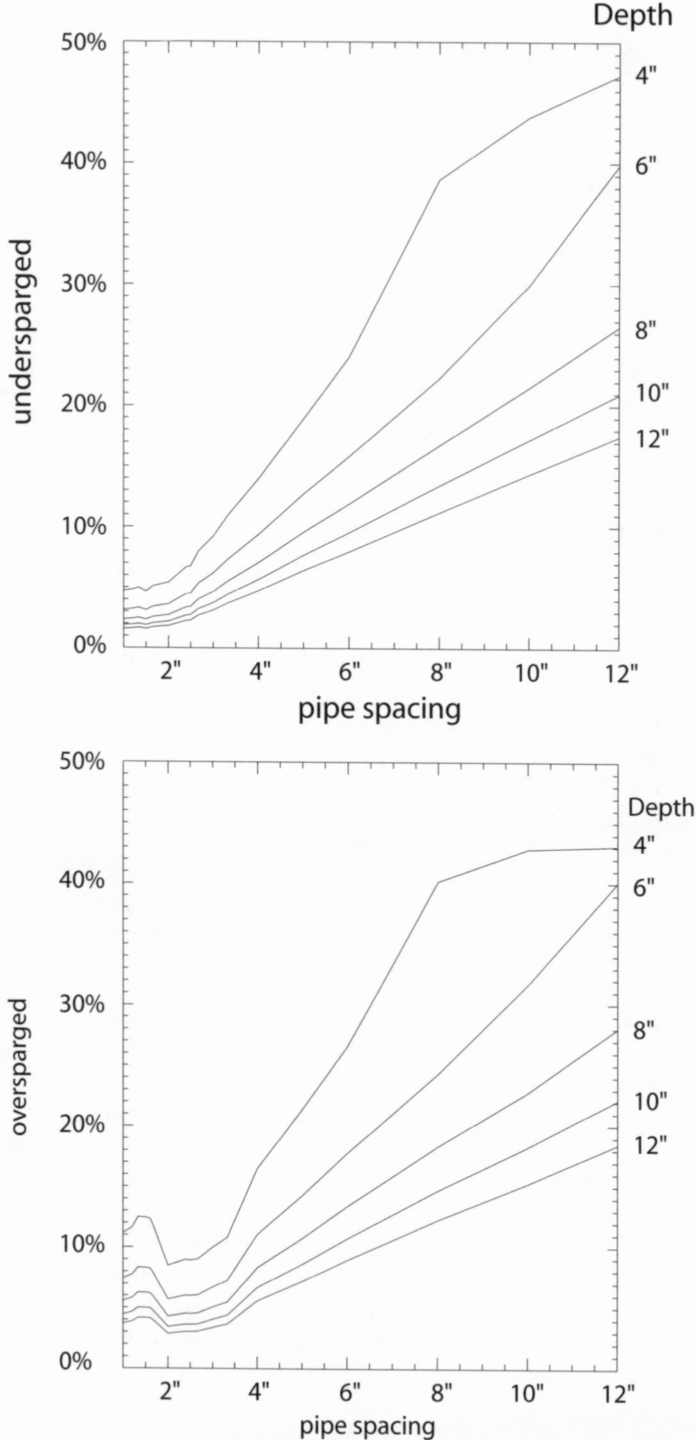

Figure 168—Lauter flow under 90% as a function of pipe spacing and grainbed depth.

Figure 169—Lauter flow over 110% as a function of pipe spacing and grainbed depth.

INTER-PIPE SPACING

Table 21—Effects for Pipe Spacing (10"W x 8"H Grainbed)

No. of Pipes	C-C Spacing	Efficiency	Under	Uniform	Over
1	10.00	91.7%	21.5%	55.7%	22.8%
2	5.00	96.2%	9.6%	79.7%	10.7%
3	3.33	97.8%	5.5%	89.0%	5.5%
4	2.50	98.6%	3.4%	92.1%	4.5%
5	2.00	98.9%	2.7%	93.0%	4.3%

Configuration Variables

My thanks to Brian Kern–an astrophysicist and brewer at Caltech, who was instrumental in helping me to develop this material.

The computer model analyzed 5184 configurations of lauter tun and manifold in order to determine the primary factors for flow efficiency and uniformity. In descending order, the factors are:

- inter-pipe spacing
- wall spacing
- grainbed depth

The analysis also determined that the pipe slots should always face down, being as close to the bottom as possible, because wort is not collected from below the manifold.

Inter-pipe Spacing By increasing the number of pipes across the width of the tun, you are effectively decreasing the inter-pipe spacing. Interestingly, analysis of the models *(see Figures 166-169)* showed a nearly linear relationship between both efficiency and uniformity, and pipe spacing, which peaks at a center-to-center pipe spacing of 4X the pipe diameter. For a half inch pipe, maximum efficiency and uniformity occur at a c-c spacing of 2 inches. Although optimum, it is not necessary for the pipes to be that close; the relationship between spacing and efficiency/uniformity starts to flatten out at 3 inches, or 6X the pipe diameter. As can be seen in *Table 21,* only 1-2% gains are realized by decreasing the pipe spacing from 3 to 2 inches, although when the grainbed is shallow (4"), the differences approach 5%.

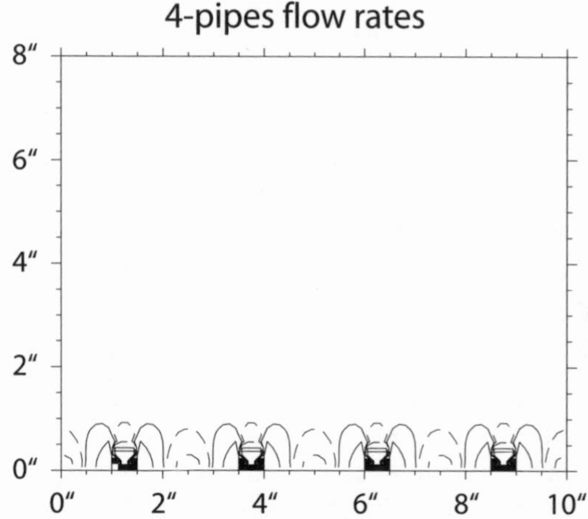

Figure 170—Over and under flow lines for 4 pipes, spaced 2.5 inches apart, in a 10″ wide tun. Compare this to the flow lines in Figures 162 and 164.

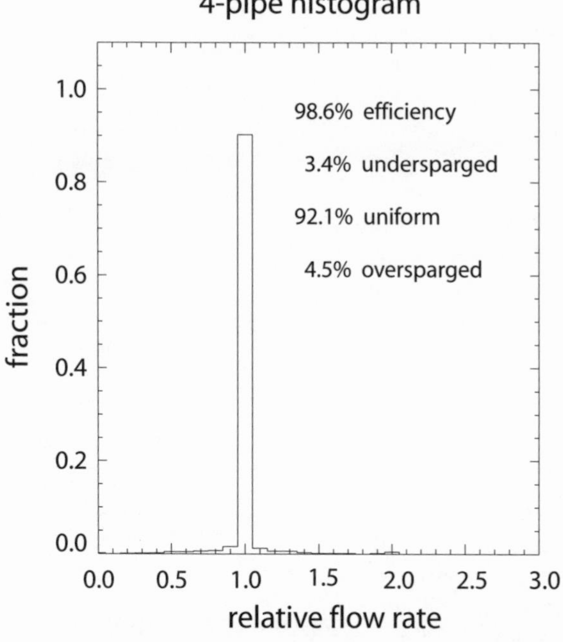

Figure 171—The histogram for 4 pipes shows a marked improvement over the single pipe histogram. These numbers may be found on Figures 166-169.

Wall Spacing The next most significant factor is the spacing of the pipes with respect to the walls of the tun. There are three ways to do this (See Figure 172):

- Edge Spacing–the two outermost pipes are placed flush against the walls and any more pipes are spaced evenly between them.
- Even Spacing–the spacing between the outer pipes and the walls is the same as the inter-pipe spacing.
- Balanced Spacing–the spacing between the outer pipes and the walls is half of the inter-pipe spacing.

As you can see in *Table 22,* balanced spacing is the most efficient. This spacing places the wall at half of the inter-pipe spacing so that flow velocity is symmetrical around every pipe in the manifold, and the manifold draws as uniformly as possible from the grainbed. Another way of looking at this variable is to say that balanced spacing covers the most area, with the closest inter-pipe spacing, using the least number of pipes, for a given tun width. This factor is most significant for large inter-pipe spacings; at closer spacings the difference and edge spacing is smaller (5% or less). But with edge spacing, you need to be aware of the propensity for preferential flow down the walls to the drain. This phenomena is often referred to as "channeling."

Fluid mechanics describes a "boundary effect," in which the flow resistance decreases at the wall, due to a lack of interlocking particles, as a function of particle size. The boundary layer for crushed malt is about 1/8 inch wide. Likewise, if the edges of a false bottom do not conform to the tun walls, the flow will divert into the gaps. These low-resistance paths can result in some percentage of the sparge water bypassing the grainbed, which decreases the yield from each volume of wort collected. This implies that balanced spacing is preferable to edge spacing for manifolds, and false bottoms should be fitted closely to the tun to minimize the affect.

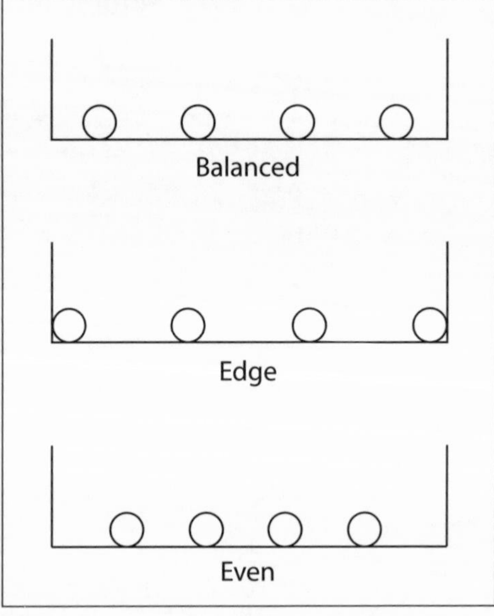

Figure 172—A comparison of balanced, edge, and even wall spacing configurations.

WALL SPACING

Table 22—Effects for Wall Spacing (10"W x 8"H Grainbed)

No. of pipes	Wall Spacing	Efficiency	Under	Uniform	Over
2	Balanced	96.2%	9.6%	79.7%	10.7%
2	Even	94.5%	14.1%	66.6%	19.3%
2	Edge	92.0%	20.4%	56.9%	22.7%
3	Balanced	97.8%	5.5%	89.0%	5.5%
3	Edge	96.4%	9.0%	80.3%	10.7%
3	Even	96.2%	9.7%	76.3%	14.0%
4	Balanced	98.6%	3.4%	92.1%	4.5%
4	Edge	98.0%	4.9%	89.9%	5.2%
4	Even	97.1%	7.1%	84.3%	8.6%
5	Balanced	98.9%	2.7%	93.0%	4.3%
5	Edge	98.6%	3.4%	92.0%	4.6%
5	Even	97.7%	5.3%	87.6%	7.1%

Grainbed Depth The depth of the grainbed is the final significant factor– not the total depth of the grain and sparge water, only the depth of the grain itself. For both false bottoms and manifolds, the amount of flow convergence depends only on the drain size and spacing. The shape of the convergence does not change significantly with depth (pressure), only the magnitude. Therefore the ratio of under-flow, uniform flow, and over-flow within the convergence zone is nearly constant, and the size (height) of the convergence zone is nearly constant. In the case of false bottoms, the drain features are quite small, so the convergence zone is narrow (less than a half inch in our model). But the drain features of manifolds are larger and more spread out, so the convergence zone is large and has a greater affect.

In other words– increasing the grainbed depth changes the proportion of the grainbed that is within the convergence zone, and as the depth increases, more and more of the grainbed is outside the zone and in a region of uniform flow, which increases the efficiency of the grainbed as a whole. Thus, the efficiency of false bottoms (small zones) are not significantly affected by grainbed depth, while manifolds (large zones) are, although you can minimize it by decreasing the pipe spacing to reduce the height of the zone.

GRAINBED DEPTH

Table 23-Effects for Grainbed Depth (10"W Grainbed)

No. of pipes	Depth	Efficiency	Under	Uniform	Over
1	4"	83.2%	43.8%	13.4%	42.8%
1	6"	88.9%	29.9%	38.4%	31.7%
1	8"	91.7%	21.5%	55.7%	22.8%
1	10"	93.3%	17.2%	64.5%	18.3%
1	12"	94.4%	14.3%	70.4%	15.3%
1	24"	97.2%	7.2%	85.1%	7.7%
1	48"	98.6%	3.6%	92.5%	3.8%
5	4"	97.8%	5.4%	86.1%	8.5%
5	6"	98.5%	3.6%	90.7%	5.7%
5	8"	98.9%	2.7%	93.0%	4.3%
5	10"	99.1%	2.2%	94.4%	3.4%
5	12"	99.2%	1.8%	95.3%	2.9%
5	24"	99.6%	0.9%	97.7%	1.4%
5	48"	99.8%	0.5%	98.8%	0.7%

For example: if you had only 1 pipe in a 10"W tun with a 8" deep grainbed, the convergence zone is about 3.5" deep, and the percentage of uniform flow is 55.7%. If the grainbed is 48" deep, the convergence zone is still about 3.5", but the percentage of uniform flow is now 92.5%. With 5 pipes, the zone height is .5" and 90% of the flow is uniform at 8"depth. When you build a manifold lautering system, both the pipe spacing and wall spacing affect the actual size of the convergence zone, and the grainbed depth affects its relative size. To get the best performance from a manifold system you should optimize all three factors.

To summarize:

- Design the manifold to have an inter-pipe spacing of 2-3 inches, closer to 2 being better.
- Use balanced spacing to get the best results with the fewest pipes.
- Choose a cooler that will give a good grainbed depth for your typical batch. I recommend a depth of 8-12 inches.

Building Copper Pipe Manifolds

Now that you know how to design a copper pipe manifold, let's build one. A manifold can be made of either soft or rigid copper tubing. Choose the form to suit your cooler and design. In a round cooler, the best shape is a circle divided into quadrants, although an inscribed square seems to work just as well. *See Figure 173.* In a rectangular cooler, the best shape is rectangular with several legs to adequately cover the floor area. When designing your manifold, keep in mind the need to provide full coverage of the grainbed while minimizing the total distance the wort has to travel to reach the drain. *Figure 174* illustrates this issue for a rectangular cooler.

In addition, it is very important to avoid channeling of the water down the sides from placing the manifold too close to the walls. The distance of the outer manifold tubes to the cooler wall should be half of the manifold tube spacing or slightly greater. This results in water along the wall not seeing a shorter path to the drain than wort that is dead center between the tubes.

The transverse tubes in the rectangular tun should not be slotted. The longitudinal slotted tubes adequately cover the floor area and the transverse tubes are close enough to the wall to encourage channeling. The slots should face down–any wort physically below the slots will not be collected. In a circular tun, the same guidelines apply but if you are using an inscribed square, the transverse tubes can be slotted where they are away from the wall.

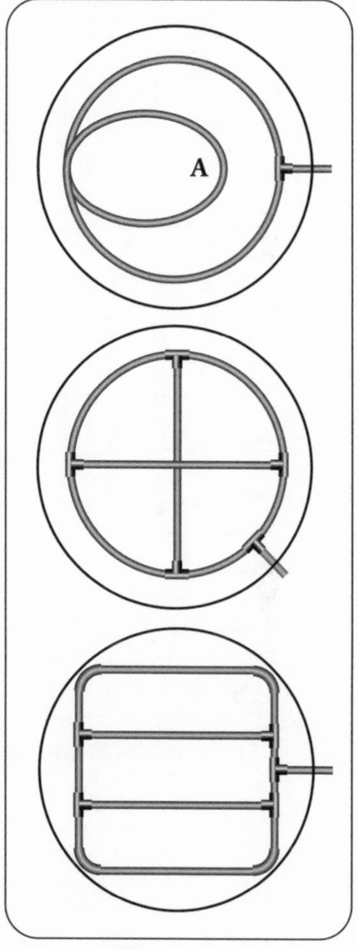

Figure 173—Difference in tubing length and area coverage for cylindrical cooler. In the first case, wort at point "A" has a comparatively long distance to travel to the drain. The second and third designs work equally well.

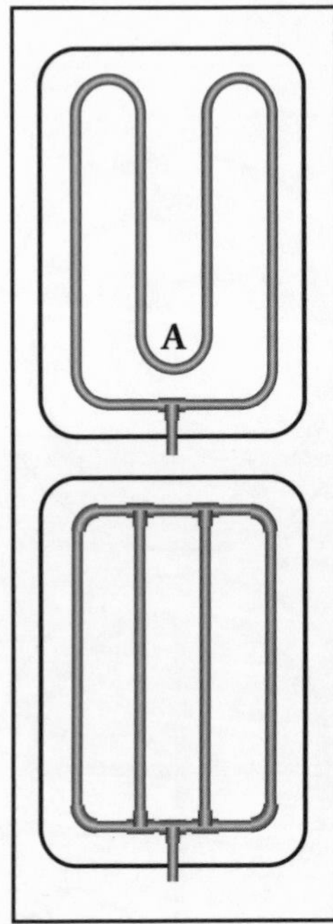

Figure 174— Rectangular manifolds. The manifold on top can be improved by providing a more direct means for wort at point "A" to reach the drain.

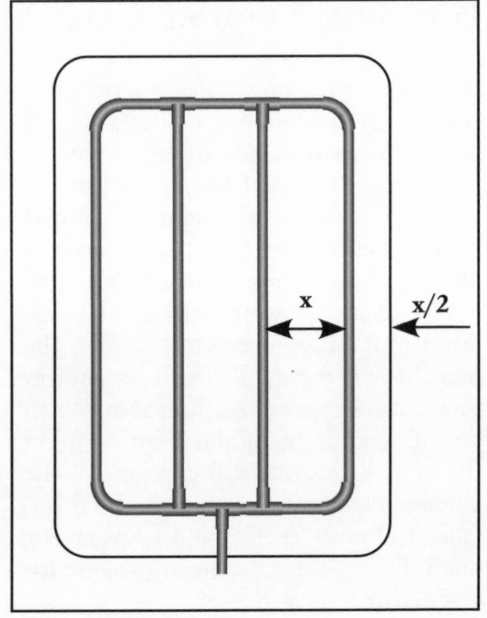

Figure 175—Design to make the best use of the space. The manifolds should fit the bottom of the cooler, covering the most area possible and not move around. Also, plan to space the manifold at half the pipe-spacing-distance to the wall to avoid channeling.

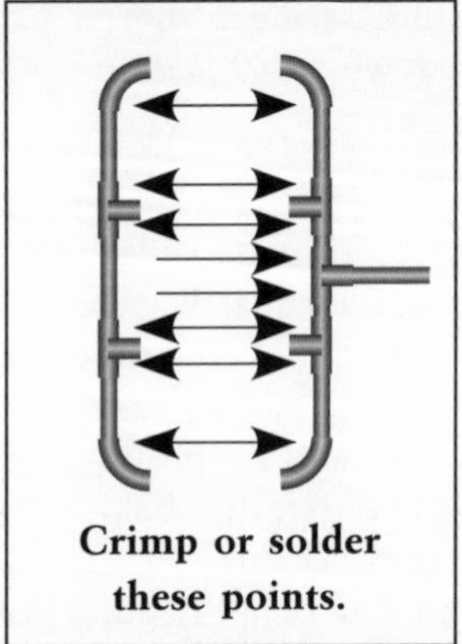

Figure 176—A useful design for rigid tubing manifolds. Solder or crimp the indicated connections but leave the other connections for the straight tubes free. This allows easy disassembly for removal and cleaning.

Choosing Your Cooler

The shape of the cooler determines your grainbed depth. In general, deeper is better. If the grainbed is too shallow (<4 inches), it won't filter efficiently and your beer will be cloudy with debris. However, if the grainbed is too deep it increases the risk of compacting due to high flow rates, and a stuck sparge can result. My advice is to pick your cooler based on your average batch; don't pick a larger one than you really need, thinking that a larger one will give you more flexibility for future batches. If you pick one that is too large for the majority of your batches, your grainbed depth will be too shallow and it won't hold the heat as well.

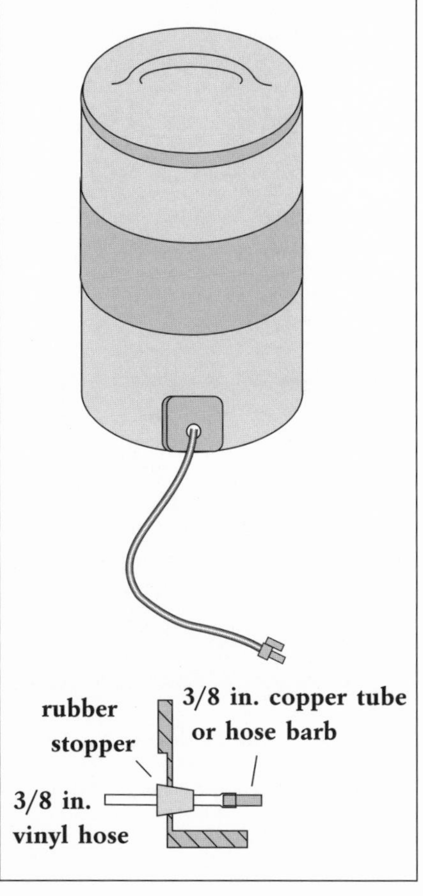

Figure 177—Beverage Cooler and Detail of Modified Spigot Hole. A suggested method for securing the manifold outlet through the cooler spigot hole using a mini-keg bung is shown here. Threaded plastic or brass bulkhead fittings can also used.

A five gallon cylindrical beverage cooler with either a false bottom or manifold works well for 5 gallon batches; it can hold 12 pounds of grain and the water to mash it. Naturally, the 10 gallon size is good for doing 10 gallon batches. These coolers have spigots which can be removed to make it easy to drain the wort via a bulkhead fitting. The rectangular ice chest coolers also work well, and are commonly sized at 20, 24, 34 or 48 quarts (5-12 gallons)–offering a good choice for any batch size. If you are using a rectangular cooler that does not have a drainage opening or spigot, lautering works just as well if you come over the side with a vinyl hose– siphoning the wort out. You should use a stopcock or clamp to regulate the flow, and as long as you keep air bubbles out of the line, it will work great. *See Figure 179.*

COOLER SIZES

Table 24—Common Cooler Sizes and Dimensions

The conversion factor for cubic inches to gallons (U.S. liquid) is 231 cubic inches per gallon.

Common Cooler Sizes (advertised size)	Internal Dimensions W x L x H or D x H (inches)	Actual volume based on dimensions (gallons)
20 Quart Rectangular	7 x 11 x 12	4
24 Quart Rectangular	9 x 14 x 10	5.4
34 Quart Rectangular	10 x 16 x 10	6.9
48 Quart Rectangular	11 x 18 x 12	10.3
5 Gallon Cylindrical	9.5 x 18	5.5
10 Gallon Cylindrical	12.5 x 20	10.6

The difficulty with using rectangular coolers for lautering is that it is hard to make false bottoms for them, and the grainbed tends to be shallow. Round false bottoms for cylindrical coolers are readily available from Listermann Manufacturing (listermann.com), but not for rectangular. Fortunately, manifolds made from copper tubing are easy to make and fit to any size cooler. My preference for 5 gallon batches is the 5 gallon cylindrical or the 24 quart rectangular coolers to ensure adequate grainbed depth. These sizes work well for 1.040-1.060 beers.

Here are all the guidelines for designing efficient manifolds and lauter tuns:

- Cylindrical coolers work well with either false bottoms or manifolds.
- Rectangular coolers are difficult to fit with false bottoms, but manifolds can be easily made.
- Choose a cooler that will give a good grainbed depth for your typical batch. I recommend a depth of 8-12 inches.
- Design the manifold to have an inter-pipe spacing of 2-3 inches, closer to 2 being better.
- Use balanced spacing to get the best results with the fewest pipes.
- A difference in the efficiency percentage between two lautering designs can be mitigated by adding the percent difference in additional grain, and may reduce the potential for oversparging in the less efficienct system by adding to the pH buffering capacity of the grainbed during the lauter.

ESTIMATING GRAINBED DEPTH

In order to estimate the typical grainbed depth in a cooler, you need to know the dimensions of the cooler and the OG of your typical batch. And you need to know that 1 lb. of dry grain has a mash volume of 42 fluid ounces, without freestanding water. (In SI units: 500g has a volume of 1.325 liters.)

Here is how you calculate it:

1. Multiply your typical batch size (5 gal.) by your typical OG (1.050) and divide by your typical yield in ppg (30) to determine your average grainbill.

   5 x 50 / 30 = 8.3 lbs

2. Multiply this weight by 42 fl.oz per lb to determine the volume of the grainbed.

   8.3 x 42 = 350 fluid ounces

3. Multiply the grainbed volume by 1.8 to convert it to cubic inches.

   350 x 1.8 = 630 cubic inches

4. Divide the grainbed volume in cubic inches by the floor area of the tun (9" x 14") to get the resultant depth.

   630 / (9 x 14) = 5 inches deep

If you want to calculate the total volume of the mash (including free-standing water), you just need to know that any water ratio beyond 1 quart per pound only adds its own volume.

For example, 8 lbs of grain at a ratio of 2 quarts per pound would equal 8 x (42 + 32) = 592 fluid ounces or 4.6 gallons.

Home Mashing Setups

To properly conduct a mash you will need room. You will need to heat the mash water and sparge water, and boil the entire 6-7 gallons of wort. Many brewers find that an electric stove is not up to the task, unless they can sit the pot on 2 burners at once. A gas stove will usually do the job, but it is often more economical (i.e., less hassle) to buy a propane burner. The total investment for a home-canning or crab-cooker type propane burner is usually less than $100.00, including the propane tank.

If you are using single temperature infusion mashes or 2 step infusion mashes in a cooler mash/lauter tun, you will only need one burner. You will need two brewpots that can each hold 6-7 gallons. Usually this translates to two 8 gallon porcelain-enamel pots.

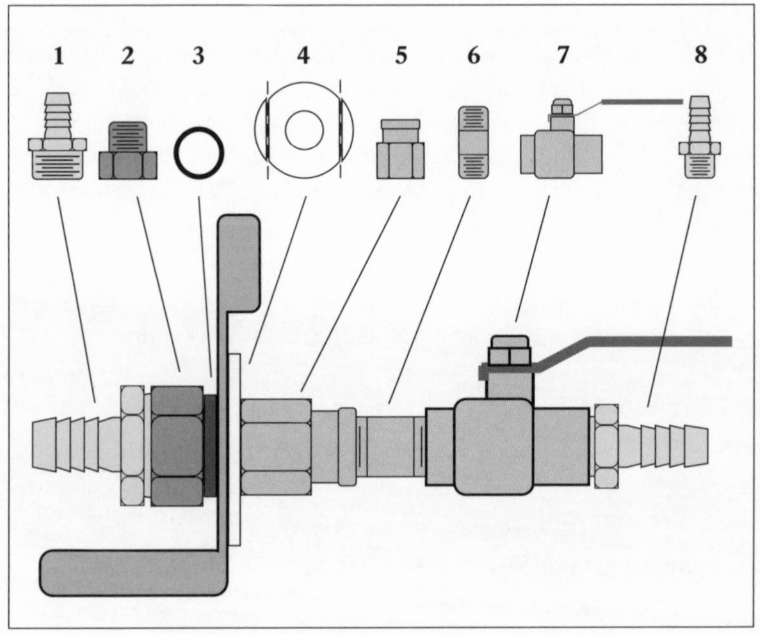

Figure 178—Suggested design for brass bulkhead fitting.

1—1/2″ Nylon Barb to 3/4′ M Hose fitting
2—3/4″ F Hose to 1/2″ MIP Adapter (brass)
3—Rubber O Ring (No. 15, 1/8″ thick)
4—Washer/Spacer, trimmed to fit
5—1/2″ FIP to 3/8″ FIP Reducer
6—3/8″ MIP nipple (1.5″)
7—3/8″ ball valve (brass)
8—3/8″ MIP to 3/8″ barb

To assemble:

1. Slip the O ring over the male threads on #2, so it rests against the flange.
2. Apply some teflon tape to the male threads of #2, and insert it through the spigot hole from the inside of the cooler.
3. Slip the spacer over the threads and hand tighten #5 to make a good seal.
4. Assemble the rest of the parts in the sequence shown.

When my wife kicked me and my mess out of the kitchen, I built a 3 tier, gravity fed system with 3 propane burners to provide the heat. (See *Chapter 18–Your First All-Grain Batch,* for pictures) This is a very popular setup among "enthusiasts" like myself. The vessels are commonly converted stainless steel beer kegs from legitimate re-sellers like Sabco Industries Inc. A cooler mash/lauter tun can be used in place of the middle mash tun, reducing the need for a third burner. Other setups make use of a pump to transfer the water to the hot water tank and use only the one burner under the boil kettle. There are many ways to design your own brewery.

Figure 179—A 6 gallon Rectangular Mash/Lauter Tun. The slotted manifold connects to vinyl tubing with a stopcock for controlling the flow.

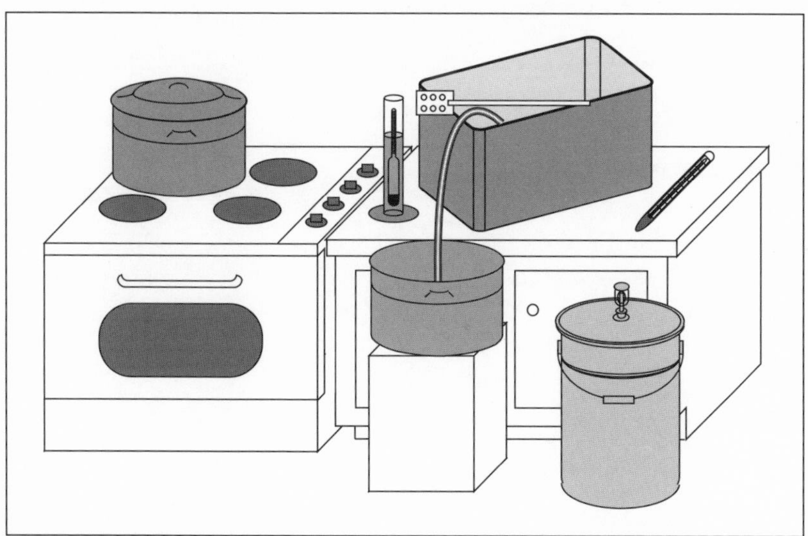

Figure 180—Mashing Procedure

This is how it works:

1. Pot A is used for heating the mash water (or conducting the mash).
2. The mash is lautered in the Mash/Lauter Tun.
3. Pot B is used to heat the Sparge Water.
4. Pot A is used to collect the 6-7 gallons of wort from the mash and boil it.

Appendix E

Metric Conversions

The tables given in this section are intended to provide a quick reference for metric users of the book don't have a calculator handy.

OUNCES CONVERSION TABLE

Ounces are bound to be confusing for the metric world. This table converts both fluid and avoirdupois ounces into milliliters and grams. (By the way, 1 Cup = 8 fluid ounces.)

Fluid Oz.	Milliliters	Ounces	Grams
1	30	0.25	7
2	59	0.5	14
3	89	0.75	21
4	118	1	28
5	148	1.25	35
6	177	1.5	43
7	207	1.75	50
8	237	2	57
9	266	2.25	64
10	296	2.5	71
11	325	2.75	78
12	355	3	85
13	385	3.25	92
14	414	3.5	99
15	444	3.75	106
16	473	4	114

TEMPERATURE CONVERSION TABLE

Find the *number* you want to convert and read its equivalent in °F or °C

°F	Number	°C	°F	Number	°C
32	0	–18	162	72	22
36	2	–17	165	74	23
39	4	–16	169	76	24
43	6	–14	172	78	26
46	8	–13	176	80	27
50	10	–12	180	82	28
54	12	–11	183	84	29
57	14	–10	187	86	30
61	16	–9	190	88	31
64	18	–8	194	90	32
68	20	–7	198	92	33
72	22	–6	201	94	34
75	24	–4	205	96	36
79	26	–3	208	98	37
82	28	–2	212	100	38
86	30	–1	216	102	39
90	32	0	219	104	40
93	34	1	223	106	41
97	36	2	226	108	42
100	38	3	230	110	43
104	40	4	234	112	44
108	42	6	237	114	46
111	44	7	241	116	47
115	46	8	244	118	48
118	48	9	248	120	49
122	50	10	252	122	50
126	52	11	255	124	51
129	54	12	259	126	52
133	56	13	262	128	53
136	58	14	266	130	54
140	60	16	270	132	56
144	62	17	273	134	57
147	64	18	277	136	58
151	66	19	280	138	59
154	68	20	284	140	60
158	70	21	288	142	61

VOLUME CONVERSION TABLE

Find the *number* you want to convert and read its equivalent in liters or quarts,

Quarts	Number	Liters	Quarts	Number	Liters
0.53	0.50	0.47	11.10	10.50	9.93
1.06	1.00	0.95	11.63	11.00	10.41
1.59	1.50	1.42	12.16	11.50	10.88
2.11	2.00	1.89	12.68	12.00	11.35
2.64	2.50	2.37	13.21	12.50	11.83
3.17	3.00	2.84	13.74	13.00	12.30
3.70	3.50	3.31	14.27	13.50	12.77
4.23	4.00	3.78	14.80	14.00	13.24
4.76	4.50	4.26	15.33	14.50	13.72
5.29	5.00	4.73	15.86	15.00	14.19
5.81	5.50	5.20	16.38	15.50	14.66
6.34	6.00	5.68	16.91	16.00	15.14
6.87	6.50	6.15	17.44	16.50	15.61
7.40	7.00	6.62	17.97	17.00	16.08
7.93	7.50	7.10	18.50	17.50	16.56
8.46	8.00	7.57	19.03	18.00	17.03
8.98	8.50	8.04	19.55	18.50	17.50
9.51	9.00	8.51	20.08	19.00	17.97
10.04	9.50	8.99	20.61	19.50	18.45
10.57	10.00	9.46	21.14	20.00	18.92

WEIGHT CONVERSION TABLE

Find the *number* you want to convert and read its equivalent in liters or quarts,

Pounds	Number	Kilos	Pounds	Number	Kilos
0.55	0.25	0.11	12.65	5.75	2.61
1.10	0.50	0.23	13.20	6.00	2.73
1.65	0.75	0.34	13.75	6.25	2.84
2.20	1.00	0.45	14.30	6.50	2.95
2.75	1.25	0.57	14.85	6.75	3.07
3.30	1.50	0.68	15.40	7.00	3.18
3.85	1.75	0.80	15.95	7.25	3.30
4.40	2.00	0.91	16.50	7.50	3.41
4.95	2.25	1.02	17.05	7.75	3.52
5.50	2.50	1.14	17.60	8.00	3.64
6.05	2.75	1.25	18.15	8.25	3.75
6.60	3.00	1.36	18.70	8.50	3.86
7.15	3.25	1.48	19.25	8.75	3.98
7.70	3.50	1.59	19.80	9.00	4.09
8.25	3.75	1.70	20.35	9.25	4.20
8.80	4.00	1.82	20.90	9.50	4.32
9.35	4.25	1.93	21.45	9.75	4.43
9.90	4.50	2.05	22.00	10.00	4.55
10.45	4.75	2.16	22.55	10.25	4.66
11.00	5.00	2.27	23.10	10.50	4.77
11.55	5.25	2.39	23.65	10.75	4.89
12.10	5.50	2.50	24.20	11.00	5.00

EXTRACT CONVERSION TABLE

A quick reference chart for converting between points/pound/gallon and Hot Water Extract (Liter Degrees/Kilogram). 1 PPG = 8.3454 HWE

PPG	HWE	PPG	HWE
1	8	24	200
2	17	25	209
3	25	26	217
4	33	27	225
5	42	28	234
6	50	29	242
7	58	30	250
8	67	31	259
9	75	32	267
10	83	33	275
11	92	34	284
12	100	35	292
13	108	36	300
14	117	37	309
15	125	38	317
16	134	39	325
17	142	40	334
18	150	41	342
19	159	42	351
20	167	43	359
21	175	44	367
22	184	45	376
23	192	46	384

GRAVITY CONVERSION TABLE

Here is a quick reference chart for converting Specific Gravity to °Plato. Balling, Plato, and Brix are basically equivalent and are the preferred gravity unit of large scale brewers.

Specific Gravity	°Plato	Specific Gravity	°Plato
1.008	2.0	1.048	11.9
1.010	2.6	1.050	12.4
1.012	3.1	1.052	12.9
1.014	3.6	1.054	13.3
1.016	4.1	1.056	13.8
1.018	4.6	1.058	14.3
1.020	5.1	1.060	14.7
1.022	5.6	1.062	15.2
1.024	6.1	1.064	15.7
1.026	6.6	1.066	16.1
1.028	7.1	1.068	16.6
1.030	7.5	1.070	17.0
1.032	8.0	1.072	17.5
1.034	8.5	1.074	18.0
1.036	9.0	1.076	18.4
1.038	9.5	1.078	18.9
1.040	10.0	1.080	19.3
1.042	10.5	1.082	19.8
1.044	11.0	1.084	20.2
1.046	11.4		

Appendix F

Recommended Reading

The following citations are recommended to provide you with more information than my book covered. Some periodicals and websites are recommended to provide more background, other references can provide more detail on particular subjects than I felt I could include. My intent was to provide a solid foundation from which to explore the world of brewing. Go to it!

Periodicals

Brew Your Own–A good magazine for the beginning homebrewer. Readily available at newsstands. Covers all aspects of homebrewing, including all-grain. *http://www.byo.com*

Brewing Techniques Archives–This magazine (now out-of-print) was the premier home and craft brewing periodical, covering classic beer styles, techniques, and brewing science with a clear prose that made the information accessible to everyone. Select articles are available online at *http://brewingtechniques.com*

Zymurgy–The magazine of the American Homebrewers Association. It covers all aspects of homebrewing, plus general interest beer topics, as well as the progress of the AHA. Zymurgy also publishes an annual Special Issue that provides in-depth information on various subjects, such as: Hops, Malts, Styles, Equipment, etc. *http://www.beertown.org*

Books

Dave Miller's Homebrewing Guide—Dave Miller

Storey Publishing, 1997

A great book for all the basics, highly recommended for beginning and intermediate brewers. Also covers kegging your beer.

Brewing the Worlds Great Beers—Dave Miller

Storey Publishing, 1992.

Another good book which explores the basics of beer making from a recipe orientation, in a simpler approach than his Guide. An excellent first or second brewing book.

Brewing—Michael J. Lewis, and Tom W. Young
Aspen Publishers, 1995

This is the best book I have read for bringing together all the mechanics and biochemistry of commercial brewing. Other books may present a particular topic more thoroughly, but this book is comprehensive and succinct. If you are really interested in the science of brewing or interested in brewing professionally, then this book is the place to start.

Brew Ware—Carl Lutzen, and Mark Stevens
Storey Publishing

Mark and Carl interviewed a lot of gadgetheads to collect the material for this book. There are a lot of labor saving devices that homebrewers have figured out how to make for themselves, and this book shows you how to make them. A useful book for those interested in building their own equipment and home breweries.

Homebrew Favorites—Carl Lutzen, and Mark Stevens
Storey Publishing

You want recipes?! They have recipes! The favorite recipes collected from scores of the best homebrewers in the world. The best way to develop your own recipe for a style is to compare lots of similar recipes, and this book is the perfect source.

Beer Captured—Mark and Tess Szamatulski
Maltose Press, 2001

This is a very special recipe book. Mark and Tess are brewshop owners and spent years choosing and developing homebrew recipes for classic beers in 150 styles from around the world. The recipes in this book are especially detailed and the brewing methods are explained very well. Want to really impress your friends with your beer? Then get this book.

Designing Great Beers—Ray Daniels
Brewers Publications, 1997

This guy thinks like I do–he looks at the variables in brewing and how to best control them to produce the different beer styles. This is a very useful book for getting into the nuts-and-bolts of brewing, and really fine tuning your beers.

New Brewing Lager Beer—Greg Noonan
Brewers Publications, 1986, 1996

For anyone interested in dedicated lager brewing and decoction mashing, this is *the book*. I referred to it several times in writing my own. Noonan is a professional brewer and a lot of the material is written with the interests of professional brewers in mind. *(Note: This may now be out of print.)*

Principles of Brewing Science 2nd Ed.—George Fix
Brewers Publications, 1989, 1998

Explains the fundamentals of biochemistry involved in malting, mashing and fermentation. A great book to really understand the whole brewing process. If you have a question about any brewing ingredient or process I have covered, Fix's books are a good place to find the answer and some background or experimental data to go with it.

An Analysis of Brewing Techniques—George and Laurie Fix
Brewers Publications, 1997.

This book complements Principles by looking at how the processes of brewing influence the ingredients and vice versa. Reading both books provides a unique stepping stone to understanding and applying the textbooks of brewing, such as Malting and Brewing Science by Briggs et al.

Using Hops—by Mark Garetz
HopTech, 1994

A good reference book for the different hop varieties and their usages. Provides a more complete discussion of hop utilization and bittering than can be found in other current publications.

Homebrewing- Volume One—by Al Korzonas
Sheaf and Vine, 1998.

A very comprehensive book covering all aspects of brewing with malt extract, including a lot of recipes. This book has more discussion of beer styles and troubleshooting than mine.

The Pocket Guide to Beer—by Michael Jackson
Simon and Schuster, 1994

The most complete book of all the worlds beers and styles. The beers of each country/brewery are rated to a 4 star system. His flavor descriptions and recommendations are very useful for recipe formulation.

Essentials of Beer Style—by Fred Eckhardt
Fred Eckhardt Communications, 1989.

A good book for targeting beer styles, provides information that can be used for formulating your own recipes for commercial beers.

The Brewers Companion—by Randy Mosher
Alephenalia Publications, 1995

Randy is a highly technical yet clear-spoken brewer who likes to answer the question: "What if...?" He has filled this book with charts and tables that answer that question, no matter what the topic. This is an extremely useful book for the all grain brewer.

Classic Beer Styles Series
Brewers Publications

These books are great references for each of the most popular beer styles, written by homebrewers who love that style. History of the style, current variations, techniques, and recipes for brewing them–you can't go wrong with these books.

Altbier—Horst Dornbusch
Brewers Publications, 1998.

Barley Wine—Fal Allen and Dick Cantwell
Brewers Publications, 1998.

Belgian Ale—Pierre Rajotte
Brewers Publications, 1992.

Bock—Darryl Richman
Brewers Publications, 1994.

Brown Ale—Ray Daniels and Jim Parker
Brewers Publications, 1999.

Continental Pilsener—Dave Miller
Brewers Publications, 1990.

German Wheat Beer—Eric Warner
Brewers Publications, 1992.

Kolsch—Eric Warner
Brewers Publications, 1999.

Lambic—Jean-Xavier Guinard
Brewers Publications, 1990.

Pale Ale—Terry Foster
Brewers Publications, 1990.

Porter—Terry Foster
Brewers Publications, 1992.

Scotch Ale—Greg Noonan
Brewers Publications, 1993.

Stout—Michael Lewis
Brewers Publications, 1995.

Vienna, Marzen, Oktoberfest—George and Laurie Fix
Brewers Publications, 1992.

Internet Resources

The Homebrew Digest–this listserver digest is available online by sending the word SUBSCRIBE to request@hbd.org It is easily the best source of homebrewing information in the world, and worth its weight in platinum. I read it daily and learn from other's experiences. A lot of the regulars have been there for 10 years or better and the discussions may seem really esoteric and technical at times, but everyone is there because they love to discuss brewing. Don't be shy.

The Homebrew Digest Archives—www.hbd.org
At the Homebrew Digest site, you can query the digest archives on any brewing topic and receive a compilation of posts discussing it. Interested in yeast aeration? Lagering? Kegging? Water Treatment? Yeast types? Malt Types? It is all there.

BreWorld—www.breworld.com
The home of Europe's largest brewing site, containing links to major breweries, the UK homebrewing page, European beer events, ingredients and publications.

The Brewery—www.brewery.org
The Brewery is the repository for all the extracted wisdom of the brewers of the Home Brew Digest, the quintessential recipe codex The Cat's Meow, and the keeper of the legacy of the Stanford brewing ftp site. A lot of well organized information is available here.

The Real Beer Page—www.realbeer.com/library/
The Real Beer Page has become the largest source of craft and home brewing information on the internet. The Library section of their site is the most useful to homebrewers, but the other links and sites are very useful too.

The Biohazard Lambic Brewers Page—www.liddil.com
Jim Liddil loves Belgium's Lambic beer style and has devoted his site to teaching you how to make it as best you can without actually being in the Lambic Valley.

The Promash Brewing Software website—www.promash.com
Promash is a Windows OS application that is a superb resource for designing and saving recipes. It is designed to meet any brewer's needs, whether you are a homebrewer or a professional micro-brewer. It does IBU calculations, gravity calculations, water calculations, et cetera–every calculation that I have presented in this book is covered in Promash. There is a large database of recipes from other Promash users available online at the website too. It is available as a download from the website or as a CD. The software includes extensive tutorials and technical support.

StrangeBrew Brewing Software—www.strangebrew.ca
Strangebrew is a Windows OS application that is another superb resource for designing and saving recipes. It has an easy to use interface and the ability to export recipes as XML. It does IBU calculations, gravity calculations, water calculations, mash calculations, plus competition forms and bottle labels. Recipes from other users are available at the StrangeBrew website along with technical support and a discusion board. It is available as a download from the website for a 30 day free trial before registering.

The Beer Judge Certification Program website—www.bjcp.org
Years ago a group dedicated brewers and judges set out to control their own destiny for the benefit of the hobby and beer in general, and the Beer Judge Certification Program was born. This nonprofit organization is dedicated to promoting beer literacy, the appreciation of real beer, and to recognize beer tasting and evaluation skills via a comprehensive examination.

All the current beer style guidelines and descriptions are maintaind online as .pdf files. This is an excellent resource for advancing brewers who would like to enter their beers in competitions or study to become part of the program.

How To Brew—www.howtobrew.com
Home of the online edition of the book, sponsored by the Real Beer Page. This edition features color graphics and search capability. If you would like to print out a color copy of the nomographs or a copy of the tables, this is the place to get them.

Palmer House Brewery and Smithy—www.realbeer.com/jjpalmer
My homepage where you can find other beer and brewing articles, links, and instructions for making chainmail armor.

The Defenestrative Publishing Co.—
www.realbeer.com/jjpalmer/ordering.html
This site covers the business end of the book, and is probably the best spot to look for notices of any errata or updates to the hardcopy that I feel are necessary.

References

The references used in the preparation of this book are listed by chapter. If a chapter does not have a listing, it indicates that the material is general knowledge and is available from several sources.

Section I–Brewing With Malt Extract

Chapter 2–Brewing Preparations

Liddil, J., Palmer, J., "Ward Off the Wild Things: A Complete Guide to Cleaning and Sanitation", *Zymurgy*, Vol. 13, No. 3, 1995.

Palmer, J., "Preparing for Brew Day," *Brewing Techniques,* New Wine Press, Vol. 4, No. 6, 1996.

Talley, C., O'Shea, J., Five Star Affiliates, Inc. discussion, 1998.

Chapter 3–Malt Extract and Beer Kits

Lodahl, M., "Malt Extracts: Cause for Caution," *Brewing Techniques,* New Wine Press, Vol. 1, No. 2, 1993.

Chapter 5–Hops

Garetz, M., *Using Hops: The Complete Guide to Hops for the Craft Brewer,* HopTech, Danville, California, 1994.

Pyle, N., Ed., *The Hop FAQ, http://www.realbeer.com/hops/FAQ.html*, 1994.

Tinseth, G., *The Hop Page, http://www.realbeer.com/hops/*, 1995.

Tinseth, G., discussion, 1995.

Chapter 6–Yeast

McConnell, D., Yeast Culture Kit Co., discussion, 1995.

Weix, P., Ed., *The Yeast FAQ, ftp://ftp.stanford.edu/pub/clubs/homebrew/beer/docs/*, 1994.

Raines, M.B., discussion, 1995.

Reichwage, R., G.W. Kent Inc., discussion, 1995.

Aquilla, T., "The Biochemistry of Yeast," *Brewing Techniques,* New Wine Press, Vol. 5, No. 2, 1997.

White, C., White Labs Inc., discussion, 1999.

Moline, R., Lallemand Inc., discussion, 1999.

Villa, K. Coors Brewing Co., discussion, 2000.

Logsdon, D., Wyeast Labs, discussion, 2001.

Chapter 7–Boiling and Cooling

Barchet, R., "Hot Trub, Formation and Removal", *Brewing Techniques,* New Wine Press, Vol. 1, No. 4, 1993.

Barchet, R., "Cold Trub: Implications for Finished Beer, and Methods of Removal," *Brewing Techniques,* New Wine Press, Vol.2, No. 2, 1994.

Fix, G., discussion, 1994.

Chapter 8–Fermentation

Miller, D., *The Complete Handbook of Home Brewing,* Storey Publishing, Pownal, Vermont, 1988.

Fix, G., *Principles of Brewing Science,* Brewers Publications, Boulder Colorado, 1989.

Fix, G., Fix, L., *An Analysis of Brewing Techniques,* Brewers Publications, Boulder Colorado, 1997.

Palmer, J., "Conditioning - Fermentation's Grand Finale," *Brewing Techniques,* New Wine Press, Vol. 5, No. 3, 1997

Alexander, S., discussion, 1997.

Korzonas, A., discussion, 1997.

Chapter 9–Fermenting Your First Beer

Chapter 10–What is Different for Brewing Lager Beer?

Noonen, G., *New Brewing Lager Beer,* Brewers Publications, Boulder Colorado, 1996.

Chapter 11–Priming and Bottling

Miller, D., *The Complete Handbook of Home Brewing,* Storey Publishing, Pownal, Vermont, 1988.

Noonen, G., *New Brewing Lager Beer*, Brewers Publications, Boulder Colorado, 1996.

Draper, D., discussion, February, 1996.

Fix, G., Fix, L., *An Analysis of Brewing Techniques,* Brewers Publications, Boulder Colorado, 1997.

Venezia, D., Venezia & Co., discussion, 1998.

Section II–Brewing With Extract-and-Specialty-Grain

Chapter 12–What is Malted Grain?

Wahl, R., Henrius, M., "*The American Handy Book of the Brewing, Malting, and Auxiliary Trades, Vol. 1,*" Chicago, 1908.

Broderick, H. M., ed., *The Practical Brewer - A Manual for the Brewing Industry,* Master Brewers Association of the Americas, Madison Wisconsin, 1977.

Noonen, G., *New Brewing Lager Beer,* Brewers Publications, Boulder Colorado, 1996.

Lewis, M. J., Young, T.W., *Brewing*, Chapman & Hall, New York, 1995.

Briggs, D. E., Hough, J. S., Stevens, R., and Young, T. W., *Malting and Brewing Science, Vol. 1,* Chapman & Hall, London, 1981.

Maney, L., discussion, 1999.

Fix, G., *Principles of Brewing Science,* Brewers Publications, Boulder Colorado, pp. 22–108, 1989.

Fix, G., Fix, L., *An Analysis of Brewing Techniques,* Brewers Publications, Boulder Colorado, 1997.

Papazian, C., *The Homebrewers Companion,* Brewers Publications, Boulder Colorado, 1994.

Chapter 13–Steeping Specialty Grains

Palmer, J., "Beginner's Guide to Using Grain in Extract Recipes," *Brewing Techniques,* New Wine Press, Vol. 4, No. 5, 1996.

Section III–All-Grain Brewing

Chapter 14–How the Mash Works

Fix, G., *Principles of Brewing Science,* Brewers Publications, Boulder Colorado, 1989.

Moll, M., *Beers and Coolers,* Intercept LTD, Andover, Hampshire England, 1994.

Noonen, G., *New Brewing Lager Beer,* Brewers Publications, Boulder Colorado, 1996.

Maney, L., discussion, 1999.

Lewis, M. J., Young, T.W., *Brewing,* Chapman & Hall, New York, 1995.

Briggs, D. E., Hough, J. S., Stevens, R., and Young, T. W., *Malting and Brewing Science, Vol. 1,* Chapman & Hall, London, 1981.

Wahl, R., Henrius, M., *The American Handy Book of the Brewing, Malting, and Auxiliary Trades, Vol. 1,* Chicago, 1908.

Broderick, H. M., ed., *The Practical Brewer - A Manual for the Brewing Industry,* Master Brewers Association of the Americas, Madison Wisconsin, 1977.

Chapter 15–Understanding the Mash pH

Fix, G., Fix, L., *An Analysis of Brewing Techniques, Brewers Publications,* Boulder Colorado, 1997.

DeLange, AJ, discussion, 1998.

Daniels, R., *Designing Great Beers,* Brewers Publications, Boulder Colorado, 1997.

Chapter 16–The Methods of Mashing

Fix, G., *Principles of Brewing Science,* Brewers Publications, Boulder Colorado, 1989.

Noonen, G., *New Brewing Lager Beer,* Brewers Publications, Boulder Colorado, 1996.

Chapter 17–Getting the Wort Out (Lautering)

Richman, D., discussion, April, 1995.

Palmer, J., Prozinski, P., "Fluid Dynamics–A Simple Key to the Mastery of Efficient Lautering," *Brewing Techniques,* New Wine Press, Vol. 3, No. 4, 1995.

Gregory, G., discussion, 1998.

Chapter 18–Your First All-Grain Batch

Schwartz, K., "A Formulation Procedure for No-Sparge and Batch-Sparge Recipes," *http://home.elp.rr.com/brewbeer/files/nbsparge.html*, 1998.

Bonham, L.K., "No-Sparge Brewing–An Old Technique Revisted," *Brewing Techniques,* New Wine Press, Vol. 6, No. 4, 1998.

Donovan, J., "Mechanics of No-Sparge Brewing," *http://www.promash.com/nosparge.html,* 2000.

Section IV–Recipes, Experimentation, and Troubleshooting

Chapter 19–Some of My Favorite Beer Styles and Recipes

Jackson, M, *New World Guide to Beer,* Courage Books, Philadelphia Pennsylvania, 1988.

Bergen, R., "American Wheat Beers," *Brewing Techniques,* New Wine Press, Vol. 1, No. 1, 1993.

Bergen, R., "A Stout Companion," *Brewing Techniques,* New Wine Press, Vol. 1, No. 4, 1993.

Bergen, R., "California Steaming," *Brewing Techniques,* New Wine Press, Vol. 2, No. 1, 1994.

Bergen, R., "Porters - Then and Now," *Brewing Techniques,* New Wine Press, Vol. 1, No. 3, 1993.

Tomlinson, T., "India Pale Ale, Part 1: IPA and Empire," *Brewing Techniques,* New Wine Press, Vol. 2, No. 2, 1994.

Tomlinson, T., "India Pale Ale, Part 2: The Sun Never Sets," *Brewing Techniques,* New Wine Press, Vol. 2, No. 3, 1994.

Slosberg, P., "The Road to an American Brown Ale," *Brewing Techniques,* New Wine Press, Vol. 3, No. 3, 1995.

Richman, D., *Bock,* Brewers Publications, Boulder Colorado, 1994.

Lewis, M., *Stout,* Brewers Publications, Boulder Colorado, 1995.

Foster, T., *Porter,* Brewers Publications, Boulder Colorado, 1992.

Fix, G., L., *Vienna, Marzen, Oktoberfest,* Brewers Publications, Boulder Colorado, 1991.

Foster, T., *Pale Ale,* Brewers Publications, Boulder Colorado, 1990.

Miller, D., *Continental Pilsener,* Brewers Publications, Boulder Colorado, 1990.

Renner, J., discussion, November, 1995.

Chapter 20–Experiment!

Mosher, R., *The Brewers Companion,* Alephenalia Publishing, Seattle Washington, 1995.

Chapter 21–Is My Beer Ruined?

Papazian, C., *The Homebrewers Companion,* Brewers Publications, Boulder Colorado, 1994.

Gold, Elizabeth, ed. *Evaluating Beer,* Brewers Publications, Boulder Colorado, 1993.

Maney, L., discussion, 1999.

Section V–Appendices

Appendix D–Building a Mash/Lauter Tun

Kern, B.D., discussion, 2001.

Appendix E–Conversion Tables

Briggs, D. E., Hough, J. S., Stevens, R., and Young, T. W., *Malting and Brewing Science, Vol. 1,* Chapman & Hall, London, 1981.

Index

(Bold typeface indicates illustration.)

A

B

D

E

F

I

K

L

N

O

P

T

V

W

Y

Z

About the Author

Metallurgical engineer by day, and beer writer, speaker, and BJCP judge whenever there is an opportunity, John has been brewing since 1991, and has written several articles for Brewing Techniques and Zymurgy. In 1992, John wrote "How to Brew Your First Beer"–a short but comprehensive document for first-time brewers which quickly became the most popular (free) how-to document for brewing in the world. Over the years, it has been requested from every continent, including Antarctica, and translated into Spanish, Italian, Korean, and Japanese. In 1995, he was featured on the Home & Garden Channel's "What's Your Hobby" show, in a segment on homebrewing.

In his goal to make good brewing information readily available to the world, John published the first edition of *How To Brew*, in June, 2000 with the help of the Real Beer Page, online at www.howtobrew.com, for free. The online edition immediately generated requests for a hardcopy, so another year was spent sprucing it up.

A person is a product of their hometown and John considers several towns to fit that designation. Midland, Michigan–where he grew up; Grand Haven, MI and Green Bank, WV–where he spent a lot of time with his grandparents; Houghton, MI–where he attended Michigan Tech, and finally Monrovia, CA–where he is raising his own family. God Bless America!

Favorite Beers: Sierra Nevada Porter, Sierra Nevada Wheat, Firestone Windsor Ale, and Victory Prima Pils.

Favorite Bands: Fleetwood Mac, Yes, Triumph, Rush, Dire Straits, Big Country, Hootie and the Blowfish, and Barenaked Ladies.

Favorite Authors: David Brin, Gerald Durrell, Robert Jordan, Julian May, J.K. Rowling

Favorite Words: The Preamble, "We the People,..."
"I have a Dream..."–Rev. Martin Luther King Jr.